SINS AGAINST NATURE

SINS AGAINST NATURE

Sex and Archives in Colonial New Spain

ZEB TORTORICI

DUKE UNIVERSITY PRESS *Durham and London* 2018

Typeset in Minion Pro and Gill Sans Std by
Westchester Publishing Services

Library of Congress Cataloging-in-Publication Data
Names: Tortorici, Zeb, [date] author.
Title: Sins against nature : sex and archives in colonial
New Spain / Zeb Tortorici.
Description: Durham : Duke University Press, 2018. |
Includes bibliographical references and index.
Identifiers: LCCN 2017051306 (print)
LCCN 2017060638 (ebook)
ISBN 9780822371625 (ebook)
ISBN 9780822371328 (hardcover : alk. paper)
ISBN 9780822371540 (pbk. : alk. paper)
Subjects: LCSH: Sex—Social aspects—New Spain. |
Sex customs—New Spain—Sources. | Sex crimes—
Investigation—New Spain—Sources. | Trials (Sex
crimes)—New Spain—Sources. | Criminal justice,
Administration of—New Spain—Sources.
Classification: LCC HQ18.N458 (ebook) | LCC HQ18.N458
T67 2018 (print) | DDC 392.60972/53—dc23
LC record available at https://lccn.loc.gov/2017051306

Cover art: Woodcut print from Francisco de Pareja's
*Confessionario en lengua Castellana, y Timuquana Con
algunos consejos para animar al penitente* (1613). Courtesy
of the John Carter Brown Library at Brown University.

I dedicate this book to three scholars

who are sorely missed and whose traces

can be found throughout its pages:

NEIL L. WHITEHEAD
(1956–2012)

JOSÉ ESTEBAN MUÑOZ
(1967–2013)

AND
MARÍA ELENA MARTÍNEZ
(1966–2014)

CONTENTS

A NOTE ON TRANSLATION

Unless otherwise noted, all translations are my own. Throughout this book I rely on contemporary Spanish orthography and direct archival transcriptions in order to preserve the original linguistic flavor and materiality of the documents. This means that many of the Spanish-language terms in the endnotes appear to be misspelled or inconsistently written, and they are often missing proper accents (or, at times, include accents where none are needed). This is especially evident in testimonies and confessions where the proper accent in the third-person preterit tense of Spanish verbs is typically omitted. Thus, when readers encounter what appear to be present-tense verbs in the first person—as in the phrase "teniendola por los cuernos la fornico doz vezes"— they are actually written in the third person, with nonstandard spellings and without proper accents. Modernized spelling would be "teniéndola por los cuernos, la fornicó dos veces" (restraining her [the goat] by the horns, he fornicated with her two times). Spelling inconsistency is also why, for example, you will see the word and legal category of "Indian" spelled both *indio* and *yndio*, depending on the document and scribes in question. With the exception of proper names, I have opted not to modernize either spelling or punctuation in the book, since direct transcriptions are more faithful to the documents themselves and give the reader a better sense of archival and linguistic conventions in flux.

Throughout the book, readers will see references to archival documents that are typically classified in terms of *ramo* (branch), *expediente* (file), *legajo* (file or bundle), *progresivo* (progressing [chronologically] toward), *cuaderno* (folder), *caja* (box), and folio or page number. Occasionally, however, no box or file number exists in a particular archival collection, and folios sometimes remain unnumbered. While I have tried to add original quotes of all of the archival document excerpts I use throughout the book, they are not necessarily direct translations. At times, I add long quotes from which I paraphrase and include shorter translations. At other times, I provide a full translation (in the main text) of the original Spanish, and sometimes only a translation of select words and phrases. At times when I paraphrase a particularly fascinating quote from a document in the book, I often include longer portions of the original Spanish than what I am translating, for readers who know Spanish and may want to read in the original language (or, rather, what was interpreted into Spanish from Nahuatl or another indigenous language). Translation—like the very process of writing history itself—is necessarily partial and always incomplete.

ACKNOWLEDGMENTS

This book has been with me for so many years that I am unsure where to begin (or end) these words. First and foremost, Kevin Terraciano has been a supportive and inspirational mentor, as well as a wonderful friend. From History 8A and Spanish paleography to Nahuatl lessons and annual Ethnohistory conference parties (the Santa Fe suite!), your ways of working with and genuinely engaging students have greatly influenced me. I cannot thank you enough. I fondly remember you once saying that my dissertation was "the filthiest" you had ever read; I hope the book lives up to those expectations. I am forever grateful for the continued generosity and support of other colleagues at the University of California, Los Angeles, who engaged closely with my research, Robin Derby, Teofilo Ruiz, and James A. Schultz. Robin, from our animal discussions to our explorations in historical method, you are an inspiration. Teo, I am simply in awe. Your kindness, generosity, and dedication to the profession of history, and to your students, is unrivaled. I am equally indebted to Michael Salman, Vinay Lal, and the late Miriam Silverberg—all three of whom pushed me to think about history creatively, and always in relation to the peculiar temporalities and classifications of archives.

I offer special thanks to my phenomenal cohort in (and around) the Department of History at UCLA, which made the many years of coursework, teaching, research, and writing productive, fun, and full of surprises. I am particularly grateful to Molly Ball, Brad Benton, Xóchitl Flores, León García Garagarza, Liz Jones, Owen H. Jones, Miriam Melton-Villanueva, Phillip Ninomiya, Margarita Ochoa, Erika Pérez, Pablo Sierra, and Peter Villella. Ben Cowan and Mir Yarfitz pushed me to think about what it means to discover, theorize, and write about (queer) sex in the archives. Dana Velasco Murillo offered support and advice when it was most needed. Phillip Ninomiya (and Diana Eguia-Armenteros at Penn) generously commented on this book's conclusions. I met wonderful people in Mexican archives over the years; special thanks go to Paul T. Conrad, Caroline Cunill, César Manrique Figueroa, and Paul Ramírez—the Archivo General de la Nación (AGN) would not have been the same without you!

I sincerely thank the following people for guiding me through the peer-review process and helping me refine my ideas: Miruna Achim, John F. Chuchiak, Lisa Darms, Kate Eichhorn, Roger Gathman, Ramón Gutiérrez, Mathew Kuefler, Erika Milam, Robert Nye, Marcia Ochoa, Kyla Wazana Tompkins, and Martina Will de Chaparro. In 2016 I co-taught "Sex in the Archives" with Marvin Taylor, head of the Fales Library and Special Collections at New York University, who left an indelible mark on this book. The same can be said for the graduate students in the course—especially Alejandro Castro, Julia Cheng, Erica Feild, Helaine Gawlica, Mercedes Trigos, Alejandra Vela, and Mon Zabala. At NYU, I am grateful to Thomas J. Abercrombie, Gabriela Basterra, Martín Bowen-Silva, Lourdes Dávila, Cristel Jusino Díaz, Gigi Dopico-Black, Nicole Eustace, Jim Fernández, Sibylle Fischer, Gabriel Giorgi, Becky Goetz, Jonathan Gómez, Karen Krahulik, Jo Labanyi, Francisco Marguch, Tess Rankin, Rubén Ríos-Ávila, Rocío Pichon Rivière, Abel Sierra Madero, Irina Troconis, Barbara Weinstein, and many more, for their close engagement with my work. Dylon Robbins and Laura Torres-Rodriguez have been wonderful *colegas* with whom to navigate assistant professorship, and Marcelo Carosi has been a great friend and interlocutor.

Several scholars—from the fields of history, literature, queer studies, animal studies, and porn studies—have invited me to give talks, shared archival documents and scholarly references, and otherwise greatly influenced my work. I am enormously appreciative of Linda Arnold, Anajali Arondekar, Etienne Benson, Chad Black, Howard Chiang, Silvia Dapía, Lina Del Castillo, Carolyn Dinshaw, Héctor Domínguez-Ruvalcaba, Elizabeth Freeman, María Elena García, Nicole von Germeten, Gayatri Gopinath, James N. Green, Jacqueline Holler, Asunción Lavrin, Sonya Lipsett-Rivera, Jane Mangan, Daniel Marshall, María Elena Martínez, Heather McCrea, Mireille Miller-Young, Kevin P. Murphy, Gabriel Paquette, Lee Penyak, Hiram Perez, Caterina Pizzigoni, Matthew Restall, Michael Schuessler, Tatiana Seijas, Todd Shepard, Maile Speakman, Susan Stryker, Danielle Terrazas Williams, Claudia Torres, Camilla Townsend, Richard Twine, Tom Tyler, Ronaldo Vainfas, Estefanía Vela, Sherry Velasco, and Farren Yero, among others. Close readings by Tamara Walker, Michelle Chase, Marcela Echeverri, Anne Eller, and Yuko Miki greatly helped with chapter drafts. Scholars such as Jens Rydström, Vicente L. Rafael, and Helmut Puff graciously answered questions from an inquisitive graduate student years ago. The warmth and generosity of such scholars are refreshing. I greatly thank Angélica Afanador-Pujol for her help with Purépecha translations.

This project benefited immensely from the following institutions: the Department of History at UCLA, the American Council of Learned Societies

(ACLS), the Andrew W. Mellon Foundation, the NYU Center for Latin American and Caribbean Studies (CLACS), the University of California Institute for Mexico and the United States (UC MEXUS), the Animals and Society Institute, the Conference on Latin American History (CLAH), the Committee on Lesbian, Gay, Bisexual, and Transgender History (CLGBTH), the Program for Cultural Cooperation between Spain's Ministry of Culture and United States' Universities, the Roger Thayer Stone Center for Latin American Studies, the Society for the Scientific Study of Sexuality, the UCLA Latin American Institute, NYU Berlin, and the Association for the Study of Law, Culture and the Humanities. Their generous financial support enabled me to carry out the archival research for this book. Constant support from the NYU Center for the Humanities (especially Jane Tylus and Gwynneth Malin) and CLACS (Jill Lane and Amalia Isabel Córdova) has been crucial in terms of teaching leave, research support, and publication expenses.

I am lucky to have worked with wonderful colleagues, students, and staff at several institutions. At Tulane University, I thank Guadalupe García, Randy Sparks, and Justin and Edie Wolfe (among others) for warmly welcoming me. My postdoctoral year in the Department of History at Stanford University—where I benefited from friendship and dialogue with Patricia Blessing, Mackenzie Cooley, Zephyr Frank, Frederico Freitas, Tamar Herzog, Patrick Iber, Matthew Sommer, Edith Sheffer, Lisa Surwillo, and Ali Yaycioglu—was especially formative. At the Penn Humanities Forum, I learned from the brilliance of people such as Kadji Amin, Jim English, Philip Francis, Heather Love, Nguyen Tan Hoang, Durba Mitra, and Sima Shakhsari, among others. For helping me navigate the ins and outs of these institutions, I thank Barbara Bernstein, Hadley Porter, and Jinny Oh at UCLA; Donna Denneen at Tulane; Monica Wheeler at Stanford; Jennifer Conway and Sara Varney at Penn; and Edgardo Nuñez, Noelia Sánchez, and, most of all, José Reyes at NYU.

Perhaps most importantly, I give thanks to the many archivists who guided me through the numerous archives and special collections libraries in Mexico, Guatemala, Spain, and the United States. There are simply too many to name here individually, though some individuals deserve special credit for facilitating my access to documents and for allowing me to take digital photos (and reproduce images here). Archivists and staff at the AGN have been so thoroughly helpful over the years; I thank Fabiola Maria Luisa Hernandez Diaz, Lilliam Pimentel, María Fernanda Treviño Campero, and Yolia Tortolero Cervantes. I also thank the wonderful archivists (and director, Germán Martínez) of the Archivo Histórico Municipal de Morelia (AHMM); it was they who led me to my first archival discovery—the 1604 *pecado nefando* trial of Pedro Quini and Simpliciano Cuyne—and I am forever grateful. I am indebted to M. H. Francisco Javier Delgado Aguilar of the Archivo Histórico del Estado de Aguascalientes (AHEA); Arturo Rojas of the Archivo General del Estado de Hidalgo (AGEH); José Miguel Romero de Solís of the Archivo Histórico del Municipio de Colima (AHMC); Jaime Reyes Monroy of the Archivo Histórico Casa de Morelos (AHCM); Rosa Martínez Pérez of the Archivo Histórico del Poder Judicial del Estado de Querétaro (AHPJQ); Rafael Morales Bocardo, Jaime César Moreno Vázquez, Rafael de Loera, and Flor de María Salazar Mendoza of the Archivo Histórico del Estado de San Luis Potosí (AHESLP); and Milena Koprivitza Acuña and Guillermo Alberto Xelhuantzi Ramírez of the Archivo Histórico del Estado de Tlaxcala (AHET). Admittedly, I owe thanks to many more archivists and archive staff, as well as to those who labor behind the scenes (appraising, conserving, classifying, describing, photocopying, and digitizing), many of whom I never met in person. I am also thankful to those whose names I once jotted down on long-lost pieces of paper and research notebooks at several archives.

Special collections libraries in the United States have offered invaluable support in the form of short-term research fellowships, knowledge and expertise, and access to rare books and manuscripts. I wholly thank Neil Safier, Ken Ward, Kimberly Nusco, Valerie Andrews, Maureen O'Donnell, and Susan Newbury at the John Carter Brown Library; Juan Gomez, Kadin Henningsen, and Carolyn Powell at the Huntington Library; Hortensia Calvo and the late David Dressing at the Tulane Latin American Library; Walter Brem at the Bancroft Library; Leslie Kan at the Newberry Library; and Joel Silver, Penny Ramon, Nils Jacobsen, Rebecca Baumann, and Isabel Planton at the Lilly Library.

The fabulous people at Duke University Press have been professional, supportive, and patient, as always. It is an honor to work with Gisela Fosado and Lydia Rose Rappoport-Hankins again. Thanks also to Sheila McMahon, Liz Smith, and David Emanuel for their help and careful copyediting. It was a pleasure to work with Jen Burton on yet another index. I am especially grateful to my two reviewers—Pete Sigal and Martin Nesvig—for their crucial feedback and support. Their mentoring, friendship, and guidance (as with people such as Leah DeVun, Martha Few, Marcy Norton, David Sartorius, and Adam Warren) have been instrumental in shaping me as a scholar. I give you my deepest thanks. Pete and Leah, in particular, remind me how historical scholarship should be tied to activism. Special acknowledgment goes to David Lobenstine for his painstaking editorial advice, his queries and critiques, and his intellectual rigor. He is everything one could hope for in an editor.

My final thanks go to the family and friends whose emotional support (and homestays!) made writing possible: Joseph Chang, Aida de Prada, Erik Fritz, Osvaldo Gómez, Gela Frutis Huesca, Caryn Furtaw, Jenny Kao, Joanne Lin, Scott Lucas, Yuki and Reiko Maeda, Jennifer Palecki, Laura Ramos, David Sada, Lorena Soto, Jonathan Yaffe, and Elza Wang. To my family—Roberta and Liberato Tortorici and Lisa and Adam Hohnbaum—I offer my most heartfelt thanks for their unwavering affection and support. Finally, I thank Su Anne Takeda, who has been with me at every step of this project, in one way or another. You inspired a lot of what is in these pages.

Earlier iterations of some of these ideas presented here have appeared as follows: "'*Heran Todos Putos*': Sodomitical Subcultures and Disordered Desire in Early Colonial Mexico," *Ethnohistory* 54, no. 1 (2007): 36–67; "Masturbation, Salvation, and Desire: Connecting Sexuality and Religiosity in Colonial Mexico," *Journal of the History of Sexuality* 16, no. 3 (2007): 355–72; "Against Nature: Sodomy and Homosexuality in Colonial Latin America," *History Compass* 10, no. 2 (2012): 161–78; "Visceral Archives of the Body: Consuming the Dead, Digesting the Divine," *GLQ: A Journal of Lesbian and Gay Studies* 20, no. 4 (2014): 407–37; "Archival Seduction: Indexical Absences and Historiographical Ghosts," *Archive Journal* 5 (fall 2015); and "Sexual Violence, Predatory Masculinity, and Medical Testimony in New Spain," *Osiris* 30, no. 1 (2015): 272–94.

Introduction

Archiving the Unnatural

In an unremarkable box on a shelf of the municipal archive of Monterrey, in the Mexican state of Nuevo León, is a document with a story that is at once extraordinary and entirely mundane. That story relates how one day in 1656, Nicolás de Lares, a citizen of Monterrey, was walking through some fields when he came upon Lorenzo Vidales, a thirteen-year-old mestizo goat herder. Vidales was, according to Lares, standing under a tree committing the *pecado nefando*—the "nefarious sin" of bestiality—with one of his flock. Lares, observing the boy "with the said she-goat in between his legs," took matters into his own hands: he interrupted the carnal act, tied up the boy, and whipped him. He then turned in the boy to the local alcalde, the colonial mayor who was, in this case, Spanish.[1] One witness noted that Lares could not help but whip the boy himself because the act was "atrocious." Out of anger and perhaps due to other, more visceral, reasons, the boy's boss had the black goat slaughtered, which certainly caused him some lost income.

For his part, Vidales was surprisingly forthcoming with the judge who, some days later, interrogated him. As was customary, the court-appointed notary transcribed the boy's testimony onto paper in the third person, altering the words of witness and suspect alike from the first-person voice to the third-person "he." The result, as we will see throughout this book, is that suspects, such as Vidales, appear to be speaking about themselves in the third person. This is a relic of notarial and archival processes, and is one of several mediations at the heart of the archive, through which documents come into history (and ended up in a box on a shelf). Vidales fully admitted his crime—"restraining the goat by the horns, he fornicated with her two times"—although he claimed ignorance that the act was sinful.[2] The criminal court tried the boy, found him guilty of bestiality, and, because of his young age, sentenced him to be tied to the gallows by his waist and whipped one hundred times. This sentence, though harsh, was far from the maximum punishment for bestiality, which, at least in theory, was death.[3] Afterward, authorities banished the boy in perpetuity from Monterrey and its surrounding kingdom of Nuevo León, sentencing him to six years of labor in a neighboring territory and specifying that he keep away from livestock and never again commit such a crime. Should Vidales ever return to Monterrey, authorities stipulated, he would face the death penalty.

This book is about the archiving of the "sins against nature" of sodomy, bestiality, and masturbation in colonial New Spain, which was Spain's largest and most important colonial possession in the Americas, established in 1535 and lasting until 1821. These chronological endpoints mark, on the one end, the creation of the viceroyalty of New Spain in 1535, which followed the conquest of Mexico-Tenochtitlan by Spanish conquistadors under the leadership of Hernán Cortés from 1519 to 1521. On the other end, 1821 signals the culmination of the Mexican wars for independence from Spain, initiated by secular priest Miguel Hidalgo y Costilla in 1810. New Spain—or Nueva España, as it was known—was the first of four viceroyalties that Spain created in the Americas, and it comprised what is today Mexico, Central America, Florida, much of the southwestern and central United States, and the Caribbean (then known as the Spanish West Indies, which included Cuba, Haiti, the Dominican Republic, Puerto Rico, the Virgin Islands, Jamaica, and other islands). Starting in 1565, with the increased colonization of the Philippines that began in 1521, New Spain also included the Spanish East Indies, made up of the Philippine Islands, the Mariana Islands, and, briefly, parts of Taiwan.

The archives of New Spain are nearly as vast as the territory it once encompassed. When I first came across the story of Vidales and others like it more than a decade ago, I was stunned. Over time, in other seemingly unremarkable acid-free boxes, I uncovered hundreds of similar archival documents. Mexico's numerous historical archives—national, state, municipal, notarial, judicial, and ecclesiastical—abound with documents related to the *pecados contra natura*— the sins against nature. The very everydayness of Vidales's case—predicated on both (human) desire and (animal) death—is its value, for it demonstrates both reactions to and perceptions of unnatural acts by officials and everyday people alike, and it raises questions as to how and why such a crime was documented in the first place. There were those, like Lares, who found such sins to be horrible, repulsive, and requiring punishment. Others took a more lenient view, did not rush off to the authorities, and contented themselves with gossiping to friends and neighbors about the scandalous nature of such acts. These diverse ways of speaking about the unnatural, we will see again and again, led to efforts to archive desire itself. Each archival document discussed here makes up part of this vast archive of unnatural desire.

While Lorenzo Vidales was spared the death penalty, his still-harsh punishment tells us much about how secular criminal courts both dealt with and documented such crimes in the mid-seventeenth century. What were the motivations of the court in assiduously—graphically—recording the details and outcome of the case? What were the social and bureaucratic mechanisms through which such a crime came to be denounced, textually recorded, and archived in a way that was meaningful for Spanish colonial authorities? How are all the emotions and motivations that created these documents eventually archived, and thus made into the basis for our understanding of history?

All these questions lead to another one: Why was I so surprised by the abundance of bestiality cases in the archives? The answer, I think, is that the histories of sodomy and sexuality are generally talked about in more narrow ways. Historians of colonial Latin America, for example, have largely examined the sins against nature through the lens of same-sex sexuality and "homosexuality." Yet how have historians and archivists, perhaps unwittingly, relegated certain acts to the margins of historical inquiry and archival ontology? And how do historical (and historicized) perceptions of such crimes—seen as "abominable," "sinful," or "against nature," for example—influence, and to some extent determine, how contemporary archivists and researchers engage with those documented desires? To what extent are we ourselves—the archivists who appraise and order documents, the researchers who consume them, and the readers of the histories written about them—implicated in a kind of historical voyeurism?

This book uses the sins against nature to examine the ways in which the desires of individuals and communities came into contact with the colonial regulatory mechanisms of New Spain, and then with its ensuing archival practices, between the sixteenth and early nineteenth centuries. To pursue this investigation, we must move from what Ann Stoler terms the "the archive-as-source to the archive-as-subject."[4] Hence, my focus here is on the social and intimate worlds of colonial sexuality and on the very practices of archiving sex and bodies, which offer archivists and historians some glimpse into the lived, conflicted desires of the past. This book demonstrates how "textual imperial power"—that is, the paperwork of the crown, the judiciary, and the Church, through which colonialism was maintained—was enacted both on and through the body.[5] The result reveals connections between the ways that events (and the desires that inspired those events) are documented, the way those documents are archived, and the way that history itself is narrated and written. In its simplest form, this book is a social and cultural history of the regulation of "unnatural" sexuality in New Spain. But I depart from many histories of sexuality in that I focus not simply on historical mechanisms of repression, or on the social practices and desires of individuals or groups. Rather, this project reveals the ways in which bodies and their attendant desires come to be archived in the first place, and points to how the archive—as both a place and a concept—shapes our own connections to the past.

To trace these connections, it is worth delineating the different stages of the archival process. First, as in the case of Vidales, we have the person who *performs the act* that is deemed worthy of being recorded. Second, we have a chain of witnesses who *view and relate the act* to authorities, who then document the "denunciation"—the formal term for describing the accusation that a crime has been committed. Next comes the *escribano*—the court-appointed notary or scribe—who documents the accusations, testimonies, and confessions, thereby *recording the act* on paper. Then we have the archivist or bureaucrat who *files away the document* in some type of archive. These documents are subsequently *appraised and cataloged* by future generations of archivists and historians, who may find the documentation (or may not), who may alter its place and classifications within the archive, and who may write about it. What we will see in all such archived desires is that there is a tension between how we, as archive consumers, want these desires to behave and how they actually do. We often want to believe that desires, whether they be those of the Church or those of the "sodomite," are archivally stable, that we can make sense of them. The reality is that the desires of either the past or the present are inherently messy, complex, and resistant to categorization.

Archival Origins

As we open the box and uncover Spanish efforts to regulate the sins against nature, we are confronted first and foremost by the terms themselves. The "sins" of Lorenzo Vidales were determined centuries before his birth—the work of a long, and institutionalized, chain of reasoning going back to early Church fathers such as Saint Augustine and medieval theologians such as Thomas Aquinas. As early as the fifth century, for example, Saint Augustine had deemed unnatural and sinful any of those sexual acts that did not take place in the "vessel fit for procreation" (i.e., the vagina).[6] Thus sodomy, bestiality, and masturbation, and even unnatural sexual positions between men and women, were all "vices against nature," included in the broader category of *luxuria* (lust). Aquinas, in his thirteenth-century *Summa Theologica*, wrote: "Just as the order of right reason is from man, so the order of nature is from God himself. And so in sins against nature, in which the very order of nature is violated, an injury is done to God himself, the orderer of nature."[7] Nature, in the eyes of the Church, is an eminently teleological structure in which proper desire was not for the sexual act itself but instead in the ideal result of that act—procreation. It is in this way that the sins against nature, which were delineated in social terms as contravening the institution of marriage, were defined centuries before New Spain ever existed, by a vision of sex that emphasized its procreative aim above all else.

Some clarification of the terms "sexuality" and "desire," as I use them throughout this book, is warranted here. How might we speak of sexuality (and sexual desire) in an epoch before the advent of "sexuality"—a term, concept, and organizing principle of the self that emerged only in the nineteenth century? The equivalent Spanish-language term, *sexualidad*, appears in not one of the hundreds of archival documents on which this book is built. Yet the concept is useful for historians despite (or perhaps because of) its anachronistic ring. As Merry Wiesner-Hanks notes, early modern peoples "had sexual desires and engaged in sexual actions that they talked and wrote about but they did not think of these as expressions of their sexuality, and they defined what was 'sexual' in ways that are different than we do."[8] These differences, archival and historiographical, lie at the heart of this book.

The second term is even more loaded; I want to be explicit that "desire" here should not be viewed as a psychoanalytic concept. To speak of desire in the colonial past, we must, I believe, do our best to conceptually unmoor desire from its nineteenth- and twentieth-century psychoanalytic underpinnings. The ways I use "desire" here are how early modern and colonial contemporaries throughout the Iberian Atlantic world would have understood the Spanish-language or, more accurately, the Castilian-language term *deseo*, which is the word that recurs most in the archives. *Deseo* is etymologically tied to the Latin *desiderium* (desire) and *desiderare* (to desire), and was used first and foremost to refer to an ardent longing or yearning, for someone or something.

The 1611 *Tesoro de la lengua castellana o española*—the first vernacular dictionary of the Castilian language, published by Sebastián de Covarrubias— defines the term *desear* (to desire) as "to have desire for some thing" and explicates the term *deseado* (desired) as "the thing that is desired."[9] Covarrubias links pleasure, desire, and consumption through *gana* (longing), which is "equal to desire, appetite, will, and those things for which we have an inclination and we long for, because we find pleasure and happiness in them."[10] The *Diccionario de autoridades*—the first dictionary of the Castilian language published by the Real Academia Española, in six volumes, between 1726 and 1739—also defines *deseo* in broad strokes: "Longing or appetite for an absent or not possessed good."[11] Desire, in this and other examples, is connected semantically to appetite, or *apeténcia*—the "interior movement with which things are desired and longed for, and especially those that the body needs for its sustenance," and vice versa.[12] Here, desire is also inextricably tied to absence.

Desire in the Iberian Atlantic world was often explicitly linked to erotic impulses, carnal desires, and sex, but not always. Desire in the early modern world must therefore be conceptualized within a much broader framework of longing, yearning, inclination, pleasure, and appetite—which were just as likely to take on both bodily and spiritual forms. It is in this vein that we will best understand desire in colonial New Spain—plural and interconnected, corporeal and spiritual, inextricable from the human, the animal, and the divine.

Given this more generous conceptualization of desire in the early modern past, this book seeks to offer a methodology of desire, interpellating the desires of the past with those of the present. We can, I think, rightly speak of individual instances of desire for the human, the animal, and the divine while we also elucidate bureaucratic manifestations of desire: colonial officials' desires to edify subject populations (through rituals of exoneration and public punishment), priests' desires to access the interiority of parishioners (through the sacrament of confession), and archivists' desires to order and preserve (through classification and taxonomy). These past desires intersect with my own desires as a historian: to access the intimate past through the archives, to theorize and grasp for the meanings of "unnatural" sex under colonialism, and to write about (and thereby re-archive) the bodies of the past, exposing them to an audience and readership for whom they were never intended.

We must acknowledge, then, the corollary desires of today's archivists and historians: to classify and commit certain acts to memory (or patrimony) and to "history." Equally important, we must reckon with a corollary set of desires—both conscious and unconscious—of archivists and historians: to obfuscate and marginalize those pieces of the archive that do not fit the story they want to tell. To try our best to conceptualize desire (through longing, appetite, will, inclination, and pleasure) as early modern peoples may have is to embody, through writing and scholarship, a methodology that opens up rather than forecloses the radical possibilities and potentialities of desire, and the ways it overlaps and deviates from our own. Early modern peoples understood desire in ways that are significantly different from (yet still intimately connected to) twenty-first-century observers, interpreters, and translators of the past. In grappling with colonial desires, we must search for proximity and points of connection but also acknowledge our distance from them.

Archival Encounters

The area known as New Spain embodies Mary Louise Pratt's concept of the "contact zone": a place "in which peoples geographically and historically separated come into contact with each other and establish ongoing relations, usually involving conditions of coercion, radical inequality, and intractable conflict."[13] But there is a second contact zone in this study: the archive itself. Antoinette Burton considers the archive as a contact zone "between past and present as well as between researchers and structures of local, national, and global power."[14] I want to push this analogy further, suggesting the archive as a space in which archived subjects, scribes, archivists, and historians are always constituted by, and in relation to, one another.

Present-day archivists and historians, when handling and analyzing archival documents, become inextricably wrapped up in all the acts of recording and archiving stretching back to the originating event. Thus, the archive should be seen as a contact zone between past and present but also between temporally diverse and interconnected processes of documenting (bodies) and consuming (information). The archive itself reflects how historical contact zones necessarily involve sex—a central component of the "ongoing relations" between the colonizer and the colonized, mediated by race, class, and gender.

The archival research presented in this study is unique in a number of ways, first and foremost in its focus on the archival encounters between the past and the present. Second, this corpus of documents has never before been assembled and studied together. My methodological approach of analyzing the initial acts of recording allows me to pay close attention to what María Elena Martínez has termed "the violent processes by which most cases of sodomy and other sexual practices became part of the historical record."[15] Historians of sexuality, when reading and writing about the bodies and desires of historical others, are, as we will see, especially implicated in these processes.

Regarding the archival sources themselves, the corpus of documents I analyze is geographically diverse, comprising records from just over two dozen historical archives in Mexico, Guatemala, Spain, and the United States. The archives most central to this project, in terms of case numbers, were Mexico's Archivo General de la Nación and Guatemala's Archivo General de Centro América. This book relies equally on local (state, municipal, judicial, and notarial) archives from the Mexican states of Aguascalientes, Chihuahua, Colima, Guanajuato, Hidalgo, Michoacán, Nuevo León, Oaxaca, Puebla, Querétaro, San Luis Potosí, Tlaxcala, and Zacatecas. Archives and special collections—including the Bancroft Library, the John Carter Brown Library, the Huntington Library, the Lilly Library, the Newberry Library, the Spanish Archives of New Mexico (microfilmed at the University of Texas at El Paso), and the Latin American Library at Tulane University—have also provided criminal and Inquisition cases, law codes, confessional manuals, religious literature, and images. Finally, the Archivo General de Indias in Seville, Spain, held colonial sodomy cases from the galleons sailing between Spain and port cities in the Gulf of Mexico and the Caribbean.

Many historians of sexuality in New Spain have relied primarily on national archives or on specific regional archives (in conjunction with national archives), and most have implicitly made male-female sexual relations the assumed category of analysis. Local archives remain largely underutilized by historians of sexuality in the colonial period, and the sins against nature remain understudied. This book, therefore, represents the first attempt to compile, analyze, and reproduce an unprecedented archival corpus of 327 documents, originating in both the criminal courts and the courts of the Inquisition, on the sins against nature in New Spain. The documents consist of complete Inquisition and criminal cases, fragments of cases, judicial summaries, denunciations and self-denunciations, correspondence between local magistrates and superior courts, appeals, private letters, royal decrees, edicts, and archival and indexical references (alongside glaring archival absences).

The word "corpus" itself purposefully connects the body—*cuerpo*—and the archive. "Corpus" comes from Latin and originally denoted a human or animal body. It only later came to signify a collection of written texts. The term, as used here, thus describes both a collection or body of texts as well as the archived human/animal/divine body as it is represented within the archival document, the archive's finding aids, and the historiographical literature. This association invites us to think through the complicated connections and relations between bodies and texts. As we will see throughout this book, bodies and archives overlap in multiple and unexpected ways, always mediated by the emotions and affective states of ensuing generations of archivists and historians. My time in the archives has prompted me to ponder, to imagine, and to articulate the interconnectedness of text and body, of archive and embodiment, in different ways.

Given that no one has written about the vast majority of cases analyzed here, it is my hope that *Sins against Nature* will be seen in and of itself as an act of archiving—a mere snapshot, but a valuable glimpse nonetheless, of colonial desires and archived bodies. Carla Freccero and Laurent Dubois, among others, have worked through the implications of "archives in the fiction."[16] Building on such formulations, I propose that we also locate *archives in the historiography*—that is, in assembling a corpus of cases, reproducing their archival classifications, and writing about them in historical scholarship, we create a historiographical archive that then becomes accessible to others in ways previously impossible. To this end, I have published a supplementary PDF file of all the archival documents employed in this study on the NYU Faculty Digital Archive (where it is supposed to last forever!), in hopes of assisting others in their research.[17] Of the 327 documents, over 170 are from the eighteenth century, and nearly 80 cases come from the first two decades of the nineteenth century. By contrast, just over 50 cases hail from the seventeenth century, and a mere 13 are from the sixteenth.

The physical reality of the archival documents is just as revealing as their chronological distribution. Found in varied states of physical preservation, they range in length from one page to nearly 250 folios (a folio being an individual leaf of paper, written on both sides but numbered only on the recto, or front, side). Thus, the significantly deteriorated thirty-five-folio sodomy case of Pedro Bravo—riddled with insect holes and water damage—actually contains seventy pages of text, given that the verso, or back, of each folio is unnumbered (fig. Intro.1). This incomplete 1658 trial of Bravo—whose neighbors in Real de los Pozos accused him of being a certain don Lucas, a "*puto* and sodomite" who had been tried for sodomy in a nearby town some years earlier, and who fled to evade justice—reminds us just how fragile the colonial archive can be in terms of its materiality. No matter how careful I was in handling Bravo's pages (with latex or cloth gloves), bits of "dust" from the slowly disintegrating document lingered on the table where I photographed the folios. Each trip to the archives thus reminds us how our own engagements with the past are mediated by the haptic and the sensory, and can quite literally contribute to the erasure of the past.

In moments like this I cannot help but wonder: Through whose hands has this document passed, and whose skin oils have marred its pages over the

Fig Intro.1 A verso page of the partly deteriorated 1658 sodomy trial transcript of Pedro Bravo in San Luis Potosí. Courtesy of the Archivo Histórico del Estado de San Luis Potosí, San Luis Potosí, Mexico. AHESLP, 1658-3, "23 diciembre, contra Pedro Bravo por somético," fol. 4v.

centuries? Whose handling of its pages has contributed to their own slow deterioration? This approach takes to heart a question proposed by Kathryn Burns: "After all, how else are we to go into archives if not through our senses?"[18] I too emphasize the haptic and the sensory to illustrate larger points about how the past touches us, and how we, in the archive, literally touch the past *and* contribute to its deterioration. We, too, will see the how the five senses—especially sight—figured centrally into these archival cases. Always worth keeping in the back of our minds is the tangible, physical artifact of the document and the ways in which it both *produces desire* (among its readers) and *is produced by desire* (through witnesses, notaries, and colonial officials). Desire itself is constantly coming undone and being sutured to historical meaning, perhaps not unlike the dilapidated pages of colonial archival documents that are bound and rebound over time.

Archival Procedures

We know about people like Lorenzo Vidales from documents that were preserved in New Spain's secular or inquisitorial court records, hence my frequent mention of these archival stories as either a criminal case or an Inquisition case. In the secular system, on the one hand, the sins against nature are seen as *criminal*—worthy of punishment by New Spain's secular courts. Ecclesiastical records, such as those of the Holy Office of the Mexican Inquisition, provide a different understanding of the sins against nature; the Church investigated and prosecuted those thoughts and behaviors that it deemed *heretical*. The primary aim of the Holy Office of the Mexican Inquisition—established in 1569 by royal decree of Phillip II of Spain and founded in 1571—was to extirpate errant religious beliefs and police the boundaries of orthodoxy. The distinction between crime and heresy—and between criminal and inquisitorial jurisdictions—is crucial, though occasionally ambiguous, and plays itself out in the chapters that follow in terms of which acts came to be denounced to (and archived by) which courts. Technically, the sins against nature fell under the jurisdiction of the secular criminal courts in New Spain, and not under that of the ecclesiastical courts, though cases that broached heretical thoughts or acts—like a priest soliciting sex during confession or erotic religious visions—are significant exceptions.

The question of jurisdiction itself was a complicated one. In New Spain's government, the executive and judicial spheres—specifically, the office of the viceroy and the High Court of Mexico (Audiencia de México), which was New Spain's superior tribunal in charge of both criminal and civil matters—were not separated. There were no juries in criminal courts, and the threat of torture brooded over many proceedings. When reading the statements of the accused—even those in which they seem to voluntarily and sincerely confess their crimes—we should, therefore, always be aware of the trying conditions under which they were offered. Colonial authorities relied on a number of oft-conflicting codes of law, including the *Siete Partidas*—the Spanish legal code promulgated by Alfonso X between 1256 and 1265—as well as the sixteenth-century *Leyes de Toro*, and the *Recopilación de Leyes de las Indias* (compiled and codified in 1680 and reissued in 1756, 1774, and 1791).[19] The implication of this reliance is that there was a vast diversity of guidelines throughout New Spain for the very same crime. In addition, there were a number of laws emanating from colonial audiencias, viceroys, and cabildos (Spanish-style municipal councils), which could also influence the outcome of cases at the level of local courts.

The Sala del Crimen—the highest-ranking criminal institution in New Spain, established in 1568—held ultimate authority over secular crimes and judicial matters. In the chapters that follow, we will find several examples of court cases that were adjudicated at the local level—that of the town or village where the crime occurred—and then appealed by a suspect's defense lawyer to the Sala del Crimen. This reflects the basic fact that most criminal cases were adjudicated locally, with the help of a local Spanish administrator (the *alcalde mayor* or *corregidor*) or, in the case of indigenous communities, by the indigenous cacique and the native officials of the cabildo. Making matters even more complicated, a separate legal body known as the Juzgado General de Indios (the General Indian Court) also held authority over native peoples, superseding that of local political leaders in indigenous communities. This convoluted complexity at the heart of the legal system plays itself out in many of the cases analyzed here.

There was also the rival system of ecclesiastical courts, many of which were set up under the Holy Office of the Mexican Inquisition, established in 1571, following a 1569 *cédula real* issued by King Phillip II, which ordered the establishment of two tribunals of the Holy Office—one in New Spain and another in Peru. In 1610 the Spanish crown established a third tribunal of the Inquisition in Cartagena. The primary goal of the Inquisition—in the Old World as in the New—was to combat heresy, though the meanings and boundaries of "heresy" shifted significantly over time. In Spain and Portugal, for instance, the Inquisition was typically concerned with witchcraft and with the religious beliefs and practices of Jews and Muslims who had converted to Catholicism. In the Americas, however, the various tribunals of the Inquisition were more concerned with punishing "superstitious" practices and bigamy—all too common among Spaniards who relocated to the Americas—and with regulating Catholic dogma that seemed to be straying too far from Rome, as well as with the content of prohibited books. The Church's efforts to stamp out heresy across multiple continents operated largely on the basis of denunciations and self-denunciations. Thus, one central act of the Inquisition was the dissemination of Edicts of Faith—published annually during Lent and posted in populous centers—the most common means of urging the masses to keep their consciences clean by denouncing their own sins and those of others. The edicts also informed the general population of which sins fell under the jurisdiction of the Inquisition and were therefore worthy of denunciation to priests and ecclesiastical courts.

In New Spain, as mentioned above, the Holy Office of the Inquisition by and large did *not* have jurisdiction over the sins against nature. This limited jurisdiction contrasts with much of the early modern Iberian world, including the Spanish cities and municipalities of Valencia, Barcelona, Zaragoza, and Palma de Mallorca, as well as Portugal and its overseas colonies of Brazil and Goa, where both sodomy and bestiality fell under the jurisdiction of the Inquisition. In Castile, Ferdinand the Catholic placed sodomy under the jurisdiction of the Inquisition in 1505, but he subsequently revoked that decree and in 1509 placed it under the purview of the secular authorities, which had important consequences for New Spain. Because the Indies was incorporated into the Crown of Castile in the sixteenth century, the Castilian legal system and its administrative and judicial bureaucracies were transposed to those territories. The law in New Spain was clear: the Holy Office of the Mexican Inquisition was allowed to prosecute cases of sodomy *only* when some overt heresy (like solicitation in the confessional) or a heretical proposition (like asserting that "sodomy is not a sin") was involved.

The result of these cumbersome layers of secular and ecclesiastical courts was a large element of uncertainty and caprice. The system of social control was set up to investigate, punish, document, and archive crimes of all kinds, and to fulfill overlapping projects: colonizing the vast territories of New Spain, converting indigenous populations to Christianity, and regulating the thoughts and actions of the populace. Spanish colonizers transplanted the terminology of "nature" to the New World, incorporating it into the colonial theological, archival, and legal lexicons of the colonial enterprise. An analysis of the formulation "against nature," archived under its many guises, therefore enables us to critique the salient dichotomies—natural/unnatural, reproductive/sodomitical, and human/animal—underlying the reproductive ideology behind colonialism. Sex in New Spain, in its many manifestations and conflicted meanings, serves as a (murky, occluded) window to observe the interplay and tension between gender, desire, and colonialism—as well as the ensuing tension between archival iterations of repression and toleration that persist to the present. Here, we will see how the contradictions, complexities, and ambiguities of colonial culture and everyday life are negotiated, first through the body and then through the archive.

Because we are dealing largely with the records of criminal trials, it is helpful to review the procedural norms in a typical criminal investigation of sodomy in New Spain. The first phase was known as the *sumaria*, a fact-gathering stage in which the court sought to determine the particulars of the case. The facts, here, were elicited from witnesses (and, if the sex wasn't consensual, from the victim), who gave testimony in response to questions posed by judicial officers. After the presentation of facts, the judge or inquisitor would next request an *auto de confesión*—an act of confession. This was the suspect's opportunity to profess what he or she had done; the suspects more often than not, however, maintained their innocence and offered their version. Transcription, all the while, was done by the escribano, the notary whose job it was to faithfully document testimonies and confessions. During this phase of the criminal proceedings, interrogation could also be accompanied by force. Judicial torture, while used relatively sparingly in New Spain, was sanctioned throughout the colonial period and was consistently used as a threat by prosecutors.

During the second phase of the criminal investigation, the *juicio plenario*, both the prosecution and the defense produced additional witnesses in order to prove their respective positions. Witnesses were occasionally cross-examined in an accepted courtroom procedure known as the *careo*, during which the accuser and the accused were both present in the courtroom to give their respective version of events. Here the court would appoint a *defensor*, or defense attorney, to give the defendant legal counsel. During the *sentencia*, the final stage of criminal proceedings, the judge, basing his decisions on the trial proceedings and expert opinion, either absolved the defendant of the charges or pronounced the defendant guilty and sentenced him or her for the crimes committed. The punishment, as we will see in the chapters that follow, could include imprisonment, public shaming, corporeal punishment, some kind of fine or seizure of personal goods, an auto-da-fé, and even death.

The actual unfolding of the investigation and trial was, just as today, often quite different from this ideal. This development becomes even more difficult to trace with the passage of time, as inconsistencies abound and procedural steps are difficult to reconstruct.[20] The issue at hand is not only whether the proper procedural steps occurred but, in addition, whether we can use the archival record to figure out if and how these steps were (or were not) followed. Using criminal and Inquisition cases alongside other published and unpublished sources enables us to juxtapose popular and official narratives while, at the same time, acknowledging the multilayered testimonies and constructed nature of archival sources. Statements by defense lawyers, testimonies by witnesses, confessions by suspects, and rulings by judges are central to this book; but we can never assume that these sources express themselves in some "authentic" way, nor should we forget that the recorded testimonies were filtered by colonial authorities and scribes, as well as by subsequent generations of archivists. For, as Kathryn Burns tells us, "notaries produced a shaped, collaborative truth—one that might shave, bevel, and polish witnesses' words a bit here, a bit there, as they were 'translated' into writing."[21] The same can be said for historians. As the following pages demonstrate, archival documents themselves are the collaborative products of entangled narratives of body, sex, and desire.

Archival Flickers

Carnal acts, colonial control, and court procedures all stem from some manifestation of desire: the desire for sex, for control, for retribution. Yet archived desire, in particular, is inherently unstable. Desire, as represented in colonial archives, provides us with a prime example of what one scholar has recently termed "archival aporia"—that is, a site of internal, and irresolvable, archival contradictions. These overlapping desires force us to reckon with representation and its limits, in both spoken words (denunciation, testimony, confession) and written texts (transcriptions, documents, finding aids, archive catalogs).[22] What, then, is at stake in archiving desire through the prism of the unnatural? The further I delved into the archives of New Spain, and the more I worked through the stakes of this project, the more I ran up against queerness. "Queerness," as a term, makes its way into the pages of Sins against Nature only minimally. However, in its methodology and theory, this is a queer project at heart.

Can scholars queer the colonial archive through the unnatural? Within the history of sexuality, "queer" is a decidedly contentious term. As a category of identitarian politics (akin to, some might argue, or against the more familiar categories of identity: lesbian, gay, bisexual, or transgender), the term "queer," I argue, has minimal relevance to colonial Latin America. However, as an anti-identitarian concept, and as a methodology, "queer" has a particular relevance to this history, which seeks to deprivilege heteronormative (and homonormative) ways of researching, writing, and archiving desire. It might be easy to assume that this book is queer because it focuses on desires that are deemed to be "against nature." That, however, would be too simple.

This book is queer because of its sustained effort to stage archival encounters across several centuries. It follows Arlette Farge's insight that "archives bring forward details that disabuse, derail, and straightforwardly break any hope of linearity or positivism," pointing to what Carolyn Dinshaw calls the "temporal multiplicities"—or queer temporality—of books, texts, and archival documents.[23] Queer conceptualizations of time oscillate between past and present (and the lure of the future), with our own desires and emotions guiding, to some extent, how we engage with the archive and why we tell the archival stories we do, in *our* present. Using a queer studies methodological approach, in mainstream historical archives, to traverse the temporal *through* the visceral—*queer archivalism*, in the words of Elizabeth Freeman—allows us to explore the fraught (and anachronistic) relations between past and present, archive and document, historian and witness, writer and written of, consumer and consumed.[24]

My project, admittedly, did not begin with such insights; I was initially interested in writing a temporally bounded social history of sodomy, "homosexuality," and "same-sex desire" in colonial Mexico. The true starting point for this book—once I realized that I needed to look beyond same-sex desire—was to complicate my own understanding of desire in the colonial past (in relation to the present). This project thus came into being only when I myself moved away from thinking about desire as teleological or as progressing toward some imagined endpoint, be that marriage, reproduction, or even the consummation of a discrete, bounded sexual act such as penetration, orgasm, or ejaculation—phenomena that in the Iberian Atlantic world came to determine which acts counted as sodomy and which did not.

This book builds on other queer archival projects in which activists, archivists, and scholars have sought to expand the very notion of "the archive," in part through feminist and postcolonial critiques of colonial and bureaucratic consolidations of power. If we recast the archives of colonial Latin America queerly, we do so by applying pressure to our own preconceptions about sex in the past, and about the archival forms through which we inherit our understandings of this past. Simply focusing on the varied sex acts that did not result in procreation does not make a project queer in any meaningful way, and it certainly does not embody a queer archival methodology. Instead, what makes this project queer, at its core, is its focus on that which is "strange, odd, funny, not quite right, improper" about how bodies and desires come to be archived in the first place (and, subsequently, how these indexes are granted, and denied, archival status in catalogs and finding aids).[25] Furthermore, my own conflicted engagements with the material I encountered in the archives—and perhaps even those of the readers of this book—also makes this project queer.

Sins against Nature ultimately grapples with the queer instability of desire, as it comes to be textually recorded and archived. In an essay on Jacques Derrida and the archive, Verne Harris questions the supposed static nature of any particular moment in time: "No trace in memory, not even the image transposed onto film by a camera lens, is a simple reflection of event. In the moment of its recording, the event—in its completeness, its uniqueness—is lost."[26] The same, of course, is true for desire: as it is being recorded, archived, and documented, it is paradoxically (in the process of) being lost forever. We are left with an imperfect trace of what was once a unique, ephemeral instantiation of desire. Yet textual and affective traces remain; a queer methodology invites us to theorize our own ephemeral encounters with these archival flickers of desire.

As *Sins against Nature* demonstrates, archival representations of desire are muddled and deteriorating (both physically and discursively): they flicker and flutter—not unlike shadows and silhouettes of objects illuminated by candlelight—and slowly disintegrate, along with the always-aging papers on which they are inscribed. Many of the archives in Mexico, as elsewhere, are now being digitized, giving us the illusion of permanence. Yet the flicker persists: microfilmed, photographed, and scanned documents will always be mere (imperfect) copies of an ever-changing, slowly disintegrating archival document (which may be a copy of another document in and of itself).

If, as Carla Freccero posits, "queer can thus be thought of as the trace in the field of sexuality," and, as José Muñoz tells us, "the key to queering evidence . . . is by suturing it to the concept of ephemera," then the queer here is an archival copy of a copy (of a copy) of an archival flicker of an original desire—a desire whose origins are difficult, and perhaps impossible, to determine.[27] Queering the colonial archive then is not about reading particular acts, desires, and subjectivities in the past as "queer" but rather about using the archive itself to elucidate the contours of ephemeral desires, ritualistic record-keeping practices, and the illusory nature of colonial hegemony as enacted on desiring bodies. Colonial archives exude these expressions of desire; they literally pour through archival inventories, card catalogs, and the very pages of archival documents. Like the inkblots that bleed through the recto side of an early modern

Iberian handwritten manuscript, becoming a shadow on its verso counterpart, desire seeps from the archive, often in unsuspecting ways.

If we return to the criminal case of Lorenzo Vidales, we see how the archive interpellates truth and fiction—original light and archival flicker. Vidales did indeed penetrate a goat, and he was indeed punished; but this brief flicker of desire in the past is completely wrapped up with (and transmitted through) the notary's written words and the archive itself, both as a system of representation and as a physical place where documents are preserved. The desires that the archival document points to were, to some degree, actually felt and acted on by Vidales, yet this does not make the representation and conveyance of those desires (into the archive) any less problematic, or any more "authentic." The archived desires of Vidales are mundane yet ritualistic (in terms of how they were initially recorded), illusory (in terms of how they allow us to construct Vidales as a historical subject), and ephemeral (in terms of the impermanence of desire and of the pages on which it is inscribed). In the case of Vidales, as in all the cases that follow, the desires of the imperial state ran up against the desires of the perpetrator, of the witnesses, and of spectators who witnessed his public punishment. Archival desires flicker; lived desires come through the document through the distortions and misinscriptions of those who created the document, and of everyone who has handled it since.

Sins against Nature ultimately explores how bodies and their desires are textually recorded and archived (through the collaboration of witnesses, confessants, scribes, colonial bureaucrats, and archivists), and thus survive into our own day. In the archive, we find not desire itself but rather the contours of desire, which we can merely begin to trace, only to be left partly frustrated (and perhaps even challenged and inspired) by the amorphous and malleable nature of desire itself. Desire as it is recorded in the archive becomes, in some ways, a mere fantastical projection of itself. Not unlike Spanish and mestizo priests who, in New Spain, penned bilingual confessional manuals—discursively creating, narrating, enumerating the sins of lust—those who participated in the many stages of secular and inquisitorial court proceedings actively sought out, constructed, and narrated those desires they deemed "against nature." In doing so, they also inevitably projected their own fantasies and desires on the bodies of others (as I, and perhaps you, do too).

As Carolyn Steedman notes, "Nothing starts in the Archive, nothing, ever at all, though things certainly end up there. You find nothing in the Archive but stories caught half way through: the middle of things; discontinuities."[28] The colonial archive exposes these discontinuous, interconnected desires. It therefore destabilizes desire at the very same time that priests and colonial authorities sought (at least in theory) to stabilize and punish unnatural acts and desires, as if they themselves were exempt from their reach.

Archival Forms

This book offers much-needed theoretical interventions on writing the intertwined histories of sexuality, desire, and archives, and, in the process, of colonialism itself. The criminal case of Lorenzo Vidales, a minimal moment in the marginalia of colonial Mexico, is nevertheless part of the vast archive of the unnatural. My contention here is that a crime such as that which Vidales committed with the goat in 1656 is constitutive of (and central to) the intimate workings of colonialism on, and through, the body. Yet scholars privilege certain archival iterations of desire over others. To put it bluntly: few historians, for example, have written about bestiality as a topic of serious inquiry and analysis.

What cultural and intellectual blinders cause us to deny the importance of these "sins"? In 2008 at the Tepoztlán Institute for Transnational History of the Americas, I presented a draft of what eventually became the fourth chapter of this book, on bestiality in New Spain. A well-known Cuban scholar approached me afterward and chastised me for writing on a topic that, according to this individual, was not worthy of research and that gave Mexicans a "bad reputation" in front of an international audience. This scholar was not persuaded by my argument that the topic was indeed worthy of scholarly attention because, among other reasons, there were *hundreds* of criminal cases of bestiality scattered throughout Mexican archives, long ignored by historians, with few exceptions. This scholar had, I think, a visceral reaction.

As Joan M. Schwartz and Terry Cook note, archives "are not some pristine storehouse of historical documentation that has piled up, but a reflection of and often justification for the society that creates them."[29] The same can be said of the historiographical engagement that results from our archival perusing. While *Sins against Nature* focuses on sexual acts and desires that have been understudied, I have no desire to merely "fill in the gaps," to simply address the lacunae of traditional historiography and offer a more complete version of the past. Here it befits us to acknowledge Anjali Arondekar's critique that the archive is too often a place for those academics and activists who "would presume that there is something about sexuality that is lost or silent and needs to 'come out.'"[30] Rather than utilize the colonial archive as a site for recovering lost historical subjects or locating agency, this book engages colonial society's own categories, concepts, and presuppositions to theorize how individuals experienced and reconciled conflicting desires at personal and institutional levels, and to theorize how archivists and historians think through those desires.

For Farge, it is only when you are "open to the forms the archive contains that you are able to notice things that were not *a priori* of interest," and this is certainly something that I learned—and continue to learn—over the course of archival research.[31] Bestiality was not initially of interest to me, yet it surfaced through the bureaucratic forms of the archive, conceptually conflated with other acts and desires deemed to be "against nature." It was only when I reconsidered my own preconceived notions of "same-sex desire" that more complex—or perhaps better yet, *queerer*—desires emerged, in myriad finding aids, catalogs, and documents. They emerged simultaneously from the very heart of the colonial archive and from its margins. Openness to archival forms—that is, the arrangements, configurations, and blind spots of an archive—is thus an obligatory step in reworking our own archival desires alongside the desires that we seek out in (and through) the archives. Only then did the impetus behind *Sins against Nature* become messier, both methodologically and theoretically, than I initially intended. The more archives I visited, the more simplistic my understanding of sodomy seemed. As a result of my unexpected encounters with the archived bodies and desires of historical figures such as Lorenzo Vidales, my previous conceptual categories—"same-sex sexuality," "illicit sex," and "deviant sexual acts"—fell apart, luring me toward "sins against nature."

I explore four major themes in this book. I begin with the visceral, and then move on to respectively discuss the human, the animal, and the divine. The book's first chapter examines how viscerality is central to archival studies of early modern sexuality (and beyond). Here I show how particularly unclassifiable acts and desires come into archival being by eliciting visceral responses—gut feelings—on the part of witnesses, both past and present. I argue that visceral reactions on the part of contemporary witnesses—like Nicolás de Lares—led to the initial archiving of particular bodies and desires, and that such gut reactions reverberate throughout history and across archival existence, thereby laying bare some of the erotic chains that structure and confuse the taxonomizing impulses of the archive itself. To get at the deeper meanings of archived bodies and desires in the past, I take up the challenge to break down "the layers of historical disgust that work to obscure them."[32] I further argue that a metaphorics of consumption undergirds historical archives and archival documents, as they are produced, ordered, read, and interpreted. Archivists and historians consume, digest, and expel the words and transcriptions of the archive, in a process that is always unfinished, that has no clear endpoint. The visceral, we will see, also mediates the tenuous boundary between the human, the animal, and the divine.

The next two chapters focus on the human, offering an extended analysis and discussion of sodomy among laypersons as it was recorded and archived by the secular criminal courts of New Spain. Chapter 2 examines the interrelated phenomena of archival misinscription and historical voyeurism largely though a microhistorical analysis of a sodomy case from 1604 in Valladolid, Michoacán, in which Spanish colonial authorities tried six Purépecha men for the crime of sodomy, publicly executing four of them. This chapter emphasizes problems of translation between indigenous languages—in this case, Purépecha—and Spanish, and looks at colonized language itself as a particular archival absence in the historical record. Finally, this chapter explores what Achille Mbembe terms the "trade between the archive and death," focusing on the ritual and symbolic use of the death penalty as a punishment for sodomy, and how it decreased over time, in New Spain.[33] I show that behind the decision to publicly burn someone convicted of sodomy lie the archival instincts of remembering and forgetting. This chapter narrates the taxonomizing impulse of the archive in relation to the voyeuristic impulses of witnesses, archivists, and historians—who at times occupy similar roles. Distortions abound in the colonial archive, which suggests that some level of misrepresentation becomes a necessary precondition for bodies and desires to enter the historical record in the first place.

Chapter 3 takes a more macrohistorical approach, utilizing just over 120 criminal cases to examine how sodomy was narrativized in both popular accounts and official registers. The bulk of this chapter looks specifically at the signs through which sodomy was read, interpreted, and narrated by witnesses, medics, scribes, and criminal courts. Secular courts privileged the ocular, but, as this chapter shows, eyewitness accounts of sodomy could be both challenged and corroborated by other types of signs, whether bodily, performative, or gestural in nature. Through such signs—particularly medical expertise, sexual violence, and public displays of gender and intimacy—sodomy becomes archivally visible to us in the present. Together, these two chapters show that throughout the colonial period, sodomy was irregularly, sporadically, and unequally prosecuted as much as it was reluctantly tolerated or conveniently ignored (and at times enacted) by priests and colonial officials.

These chapters demonstrate how the language of individual testimonies is problematic for archivists and historians, especially when court-appointed interpreters translated indigenous-language testimonies into Spanish. This is indeed part of how misinscription is enacted. Words like *echarse* (to throw oneself on another), *dormir* (to sleep with someone), *cabalgar* (to ride), *joder* (to fuck), and *acceso carnal* (carnal access) were all commonly used in denunciations and confessions alike, indicating a vernacular register of sexuality that was sometimes distorted as it was processed in official registers. The formulaic language used in criminal and Inquisition cases thus obscures popular conceptions of bodies, desires, and devotions but does not completely occlude them.

My decision to commence the book with the "human" should not be seen as an attempt to foreground the human subject. Rather, it is a means of critiquing a category that, as we move throughout the chapters, becomes increasingly unstable. Humanity is bereft of meaning without animality or divinity, and carnal desires attain much of their semantic drift from what the Church conceptualized as animalistic and monstrous "lust." Chapter 4 moves us therefore into the realm of the animal, focusing on a corpus of 144 archival references to bestiality, made up of complete criminal trials, fragments of cases, and ecclesiastical records. This chapter alludes to animal erasure, and this provocation has multiple aims. First, I highlight how the subjectivity of the nonhuman animal quite literally disappears—or perhaps never appears in the first place—and is effaced from the historical archive. Second, I show how in contrast to their human counterparts, the European domesticated animals—donkeys, mares, goats, cows, dogs, and hens—that criminal courts implicated in the crime of bestiality were regularly put to death by secular courts, so as to "erase the memory of such acts." Archives in this sense mediate spectacles of animal suffering and death, offering us only imperfect glimpses of the animal body in colonial archives. Finally, I posit that the human is, in fact, a disappearing animal—an archival animal that hides its true nature behind the conceptual cloak of "humanity."

In the final two chapters, I move to the divine, first by looking at priests as intermediaries between the human and the divine, and then by focusing on erotic religious visions and acts that, according to the Church, polluted and desecrated both human body and sacred space. Chapter 5 analyzes a corpus of some forty cases of Catholic priests who were tried by, or denounced to, the Holy Office of the Inquisition for the solicitation of sexual favors from male penitents (and often female penitents as well) in the confessional. The historiography of solicitation in the early modern Iberian Atlantic world has largely been skewed toward the study of priestly sexual advances and abuse that were directed toward women and girls—an imperative topic on which more research is needed. And while the topic of priestly abuse of boys and young men in the twentieth century has received ample attention in scholarship and in the media, the topic is underresearched in the early modern world. Although solicitation in the confessional was technically defined as heresy, the corpus of documents I examine here shows that many priests successfully evaded that charge. Many priests willfully distorted the discourse of religious desire and experienced an erotic charge by desecrating sacred space. Yet the punishments that priests received for the crimes of solicitation, sodomy, and mutual masturbation were lenient in comparison to those laypersons received. For this reason, I theorize this corpus of Inquisition documents as archives of negligence—another side to what Anthony M. Petro has called the "queer archive of Catholic sexual abuse."[34] This is an archive of desire that, despite (or perhaps because of) its preservation among the many files of the Holy Office, points repeatedly to individual and institutional cover-ups that were largely sanctioned by the Catholic Church. Here, the tension between forgetting and remembering in (and through) the archive is especially evident.

Finally, chapter 6 traces "pollution" (an early modern term for masturbation) and eroticized religiosity in New Spain through a handful of particularly fascinating Inquisition cases, which shed light on the shared intimacy between the sacred and the profane. This chapter focuses on eroticized desires for the divine, largely in relation to how "pollution," "obscene acts," "claiming sexual intercourse with saints," and "other errors" came to be archived in colonial New Spain up to the present. In articulating the intimate connections between spiritual and corporeal desires, this chapter uses the archives of the Mexican Inquisition to offer an unrivaled glimpse at how some priests, nuns, and laypersons in New Spain interpreted and experienced the divine in ways that intersected with, and challenged, communal religious beliefs and practices. I argue that those individuals who, for one reason or another, eroticized the divine simultaneously expanded both the devotional and erotic imaginary of the colonial archive. The explicit details of desires and devotions that emerge in this chapter remind us of the ultimately ineffable (and unarchivable) nature of private, intense religious experiences.

Together these chapters recast Iberian Atlantic history through the prism of the "unnatural," showing that colonialism itself relied on nature as a category of difference; that category, however, was ultimately as unstable as the bodies and desires that came to be documented in the archives. If we think about both the act of archiving and the writing of history as embodied practices, it makes sense to interrogate, as does Diana Taylor, how "materials from the archive shape embodied practice in innumerable ways, yet never totally dictate embodiment."[35] *Sins against Nature* shows how textual and embodied representations of desire—like that which the young Lorenzo Vidales experienced and acted on in 1656 with one of the goats from his flock—come to be documented and transcribed, eventually making their way into historical archives, and thus into history itself. While priests and criminal authorities in New Spain sought to punish offenders in order to "deaden the memory" of the sins against nature, paradoxically these bodies and desires came to be permanently archived through the very attempts of colonial authorities to suppress them.

Sins against Nature maintains that historical archives destabilize bodies, desires, and social categories—an assertion that has significant implications for those of us who create and use historical archives. The goal of this book is to peel back the layers of the colonial archive, first by focusing on the sins against nature and engaging documents for the rich ethnohistorical details that they provide, and then by subjecting all archival representations of desire to scrutiny. Only then can we hope to reveal the messy, murky terrain that lies beyond the deceptively simple words and scribbles annotated on an archival folio—hopefully making us even more aware of and vulnerable to the engagements, the affects, and the seductions of the archives.

CHAPTER I

Viscerality in the Archives

Consuming Desires

This book begins, perhaps counterintuitively, with an archival outlier. On February 15, 1810, a Spanish woman named Ignacia Gómez went, accompanied by a female friend, to the cemetery of San Juan de Dios in Mexico City. Their plan was to offer up prayers and light candles for Gómez's elderly aunt, Antonia Fontecho y Hurtado, who had died the previous day at nearly one hundred years of age. Upon entering the graveyard, the two women were affronted by the spectacle of a man on top of the elderly woman's corpse, with his genitals exposed, moving in a manner that left "little doubt" as to the "carnal act" he was carrying out. The description that eventually made its way into the criminal case, and thus into the archive, hints at a visceral response on the part of these women. Gómez and her friend shrieked, shocked and disgusted by what they were witnessing—a spontaneous reaction to an incomprehensible event. The man fled over the cemetery wall into the kitchen of the convent next door but was immediately apprehended by the resident priest, who had heard the women's screams.

The suspect, José Lázaro Martínez, was an eighteen-year-old unmarried indigenous man from Oaxaca. He was the servant of a bedridden man in the hospital adjoining the graveyard and was "uninstructed in the Christian doctrine." After detaining Lázaro Martínez, the priest handed him over to the Tribunal de La Acordada—a court that included its own autonomous police force, established in 1710 to punish highway robbery and contraband, among a variety of other crimes—to be imprisoned and tried for his crimes. Court officials first took statements from the two female witnesses. They then interrogated Lázaro Martínez, with a court-appointed clerk transcribing his confession. As usual for criminal and Inquisition trial records, notaries and scribes formulaically altered the speaker's first-person testimony into a third-person narrative. When, as was customary procedure, court officials asked the suspect if he knew why he had been imprisoned two days earlier, Lázaro Martínez confessed that on Wednesday of this week, at around two o'clock in the afternoon,

> two women found him in the graveyard of San Juan de Dios on top of a dead woman with whom he was fornicating, [and] that he did this because Miguel, the young servant of Father Lastra, sacristan of the same convent, had advised him so. [And] who, on two occasions, he saw that he [Miguel] locked himself in the cemetery, and he told him that he was going to fornicate with the dead women because his *amasia* [lover], who had died pregnant in that same hospital, was buried there. The abovesaid Miguel also advised that he make a hole in the underskirt of the dead woman to be able to fornicate with her.[1]

The day Lázaro Martínez was caught, he told tribunal officials that he and Miguel drank pulque—a traditional Mesoamerican alcoholic beverage made from the fermented sap of the maguey, or agave, plant—and, in a state of intoxication, they entered the graveyard with the intent of engaging in "carnal acts" with corpses. Lázaro Martínez swore that this was the only time he had carried out such an act, and Miguel, he said, fled before witnesses saw him.

One week later the court appointed a *curador*—a public defense lawyer—to represent Lázaro Martínez, and the trial proceeded, with the illustrious don Manuel Campo y Rivas as judge. In order for the suspect to swear an oath to the court, the judge, citing Lázaro Martínez's inability to make the sign of the cross as evidence that he was ignorant of Christian doctrine, deemed it necessary that he receive rudimentary religious instruction first. To this end, he was placed in the care of the prison's infirmary for several weeks. A second deposition was taken on April 12, 1810; this time he changed his story (though he was noticeably reticent, not wanting to respond to questions posed to him): "He said that he is in prison because in San Juan de Dios they found him in the graveyard on top of a dead woman, but that he does not remember because he was drunk."[2] Despite the court's instigation, Lázaro Martínez, now understanding the potential gravity of his situation with the help of legal counsel, asserted that his previous testimony was false, and that he was never found "carnally mixing with the dead woman."

The tribunal did not find Lázaro Martínez's change of heart convincing, concluding that "without a doubt" he had either been counseled to prevaricate or was trying to evade being punished for his crime. The very politics of memory were at stake. But, what exactly *was* the crime that Lázaro Martínez had committed? For twenty-first-century readers, the answer is obvious: this is a case of necrophilia. Yet that term, like "homosexuality," did not yet exist. It was not until 1850 that a Belgian physician and head of the psychiatric hospitals at Ghent, Joseph Guislain (1797–1860), coined the term *nécrophiles* in a lecture he gave in reference to the contemporary case of François Bertrand, a French sergeant who dug up dozens of corpses from a Paris cemetery to have sex with them (and was sentenced to one year in prison).[3] Lázaro Martínez's crime thus remained not entirely understandable, or classifiable, to his contemporaries—just one of the crucial terminological and conceptual points of disjuncture between the past and the present to which we will return in the pages that follow.

The tribunal faced a predicament: there was simply no law in Spain or in New Spain that dealt *specifically* with the act of "carnal congress with a corpse." Instead, Lázaro Martínez's defense interpreted the eighteenth-century Spanish legal code—specifically, the 1785 *Compendio de los comentarios extendidos por el maestro Antonio Gómez a las ochenta y tres leyes de Toro . . .* , compiled by Antonio Gómez—to mean that the act would be subsumed under the sins against nature. Chapter XII of Law LXXXII stipulated that "the crime *contra naturam* be punished with the customary penalty [death], even though it is neither perfect [i.e., in the anus] nor consummated [with ejaculation], but only attempted and prepared [for], by reason of its singular gravity."[4] The same segment of the code specifies: "only an arbitrary punishment is deserved if [carnal] access with another is not in the exterior vessel [i.e., the anus], but rather in another part of the body, or if there is only touching by hands with the spilling of semen."[5] The defense understood the act as falling within the sins against nature, but only in relation to carnal access with "another part" of the (dead) body, which carried less gravity than anal penetration. Lázaro Martínez's defense also (contradictorily) referenced other laws under which "a similar crime" could either enjoy immunity from the law or receive a ten-year sentence of forced labor on a presidio. Citing the boy's youth, status as an Indian, rusticity, and lack of understanding of Christianity, the defense pleaded that Lázaro Martínez be shown mercy.

The judge found no legal precedent in New Spain's criminal and ecclesiastical courts to which he could turn. Indeed, my years of research at dozens of archives have turned up only one other reference: a one-page denunciation made by fray Miguel de Zárate to the Inquisition in 1581.[6] Conceptually, the judge made sense of Lázaro Martínez's act by invoking the unnatural: "taking into account that he should be given a punishment for an act so scandalous, horrible, and repugnant to nature itself and even unto brute animals, and much more [so] having verified it in a sanctified place, dedicated to the burial of cadavers [of those] that died in that Hospital [of San Juan de Dios]."[7] The court transcripts also describe the act of carnal congress with a corpse as a grave "excess" deserving of punishment but reference no specific law or established punishment.

On May 14, 1810, a judge from Mexico's highest criminal court, the Real Audiencia, sentenced Lázaro Martínez to receive "twenty-five corrective lashes inside of the prison" and to labor for four years at the Fort of Perote, where he was to be instructed in the tenets of Christianity. The punishment was an arbitrary one but was in line with other late colonial criminal sentencing, that is, after the Bourbon Reforms were enacted in the eighteenth century. No doubt, Lázaro Martínez was to be whipped in private so as not to scandalize the public with, or fuel local gossip about, the obscene and practically unimaginable nature of his acts. The decision of the colonial court to *not* employ a town crier, or a *pregonero*—as was customary, to publicly shame the subject and proclaim the details of the crime to the masses—is instructive, highlighting some of the ambivalences of archiving. Despite leaving behind highly detailed bureaucratic records about the case—thereby permanently archiving this body and its "criminal" desires—the court sought, at some level, to publicly eradicate the memory of the defiling nature of his acts.

Beginning with two women's horror in a graveyard on the afternoon of February 15, 1810, this chapter examines viscerality in the archives. This is a theme that resonates throughout this book. How do visceral reactions affect the ways that a document comes to be archived? How do they alter the contents of the archive, and how do particular histories—and documents themselves—come to be encountered, classified, and interpreted? This chapter moves between two late colonial case studies: the 1810 criminal case of Lázaro Martínez and the 1775 Inquisition case of Manuel Arroyo, whose particular act of "sucking semen," we will soon see, confounded inquisitors nearly as much as Lázaro Martínez's sex with a corpse had perplexed authorities. In the historical past, in the archive, and beyond, these (and other) sins against nature have provoked a vast range of responses across time, from disgust to desire, indignation to indifference.

What conceptually unites these two cases—and many more, especially in the final chapter—is that these desires (and the bodily emissions that may have resulted) do not necessarily comply with the standard official and notarial terminology of the archive, despite the fact that they fell broadly within the purview of the sins against nature. The acts of Lázaro Martínez and of Arroyo are less legible and more historiographically marginalized than, for example, more straightforward cases of bestiality, sodomy, or masturbation. This chapter is thus partly about how official, standard, and bureaucratic language and categories shape (and are shaped by) the visceral, which in turn shapes the archive. To this end, I am interested here in practices of archival naming—which corporeal acts get specifically named and which do not.

This chapter explores the ways that the archive classifies the desires of the past and, in particular, the visceral, as illustrated in the criminal case of Lázaro Martínez and the Inquisition case of Manuel Arroyo. I then analyze the meta-phorics of consumption that undergird the archive (in both a textual and a cor-poreal sense). In particular, I show how the idiom of consumption has, by no small coincidence, filtered through archival theory and historical scholarship, and why this is relevant for the rest of the book. One thread weaving through this book is how scholars and archivists encounter documents—as well as the human protagonists and marginalized desires found within—through a type of cross-temporal affective engagement. This chapter stages an initial archival conversation about the past and present, telling a story about how people, including myself, engage with the archive over time. Focusing on viscerality in the archives, and on what sometimes gets left out of archival descriptions and scholarly analysis, enables such a conversation to take place. Viscerality, as we will soon see, has significant implications for those who create, order, and use archives.

Archiving the Visceral

I came across the criminal case of Lázaro Martínez years ago, by accident, through an exceptionally vague reference in the computer database of Mexico's national archive, the Guía General (General Guide) of the Archivo General de la Nación. I was then researching cultural, legal, and religious attitudes toward "unnatural" death—suicide, abortion, and infanticide—in colonial Latin America for a distinct but related and ongoing research project.[8] Unlike the nineteenth-century categories of "necrophilia" and "homosexuality," which do not appear in colonial Mexican archival catalogs and digital finding aids, the words "abortion" (*aborto*) and "infanticide" (*infanticidio*) appear with some frequency. "Suicide" (*suicidio*), in contrast, appears rarely, and typically only in relation to late eighteenth- and nineteenth-century records. My search for suicide in the archives thus necessitated creative digging for correlated terms, often framed in the self-reflexive tense, such as having "hanged" (*ahorcado*), "drowned" (*ahogado*), or "poisoned" (*envenenado*) oneself.

On a whim one day in Mexico City, I searched for the word "cadaver" (*cadáver*) with little hope that it would lead me to suicide cases (it did not). What I did come across, however, was a case that—in the perfunctory, euphemistic language of the anonymous late twentieth-century archivist responsible for classifying the document—referred vaguely to the "profanation of cadaver," or *profanación de cadáver*. This turned out to be the 1810 criminal case of Lázaro Martínez, though based on the description one would never know what his crime was. The database entry appears in the archive's computer database as such:

General Archive of the Nation / Colonial Institutions / Real Audiencia / Criminal (037) / Container 313 / Volume 705
Title: File 24
Date(s): YEAR 1810
Level of description: Composite documentary unit (File)
Volume and support: Pages: 237–250
Producers: (Pending)
Scope and content: CRIME: PROFANATION OF CADAVER; ACCUSED: JOSE
LAZARO MARTINEZ; AFFECTED: ANTONIA FONTECHO Y HURTADO;
PLACE: MEXICO [CITY].[9]

That day in the archive, I filled out the necessary forms to access volume 705 of the colonial criminal records, waited some ten minutes to receive the tome, and turned to folio 237. I was immediately and unpredictably shocked and enthralled. My vision narrowed on the page; I could barely believe what I was reading. The document, despite archival equivocation about its contents, turned out to be unlike anything I had expected, in part because the archivist's classification had distorted my expectations.

In extreme contrast to the database entry, the cover page, affixed to the criminal case when the documents were compiled in (or shortly after) 1810, read: "Mexico [City], Year of 1810. Against José Lázaro Martínez for having been found carnally mixing with a dead woman" (fig. 1.1).[10] That singular archival discrepancy, between catalog and document, triggered something that, in my years of research in the archives, I had never quite experienced; it was something not quite articulable—a cross between a vague sense of disgust at the details of the act (especially Miguel's advice that he cut "a hole in the underskirt

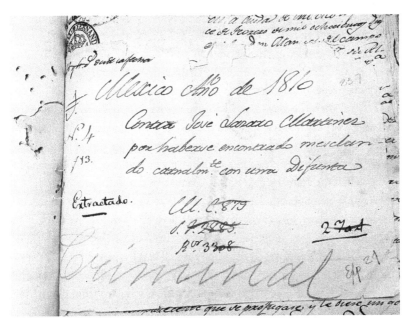

Fig 1.1 Title page of the 1810 criminal trial of José Lázaro Martínez. Courtesy of the Archivo General de la Nación, Mexico City, Mexico. AGN, Criminal 705, exp. 24, fol. 237.

of the dead woman to be able to fornicate with her"), a lurid fascination with the graphic descriptions of witnesses and suspect, and a burning, unrealizable desire to know more about the motivations of both men, especially those of Miguel.

What I felt that day in the archives, in other words, was visceral—an abrupt, intense, intuitive gut response to some external stimulus, experienced through conflicted and partly incomprehensible corporeal and emotive sensations. Viscerality, I believe, has an untapped potential for archival studies of early modern sexuality (and beyond). For Brian Massumi, viscerality "registers *intensity*" and "excitations gathered by the five 'exteroceptive' senses even before they are fully processed by the brain."[11] Those five senses—sight, hearing, touch, smell, and taste—help, through proprioception, to perceive one's own bodily position, motion, and state in relation to the external environment. Attentiveness to the visceral has the potential to seduce (and nauseate), for it emerges from "that abject and erotic territory—the blood and guts, cum and shit" of the archive, provoking us, sometimes unwillingly, to feel our own bodies, desires, and gut reactions in intimate relation to archival narratives of sex and desire in the past.[12] Visceral reactions unsteadily guide us into the uncharted territory of how we ourselves, as archive users, can be physically and affectively moved by the archive in ways that we might not fully like, expect, or understand. In opening our analysis up to viscerality, we may find surprising points of connection (and disjuncture) between the past and the present, between the ways that historical actors and we ourselves may (or may not) share certain responses in the face of a particular image or event.

Several concepts central to this book emerge through the case of Lázaro Martínez, in the details of his trial, in the unclassifiable nature of his crime, and in the ways that the court records are archived across time. To the final point, I propose that we understand archiving itself as an ongoing process set in motion, at least in part, by a chain of visceral reactions: from historical actors to colonial officials, from notaries and scribes, from archivists and historians. The visceral, as we will see, comes into criminal and Inquisition cases at multiple stages: from the initial accusation to the response of authorities, from the archiving of these cases to our readings of them as scholars, from the writing of history to the reading of historiography. Herein lies its cross-temporality, which also implicates me, the author of this book, and you, its reader. If it is true that, as Arlette Farge asserts, "the archival document is a tear in the fabric of time, an unplanned glimpse offered into an unexpected event," then each archival document—and each asynchronous interaction that people have had with that document over the centuries—connects the past and the present together in ways that are not entirely anticipated or resolvable.[13]

The criminal court viewed Lázaro Martínez's defiling of Antonia Fontecho y Hurtado's cadaver as *exceso*—an "excess" that ruptured the boundaries of permissibility and comprehensibility, much more so than other sins of lust. Criminal courts throughout New Spain formulaically resorted to the term "excess" when referring to everything from sex out of wedlock and violent outbursts to idolatry and superstition.[14] But *this* excess was different, because of both its rarity and its unclassifiable nature. Indeed, my own shock at encountering this case in the archives had partly to do with the infrequency with which such acts are documented at all. The criminal court ultimately accepted the interpretation that the act itself was "against nature," but the basis of that interpretation, the 1785 legal text compiled by Antonio Gómez, fails to mention sex with a corpse by name. In contrast to sodomy, bestiality, and masturbation, this particular act does not figure into a long tradition of naming, classifying, and writing about lust in European legal and theological tracts.

One rare exception (not cited in the 1810 criminal case) is Alphonsus Maria de' Liguori's 1748 *Theologia moralis*, in which the Italian bishop, writing in Latin, broaches the act in his taxonomy of sexual sins. Liguori inquires: What type of a sin is it "to come together [carnally] with a dead woman?" His reply, based on a handful of esoteric medieval and early modern theological treatises, is that "together [these texts assert] it is not really [a sin of] fornication because it is done to a cadaver; nor is it bestiality, so that one may determine; but it is pollution, and affective fornication."[15] Thus, for Liguori, sex with a corpse fell somewhere between "pollution" (the general term for masturbation) and *fornicationem affectivam* ("affective fornication," which signified the act stemmed from will and desire rather than reason). For Gómez, sex with a corpse was an act of "imperfect sodomy," which took place not in the anus "but rather in another part of the body."[16]

Throughout the trial of Lázaro Martínez, the judge and court officials embedded a lexicon of viscerality in their descriptions: carnal congress with a corpse was understood juridically as being quintessentially *repugnant* to nature as well as to the very conceptions of the human (and the animal). Such repugnance, however, is not confined to the past. We can only speculate about the anonymous twentieth-century archivist who manually entered a redacted description of Lázaro Martínez's criminal case into the computer database in such a way that obfuscated the actual contents of the archival document. But we can guess that, upon digesting the historical texts of the past, he or she experienced *some* visceral response, possibly disgust or moral offense, that rendered it necessary to describe this early nineteenth-century case of "carnally mixing with a dead woman" in more sanitized terms—"profanation of cadaver." Perhaps this alteration was unconscious, though this seems unlikely given that standard archival practice is to copy word-for-word (or as closely as possible) the case description on the cover page of a criminal or Inquisition case. For Sara Ahmed, in visceral reaction of disgust, words tend to be involuntarily "cast out or vomited."[17] That archivist consumed particular words (not unlike earlier colonial scribes or later historians like myself), partly digested them, and then vomited euphemistic terms for future researchers to more easily eat up (or, more likely, to ignore). The visceral reactions of this archivist are registered only in negation, through their absence from the archival database and finding aid.

In "On the Visceral," Sharon P. Holland, Marcia Ochoa, and Kyla Wazana Tompkins posit that viscerality emerges "from the carnal language of (colonial) excess."[18] Here, the *colonized* subject—indigenous and purportedly "ignorant" of Christian doctrine—acts out and embodies (both physically and conceptually) colonial "excess," which is subsequently described in visceral terms by both witnesses and the criminal court, and granted (or denied) an archival name by the early nineteenth-century scribe (or the twentieth-century archivist). Secular and ecclesiastical authorities throughout New Spain, however, also harnessed the power of the visceral to ensure that colonial rule was not merely tolerated but profoundly *felt* and experienced by the populace. Lázaro Martínez was spared from being publicly shamed and whipped, but in the following chapters we will encounter horrific spectacles of the shaming, whipping, and execution of "sodomites" (and other "criminals" and "heretics") that were publicly carried out by colonial authorities to punish convicts and dissuade against following in their footsteps. In doing so, colonial officials and courts aimed to produce visceral responses—through the tactile, the visual, the olfactory, the aural—deep within the bodies of convict and spectator alike, in ways that were meant to leave indelible traces in the mind. Excess is thus performed, and viscerality produced and experienced, by a range of historical subjects, to radically different ends.

We can only imperfectly access experiences of, and meanings behind, the visceral for any given historical subject. To mine colonial documents, and their archival classifications, for evidence of viscerality thus requires speculation (as a methodology) to imagine partly how archived subjects *might* have experienced a range of conflicting corporeal and emotive sensations upon encountering certain spectacles, staged (as in public executions) or otherwise (as in the graveyard that day in 1810). To return to Massumi's terms, what sensory *excitations* and *intensities* might witnesses and court officials have experienced in 1810, when they (visually or verbally) encountered the spectacle of sex with a corpse? Do they share something in common with the twentieth-century archivist, or maybe even with other nineteenth- and twentieth-century historians and archivists, who (textually) encountered the same spectacle, though with a degree of temporal detachment? What of the sensory and what of the visceral are lost with temporal and physical distance?

The experiences of Ignacia Gómez and María Brigada Salazar, friends and witnesses to Lázaro Martínez's crime, serve as a case in point. We know, for example, that whatever each of the women experienced that day in the graveyard *translated* almost immediately into the mutual act of screaming, likely out of shock, fear, and disgust. But viscerality itself was experienced just moments *before* the visual image translated into action. For Massumi, the space into which a visceral experience or sensation momentarily jolts the flesh "is one of an inability to act or reflect, a spasmodic passivity, so taut a receptivity that the body is paralyzed until it is jolted back into action-reaction by recognition."[19] Viscerality, thus, begins in a suspended space of perception, that brief instant right when the two women first encountered the affronting scene, right before they screamed. The second witness later recalled that she and her friend "saw that the underskirt of the deceased was not lifted up, but there was a hole in them, leading to her pudenda," one of innumerable instances in which archival narratives privilege the visible.[20] The overemphasis on the visible, of course, comes to the detriment of registering (and archiving) other sensory cues—the faint but unmistakable smell of Fontecho y Hurtado's barely decomposing body, perhaps, or the sickening sound of Lázaro Martínez's heavy breathing. For these are details that do not make it into the archive, but they were presumably at play in generating visceral responses, unique to each, in both witnesses. Such details are lost within, and absent from, the language and form of the archival record.

Our own emotional responses to the act of fornication with a corpse are as varied as those of the subjects we encounter in the archives. Some of us feel shock, others repugnance; still others take offense at the defilement of the deceased or at what seems like a violation of human dignity, which we accord even to the nonliving. At least some readers might feel a faint stir of desire, some lurid curiosity bordering on the erotic. Each of these emotions has the potential to be visceral in its own way. Pointing again to the ultimate illegibility of the act, it is possible too that "carnally mixing" with the dead was an act of intimacy. If we are to believe Lázaro Martínez's assertion that Miguel only engaged in these acts *after* his pregnant lover died and was buried in the cemetery, perhaps sex with a corpse was meant to approximate an intimacy that he once shared with her in life. Or, perhaps Miguel's acts were largely born of prurient desires, which he fulfilled (for reasons unknown) only after the death of his lover, not with her body but rather with the corpses of those to be buried in her proximity. We never find out if Miguel had sex with the corpse of his lover or only those of other women. Going one step further, we will never know if Lázaro Martínez's story about Miguel was even true.

All people react differently to different things. This may seem a facile observation, yet its complexity, when seriously considered, cannot be overstated. Though two people, like the witnesses above, may react to a given spectacle or experience in a similar manner, they never react *identically*. No two individuals felt quite the same thing or reacted in quite the same way when, for example, they stumbled upon an adolescent engaging in bestiality on a rural pasture, when they attended the public execution of a sodomite in a town plaza, or when they almost imperceptibly, and perhaps unconsciously, sensed a priest's clammy hand edging surreptitiously closer to his or her body while confessing the sins of the flesh. Viscerality encompasses an array of responses, many linked to disgust, or something akin to it (though not always), which could manifest physically as an adrenaline rush, pounding heart, shallow breathing, flash of nausea, distorted vision, loss of balance, sinking stomach, shivering, sweating, and any number of other reactions.

Whether talking about the women who encountered Lázaro Martínez that day in the graveyard, or the archivist who altered the language of the case file's title page, we can only speculate as to what their visceral responses may have been, and what meanings they might have held for those who experienced them. Such speculation helps us analyze how certain affects, in relation to some specific event in the past, can and do reverberate across individuals who are separated by place, time, and experience. Attentiveness to viscerality elucidates the intimate connections between affect (feelings and emotions) and archiving, but it also leads us to that uncomfortable place of suspension, where our own analytical tools both illuminate and obscure. The visceral remains ineffable, a reminder that for all our desires to know more, there are still more desires that elude us.

Liquor, Pustules, Semen

Sometimes, perhaps consciously and unconsciously, we mitigate the visceral effects of (unsavory) desires by euphemizing the past; we turn sex into "profanation." I turn here to the 1775 Inquisition trial of Manuel Arroyo, which further explores the vast range of (speculative) corporeal and affective reactions to archival material. This case is one of only three Mexican Inquisition cases from my corpus that is archived in the United States, in this case in the Bancroft Library at the University of California, Berkeley. As such, some history behind the document's acquisition is warranted. According to the Bancroft's newsletter: "In February 1996, a collection of particular interest to the Bancroft Library was offered for sale, a remarkable cache of 61 volumes of Mexican Inquisition manuscript records covering the years 1593–1817." This purchase was made possible by then director of the Bancroft Library, Charles Faulhaber, who reached out to friends and benefactors. The result was that some 198 donors made gifts totaling over $100,000, making possible the acquisition of these documents, which immediately underwent extensive conservation treatment "to mend iron gall ink damage, after which pages were sewn into individual folders and boxed in groups," and were then made available to researchers.[21]

Whereas an anonymous archivist at Mexico's Archivo General de la Nación opted to euphemize Lázaro Martínez's 1810 necrophilic act as "profanation of cadaver," the archivists at the Bancroft Library (who, in the mid- to late 1990s, created the catalog and computer database entry for the Arroyo case) were more forthcoming in their description:

BANC MSS
[Volume 13:1]
Dates:
1775
Place and Name:
Pachuca
Manuel Arroyo
# of Leaves/pages:
96
Accusation/Subject:
Counseling that sucking semen from men was not a sin[22]

In these and all other cases, archivists necessarily resort to "essential identifiers" to outline basic information for each set of documents, which are reductionist by nature. According to Francis X. Blouin and William G. Rosenberg, these identifiers, such as Library of Congress subject headings, inescapably simplify "the complexities of subjects that many documents reflected into a rigid set of subject constructions, reducing the range of descriptive tags."[23] The descriptive tag above, for example, is "counseling that sucking semen from men was not a sin," which necessarily simplifies the acts and beliefs of Arroyo, the subject who is reflected in the document.

Arroyo's entry is one of only two in the Bancroft Library's collection of Mexican Inquisition documents that deal with the sins against nature. The other case, which we will encounter in the final chapter, is the 1621 Inquisition case against a young woman, Agustina Ruiz, whose crime, according to the descriptive tag, was "claiming sexual intercourse with saints," though from this phrasing one would not be led to believe that it focuses centrally on Ruiz's act of "pollution," or masturbation, accompanied by explicit fantasies of Jesus, the Virgin Mary, and Catholic saints. The other cases in the collection deal with a variety of topics, including bigamy, solicitation in the confessional, witchcraft, superstition, and religious offences (such as the maintenance of Jewish or Lutheran beliefs). The cases of Manuel Arroyo (1775) and Agustina Ruiz (1621), however, stood out among the collection, and it was indeed the Bancroft's archival descriptions of both cases that piqued my interest.

Arroyo's case focuses on a literal act of consuming human semen, which the Church defined as inherently "against nature," though the act itself ranked lower within the hierarchy of unnatural sins than did sodomy or bestiality, and higher than masturbation. On the surface, the archival description above seems devoid of visceral reactions. But we can perhaps imagine a certain voyeuristic glee or excitement—itself an affective reaction—as the archivist penned the catalog description. The language of this archival description, however, contrasts greatly with that of other archival documents housed in Mexico's Archivo General de la Nación, in which Manuel Arroyo also makes an appearance for the very same crime.

In comparison to the Bancroft's candid description, the colonial scribes who originally recorded this case rendered its details in vague, bureaucratic language. Our points of comparison here are two fragmentary summaries of Arroyo's Inquisition case housed in Mexico's Archivo General de la Nación, both from the late eighteenth century. In one instance, rather than mention the thoughts behind the act of "sucking semen" around which the case revolves, the scribe summarizing the case in 1776 refers simply to Arroyo "having engaged in obscene touches [*tocamientos obscenos*], and defending that they are licit and good."[24] Unlike in the case of Lázaro Martínez, the twentieth-century archivist responsible for writing a description of this document reproduced its original language almost exactly in the catalog entry. The second fragment—a 1775 publication of the witnesses who testified against Arroyo—is also missing its title page, but the language of archival description is equally illustrative. The twentieth-century archivist, who offered a case description for the national archive's catalog and computer database, describes the document as follows: "Publication of the witnesses who have testified in the case that, in this tribunal, the prosecutor has pursued against Manuel Arroyo, mestizo or mulatto, about the acts observed, and [for] having defended them as licit and Christian."[25] This particular case descriptor opts for euphemism in a way that overlaps with the Lázaro Martínez archival entry: for one reason or another, the archivist reclassified the "obscene touches" and "sucking semen" of the document itself as *hechos observados*—acts observed—within the document.

As with the Lázaro Martínez entry, it is difficult to parse exactly how archivists responded to the details of this case, and how their responses did or did not influence the descriptions they wrote. How then *might* viscerality be central to Arroyo's case, and to the archival descriptors in the Bancroft Library and in Mexico's national archive? To answer this, we turn to the particulars of Arroyo's trial and to the denunciations against him, where we first see traces of viscerality. On July 26, 1775, don Josef Badiola, a priest and missionary in the central Mexican town of Pachuca, denounced to the Inquisition a "damned doctrine" he had heard about from don Mariano Yturria, a priest and ecclesiastical judge. Badiola described this heretical belief: "it is not a sin to suck human semen from men with one's mouth for reasons of health . . . and that this act is good to rid them of bad thoughts with women, and to stop them from walking around and sinning with them . . . [and he said] *that it is a sin not to let one suck semen.*"[26] Given that the primary purpose of the Mexican Inquisition was to police the boundaries of orthodoxy and root out heresy, it is no surprise that the Mexican Inquisition would take an interest in the fate of one who had uttered such heresies.

It is important here to convey a crucial difference between the cases of Lázaro Martínez and Arroyo in terms of how their crimes were defined and constituted. Lázaro Martínez was tried and punished by a secular criminal court for the *act* of carnally mixing with a corpse. For the secular courts, the crime consisted of the execution of the act itself. Arroyo, in contrast, was tried and punished by the Holy Office of the Mexican Inquisition not for the act of "sucking semen" but rather for the heretical *thoughts* and unorthodox *beliefs* that accompanied such acts. Inquisitors were therefore primarily concerned with Arroyo's purported assertion that "it is not a sin to suck semen" from another man. In Arroyo's case, it was both the act of fellatio and its accompanying heretical thoughts that generated visceral responses.

The notion that sucking semen was not a sin first appears in the archive in 1775, through the denunciation of a mestizo man in his midtwenties, José Antonio de la Peña, who had confessed his sins to Father Yturria in the local church of Real del Monte. After hearing Peña's confession (no records of which exist), the priest told Peña that, as it was out of his power to absolve him, he should denounce himself to the Inquisition. Peña complied, testifying to inquisitors that one year earlier, while working on a nearby hacienda, he befriended a jobless mulatto, Manuel Arroyo, who began spending increasing amounts of time at Peña's workplace. The two men grew closer, and one day, according to Peña, Arroyo requested that, "out of charitableness, he give him a mouthful [*un bocado*]."[27] Only later would he find out what this meant. Peña declared that he and Arroyo began sharing a bed, and that one night he awoke to the sensation of Arroyo touching his genitals. He continued:

> Arroyo assured him that one night he had also touched his parts but that he just had not felt it, and that the reason for doing so was because he knew that this witness [Peña] had a hidden sickness, that only he [Arroyo] would be able to cure, and that he would do this in the charity of God. With this, he [Arroyo] persuaded this witness, and that same night he performed the remedy on him in this manner: . . . he [Arroyo] sucked it with his mouth, telling him that he did not know the benefit of what he was doing, because he would no longer have bad thoughts, nor would he sin with women.[28]

In the narrative he constructed for inquisitors, Peña went on to say that although Arroyo either played with his genitals or "sucked" him almost nightly over the course of a year, he never felt ill, and did not know what his "hidden sickness" was.

The explicit details of the case, however, go much further, implicating us— author and reader of this book—in a chain of visceral reactions that can be traced back to the original acts and denunciations that took place in the late eighteenth century. It is here that my own visceral responses, as researcher and historian, came to surprise even me, and subsequently informed my selection of texts, my decisions about which quotes to include or omit, and how to analyze the relationship between Arroyo and Peña. As I read through the ninety-six-folio Inquisition case of Manuel Arroyo in the Bancroft Library's reading room, I realized that little in the archival description of the case had prepared me for the convergence of intoxicants, disease, and bodily emissions—liquor, pustules, and semen—embedded in this act. From the pages of archival documents unexpectedly seep, in the words of Farge, the "raw traces" of the past, often catching archivists and historians off guard.[29]

Following the denunciation (and imprisonment) of Peña, Arroyo was apprehended and interrogated by inquisitors. Upon questioning, Arroyo asserted that his own priest and confessor had first counseled him to eliminate sickness and lust (toward women) by sucking Peña, telling him that the hidden sickness would eventually result in the death of Peña, and that he alone would be responsible. Perhaps Arroyo fabricated this rationale, or perhaps he had confessed with a priest who, as we will see in the chapter on solicitation, had some ulterior motive in making such assertions. The archival document is silent on the topic.

What, however, did the "remedy" consist of, and why was it administered in the first place? Here, Arroyo's statement differed noticeably from Peña's. Arroyo told inquisitors that the first time he touched Peña's genitals, he saw that "his foreskin was full of pustules," a fact that, if true, Peña failed to mention to the inquisitors, perhaps out of fear, shame, or guilt.[30] Arroyo said that he thought Peña had contracted either gonorrhea (*purgación*) or syphilis (*bubas*) from sexual contact with a woman, and that Arroyo knew how to cure his pustules. Arroyo described the treatment as such: "having taken a mouthful of camphorated liquor [distilled with the medicinal bark camphor] and, at the same time, putting the foreskin in his mouth with the aim of cleansing it, and this cleanse was executed some fourteen times."[31] Perhaps unsurprisingly, the very idea of sucking another person's foreskin full of pustules, with a mouthful of liquor, prompted my own revulsion as I read the case. I was not alone in my unease; one of the peer reviewers of a journal article of mine that discusses this case declared, amid other more formidable comments, "this is just so gross on so many levels."[32]

Viscerality reverberates over the centuries: even though their affective responses are often absent from the trial transcripts, some of the eighteenth-century inquisitors who interrogated Arroyo, and the scribe who assiduously recorded his words, undoubtedly reacted from the gut. Arroyo admitted to irregularly sucking Peña and "curing" him some fourteen times, but he qualified his actions: if Peña had told inquisitors that it had been more frequent, it must have been that Peña dreamt it. Inquisitors were not convinced. In November 1775 Arroyo—described as being of "regular height, brownish skin [*trigueño*], dark eyes, a flat nose not very high up, black hair and wearing a rosary around his neck"—was charged one hundred pesos by the ecclesiastical court to cover the costs of his imprisonment, his goods were confiscated, and he was moved in shackles from the prison in Pachuca to the secret prisons of the Inquisition outside the city.[33] Only then did Arroyo confess that he had "cleansed" his friend over thirty times, in two of which he had substituted liquor with "medicinal herbs."

Arroyo's acts, and his insistence that "it is not a sin to suck human semen," drew inquisitors into a space of rhetorical repugnance. The act itself was "obscene and repugnant to nature," and inquisitors declared that the "extremely vile act of sucking the spillage [of semen] appears more canine than human, and is so shameful and contradictory to rational beings that not even among the Roman Gentiles, artefacts of obscene evils, was this seen."[34] Yet nature is inconsistent: according to Thomas Aquinas, writing in the thirteenth century, sodomy was "contrary to the union of male and female which is natural to all [brute] animals."[35] How, then, could sucking semen be "more canine than human" if male-female coupling was inherently natural to brute beasts? To apply the formulation of Mel Y. Chen, this is an archival moment in which "animality, the 'stuff' of animal nature that sometimes sticks to animals, sometimes bleeds back onto textures of humanness."[36] In that very bleeding back, as we will see in the chapter on bestiality, nature itself comes partly undone.

Not unlike the sticky, messy conglomeration of liquor, pustules, and semen, disgust and desire have their own stickiness, and adhere to the archive across time. William Ian Miller notes how particular excreta of the human body— menstrual blood, semen, excrement, vomit, and mucus—all "have a gravitational attraction that bends social and cognitive structures along their lines of force."[37] These substances, inscribed in documents, have the potential to rupture some of the classificatory systems of the archive. This rupturing potential is evident repeatedly in the archives. We see as much in the ongoing struggles of Spanish priests, colonial notaries, archivists, and historians to describe the partly unclassifiable acts and desires of individuals such as José Lázaro Martínez, Manuel Arroyo, and José Antonio de la Peña.

Arroyo's trial came to a close on February 29, 1776; the Holy Office proclaimed that the following day Arroyo would be paraded through the streets of the city to the central plaza, where he was to receive two hundred lashes for his heresies. Afterward, he was banished from the city for ten years, the first three of which he was to labor in a fort, and then to work with rations, but without pay, at the Castle of San Juan de Ulúa, on Mexico's eastern coast. Inquisitors specified that Arroyo was to confess regularly and pray the rosary throughout the first year of his punishment. Not surprisingly, out of fear of "scandalizing the Christian community," inquisitors made it clear that Arroyo's crimes were *not* to be publicly proclaimed, as was customary, by a town crier. We see a similar logic at play with Lázaro Martínez: authorities feared that any detailed announcement of such acts might disseminate (rather than eradicate) the memory of the crime, thus potentially serving as an impetus for others to engage in similar acts.

Consuming Archives

As we have seen, sex enters the archive in a contingent and highly charged relationship with (and between) bodies and texts, the latter of which are metaphorically consumed—and later digested—by scribes, archivists, and historians in order to make meaning out of them. To explore this relationship, especially as it is mediated by affect, here I reflect on how archival theory has purposefully situated itself within a particular lexicon of food and consumption. If in a colonial context, as Sara Ahmed asserts, "the politics of 'what gets eaten' or consumed is bound up with histories of imperialism," then we might say that the politics of consumption are intimately connected to specific modes of documenting, remembering, and recounting those very (everyday) histories of imperial encounter. Both archival practice and historiography *are* forms of consumption: our appetites are especially voracious in, and around, the colonial archives.[38]

Theorists of the archive have often turned to the (sweet, savory, bitter) tropes of consumption to make sense of archival research and our encounters with archived subjects. Ann Stoler, for one, suggests that the "consumption of facticities" lies at the heart of colonial archives.[39] Colonial archives in the Dutch East Indies are, for Pramoedya Ananta Toer, analyzed by Stoler, "the bitter aftertaste of empire, the morsels left for us, their voracious contemporary readers."[40] Arlette Farge says, "Archival discoveries are a manna that fully justify their name: *sources*, as refreshing as wellsprings," for the French word *source*, as Thomas Scott-Railton (translator of Farge's text from French to English) notes, refers to both sources of information and natural springs of water.[41] Cristian Berco notes that the archive is "a scholar's heaven where the sought-after records of a past society flow like manna from thousands of dusty volumes in their archival repository."[42] The comparison of archival documents to manna—the flowing edible substance that, in the Bible and the Koran, God provided for the Israelites during their travels in the desert—is a calculated one: archival documents are the very sustenance that nourish, both figuratively and metaphorically, historians and archivists alike. The archive thus becomes refuge where documents are voraciously consumed, avidly digested.

Carolyn Steedman offers a different image of archival consumption: the literal inhalation of "the dust of others, and of other times."[43] For Steedman, in dialogue with the nineteenth-century French historian Jules Michelet and with Jacques Derrida, "archive fever" is literal, produced by "the historian's act of inhalation."[44] Especially as nineteenth-century historians and archivists were increasingly exposed to the toxic chemicals, tanning agents, and tiny particles emitted from early printed books, old documents, leather bindings, parchments and vellums, glues and adhesives, they too breathed in "the dust of the workers who made the papers and parchments; the dust of the animals who provided the skins for their leather bindings."[45] Even today, as anyone (like myself) who has suffered from itchy eyes, runny nose, and headaches in the archive knows, the mold, spores, dust, and airborne fragments of early modern books and manuscripts have an uncanny ability to produce allergic reactions—from the passing to the severe—in those of us who breathe them in.[46] Our inhalation is yet another dimension of the intimate relationship between body and archive.

Scholars have thus situated archives, and archival documents themselves, as morsels, manna, and dust—ingredients that both sustain and afflict. I propose therefore that we think metaphorically about archiving as a mode of digestion. Archives are first consumed, then digested, and in the process—especially if we turn to the Latin word for digestion, *digere*, which centers on the need to "separate, sort out, order or classify"—we taxonomize in our attempt to make sense out of the messiness of the (desires of the) past. That separating and sorting out, needless to say, happens physically, in our stomach and intestines; but it also happens in the archive.[47] This maneuver allows us to situate the colonial archive—as well as its documents, conventions, catalogs, and finding aids—within a long chain of affective responses inextricably linked to the act of consuming, and digesting, the past. Yet archival consumption is an always incomplete process: as Steedman notes, in the archive, "you know that you *will not finish*, that there will be something left unread, unnoted, untranscribed."[48] There will always be that "something" left untouched, unconsumed, undigested. Seeing archiving and archival research through consumption invites us to ask: Which histories get eaten, digested, and excreted, and which do not? Which are indigestible, get regurgitated, and why?

For Elizabeth Freeman, the "visceral encounter between past and present figures as a tactile meeting, as a finger that in the stitching, both touches and is touched, and that in reading, pokes and caresses the holes in the archival text even as it sutures them."[49] Freeman uses *haptic historiography* to refer to "ways of negotiating with the past and producing historical knowledge through visceral sensations."[50] This chapter then might be seen as a microhistorical exercise in haptic historiography, one that explicitly links visceral sensations (and archival affects) to the production of historical knowledge and the very processes through which the bodies and desires of others come to be archived in the first place. For, if as David Hillman asserts, the entrails are "the place where the other is taken in, is acknowledged in his or her otherness," then being attuned to the visceral encounters of the archive allows for a more nuanced critique of the formulaic language of colonial documents (and their occasionally euphemized catalog entries) as they are tied to the literal and metaphorical consumption of the historical other.[51] Viscerality in the archives ultimately invites us to examine the spaces between affective and bureaucratic impulses—between embodiment and documentation.

This chapter has focused on a handful of thoughts, acts, and desires that both intersected with, and fell outside, more easily classifiable sins against nature. The archives of the unnatural, assembled here, encompass a wide spectrum of responses to these "sins," many of which were visceral. Each reaction falls, sometimes at multiple and contradictory points, within this spectrum— from extreme to mundane, illegible to legible, intolerable to acceptable— depending on who encountered the act, when, and how. If I think back to that day in the archive when I first encountered the criminal case of Lázaro Martínez, I have trouble recalling exactly what I felt the very moment I laid eyes on the title page. I did not squirm in my seat or look away, the walls of the archive did not narrow, and I felt no nausea, and only minimal feelings of disgust. But I remember feeling some strong and conflicted emotional response, not unlike what I felt in the Bancroft Library when I first encountered the catalog entries relating to Manual Arroyo and Agustina Ruiz—an anxious rush of excitement and trepidation, of impulsiveness and perplexity, and perhaps even some sense of connection to the "queer" desires of the past.

Perhaps not unlike Ignacia Gómez and her friend, who unwittingly stumbled upon a scene that shocked and disgusted them, historians and archivists constantly come into contact with archival references and documents that elicit visceral responses of one kind or another. Sometimes we are disgusted; sometimes we are fascinated. And sometimes it is our own disgust that mesmerizes us. Too often, however, we ignore the visceral altogether. Our "rational" analysis dominates those "systems of meaning that have lodged in the gut."[52] And yet the visceral sneaks up without warning, sometimes accompanied by a gag reflex, a hint of bile in the back of one's throat, the churning of one's stomach, blood rushing, heart stopping. By working deliberately through the bound phenomena of consumption and viscerality—issues that are central to the archive and to the very writing of history—and by acknowledging that each of us will experience, and feel, the archive in a slightly different way, we get a glimpse of the affective and erotic chains that both structure and confuse the taxonomizing impulses of the archive itself. Viscerality plunges us deep into the guts of the colonial archive, and it does not let go.

CHAPTER 2

Impulses of the Archive

Misinscription and Voyeurism

In the Archivo Histórico Municipal de Morelia, in one of dozens of acid-free cardboard boxes in which archivists have long stored colonial documents, there lies an exceptional trial from 1604, in which a group of indigenous Purépecha men became wrapped up with the colonial criminal justice system for the crime of sodomy. I first learned of the existence of this case in the summer of 2003, when I traveled to the state of Michoacán in search of documents dealing with gender and sexuality in New Spain. The municipal archive—which, like so many other archives, has changed location several times in the past decades due to space constraints, humidity problems, and economic factors—was then housed in a small but centrally located governmental building on Calle Allende, just a few blocks west of Morelia's cathedral and the Plaza de Armas.[1]

The archive's reading room then had enough tables and chairs for perhaps a dozen researchers. The archivists themselves were nothing but friendly, knowledgeable, and helpful, providing access to the documents and helping me make sense of some of the more difficult early modern Spanish handwriting. Fifteen years ago, there was little scholarship on sodomy and "homosexuality" in colonial Mexico. I was therefore ecstatic—itself a potentially problematic response on the part of the historian—to find a catalog reference in Morelia's municipal archive to this criminal case in which two Purépecha men, Simpliciano Cuyne and Pedro Quini, were tried for the pecado nefando—the "nefarious sin"—of sodomy. I requested *expediente* (file) 20 within box 30 and delved into what was to be my first significant archival find, which in many ways turned out to be the impetus for this entire study (fig. 2.1). The file itself was made up of nearly one hundred folios, and it was penned by sev-

Fig 2.1 Title page of the 1604 sodomy trial transcript of Simpliciano Cuyne and Pedro Quini. Courtesy of the Archivo Histórico Municipal de Morelia, Morelia, Mexico. AHMM, caja 30, exp. 20, fol. 1.

eral notaries. This case, like most, is thus a composite document and a collaborative effort, compiled throughout (and likely after) the investigation and sentencing.

That document told the following story. At around 2:00 p.m. on August 15, 1604, the day of the local Feast of the Virgin in Valladolid (now Morelia), Michoacán, two indigenous Purépecha men, later identified as Cuyne and Quini, were caught in flagrante delicto. They were committing the nefarious sin in a *temascal*—a type of enclosed, pre-Hispanic steam bath or sauna used widely by Mesoamerican peoples for its ritualistic, ceremonial, and therapeutic effects. Thus, at the outset of this criminal case, we see the colonial influence, shifting the temascal from a Mesoamerican space of purity and cleanliness to one that harbored the potential for the sins of lust. The temascal was housed on the property of a priest, Juan Velázquez Rangel.[2]

It was the fourteen-year-old nephew of Velázquez Rangel who first saw the men, thereby initiating a chain of reactions and accusations that violently thrust these individuals into the colonial archive. The case is unlike most sodomy cases from New Spain in that the judge sentenced these Purépecha men, and several accomplices, to death. By analyzing this case—in conjunction with a handful of other cases from New Spain in which colonial judges pronounced the death penalty for sodomy—this chapter works through how certain sex acts, and the spectacular punishments they sometimes invoked, came to be remembered, both popularly and officially, and archived around the slippery categories of language and desire. By working through the particulars of this case, I articulate the larger politics of documentation, translation, and remembrance—all of which can be colonizing acts.

As with most criminal cases in this period, the 1604 document began with an act of witnessing and a subsequent denunciation. Whether we are to believe that the fourteen-year-old witness uttered the actual words that were attributed to him on paper, once called to testify, the boy stated that he had seen two men in the steam bath, "the one on top of the other with their pants undone, as if they were man and woman."[3] The boy related how, that afternoon, he was searching for a lost horse that had escaped from his uncle's corrals when noises coming from inside the nearby temascal caught his attention. Through cracks between the walls of the temascal, he saw what he initially thought were "a man and a woman and that they were there committing something carnal," noting specifically that he saw the man on top *dando rrempuzones*—thrusting or, literally, "giving thrusts"—as if he were on top of a woman.[4] The boy quickly realized, however, that the person on the bottom also appeared to be a man. He hastily called his uncle's young Nahuatl-speaking indigenous servant, Gaspár, to verify that two men were indeed committing the "nefarious sin against nature."

Here, I want to focus briefly on language, terminology, and the archive. It would not be amiss to say that these two men were figuratively *thrust* into the archive. In the singular, the word used by the witness, *rrempuzon*—an antiquated, unstandardized spelling of the modern-day *rempujón*—refers to the violent impulse (be it a push, a shove, a thrust, or a blow) with which someone or something is forcibly moved. Though written more than a century after criminal authorities in Valladolid investigated this sodomy allegation, the 1737 dictionary of the Castilian language, the *Diccionario de autoridades*, is instructive; it speculates that the term *rempujón* is etymologically linked to the Latin words *impulsus* and *impulsio*. And here we find an intriguing connection between the ways that certain bodies are—as the Latin terms would have it—pushed, incited, and urged to act, both in the real world of lived desires as in the archival world of representational desires.

As the archival narrative unfolds, we glimpse a better understanding of what compelled the two men *inside* the temascal to act, but what incited the boy outside to come closer and to take a look? And how did what he saw significantly alter the documentary processes set in motion by (and as a result of) his watching? The boy's initial impulse to approach the steam bath, having heard those unmistakable noises coming from within, most likely stemmed from a certain curiosity or a prurient desire to see what was taking place inside. Yet the shocking realization that the two individuals were both men, acting "as if they were man and woman," radically altered the implications of the boy's act of watching. While we can never know for sure, we can speculate that had the boy found a man and woman having sex, he may have felt no pressing reason to denounce them for their indiscretion. But because the sexual encounter he had seen was an act of sodomy, the boy realized he was witnessing a "crime" rather than merely spying on a sex act. Might not we metaphorically view these specific "thrusts" (as they came to be archived) as part of those "steady and feverish rhythms of repeated incantations, formulae, and frames" that, for Ann Stoler, make up "the pulse of the archive"?[5] That is, the physical thrusts of Cuyne's and Quini's bodies come into archival being through a separate—though linked—set of "feverish rhythms" on the part of witnesses, interpreters, and scribes as they transmit and record the details of those original thrusts.

All this points to what I am terming the *impulses of the archive*: the taxonomizing impulse of the archive itself; our own compulsion to touch, hold, and possibly even possess the documents in the archive; the occasional voyeuristic impulse to look with intent at the bodies of others (whether material or textual); and the desire to circulate narratively constructed knowledge about those bodies. One inevitable by-product of the impulses of the archive is distortion. In the space between that which is perceived through the senses and that which is subsequently *represented* as having been seen or heard or felt, we find all manner of misinscription, several examples of which I flesh out below.

In Derridean terms, "inscription" can perhaps be best understood as "the processes through which traces of a lived past life are 'archived' by individuals or societies in ways that make the place of uncovering—the archive—a point of intersection between the actual and the imagined, lived experience and its remembered (or forgotten) image."[6] Archival misinscription—working along-side, and not necessarily in opposition to, archival inscription—goes one step further, showing how misrepresentation becomes a necessary precondition for (representations of) the body and its desires to enter the historical record in the first place. It participates in, and thus pushes on, what Marisa Fuentes has called *mutilated historicity* to refer to "the violent condition in which enslaved women appear in the archive disfigured and violated," exemplifying, in the process, how their "bodies and flesh become 'inscribed' with the text/violence of slavery."[7] For the bodies and flesh of "sodomites" also come to be violently mis/inscribed in the colonial archive—mutilated and effaced—but in ways that differ significantly from those of enslaved women. Those, like myself, who seek out and access the archive are inevitably implicated in the processes of archival inscription and misinscription, thereby confounding the very impetus behind the act of uncovering that which we seek in and through the archives.

Misinscription of the body thus becomes one of the phenomena that partly governs the ways that historians and archivists interact with the archive (and with its archived subjects), and is ultimately linked to a voyeuristic impulse. In some sense, these impulses become the driving and motivating forces of the archive, and of history itself. For as Steedman tells us, "If you are a historian, you nearly always read something that was not intended for your eyes."[8] Those of us in the archive, in other words, can be guided by voyeuristic impulses that might not be so distinct from the curious gaze of a teenage boy staring into a temascal.

From Desire to Testimony

What began as an individual (and potentially autoerotic) act of voyeurism quickly spiraled into a selectively public chain of seeing and telling, witnessing and denouncing. The indigenous servant, Gaspár, confirmed that the individuals inside the temascal were indeed men; Valázquez Rangel's nephew ran to the nearby plaza and alerted the first two Spaniards he saw, García Maldonado and Juan Hernández. Both men accompanied the boy to the temascal, where they too witnessed the sex between Cuyne and Quini. The Purépecha men realized, at some point, that their own bodily impulses had attracted the voyeuristic impulses of others. Immediately, the man on top, Cuyne, fled to the nearby church of San Agustín, where he had served as sacristan, and from which he was later forcibly removed, against the wishes of the priest, by local authorities and imprisoned. Quini, however, was not so quick. He vehemently argued with the growing number of witnesses, and then tried to escape the temascal, but was apprehended in his "white underwear wet with fresh blood," according to one of the Spaniards. That same witness, proficient in the Purépecha language, ascertained from Quini in his native tongue that Cuyne had been drunk.

Here, we have one of our first hints as to how bodies and objects are inscribed into the archive, and in turn imbued with multiple meanings by the many makers of the historical document—witnesses, notaries, judges, archivists, and historians. The bloodied underwear—*calzones blancos mojados de sangre fresca*—that Quini was wearing came to play a key role in the trial. According to Gaspár, "He was certain that both were committing the said sin and even more so, he saw the said Indian and the first thing he recalled [*deprendio*] was that he was wearing white underwear wet with fresh blood, and what he has said is the truth."[9] Temporarily leaving the question of language aside (Gaspár made his testimony in Nahuatl, but, as was common, only a Spanish translation of his original testimony is recorded), I want to consider the memory, and the description, of the physical object. The court-appointed interpreter in this case rendered an unspecified Nahuatl word for memory as the Spanish-language term *deprendio* (that is, *deprehendió* in modern-day orthography)—a past-tense conjugation of the antiquated Spanish *deprehender*, which means to recall, to commit something to memory, or to acquire knowledge of something through experience.

The bloodied underwear thus functions within the criminal record both as a mnemonic representation (for the witnesses) and as physical evidence (for the court) that was saved as evidence and later examined in order to determine if two men had consummated the act of sodomy. Here we see how memory and evidence come together to create juridical "truth." Throughout New Spain, both criminal and ecclesiastical courts tried to create such results, interpreting physical evidence and the oft-conflicting memories of that evidence in order to establish culpability. The conclusion of Gaspár's testimony—the formulaic assertion that "what he has said is the truth"—insists on the intimate link between personal memory and veracity. For Gaspár, or at least for the interpreters and notaries who retrospectively translated and transcribed his statement, the act of committing Pedro Quini's bloodied underwear to memory amounted to a particular "truth" that, given the circumstances through which it was produced, weighed greatly in the criminal court.

This 1604 sodomy trial from Michoacán provides us with several examples of how bodies and objects—the first of which are Quini and his underwear—are simultaneously inscribed *and* misinscribed in the archive. Not unlike the Nahuatl-speaking Gaspár, both Cuyne and Quini testified through court-appointed interpreters who translated from the men's native language, Purépecha (*tarasca* in the document), into Spanish. Not surprisingly, the written records do not include the original language that Cuyne, Quini, and the other indigenous men used to confess and testify. None of the native peoples involved in this case spoke enough Spanish to make their formal confessions and declarations in that language. Because the entire criminal case was recorded in Spanish, the very words themselves are imperfect and imprecise. Yet, despite the methodological problems associated with this colonial process of translation, these testimonies nonetheless offer vital clues. This "imperfect" use of language is, as we will soon see, only one part of the story of misinscription.

In his testimony taken on August 16, Cuyne asserted that he was twenty years old and married to a Purépecha woman in San Agustín, Vitoria, and made no attempt to deny that he and another man (unknown to him by name but later identified as Quini) were found together *entrepernados*—legs intertwined—in the temascal. On that day, he said, he was at a house near the convent of San Agustín with other Purépecha friends when two black men—most likely African slaves, free blacks, or mulattos—sold them wine and pulque. The men had been drinking when an unknown Purépecha man, Quini, came to them trying to sell a piece of cloth. Cuyne, according to his testimony, eventually went with the man because he was "defeated by his pleas," and because the man suggested they drink together and go to a nearby temascal, where he might nap.

According to Cuyne, "He went with him to the said temascal and this witness [Cuyne] entered first and he threw himself on the floor to sleep, and then the said Indian who was in prison [Quini], and whose name he does not know, came up to this witness and began to hug him and kiss him, and he touched him with the hand that he had placed on the fly of his pants."[10] While Quini purportedly "told him that he had much desire, and that if he consented he would give him the blue cloth," Cuyne insisted that he was without desire.[11] Nevertheless, his testimony is full of intimacy in the form of hugs, kisses, and caresses. Yet "desire," as archived here, is particularly problematic. To what spiritual or corporeal desires might the term point? And how is this very concept distorted in the linguistic shift from the unrecorded Purépecha word that Quini uttered (which Cuyne repeated to authorities) and its translation into the word *deseo*? The legs of the two men, it is clear from the testimonies, were "intertwined"; yet their spoken words unravel as they are irrevocably translated in the historical record, alienated from their original cultural and linguistic contexts.

We will return to such unraveling again and again. For now, suffice it to say that desire—sexual or otherwise—only exists within the historical moment and linguistic contexts in which it was uttered; thus, any textual representation of desire simply cannot be perfectly authentic. That is, the invocation of "desire" in the document points to something that we may facilely seek to classify and comprehend as "sexual," "corporeal," "spiritual," "marital," or otherwise, but which confounds our impulse to truthfully, or fully, represent that which was experienced. By framing sexual desire as a category of historical analysis—partly through historicizing the subject of desire and interrogating how archival documents record overlapping and conflicting desires—historians can better grasp the reasons behind everyday manifestations of desire in relation to both bodily and archival impulses. And, as we will see in this document, and many others like it, sexual desire often blurs the boundaries between nature and the unnatural, order and disorder, thus challenging systems of archival classification.

For the women and men of colonial Mexico, desire—in its many manifestations, sexual and spiritual, corporal and emotional—was omnipresent. This assertion may seem banal, but it is important to acknowledge that sexual desire is wrapped up in and obscured by a wide spectrum of desires, many of which were inscribed in colonial archival documents. We find evidence of this in the life histories of Cuyne and Quini, both of whom were married to Purépecha women and were without children. Here, the "natural," orderly, and potentially procreative desires that took place within the bonds of matrimony overlapped with other desires, which colonial authorities deemed "against nature" and therefore punishable.

It was the desire that Quini felt for Cuyne (perhaps fueled by the consumption of pulque) that led him to initiate sex in the temascal: "The said Indian [Quini] removed the belt of this confessant's pants and then untied them, and he untied his own and stretched out on the floor, and [his body] lifted upward, this witness [Cuyne] threw himself on top of the said [Quini] and placed his virile member in Quini's anus, and having it inside as if he were with a woman he completed [i.e., ejaculated] and had carnal copulation through this part with the said Indian."[12]

It was precisely at this moment, "when Cuyne finished having the said carnal copulation and ejaculated in the anus of the said [Quini]," that Cuyne turned his head toward the door, saw the observers, and fled to the nearby church.[13] Later in his testimony, Cuyne asserted that this was the only time that he had ever committed sodomy. In response to questions posed to him in the course of the interrogation, he also stated that he did not know where the large quantity of blood on the white underpants came from, and that the blue cloth was not given to him in exchange for sex but rather that he had purchased it.

Quini's testimony yields even more intricate details. In the first testimony, also taken on August 16, Quini said that he was from Tzintzuntzan and was married to an indigenous woman named María. He did not know his age but, according to the criminal authorities, looked about twenty-five. Quini verified that he was found with another indigenous man (whose name he did not know) in the temascal, but that they had only gone there to temporarily hide because they had been drinking pulque and were afraid of being caught by authorities. Quini said that he sold him the piece of blue cloth for a small sum, and denied that anything more had taken place, and that he was drunk and did not remember. In a second testimony, taken on August 18, face-to-face with Cuyne in the judicial confrontation known as the *careo*, Quini changed his story dramatically. He not only admitted to the events in the temascal but said he had committed sodomy with a number of other men—men he popularly termed *putos*, that is, "a man who commits the nefarious sin"—in and around Valladolid.[14] These men, too, became the targets of Spanish colonial authorities. The story of Cuyne and Quini in the temascal thus became the beginning of an extensive criminal trial, set in motion by one act of witnessing, that sought to extirpate sodomy among a group of Purépecha men accustomed to committing the nefarious sin in colonial Valladolid, as well as in the nearby indigenous towns that surrounded Lake Pátzcuaro some thirty miles to the west.

Transcribing Sex

For this 1604 sodomy case to make historical sense, it must be contextualized within a long-standing practice of documenting, remembering, and forgetting sodomy accusations in the early colonial period. While I have been unable to locate earlier archival cases of sodomy from colonial Michoacán, there is one case that has garnered attention for centuries: the infamous 1530 criminal trial and execution of Tzintzicha Tangaxoan, el Caltzontzin, the noble indigenous ruler of the Purépecha peoples. The extant documentation on el Caltzontzin's crimes and execution deals only tangentially with the charge of sodomy, but, as we will see, this is illustrative of the ways that historians inscribe (and misinscribe) individuals in the past.

While the Spanish conquest of the province of Michoacán began shortly after the conquest of Mexico Tenochtitlán—Mexico City today—in 1521, Spanish power was not consolidated in the region until 1529–30 when the expedition of conquistador Nuño de Guzmán, the president of the first audiencia of New Spain, passed through the region on his way to the town of Tzintzuntzan with Spanish soldiers and indigenous allies.[15] Among those allies was el Caltzontzin, known also by his Spanish name don Francisco, who was accused of grave crimes on January 26, 1530, by a Spanish encomienda owner from Uruapan, Francisco de Villegas, who was also traveling with the campaign. The most serious among these charges were that el Caltzontzin had repeatedly ordered Spaniards to be killed in Michoacán, and that he habitually committed sodomy.

For these crimes, Guzmán pronounced the death sentence on February 14, 1530:

> That from the prison where he is, he be taken, hands and feet tied, with a rope around his neck, and with the voice of a town crier that manifests his crimes, and he be put in a *zerón* [a basket made of reeds or wicker to load on an animal], if there is one, and tied to the tail of a nag, and he be dragged around from the place where this royal [court] is established and he be taken alongside this river, and there he be tied to a [piece of] wood and burned in live flames until he dies naturally and is turned into ashes.[16]

The sentence also stipulated that if the Purépecha noble were to receive the sacrament of baptism prior to death, he would, out of mercy, die by garrote—strangled by an iron collar—prior to the burning of his corpse.

What comes out in the 1530 trial transcript is that some years earlier, a Spanish *visitador* to the province of Michoacán, Pedro Sánchez Farfán, also "held a trial against the said Caltzontzin for sodomy in which he found a large amount of information."[17] The fact that the sodomy trial from the 1520s is lost or no longer extant, and that there are few references to sodomy in the extant 1530 trial, points to a particular archival absence. The original case has been lost, and all we are left with is an archival fragment to which it gestures. It would be easy, in some senses, to fetishize the now-absent sodomy trial from the 1520s as, in Arondekar's formulation, a "lost object of archival desire."[18] And yet I myself have, at times, been guilty of such fetishization. That earlier trial, *were* it ever to be found, seems to promise, in the words of Villegas, "a *large amount* of information." Yet my own search for this trial—it was always in the back of my mind each time I stepped into an archive in Michoacán—frustrated my desires to access the very information that it would presumably contain. Here, a particular type of archival absence materializes—one that disorients "the teleological promise of archival claims."[19] Such absences, as we will see, play an integral part in the archival terrain of colonial sexuality, reminding us that what is not in the archive can be just as important as what is.

In the 1530 trial, it becomes clear that el Caltzontzin did in fact order Spaniards to be killed on several occasions; but what the trial records tell us about sodomy is vague. Although many witnesses called forth had *heard about* the earlier sodomy trial by Farfán against el Caltzontzin—hearsay being particularly charged in this instance—only one detailed description was offered, by a Purépecha man named Cuaraque, who explained:

> That he knows that he has *indios* with whom he sleeps, and that the one is named Juanico, who is in Apascuaro and will arrive soon. And another he knew, who is now deceased, is named Guysacaro. And this is what he has heard spoken and is notorious among all the indigenous servants of the said Cazonzi [el Caltzontzin]. And that when the said Cazonzi is drunk, he has seen him put his tongue in the said Juanillo's mouth and kiss him. And that since he was little the said Cazonzi has been accustomed to having those [servants] for such use, and that it is notorious that he has them for that use, and as for them, they are had and possessed among each other.[20]

The hearsay nature of this account is particularly problematic, yet fruitful for examining the archival implications of such reports. Cuaraque's testimony suggests that, unfounded or not, rumors about el Caltzontzin's proclivities for young indigenous boys circulated throughout the region, and held particular weight in a court of law that was already set on convicting the culprit in question, at least for having mandated the killing of Spaniards.

The many rumors about el Caltzontzin, and Cuaraque's eyewitness account, *might* make it more likely that the charges of sodomy were accurate. Yet this begs another question: Why did Farfán not convict el Caltzontzin of sodomy in the 1520s? It may have been the case that Farfán did not find enough information to secure a conviction, or it may have been that the information he found was contradictory or that it had absolved the Purépecha leader. Another possibility is that el Caltzontzin's wealth and status protected him. Indeed, Francisco de Villegas tells us in his original complaint that "the said Caltzontzin, with his crafty skills and large quantities of gold and silver, exempted himself from the punishments that he deserved."[21] Is it possible that el Caltzontzin was found guilty of sodomy but that he offered the Spaniards precious metals in exchange for his freedom? It is perhaps equally possible that the sodomy charges were fabricated and were meant to vilify an indigenous leader who resisted the Spanish colonial presence.

No matter how we analyze the 1530 trial of el Caltzontzin, it offers limited information on sodomy and same-sex desire among native elites in early colonial Michoacán. It does, however, provide us with a clear example of how scholars have failed to look closely at the representations of sodomy, reading this case primarily through a discourse of alterity. One scholar, for example, has posited that Nuño de Guzmán's interest in the charge of sodomy functioned primarily to demonstrate "the construction of an image of the Cazonci [el Caltzontzin] as a 'perverse other' in the eyes of the Spanish interrogators."[22] Most have ignored the possibility that el Caltzontzin might have had sex with other men, thereby implying that the accusations were rhetorical. Given, however, the rumored notoriety of el Caltzontzin's ways, Cuaraque's account of having seen his tongue in Juanillo's mouth, Farfán's missing sodomy trial from the 1520s, and the possibility that el Caltzontzin could have bribed the Spaniards, we ought not to discount this coalescence of archival traces as mere strategy on the part of the Spaniards to depict el Caltzontzin as a "perverse other." We should, however, be equally wary of assuming that el Caltzontzin was a "sodomite," both because of the potential pitfalls of the (missing) historical sources and because of the inherent problems of imposing that term on an early sixteenth-century Purépecha noble. Either way, we distort el Caltzontzin and his desires.

The existing evidence might tell us more about the nature of rumor and how sodomy accusations played out than about the historical realities of men who desired other men in early colonial Michoacán; yet the missing records of his 1520s trial, and the extant records from 1530, point to the ways that certain indigenous bodies come to be inscribed within the colonial record. They also intimate certain kinds of misinscription, especially the way that Spaniards read el Caltzontzin's acts and desires through the European concepts of "idolatry," "sacrifice," and "sodomy." James Lockhart has theorized early cultural interactions between Europeans and Mesoamericans through a process he calls Double Mistaken Identity, in which "each side of the cultural exchange presumes that a given form or concept is functioning in the way familiar with its own tradition and is unaware of or unimpressed by the other side's interpretation."[23] Archival misinscription alludes to Lockhart's confusion of categories and to the ways that mutual misunderstandings come to be grafted onto the body and enter the historical record. In the case of el

Caltzontzin, both archival presence (here, the extant 1530 trial) and archival absence (the missing 1520s trial) invite us to question the reliability of the historical record and the resulting historiography. Archival presence and absence each harbor an enormous potential to generate misinscriptions, in terms of how bodies and desires are transcribed in the past and how they are remembered and written about in the present.

Webs of Accusation

In all, thirteen men were eventually implicated in what began with two men in a temascal. This web of sodomy accusations began with Quini's second confession. When asked about why he was relating explicit information about the other putos he knew, Quini replied: "Because God has wanted to declare and discover the truth."[24] In this case, transcriptions of sex come about partly through Quini's impulse to confess to God, and subsequently to reveal the truth to colonial authorities (who, in turn, authenticated this "truth" through their acts of listening to, translating, and recording Quini's spoken words). Quini confessed that he and Joaquín Ziziqui, an indigenous servant he knew, had sex twice. Ziziqui, accustomed to committing sodomy, "served him both times as a woman," and Quini ejaculated both times.[25]

Quini then stated that the first time he had committed the nefarious sin was some four years earlier with Ziziqui, and that it took place in the company of two other indigenous men: the already deceased cook (later identified as Marcos) of the Spanish treasurer Pedro de Aguaya and a young painter from Uruapan (later identified as Miguel) who was de buen cuerpo y buen parecer— "of good body and good looks." According to Quini, he himself had heard from Ziziqui that heran todos putos: "they were all putos, who were used to committing the nefarious sin" (fig. 2.2).[26]

Years ago, as I sat in Morelia's municipal archive reading through the trial transcripts, what initially appeared to me to be a web of false accusations became increasingly plausible. Quini's testimony prompted Valladolid's particularly zealous criminal court to investigate. My own misguided assumption—that Quini had merely begun to list off (and possibly even invent) the names of other men he had labeled "putos" in an effort to mitigate his own guilt—began to fall apart the further I delved into the case. As the web of accusation grew wider and increasingly complex, the criminal court was largely successful in its attempts to corroborate denunciations, testimonies, and confessions that spread through several towns in the region. Quini's accusation

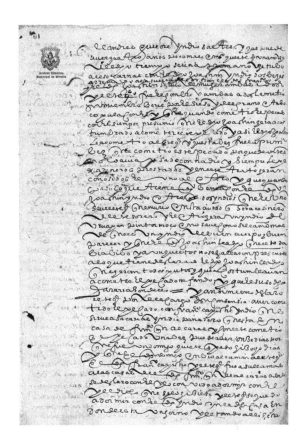

Fig 2.2 A verso page of the 1604 criminal case against Cuyne and Quini, with the phrase *"heran todos putos"* in the middle left. Courtesy of the Archivo Histórico Municipal de Morelia, Morelia, Mexico. AHMM, caja 30, exp. 20, fol. 16v.

was substantiated by Ziziqui's confession, in which he too admitted to having been penetrated twice by Quini. Ziziqui did not know, however, if the young painter and the deceased cook from Uruapan were "putos" or not. In spite of his own admission, Ziziqui, who was unmarried and approximately twenty-five years old, attempted unsuccessfully to negate his agency (and thereby exculpate himself). He "said that he is a Christian and that it could have been about six years ago when the witness was only a boy living in the neighborhood of San Francisco, the said *yndio* [Indian] Pedro Quini had committed on this witness and persuaded him to commit the nefarious sin, and that the witness, being a young boy not knowing what he was doing, fell into it."[27]

The next individual inscribed in the historical record was a Purépecha baker, Francisco Capiche, with whom Pedro Quini had sex eleven days earlier. According to Quini, that night Capiche invited him to sleep at the house of don Francisco Muñoz, where he worked. Around midnight the two entered the house, where Capiche "begged him to do it," at which point "the witness had copulation with him, and he put his virile member inside his anus and he had access with the said Francisco Capiche, ejaculating."[28] Quini then related his relationship with an indigenous man from Cuisco, Miguel, with whom he had sex one month earlier. Miguel apparently invited Quini to enter the *colegio*—where a community of religious men lived and studied—where he worked washing clothes. There, they "entered to sleep in the kitchen, and lying there the said Miguel began to insist that Quini try to put his genital member inside of him," and Miguel thus "served him as a woman."[29]

While Miguel from Cuisco was neither located nor mentioned again in the trial transcripts, Capiche was eventually caught and tried. During his interrogation, Capiche adamantly denied any sexual involvement with Quini. At this point, to elicit the "truth" it wanted to hear, the court threatened to torture Capiche. The decision produced the desired results: Capiche confessed his crimes. Torture gives us some sense of the plasticity of archival narratives and the "fictional" impulses of the archive, that is, "their forming, shaping, and molding elements" that were set in motion first by witnesses, and subsequently by notaries, archivists, and historians.[30] The use of torture, and even the very threat of it, amplifies the realm of possibilities within which archival misinscription can take place. Torture and the archive are, of course, intimately connected. As Lisa Silverman articulates, "There is the question of the preservation of documents pertaining to torture, whether those documents are the physical implementation of torture, the written records of interrogations, or the written or oral recollections of those who witnessed, participated in, or suffered acts of torture. Why are such documents created in the first place, and preserved, in the second place? What does the preservation of such documents mean?"[31] In the case of the Purépecha men, the preservation of their sodomy trials means that they are permanently misinscribed—partly through torture—in the historical record.

In the case of Capiche, we are not merely speaking of the threat of misrepresentation through the imposition of European concepts onto native bodies, the mediation of testimony through interpretation, or the temptation to interpret the past through anachronism. Rather, the archived subject unwillingly submits his or her own body to the judicial apparatus in its attempt to construct legal evidence through (the threat of) pain and suffering. The archival document itself becomes inextricable from the instruments of torture that coerce a subject to speak, and that produce a particular narrative. Confession produced in such a manner could, of course, maintain any number of relationships to actual truth. But the evidence that the court strove to produce through torture, when inscribed in the archive, is already partially misinscribed by and through the means of production. In the end, it mattered little whether the confessions elicited through torture were veridical in nature; what mattered was that the ritual of producing "truth" was transcribed, documented, and entered into the archive.

Perhaps the most intriguing in this web of accusations is Quini's accusation that Francisco Conduyi, an unmarried baker in his midthirties from Tzintzuntzan, was a puto who may have habitually sold sex. It was at Conduyi's house, next to Tzintzuntzan's church, where, a few years prior to 1604, "this witness learned to commit the pecado nefando." Quini also stated that he knew that Conduyi was "a puto and that he has committed the nefarious sin, and he is ancient in the trade of committing it because he has seen him commit it about three years ago, and he saw him serve as a woman many times."[32] Quini also asserted that an indigenous man named Ticata "lives together with the said yndio Francisco [Conduyi]."[33] Quini, only slightly later in this testimony, also made vague reference to "the other yndio [who] served the said Francisco Conduyi as if he were his woman."[34] Given Quini's description, Ticata may have lived (and "served") as a woman in terms of dress, traditional tasks and chores, and sex over a long period of time.

There are striking semantic (and temporal) differences in the verb tenses and terminology Quini used to differentiate these two versions of serving. Here, to describe this man who "served," Quini employed the long-term and habitual, imperfect conjugation of the Spanish verb *servir*, as if he were a woman over a long period of time (*servía como si fuese muger*). In reference to any other man who, in a single or repeated act of sodomy, was sexually penetrated, Quini and others employed the short-term preterit tense of the verb to show that they "served" as a woman (*sirvió de muger*). Because Quini was speaking Purépecha and not Spanish, however, we cannot know if he made this same imperfect-preterit distinction in his original testimony or if this temporal distinction was imposed in translation. Here is yet another space for archival misinscription, enacted through grammar and translation. Importantly, Quini saw Conduyi repeatedly serve "as a woman" in the act of sodomy while, at the same time, Conduyi had an indigenous man who served him "as if he were his woman."

Even more intriguing than the fact that Conduyi's home served as a meeting place for men seeking out sexual activity with other men (and possibly a place for the sale of sex) is that, as Quini related, about three years earlier, local authorities in Tzintzuntzan had tried to imprison Conduyi for sodomy.

Authorities never caught him because Conduyi fled, only later secretly return-ing to the town. Fortunately for Conduyi, he absconded again in 1604, most likely after hearing that Quini had been imprisoned. That Conduyi's house served as a meeting point brings up numerous unanswerable questions about privacy and local levels of tolerance. Did his neighbors know about the men who had sex in his house, about the man named Ticata who lived with him, or about the indigenous man who over a long period "served as if he were his woman"? How did authorities in Tzintzuntzan, in the years prior to 1604, find out about Conduyi's sodomitical activities, and what happened to the transcripts of those efforts? Authorities' repeated attempts to locate Conduyi failed, and he drops out of the historical record.

In one final string of accusations, Quini mentioned two men, Pedro Zinzo and Joachinque, both from Tzintzuntzan, whom he saw have sex once. Nei-ther was ever located by colonial authorities, although officials accidentally im-prisoned the wrong man, Pedro Ziziqui, for a short time, thinking that he was either Pedro Zinzo or Joachinque. Lastly, Quini mentioned a boy identified only as the fifteen-year-old Juan, indigenous servant of Francisco Ruiz, with whom, according to Quini, he had never had sex despite the boy's pleas on two separate occasions they do so. In spite of exhaustive accounts of sex with others—specific dates, times, places, and positions—here, when discussing Juan, Quini is evasive. Juan was nonetheless also imprisoned and interrogated. Juan gave a detailed account of how a few weeks earlier, in the pasture behind the corrals of the butcher's shop where he worked, Juan "undid his underwear and threw himself on the ground . . . and he [Quini] ejaculated as if he were with a woman, which this witness felt."[35] Juan also implicated another "yndio," Miguel Hidalgo, who pressured him to have sex on a hacienda. Most likely act-ing on the advice of his lawyer, Juan later recanted his confession and denied these stories; it helped little given that Quini, in a face-to-face careo with Juan on August 23, finally confessed to having had sex with Juan. Quini stated that initially he was too scared to tell the truth, and we can only surmise that this may have had to do with the boy's young age. Juan much later, and only under threat of torture, admitted once again that these stories were, in fact, true.

As I navigated this complex web, the case's uniqueness became clear to me. As mentioned, it is (thus far) the earliest sodomy trial to be located for all of New Spain through which we can trace extensive networks of indigenous men who knew when and where to engage in sex with other "yndios." But the case is also unique in terms of what the testimonies within its pages say and, perhaps unintentionally, hold back from its intended readers. There is, for example, a tension throughout between efforts to deflect one's own culpability—which leads, as in the case of Quini, to a proliferation of accusations—and an effort on the part of some to conceal and limit information in order to protect themselves, their friends, sexual partners, lovers, and acquaintances.

Such efforts directly influenced not only the scope and outcome of the criminal case but also the ways that certain individuals made it into the archival record while others eluded the encounter with colonial justice (and with the scribes whose transcriptions would eventually become part of Morelia's municipal archive). That el Caltzontzin, in the early sixteenth century, and Francisco Conduyi, in the early seventeenth, both evaded colonial authorities, at least for a time, and presumably went years without attracting excessive attention for their alleged sodomitical tendencies points to the piecemeal nature of colonial justice, the historical archive, and the "evidence" found within.

In the end, a total of thirteen Purépecha men were implicated, though only young Juan, Joaquín Ziziqui, Miguel Hidalgo, and Francisco Capiche were apprehended by colonial authorities and tried alongside Simpliciano Cuyne and Pedro Quini for having committed "such an abominable crime and such a great offense to God."[36] The 1604 criminal trial had a grim outcome for all involved—one that eradicated the corporeal evidence of the crime while diligently archiving the textual evidence.

As If They Were Man and Woman

Archival misinscription takes many forms. One of those is the inherent problem of translation, especially between indigenous languages and Spanish. Nowhere in the document is this clearer than in the Spanish terms and expressions that colonial courts, translators, and notaries in New Spain employed to refer to the physical positioning of men's bodies during the sodomitical act. Colonial criminal courts, as we will see, almost always understood and (linguistically) represented the act of sodomy in highly gendered terms. Here I focus on a particular type of archival misinscription that came about when witnesses and authorities conceptualized male-male penetration with the formulaic phrase *como si fueran hombre y muger*—"as if they were man and woman."

One methodological problem with using official, bureaucratic documents to trace desire is the way the formulaic language of bureaucracy obscures popular terminology and classifications. Translation of native testimony and confession into Spanish obviously exacerbated this. Yet even when an individual testified and confessed in Spanish, there is a chance that some of the original language and terms used by the speaker were lost through the paraphrasing of popular expressions into official discourse. It is highly unlikely, for example, that the fourteen-year-old nephew of Velázquez Rangel, or the even younger Nahuatl-speaking indigenous servant Gaspár, would have described what they saw as the *pecado nefando contra natura*—"the nefarious sin against nature." Other terms, including *sodomía* (sodomy), *acceso carnal* (carnal access), *cópula* (copulation), and *abominable delito* (abominable crime), recur in official narratives and are products of theological categories and concepts, common in legal discourse, as opposed to colloquial terms. We have no indication of what words Purépecha speakers would have used to refer to the act of "sodomy," although fray Maturino Gilberti's 1559 *Vocabulario en lengua de Mechuacan* perhaps offers us some clues. In that work, he lists the Purépecha translation of *pecado contra natura* (sin against nature) as *no thantziqua thauacurita, thiahchucuh peraqua* (fig. 2.3). Gilberti tells us that *thauacurita* translates to "sin" and that *thiyahchucuhpeni* refers to one man "doing it with another" (with the root *thia-* or *thiyah-* signifying "excess"), thus helping us better approximate the meanings behind these Purépecha phrases.[37]

We do, however, occasionally catch a glimpse of popular terms through the archival record. The word *puto*, for example, is used to describe those accused by Quini, not simply to refer to someone who has committed sodomy but rather to someone habitually *accustomed to* having sodomitical relations. The adjectives *ensima* (on top), *abaxo* (on bottom), and *boca abaxo* (face down) are also regularly employed to describe the physical positions in sex acts between men. Prevailing notions of gender were often grafted onto these positional terms. Witnesses and criminal courts, for instance, regularly referred to the man "on top" as occupying the presumably manly role of penetrating. Conversely, the man "on bottom" was receptive, and therefore thought of as the womanlike partner in the act of sodomy.

As we have seen, the colonial court employed the words *hombre* ("man") and *muger* ("woman") to gender the roles of the "top" and the "bottom," the penetrator and the penetrated. Several witnesses and suspects do this too, though we cannot be sure if these were distinctions that they themselves would have made or if these categories originated from colonial bureaucratese. The type of misinscription that takes place here is not the mere result of an imposition of gendered language onto the bodies of two Purépecha men committing sodomy. Rather, misinscription comes about when either colonial contempo-

Fig 2.3 Title page of Maturino Gilberti's *Vocabulario en lengua de Mechuacan* (1599). Courtesy of the John Carter Brown Library, Mexico Incunables Collection, Brown University, Providence, Rhode Island.

raries or present-day historians take these dyads (man/woman, top/bottom) and graft them onto an assumed dominant-submissive dichotomy.

Left unchallenged, these misinscriptions of gender obscure lived histories of desire and sex. On first inspection, the 1604 sodomy case from Michoacán indeed appears to reify the dichotomy between the penetrator (serving the role of the "man") and the penetrated (serving the role of the "woman"). A closer analysis, however, calls into question the presumption—made by colonial authorities, judges, witnesses, notaries, and even some historians— that either masculinity or femininity could be reliably mapped onto an act of sodomy. Due to the inherent problems of linguistic, cultural, and ideological translation, we cannot know if the notion that the penetrated bottom served as "woman" or that the penetrator served as "man" came from the Purépecha speakers themselves or if these were rudimentary mistranslations of more intricate Purépecha concepts of body and sex. It seems likely that these were categories imposed by the Spanish in order to classify—and denigrate—sexual relations between men.[38] It is also worth noting that the Spanish subjunctive verb tense of *ser* (to be) is used here—"*as if they were* [*como si fueran*] man and woman"—thereby registering some sense of doubt, and perhaps even desire, on the part of the translator or speaker. Again, we cannot be sure if the Purépecha speakers would have used a verb mood similar to the Spanish subjunctive to register similar emotions of doubt on the part of the speaker.

What we find on closer inspection is that the "as if they were man and woman" description of male sodomy does not correspond to masculinity or femininity, or to stereotyped notions of masculine and feminine behavior. Furthermore, the imposition of the categories "man" and "woman" in early modern sodomy trials (and even in some historiography) does the work of misinscribing indigenous bodies through the colonizing tendencies of juridical language. If we turn our attention to the group of thirteen Purépecha sodomy suspects, it appears that most men typically assumed *either* a top or a bottom role in most encounters with other men. Quini, for example, almost always assumed the role of the top. From the rich yet incomplete information that the file provides, it seems that Quini and possibly Conduyi regularly assumed both top and bottom roles. And, while Quini repeatedly saw Conduyi at his house with a variety of men, assuming the role of the bottom, he also said Conduyi had a man who served him "as if he were his woman." Significantly, in none of the testimonies are tops described as being more masculine, bottoms as more feminine or effeminate, or of either as being more or less worthy of punishment because of the gendered implications of this formulaic phrase.

Historians, analyzing the gravity of penetrating or being penetrated by another man, have long debated whether the top or the bottom in sodomy cases—phrased within the documents as the "active" or "passive," "male" or "female" partner—was punished more harshly. The answer to this question depends entirely on local context and jurisdiction. Given the frequency with which witnesses, judges, and even suspects tended to frame sodomy in terms of gender, it may come as a surprise to learn that the colonial criminal court in Valladolid in 1604 also made absolutely no distinction between the "man" and "woman," indiscriminately punishing those who had occupied either role. The implications of such gendering did, however, have severe (and sometimes fatal) consequences for hundreds of men throughout early modern Iberia.

Historiography on the topic is illuminating. Rafael Carrasco's study of sodomy in Valencia between 1565 and 1785 concludes that in early modern Spain, "active" participants in anal sex were typically punished more harshly than their "passive" counterparts.[39] Mary Elizabeth Perry's research on sodomy trials from the secular courts of Seville similarly led her to the conclusion that "the real crime of sodomy was not in ejaculating nonprocreatively, nor in the use of the anus, but in requiring a male to play the passive 'female' role and in violating the physical integrity of the male recipient body."[40] Cristian Berco, analyzing sodomy trials of the Aragonese Inquisition in Spain, tells us that the "question of who was the inserter/dominator/man and who acted as the receptor/submissive/female gained vital relevance when conjoined with social, ethnic, and political status."[41] As such, the severity of the punishment depended largely on class and race; Berco demonstrates that those of the disadvantaged classes, regardless of their role, were routinely punished more harshly than their socially elite counterparts. My research on New Spain confirms Lee Penyak's assertion that "willing participants convicted of sodomy could expect to receive the same penalty whatever sexual position they used."[42]

It is true that in early modern Spain, as in New Spain, witnesses and courts often ascribed to the misogynistic perception that the top inevitably had more agency than the bottom in terms of orchestrating and carrying out the sodomitical act. Yet to explain the rhetorical weight of the "as if they were man and woman" formula, we must turn to the hidden assumptions behind the expression. To be sure, this formulaic phrase held enormous sway in terms of gendering sodomy and making the act comprehensible. The model helped in determining the facts of the case, conveying its details, and transcribing the sex that took place. Simply put, it helped courts and witnesses make conceptual (and bodily) sense of sodomy. The phrase, however, did not necessarily hold as much sway in terms of determining culpability, at least when we look at instances of sodomy that appear to be consensual.

The closer we look, the more that the male-masculine-penetrator and female-feminine-penetrated paradigms fall apart. The historiography on sodomy in Spain tends to overemphasize the punishment of tops largely because many of the tops' sexual relations with the men and adolescents who bottomed for them reflected hierarchies of age, social status, language, and ethnicity. Many boys and adolescents—not deemed to be adult until they reached the age of fourteen—for example, could not be sentenced to death for their crimes because of age restrictions. This creates one distortion in the ways historians subsequently read the historical record. In medieval and early modern Spain, tops were punished more harshly than bottoms, but not because they were tops, nor because they had violated the integrity of the male recipient body. Rather, this reflects how bottoms were sometimes coerced into the act, how they tended to be younger than tops, and how courts tended to ascribe more agency to the top than to the bottom. Some historians appear to have done the same.

Another distortion arises from the fact that some criminal courts, several witnesses, and even historians have made the assumption that the top was the person who initiated sexual contact. The 1604 sodomy case presents us with several graphic instances of penile-anal penetration, yet I argue that a certain level of penetrational ambiguity adheres to sodomy trials—both in the ways sodomy appears in the archive and in how historians later interpret the case details. While it is often clear which bodily orifices are being penetrated, the individual motives behind wanting to be penetrated by (or wanting to penetrate) another are harder to tease out. The individual who initiated sexual activity with another was often *not* the one who performed the act of penetration. We see this, for example, in Quini's drunken seduction of Cuyne, as well as in Capiche's seduction of Quini. In both instances, the one who assumed the receptive role in anal sex was the one who initiated the sexual act, and not the other way around. Examples of penetrational ambiguity abound in the colonial archives, yet there remains a danger of misreading the power dynamics behind an act of penetration in ways that might confirm gendered stereotypes rather than acknowledge the ambiguous positionalities behind sodomy. Such ambiguities point to an epistemological issue at the heart of the history of sexuality—namely, there are many things about the meanings of sex and desire in the past that we simply cannot know.

What then is the ultimate cultural and juridical significance of the "as if they were man and woman" formula for making sense of sodomy? It is partly a vestige of the Spanish legal system, which sought to ascribe agency to one or both suspects of sodomy. But it was also a convenient rhetorical model for individuals and courts to envision the physical, bodily realities of the act (and therefore determine the contours of the crime). The motives and desires behind *any* act of penetration are obscured partly by and through the formulaic language of the archival documents, partly by archival misinscription, and partly by the historian's own act of interpretation.

Documenting Death

The case of Cuyne and Quini points to the extraordinarily violent ways that sodomy makes its way into colonial archives. On August 26, 1604, less than two weeks after Cuyne and Quini were arrested, the court ordered that all the goods of all those charged with sodomy be confiscated. In an interesting twist of events, as we have seen, Cuyne was granted immunity from the judicial process due to his having fled the temascal to the nearby church. The priest successfully petitioned for Cuyne, "an obedient son of the Holy Church," to be granted sanctuary. As far as we know, he was never tried for sodomy. This was, however, in spite of the recommendation of the alcalde, who argued that due to the severity of Cuyne's crime, and the fact that he had confessed everything under oath, he should be prosecuted to the full extent of the law. Priestly power ultimately protected Cuyne, a hint at the ongoing jurisdictional tensions between ecclesiastical and secular authorities over sodomy. A further blow to the pride of secular authorities came when the criminal court forced the local alcalde to pay "two pounds of wax for the holiest sacrament [*santissimo sacramento*]" and fined the *alguacil* (constable) one marco of silver for having removed Cuyne against the priest's wishes.[43]

On September 20, 1604, the criminal court sentenced Miguel Hidalgo, the only one who had not confessed to the crime of sodomy, to be publicly tortured by garrote and ropes (*cordeles*)—that is, he was to be strangled and painfully stretched on the rack, but not killed. On that very same day, the court also sentenced Pedro Quini, Joaquín Ziziqui, Francisco Capiche, and Juan:

> That they be taken from the jail and prison in which they are held on beasts of burden, with ropes around their necks, their feet and hands tied, with the voice of a town crier that declares their crime, and taken through the public streets to the place where similar justice is customarily carried out. And there they will be garroted in the accustomed manner until they die naturally, and, once dead, their bodies shall be burned in the flames of fire and turned to ash, and I declare that all of the belongings of the abovesaid that are found shall be confiscated for the Supreme Council of Your Majesty.[44]

Four of the six men tried for sodomy received the death penalty. That punishment had nothing to do with whether these men were the top or the bottom, masculine or feminine, "active" or "passive," married or single, or whether they had committed sodomy once or multiple times. The defense lawyer for these four men appealed the sentence; that appeal to the Real Audiencia in Mexico City, New Spain's highest court, was rejected nearly a month later, on October 15, 1604. We can safely assume that the executions were carried out sometime later that year.

These 1604 executions make most sense within a larger historical tradition of death sentences meted out for sodomy in New Spain between the sixteenth and early nineteenth centuries. In 1658 more than one hundred men—mestizos, Indians, Spaniards, blacks, and mulattos from Puebla and Mexico City—were accused of committing the nefarious sin in Mexico City; fourteen were sentenced to death.[45] A seventeenth-century contemporary, Gregorio Martín de Guijo, wrote that the fourteen men were paraded to the neighborhood of San Lázaro, where, one by one, they were garroted and their bodies subsequently burned in a fire that began around eight o'clock at night and "lasted the entire night."[46]

Some historians have maintained that this 1658 spectacle was unique. Serge Gruzinski, for one, called it "an unprecedented wave of repression."[47] Federico Garza Carvajal asserts it marked an apex: "Between 1657 and 1658 the Mexican High Court unleashed an unprecedented prosecution of sodomites that culminated in the arrest and the interrogation of at least 125 of its metropolitan citizens."[48] This figure is, however, misleading. It is true that well over one hundred men were implicated in accusations of sodomy; but, in fact, only nineteen were actually imprisoned and tried by secular courts. Of those, fourteen were sentenced to die and one fifteen-year-old boy was sentenced to receive two hundred lashes and six years of forced labor. The local courts employed town criers to *summon* approximately one hundred other men who were accused, but the vast majority were neither caught nor arrested. Thus, even if a moral panic linked to sodomy did ensue in Mexico City in the mid-seventeenth century—the end result of which was the extraordinary execution of fourteen sodomites—these deaths were not atypical. My archival research shows that the death sentences meted out to "sodomites" in both 1604 and 1658 are consistent with sodomy punishments throughout the Iberian Atlantic world, especially between the early sixteenth century and late seventeenth. In other words, across these 150 years, it was not uncommon for a man convicted of "perfect sodomy" (which entailed anal penetration between men, usually with ejaculation) to be garroted or burned to death.

Like the 1604 case, the 1658 records demonstrate the "dramatic clash between the repressive colonial apparatus and the individuals who were sexually active, and, even more, a subculture on the margins of the rules in force."[49]

Comparisons of sodomy death sentencing between New Spain and early modern Iberia are revealing. In the Spanish province of Aragón, the Inquisition sentenced over 150 men to death for sodomy or bestiality between 1570 and 1630 (the majority for the latter crime).[50] However, after 1633, according to William E. Monter, there were no more sodomy executions in Aragón.[51] In Seville, Spain, at least seventy-one men were burned to death for sodomy and bestiality between 1567 and 1616.[52] In Madrid, secular courts were responsible for the deaths of over one hundred sodomites from the 1580s to the 1650s. And in Palermo, Sicily, then under Spanish dominion, between 1567 and 1640 at least eighty-three men were publicly executed for sodomy.[53] In contrast, the records of the Portuguese Inquisition, which had jurisdiction over Portugal and its overseas colonies of Brazil and Goa, indicate that only approximately thirty men were put to death for sodomy, most of them in the seventeenth century.[54]

The Iberian numbers diverge in important ways from those of the thirteen British colonies on the Atlantic coast of North America, especially in terms of chronology. There are records of twenty-six charges of "buggery," sodomy, and bestiality against twenty-three men in Pennsylvania between 1682 and 1800, but only one of those is prior to 1730. In colonial New England—made up of the Province of New Hampshire, Province of Massachusetts, Colony of Rhode Island and Providence Plantations, and Connecticut Colony—the story was different: seven men were executed for bestiality between 1642 and 1674, and none, so far as we know, afterward.[55] As late as 1796, an eighty-five-year-old Massachusetts man was sentenced to hang for the same crime as was an eighty-three-year-old Connecticut farmer only a few years later, though the court records are incomplete, and we do not know if these sentences were carried out.[56]

The Iberian and British American figures on sodomy and the death penalty are perhaps more of a reflection on the fragmentary nature of archival holdings and historical records preservation than anything else. Nonetheless, there are fascinating points of convergence and divergence between the European, Iberian American, and British American contexts. Most prominent is that the corpus of extant sodomy and bestiality cases for colonial North America pales in comparison to that of New Spain. Furthermore, there are many more executions for sodomy than for bestiality in New Spain. The converse is true for the British North American colonies—which may be because of differences in traditions of punishment, or, given the fragmentary nature of the archives, because of differences in recordkeeping practices.

New Spain's death sentence for sodomy, of course, has a long genealogy, tied, first and foremost, to the Book of Leviticus in the Old Testament, which states: "If a man also lie with mankind, as he lieth with a woman, both of them have committed an abomination: they shall surely be put to death; their blood *shall be* upon them" (Leviticus 20:13). While the Council of Toledo in 693 concluded that those found guilty of sodomy would be punished (merely) by castration and subsequent banishment, by the eighth century, the Fuero Real (which brought together a number of local *fueros*, or local law codes, from diverse territories) stipulated that those who had committed sodomy or bestiality would be publicly castrated and then would be hung upside down until death.[57]

The most important medieval Spanish law on sodomy was the *Siete Partidas*, compiled under the direction of Alfonso X between 1251 and 1265. Title XXI of the seventh *partida* reaffirmed the death penalty for those found guilty of the sin against nature: "If it should be proved, both the party who commits, and the party who consents to it, must be put to death; except where one of them was compelled to perform the act by force, or is under fourteen years of age."[58] The *Siete Partidas* mentioned only men in reference to sodomy, but in the mid-sixteenth century Gregório López, who prepared the standard gloss on the Salamanca edition of the *Siete Partidas* in 1555, argued that the law applied to women as well. López wrote that "women sinning in this way are punished by burning according to the law [*pragmática*] of their Catholic Majesties which orders that this crime against nature be punished with such a penalty, especially since the said law is not restricted to men, but refers to any person of whatever condition who has unnatural intercourse."[59]

In August 1497 the Catholic monarchs Ferdinand of Aragón and Isabella of Castile issued the *Pragmática de los Reyes Católicos acerca de los reos de pecado nefando*, which stated that any person found guilty of the *delito nefando contra naturam*, "the nefarious crime against nature," would be burned and their goods confiscated by the Crown—as was specified in the 1604 sodomy case.[60] The pinning of both *crimen* (crime) and *pecado* (sin) to *nefando* (nefarious) perhaps implies that sodomy in Castile was beginning to be viewed as a "crime" that eventually came to fall under the jurisdiction of secular rather than ecclesiastical courts, as it did in the Spanish American colonies. It also stipulated "that any person, of any state, condition, preeminence, or office, who commits the nefarious crime against nature, as established by means of proof, which according to the Law is sufficient to confirm the crime of heresy or the high crime of treason, shall be burned in live flames in the place [where the crime was committed]."[61] Here, the royal edict associates the burden of proof necessary to substantiate sodomy with that needed to determine either heresy or treason, which shows how sodomy was seen as one of the gravest crimes in the Catholic world. Equally significant is the specification that even when a "perfect and complete" act of sodomy could *not* be proven juridically, acts that were "very proximate and close" to it, such as fellatio, could merit the same punishment and fate.[62] These Iberian laws had fatal consequences for Pedro Quini, Joaquín Ziziqui, Francisco Capiche, and the young Juan, alongside dozens of other men in New Spain—all of whom were physically eradicated and symbolically erased from memory, even though their textual traces (and documented desires) live on.

Absent Archival Referents

We can safely assume that the recorded figures for sodomy death executions in the Iberian Atlantic world represent a mere fraction of those who were actually sentenced to death. To complicate matters even more, in New Spain, even as late as the end of the eighteenth century, local courts pronounced death sentences for sodomy and bestiality, often only to be overturned by the high court in Mexico City. Yet when archival documents are incomplete, miscategorized, or simply not centralized, we may not have enough evidence to show whether these sentences were challenged, successfully appealed, or carried out. This, once again, points to the incomplete nature of the historical record and to the methodological difficulties of assessing the connections between sodomy, death, and archives. Even in Lisbon's Torre do Tombo, where archivists eventually centralized Inquisition sodomy trials from Portugal and its colonies between 1610 and 1795, the first of twenty-one individual sodomy binders—Cadernos do Nefando, or "Folders of the Nefarious"—has been lost, leading to inevitable gaps in the historical record. This tension between archival absence and presence is even more evident in New Spain, where secular sodomy and bestiality cases were never centralized, and where surely there are many cases yet to be found, and many more that have been lost to the ravages of time.

Documenting death as it relates to sodomy is, to say the least, a tricky business. Yet even in the context of New Spain, our attempts to do so do not lead to what Arondekar terms the "empty archive" of colonial sexuality.[63] Colonial New Spain's archives of sexuality are teeming and, at the same time, riddled with holes, gaps, and inconsistencies. Here, I connect my discussion of documenting death to archival fragments and what I am terming *absent archival referents*, which emphasizes archival documents that are no longer extant or locatable.

The corpus of colonial sodomy cases I have gathered here indicates that at least fifty-four men—and certainly many more—were executed in New Spain for the crime of sodomy. These executions occurred between the years 1530 and 1786, though there could be other missing or undocumented cases from elsewhere in the viceroyalty of New Spain's existence, from 1521 to 1821. This figure includes el Caltzontzin, executed in 1530, and the Purépecha men, killed in 1604. There are several references to sodomy executions in early colonial Guatemala, though trial records have thus far been impossible to locate. A brief archival entry in Seville's Archivo General de Indias relates that in Guatemala, in 1596, an unspecified number of "delinquents" were burned in Guatemala for the pecado nefando and *otras especies de sodomía*, "other kinds of sodomy."[64] Whether this referred to the burning of two or twenty individuals convicted of sodomy, we will likely never know. We will also never know if those "other kinds of sodomy" refer to female sodomy, masturbation, fellatio, cunnilingus, or other acts that approximated the unnatural.

Based on archival documents found in Guatemala's Archivo General del Gobierno—established as the national archives in 1846, after the consolidation of Guatemalan independence—an 1851 copy of the *Memorias para la historia del antiguo reyno de Guatemala* makes reference to other early colonial sodomy death sentences. The tome briefly relates that in November 1601, don Pedro de Carranza and Juan Ucelo, both indigenous from Chiquimula, were "condemned to burn" for sodomy (with all their goods confiscated for the *real cámara*), and another man, Andres Pérez, was to be tortured for the same crime.[65] A 1937 copy of the *Boletín del Archivo General del Gobierno*, using the same archival database, similarly made reference to "evidence [*constancia*] of the incident in the city of Santiago de Guatemala, December 10, 1583—the date on which the *indio* Juan Martín was to be executed by means of fire in the *plaza mayor* of the said city. On that date, three clerics and a retailer, assisted by various particulars, saved the condemned, raising great scandal in the said plaza in the exact moments that the *indio* Martín was led to the stake, for having committed the nefarious sin."[66]

These historiographical and archival references make clear that it was not unusual to sentence convicted sodomites to death in early colonial Guatemala. In 1968 the Guatemalan government renamed the Archivo General del Gobierno as its present Archivo General de Centro América, yet despite my efforts to locate there the original cases on which these references were based, I have not been successful, nor to my knowledge have other researchers. These references thus point ultimately to absent archival referents. These and other documents may be missing from the archive due to any number of reasons, spanning from colonial times to the present. As Sylvia Sellers-García tells us for the colonial Guatemalan context, "Much like correspondence that might be ruined by water, lost during travel, or stolen as it changes hands, documents in the archive ran analogous risks due to poor storage conditions, poor organization, and theft."[67] The documents from Juan Martín's 1583 sodomy trial may be lost, misplaced, or simply misclassified, yet historiographical traces of the archive's own records persist.

Another important cache of sodomy death sentences originates in and around Mexico City, including those from 1658 analyzed by Gruzinski. Similar repression took place throughout the seventeenth century. Mexico's Archivo General de la Nación contains a succinct judicial summary—once again, the original case is lost—that mentions two black men, Juan Chapinero and a slave named Nicolás, who were sentenced in 1651 to be publicly garroted until they died, their corpses subsequently burned.[68] This same document refers to a prior case with no date given in which a mulatto, Agustín de Ávalos, and two indigenous men, Juan Quessar and Bernardino de Pinedo, were convicted of sodomy around the same time, but no information on the sentences is provided. While it is possible, and perhaps even likely, that these three suffered the same fate as Chapinero and Nicolás, we cannot be sure. In the historical archive of the Museo Nacional de Antropología e Historia, Camilla Townsend has uncovered several extraordinary references in the Nahuatl-language "Annals of Puebla" to indios and mulattos who were burned for sodomy in Puebla in 1682, 1690, and 1691.[69]

Several other seventeenth-century sodomy executions come to us through the diary of Mexican priest Antonio de Robles, Diario de sucesos notables (1665–1703). Robles has four separate entries about sodomy and capital punishment, the first from March 1670: "Monday at four in the afternoon in the public market of San Juan they burned Juan de la Cruz, an Indian from the neighborhood of La Lagunilla, for the nefarious sin."[70] Robles tells us that on June 25, 1671, two mulattos and three black men—caught in Juan de Ávila's textile mill in the town of Mixcoac, on the outskirts of Mexico City—were burned "for sodomy" (por sométicos) in Mexico City's neighborhood of San Lázaro, where Mexico's national archive stands today.[71] At that same spot, on November 13, 1673, authorities burned another "seven mulattos, blacks, and mestizos," who had also been caught in Ávila's textile mill, for the crime of sodomy.[72] Finally, Robles mentions that over a decade later, on November 20, 1686, "a mulatto and a mestizo" were executed by fire for sodomy, and "they took a black man to be publicly shamed for being an accomplice."[73] My efforts to cross-reference Robles's reports of sodomy executions with archival evidence have been unsuccessful, yet another instance of the fragmented (and always partly absent) nature of the colonial archive. Thus, the fates of these fifteen individuals—all racially marked as Indians, blacks, mulattos, and mestizos—likely enter historicity only through Robles's diary.

This tradition of capital punishment for sodomy also stretched west, from the Atlantic to the Pacific. An archival fragment from 1671 refers to two *sangleyes*—Chinese men temporarily living and working in the Philippines, which were colonized by Spain, and incorporated into New Spain in 1565—who were condemned to death for sodomy, although the governor of Isla Hermosa (present-day Taiwan) successfully intervened on their behalf and prevented the sentence from being carried out.[74] Though the archival record is sparse, it would be naïve to assume that these two were the only men in the colonial Philippines whom Spanish authorities sentenced to death for sodomy. In the Caribbean, several sodomy cases were initiated in the ports of Havana, Santo Domingo, and San Juan de Ulúa (near Veracruz, Mexico), but, because these men were tried by the Audiencia de la Casa de la Contratación—the House of Trade—in Seville, they were sentenced and executed for sodomy in Andalucía, Spain, and not in New Spain, and the records reside in Seville's Archivo General de Indias. This was the case with two mulatto men, Gerónimo Ponce de Leon and Domingo López, executed in 1603, and with a Portuguese mulatto named Francisco, executed in 1648.[75]

Finally, there are several late colonial newspaper references to the death penalty being meted out for sodomy as late as 1786. These sources offer representations of death for sodomy in the historical record, but they also serve as possible examples of the *death of the historical record itself*—the original documents appear to have ceased to exist. To my knowledge, no archival documents have surfaced that can corroborate these reports, but this does not invalidate them as historical sources. Instead, it complicates them as absent archival referents, which speak to the relationship between sodomy, death, and the missing archive. The February 1735 edition of a late colonial newspaper, the *Gazeta de México*, mentions two men who were sentenced to death, their corpses subsequently burned, "for the grave crime of Sodomy."[76] On August 27, 1738,

the same *Gazeta* relates that the court sentenced two indigenous men convicted of the "nefarious crime" to die by fire.[77] The newspaper also reported
that members of the local *cofradía*—a lay religious brotherhood dedicated to
the worship of a patron saint—accompanied them and offered solace on their
way to meet their fates. The June 30, 1784, printing of the *Gazeta* notes: "On
the 23rd the penalty of death and fire was executed on the nefarious offender
of this royal jail of the court, whose body was reduced to ashes in the accustomed site."[78] Nineteenth-century Mexican historian Manuel Rivera Cambas
also refers to a case of two men who "for the crime of sodomy and bestiality"
were executed alongside four other men, for theft and arson, by the Tribunal
de La Acordada on June 24, 1786.[79] The severed heads of all six criminals were
nailed to posts across the city, in the places where each crime had been committed. These archival fragments of death are especially valuable in that they
enable us to see the regulation and punishment of sodomy in New Spain in
terms of a continuum—albeit an uneven one—of repression. Although, so far
as I know, there are no extant archival cases indicating sodomy was punished
by death in the eighteenth century (again, the latest document in the archives
is from 1691), the matter-of-fact nature of these late colonial newspaper clip-
pings, and the unambiguous 1784 reference to the *sitio acostumbrado*—the
accustomed site where sodomites were burned—intimates that capital punishment for sodomy was anything but out of the ordinary.

Archive as Sepulcher?

In recent decades, theorists have articulated the intimate relationship between
archives and death. Arlette Farge, for one, notes how "history remains first and
foremost an encounter with death."[80] Certainly in the documents that demonstrate the link between sodomy and death, that "encounter" is impossible to
avoid. Achille Mbembe goes further, suggesting not only that the archivist and
the historian conjointly inhabit a sepulcher but that archiving itself "is a kind of
interment, laying something in a coffin, if not to rest, then at least to consign
elements of that life which could not be destroyed purely and simply."[81] Yet to
what extent does the archive itself mediate our own interactions with archived
representations of death? If, for Mbembe, the archive is a cemetery—a place
where "fragments of lives and pieces of time are interred there, their shadows
and footprints inscribed on paper and preserved like so many relics"—then
what relationships do we have to the archived dead, and how do we encounter
deadly desires in the archive?[82] This is a question we cannot resolve, but its

impossibility should prompt us to look more closely at our relationships to death and the archive. What, for example, are our ethical responsibilities to the archived dead? Can the history of sexuality attend to these? And what are our relationships to the various types of death—spectacular, mundane, ritualized, punitive, or otherwise—that the archives depict?

It is here, with some chagrin, that I share an archive story—one that has perplexed me in the decade and a half since I first encountered the 1604 sodomy case. When I came across those files in Morelia's municipal archive, I was intrigued, but I thought it would likely prove to be a series of false accusations, or that it would contain more rhetoric against native subjects than evidence of sodomy among them. As I delved into the early modern Spanish paleography— that is, the interpretation of forms of writing—necessary to read the notaries' various scripts in the file, I came to realize that this case was unique, more detailed, and more valuable than anything I had anticipated. Anxious, I simply could not wait to read through the dozens of folios to ascertain the outcome of the case. One afternoon, I impatiently skipped ahead to read the final folios of the case, in hopes that they would reveal the fates of the accused. I found my answer: four of the implicated Purépecha men had been publicly executed for their "crimes against nature." Though I was reading about the torture and eventual killing of fellow human beings—individuals for whom I felt a certain affinity—my first reaction was one of exhilaration. I was ecstatic—a feeling that I can barely describe even now. I had my first significant "archival find" in the history of sexuality. Could this document, I wondered with anticipation, challenge previously held assumptions about sodomy among native peoples in rural New Spain?

The more archives I visited, the more archival "finds" I found, the more discomfited I was by my sense of exhilaration. Did my own affective reactions to the archived subjects and their stories play into a certain historical objectification? My sense of elation at having "discovered" definitive proof of the death penalty in 1604 was, to say the least, problematic. I had gone into the colonial archive looking for "sodomites" and "homosexuals" in New Spain, and my first sustained encounter with same-sex desire ended in torture and death, in the spectacle of public punishment enacted on the bodies of Purépecha men and adolescents. This was an archival encounter that, unsurprisingly, confirmed weighty differences (of temporality, identity, situation, and experience) between the historical subjects that I was researching and myself. Their bodies and desires were profoundly misinscribed, as we have seen—through language, gender, colonialism, and the trappings of representation—in the historical record but also through my own imagined identification with, and use of, them in the writing of this book. I too am complicit in processes that misinscribe and misrepresent, despite my best intentions as a historian and queer studies scholar. For to write about the desires of another—a historical other—and to mold archival narratives about that person into "history" is to always partly misinscribe.

How might my affective response to the material have been altered, I subsequently pondered, if those folios had ended differently? Would I have been more or less elated at my archival find had the Purépecha men escaped from prison prior to sentencing? What if the intricate webs of accusation had been opaque, so as to better protect friends, neighbors, lovers, and sexual partners? Or what if the criminal case were an archival fragment, with no clear resolution (for either the Purépecha men or for myself, the historian)? Then, at least, the incompleteness of the archival document would have offered a glimmer of hope—a chance that the men had avoided public whipping and shaming, the indignity of a town crier pronouncing their crimes, and the vulnerability of a public death at the hands of colonial authorities. Indeed, these hypothetical questions suggest that I *wanted* these men to have escaped the death penalty. But, were that the case, I would not have written this chapter on the desires (and horrors) of the past. The terrible reality is that, both here and in the chapter on bestiality, I necessarily rely on horrendous human and animal deaths to make my arguments. This points to my complicity in the process of misinscription—to how we inevitably read our own desires into the archives, doing so in ways that ultimately confound the reasons behind why we seek what we do in the past. My own archival voyeurism thus both elucidates and occludes the lives and desires of Cuyne, Quini, and the other Purépecha men—inscribing and, once again, misinscribing by and through the very process of writing them into history.

I am left with nagging questions: How does it alter the stakes of historical writing to acknowledge our own (occasionally problematic) affective responses to the archival material at hand—to confess my own elation at having uncovered evidence of gruesome sodomy executions? How can the field of the history of sexuality sufficiently attend to that which Kate Eichhorn calls the "impure methodology" (and "dirty history") of doing archival work?[83] Does the mere acknowledgment and analysis of my own conflicted response to the 1604 sodomy trial sufficiently address this "dirtiness"? In my case, it may be that

I put my own interests—finding remarkable documents, getting an academic job, impressing my colleagues—before those of the historical subjects I encountered in the archive (despite writing about them with sympathy). Of course, I am not alone, and many historians whose historical subjects are no longer living struggle with similar methodological quandaries. And while the above questions are worth asking, perhaps there is no option other than to prioritize my own research interests within the archives, and to write as ethically about historical subjects as I can. After all, how could I prioritize their interests over mine without presuming to know what they themselves would have wanted?

In my teaching, research, and writing, I focus attentively on the tragedies that colonialism has wrought on the bodies and subjectivities of colonized peoples, but in *that* moment of archival discovery—in *that* archival encounter—my elation at having found unrivalled evidence of sodomy among indigenous men in Michoacán overshadowed all else. I share this archive story not with the intent of feeling better about myself, or achieving some archival catharsis, but rather to highlight the messy, dirty methodologies that mark the discipline of history. This focus brings us back to the impulses of the archive: archival misinscription and historical voyeurism—two phenomena that we see at work within the documents as well as in our interpretations of those documents. There are no easy answers, yet I hope that asking self-reflexive questions and analyzing the content of archival documents in conjunction with our own affective responses (and attractions) opens up imaginative possibilities for practicing the history of sexuality. The archive itself is indeed a sepulcher that we will all, eventually, come to inhabit. The archived bodies, recorded subjectivities, and documented desires of historians and archivists may also one day circulate in ways that we ourselves may have never imagined. Perhaps they already do.

Despite this chapter's emphasis on death, the colonial archive is, to be sure, a vibrant space of life. On so many levels, the archive represents traces of lived experiences and desires that come to us through the documents, and through the subjectivities that we construct for historical subjects out of those archival narratives. The corpus of cases discussed in this chapter is rich in ethnohistorical information, suggesting that multiethnic sodomitical subcultures existed throughout New Spain, in both rural towns and urban centers. Pedro Quini, Joaquín Ziziqui, Francisco Conduyi, and the other men termed "putos" were part of a formidable group of men in and around colonial Valladolid who knew where to engage in sex with other men. The case also evidences some of the contradictions of colonialism, especially in the legal defense invoked by judges, prosecutors, and lawyers in this case. In an attempt to exculpate Quini, for example, the court-appointed *defensor* referred to the accused as an "incompetent Indian without any understanding, who neither knows nor understands the gravity and abomination" of his crime.[84] Similarly, Ziziqui, Capiche, and Juan were referred to as *yndios ignorantes de poco razon y entendimiento*—"ignorant Indians of little reason or understanding"—which is why, according to their legal defense, they had confessed to crimes that they did not actually commit.[85] These tropes of indigenous ignorance, lack of reason, and inability to understand thus bolster the colonial project through the very legal maneuvering that was meant, in the first place, to exonerate and protect them from the repressive nature of colonial justice. This logic also does the work of misinscribing, yet again, the archived representation of the yndio ("Indian") in New Spain.

Perhaps the most radical misinscription of the body here is the colonial archive's move to legitimate—through documentation and preservation—the killing, burning, and literal disintegration of the body of the sodomite into "ashes." Achille Mbembe explains, "The best way to ensure that the dead do not stir up disorder is not only to bury them, but also to bury their 'remains,' the 'debris.'"[86] Here we evince the reasoning behind the death penalty and the contradictory logic of the colonial archive, poised between remembrance and forgetting. The bodies of sodomites were burned into ashes and denied burial so that, as we will also see in bestiality trials, no trace of the nefarious act would remain. Yet, at the very same time, the colonial archive documents, in explicit detail, and makes visible (and legible) the delineations and silhouettes of nefarious desire, thereby committing them to historical memory and unwittingly enabling future archivizations of desire. Similarly, the use of the pregonero—the town crier—to publicly pronounce the crimes of convicts also disseminated information, thereby committing to popular memory the very desires colonial authorities sought to eradicate through the ritualized burning of sodomites.

The very concept of misinscription hinges on the idea that there is some gap or infidelity between what an individual actually said—and as important, what an individual actually did—and how their words were translated and transcribed. Misinscription is provocative because in most cases we can really only speculate on whether, or how much, any given body or desire was misinscribed. Yet I also use this term to refer to the ways that the actual details of original events are continually altered, and potentially misproduced, by the presence of later generations of archivists and historians, as we saw in my discussion of viscerality in the archives. Of course, archival transcription is the first of many steps—on a spectrum from witnessing a crime to archiving it—for bodies and desires to be misinscribed. This chapter has invited us to think through the implications of voyeurism and misinscription, not only in how the bodies and desires of historical agents came to be archived in the first place but also how we ourselves, as transmitters and consumers of bodily knowledge, participate in overlapping modes of circulation and reproduction.

The value of the 1604 sodomy trial also lies in the ways it asks us to confront our own perceptions (and misperceptions) of the nature of colonial repression. Colonial archives show that some men and women looked upon sodomy and sodomites with a derisive sense of humor, a lurid intrigue, or even a certain disinterest. Others were offended, but not to the extent that they would want to see their neighbors imprisoned, whipped, banished, garroted, or burned at the stake. And, of course, many were willing participants themselves. These conflicting reactions to sodomy help to explain why, as we will see, it sometimes took years before some notorious sodomites were denounced to criminal authorities, and why many never were.

Colonial repression definitely existed—but not necessarily in opposition to tolerance or toleration. This 1604 case lays bare some of the many impulses of the archive that we will encounter again throughout this book—taxonomizing language, effacing acts of translation, and transcriptions of desire. Here we have, largely through a microhistorical interpretation of one case, explored the meanings behind the archiving of sodomy in New Spain. This exercise has led us into the murky terrain of the archive, and the inevitable list of partly unanswerable questions that accompanies any attempt to interpret the subjects of the archive. That uncertainty speaks to the troubled methodology of researching and writing about sex and desire in the past—in short, the trouble with *doing* the history of sexuality. My discussions of archival impulses, sodomy and the death penalty, and my own conflicted affective archival engagements have, I hope, shed new light on the ways that sexuality enters (and exits) the colonial archive. Ultimately, historical voyeurism and its resulting misinscriptions stem from the very *impulse* to watch in the first place, which can itself be experienced viscerally. Visceral impulses—like the young boy's spontaneous peek into the temascal one day in August 1604—thus set the colonial archive in motion.

In her 1966 articulation of the connections between pollution, cleanliness, and taboo, Mary Douglas wrote, "Sometimes bodily orifices seem to represent points of entry or exit to social units."[87] In the 1604 case discussed in this chapter, the *sieso*—the anus—is named with specificity, and it functions symbolically as one such orifice. It becomes an ideological entry point to social networks, sexual subcultures, colonial regulatory mechanisms, and the archive. Leo Bersani, writing about the AIDS crisis in the 1980s, famously asked: "Is the rectum a grave?"[88] Given that the archive functions as sepulcher, with slight reformulation of this query, we can find ourselves asking this question instead: "Is the rectum an *archive*?" If so, how (and what) does it record? How is it read, documented, and remembered, and by whom?

CHAPTER 3

Archiving the Signs of Sodomy

Bodies and Gestures

In Mexico's national archive there is one particularly perplexing set of records—officially designated Indiferente Virreinal—that contains a diverse and disordered collection of 254,039 documents, dating from 1524 into the 1880s, distributed among 6,743 boxes. According to the archive's website, "The documentary group designated Indiferente Virreinal is a collection of documents that is made up of files coming from diverse institutions that (principally) existed during the colonial period; a kind of miscellany inherited by the Archivo General de la Nación from its predecessor, the Secretaría de Cámara del Virreinato."[1] Yet despite the website's assertion, historian Linda Arnold confirms that most of the documents do not come from the Secretaría de Cámara but rather from diverse colonial institutions including the Church, the Inquisition, the courts, and the treasury department. In general, the colonial documents not identified with any of the previously existing *ramos*, or branches, of the archive eventually came to be labeled "Indiferente Virreinal"— an archival miscellany of the Viceroyalty of New Spain.

When I commenced the archival research for this book, relatively few Indiferente Virreinal documents had been described, cataloged, or digitized. Yet in the first decades of the twenty-first century, with joint financial support from Spain's Ministry of Culture and Mexico's Ministry of the Interior, a diverse group of eighty-three individuals—historians, archivists, and recent university graduates—processed the hundreds of thousands of documents that made up this collection, classifying and describing them as best as possible given the daunting task.[2] Part of this initiative was to make many of the documents digitally available to researchers. Only because of this collaborative effort was I myself able to uncover dozens of archival references to sodomy and bestiality that otherwise would have remained invisible among the documentary chaos of this particular record set. The judicial summary of the (absent) criminal case that follows is one of many Indiferente Virreinal documents that illustrate the peculiar ways sodomy is rendered visible in the historical past and the archival present.

Around 1710, in the town of Coyoacán, just south of Mexico City, a black slave named Lorenzo Joseph Carrion verbally denounced two men to a local priest, who alerted secular authorities, for having committed the crime of sodomy in a textile mill some nine months earlier.[3] According to Carrion, he saw that "a free mulatto named Juan de Dios, an apprentice and tailor, and Joseph de Santiago, an unmarried [indigenous] man, met to commit the nefarious sin. The said mulatto served as a woman, and the Indian as a man. And although this deponent was sleeping, he had awoken due to the movements that they were making, and he watched them with attention until they had finished committing the said sin."[4] Carrion's voyeurism, watching the two men *con atención*—with attention, in his words—initiated the judicial machinery once it reached the ears of colonial authorities. Carrion "also saw them" (*también los vido*) on another occasion at three o'clock in the morning engaged in the same act in a dark corner of the mill.[5] An unmarried indigenous man, Lucas Lorenzo, also witnessed similar acts, after which he approached the owner, don Juan Pabia, who, upon hearing the charges against him, expelled Juan de Dios from working and living at his textile mill.

After being informed of Juan de Dios's activities, the *alguacil mayor* of Coyoacán apprehended Juan de Dios, Joseph de Santiago, and two mulatto slaves who were also implicated. When faced with the overwhelming eyewitness testimony against him, Juan de Dios chose to fully confess his crimes, stating that he had in fact served "as a woman" in repeated acts of sodomy. In an attempt to mitigate his own punishment, he claimed that Joseph de Santiago, two mulatto slaves named as Gaspár de los Reyes and Andrés de la Cruz, and two other mulatto slaves and a mestizo man (never located by authorities) had committed the sin of sodomy far more frequently than he had. The complete transcripts of the trial, no doubt, contained the explicit details that are characteristic of early modern sodomy cases; yet this judicial summary, like so many other records, leads to an archival absence. The transcripts of the original case are lost. All that has surfaced thus far is this thirty-folio judicial summary, presumably written by the notary after the sentencing, from which we can piece together the details of the case. Gaspár de los Reyes was tortured three times but maintained his innocence, and he was not punished. The criminal court did find Juan de Dios,

Joseph de Santiago, and Andrés de la Cruz guilty of sodomy, and sentenced them to be paraded through public streets, whipped two hundred times each, and imprisoned for life, with only bread and water given to them every day (except Sundays) for the first seven years of their confinement.[6]

Seeing Sodomy

How do we see sodomy, both historically and archivally? More specifically, what acts of viewing, imagining, and speaking of the desires of others culminate in the recording and transcription of those desires (first onto paper and eventually into the archives)? By what means do certain bodies become legible and enter the historical record at specific moments, and why? Finally, how are the bodies of "sodomites" classified? As we saw in the previous chapter, the question of the visible in the above accusations is key. Based on Joseph Carrion's accusation in the 1710 sodomy case from Coyoacán, we get a sense of just how much weight criminal courts placed on eyewitness testimony in terms of bringing the crime to its attention and adjudicating the outcome. Such visual accounts were often corroborated (or challenged) by the reading of "signs"—a seemingly simple but endlessly ambiguous term that refers to something that could be interpreted, something from which conclusions could be drawn. All signs, physical or otherwise, had to be seen (or heard), assessed, and interpreted. This interpretation occurs via any, and sometimes all, of our senses. Misinscription is, of course, a problem fundamental to how colonial courts interpreted the signs around them. As we will see in this chapter, the visual tends to dominate the process of interpretation, both in the past (for criminal courts) and in the archives (for historians and archivists). For, as Kathryn Burns notes, we inevitably encounter the archives with all our senses.[7] But our reading of the documents—and hence our interpretation of them—is enabled primarily by our eyes.

This chapter focuses on the ways sodomy was rendered historically and archivally visible through select interpretations of the signs of the body—its physical state, its affective gestures, and its everyday performances of gender and morality. Through these signs, sodomy became both legible and meaningful for witnesses and courts in the colonial past—thereby directly influencing how they also acquire meaning for archivists and historians. I conceptually divide my discussion between corporeal, gestural, and affective signs, knowing fully well that witnesses and courts analyzed such markers in conjunction with one another, and not independently. According to Stuart Hall, a sign "connotes a quality, situation, value or interface, which is present as an implication of implied meaning, depending on the connotational positioning."[8] My discussion here relies on Hall's formulation but moves us away from linguistic understandings of signs and toward archival readings of how certain signs—things to be interpreted—could imply sodomy. Furthermore, some of the "connotational positioning" of the signs of sodomy are constructed by and through the very act of documenting. The body, its gestures, and its affective states provide us with an entangled set of signs that, as we will see, could have radically different implications for sodomy suspects in terms of how criminal courts made sense of the charges against them. The body and its moral and emotional states are thus witnessed (and constructed) in different ways; those differences could—and often did—establish distinctive burdens of evidence and truth for colonial courts. Categories of testimony and evidence fit together, juridically speaking, in complicated ways, especially given the disproportion between eyewitness testimony and physical evidence. There was, to be sure, more eyewitness testimony than physical evidence in most sodomy cases. As such, eyewitness testimony was considered as important as physical evidence, and sometimes even more so.

Whereas the previous chapter took a largely microhistorical approach to explore the archival impulses of misinscription and voyeurism, here I expand my approach both chronologically and thematically. This chapter examines the wide array of seemingly arbitrary signs that people—including everyone from criminal authorities, judges, witnesses, surgeons, and neighbors to wary parents and potential sex partners—looked for to indicate sodomitical proclivities. On the one hand, this chapter looks at the demographics of sodomy, eliciting ethnohistorical information about how the charge of sodomy was construed according to differences of caste, race, and gender. On the other hand, it decodes the conceptual models used by colonial contemporaries (and, more recently, by historians) to understand the permutations of those acts in the legal and medical spheres. To do so, I work across my archival corpus; within those 327 documents, I have uncovered 129 archival references to sodomy among laypersons. In one way or another, all these documents lead us to the same question: What counted as reliable evidence for colonial courts? Intertwined with this question are others: What counts for historians today as "reliable" archival evidence, and by what means do historians, with the help of archivists, uncover sodomy within the archives?

These records reveal conflicting testimonies, inconsistent details, unstable desires, and shifting perceptions of what may (or may not) have taken place. All this ambiguity should caution us against thinking that rigid legal or cultural codes governed the historical pasts with which we are dealing. We know that medieval legal codes, like the *Siete Partidas*, as well as early modern laws relating to sodomy emphasized definitive proof and tangible evidence; not surprisingly, establishing (or for the accused, refuting) a sodomy charge through corporeal and affective signs was central to the adjudication process. In trying to determine either that an act of sodomy took place (a question of "fact") or that a given individual had sodomitical tendencies (a question concerning moral character, reputation, and gender), witnesses and authorities made assumptions about sex acts and their meanings. In short, they inferred meaning from an assemblage of signs. To see how the signs of the sodomitical body were perceived, transmitted, transcribed, and recorded, we must delve into contemporary ideas about the significance of eyewitness testimony, the reliability of tangible evidence, and the role of medical examinations of the penetrated body, especially in cases of coercive sodomy.

The archival texts upon which this chapter is largely based consist of every reference to sodomy that I found in New Spain's secular criminal court records, from well over a dozen archives. Thus, my corpus includes a disparate blend of complete sodomy trials, fragments of criminal cases, judicial summaries, and false accusations. Equally important, however, are denunciations of sodomy received by the Mexican Inquisition, which because of jurisdictional limits were supposed to be ignored, save in some instances, by ecclesiastical authorities. This was nearly always the case if there was no prima facie reason to believe heresy, blasphemy, or a priest was involved, because then the charge of sodomy fell outside the Inquisition's jurisdiction. The Inquisition could, however, prosecute someone—as it sometimes did—for merely *asserting* that sodomy was not a sin. Nonetheless, as we will see, sodomy was sometimes popularly yet erroneously *perceived as* heresy, though in reality it was not. The impression left by this geographically diverse corpus of sodomy cases is—as we began to see in the previous chapter—one of sporadic and uneven repression, which shows how sodomy was sometimes ignored by all levels of society, so long as the act was kept private. Sodomy did not always elicit horror, fear, shock, and scandal among those privy to instances of it—a fact that begs us to move beyond polarized categories of tolerance and repression in theorizing the relationship between sexuality, the Church, and the colonial state.

He Saw It with His Own Eyes

A phrase that, with some variation, recurs in more than half of these sodomy cases—*lo vido ocularmente*—refers to sight and the eyes; the literal translation is "he or she [the witness] saw it visually." To what the "it" referred changed with the context, but the importance of the visual did not. Eyewitness evidence operated alongside other forms of physical evidence, despite the fact that it was, by definition, more ephemeral than, say, wet or bloody underwear or an "instrument" used to penetrate another.

All sodomy cases began with a denunciation, be it a self-denunciation or the accusation of another, which, by the time it was transcribed and recorded, may have already gone through several stages of construction, transmission, and transcription. Thus, the eyewitness testimony of the denouncer, whether genuine or not, was one of many ways that she or he sought to construct a plausible narrative that would be taken seriously by criminal authorities. In New Spain, at least one witness was required to initiate a trial for the charge of sodomy, with the possibility of securing a conviction. According to law, if there was *only* one witness, his or her testimony had to be corroborated with confessions or other forms of medical or physical evidence. The tremendous reliance on eyewitness testimony in sodomy cases develops, as Berco notes, "because the crime of sodomy legally entailed a strict physical occurrence, that is anal intercourse with *efusionem intra vas*, or ejaculation inside the rectum."[9] Apart from a person confessing that he had ejaculated into the anus of another man, or confessing that he had received the ejaculate of another man, verification gets murky. In other words, these testimonies relied not on absolute corroboration with "fact" but rather on tactile, aural, and visual *signs* from which a witness inferred that an act of sodomy had taken place, and that he or she could then articulate in court. The ambiguity inherent in those signs, and in their interpretation, almost always left room for the accused to refute the claims against them.

The significance of corroborated eyewitness testimonies could, as they did in the 1710 case with which I opened this chapter, lead to seemingly full confessions on the part of the accused. Regardless of their veracity, eyewitness accounts could also bring about imprecise and contradictory confessions. Thus, witnessing itself existed on a spectrum of sorts, ranging from testimony so full of detail to that which lacked specificity (and hence credibility). The very act of witnessing—of watching attentively, of striving to perceive as many details as possible—was thus encouraged by the judicial system, a fact that places a certain voyeurism at the center of colonial justice.

In a 1731 case from New Mexico, the omniscient gaze (and wrath) of God seems to have been channeled through the body of one Spanish witness, Manuel Trujillo. One day while he was out searching for some goats that had damaged his plantation, he encountered two indigenous men, Asención Povia and Antonio Yuba, committing the nefarious sin.[10] Upon seeing them, Trujillo "easily recognized the act" as that of sodomy, and he dismounted his horse and severely whipped both men for their sins against God.[11] By taking punishment into his own hands, Trujillo served as a witness both to colonial authority and to God. In prison, the two Pueblo men denied that they had committed sodomy, although they admitted to having been caught lying naked together and caressing each other. According to Povia, the two were lying *barriga con barriga*, "stomach to stomach," when Yuba, who was on the ground, "grabbed his [Povia's] virile member and brought it closer to his [Yuba's] posterior part, but Yuba could not rouse it to put it inside; the abovementioned *indio* was caressing it so that he would incite it, but could not rouse it; and it was because of God that he could not become inflamed."[12] While Povia imagined God watching him, inducing shame so as not to get an erection (and, eventually, to confess his sins), it was the Spaniard who saw them in this state. Due to lack of proof that the two had actually committed sodomy, Povia and Yuba were merely exiled by the court in Santa Fe to different towns in New Mexico for a period of four months each. Individual acts of witnessing can thus be both communal and divine, rendering visible for the criminal court that which God had already witnessed.

A surprising number of cases involved a sort of participatory voyeurism, in which one of the sexual partners initiated charges against the other, often with unwelcome results for both. Such was the case with two men in their early forties, the Spaniard Bernardo Zerón and the free mulatto Miguel Díaz de Zepeda, whose bodies and desires entered the archival record in the late seventeenth century. In 1694 in the city of Tlaxcala, Zerón alleged that Zepeda had repeatedly solicited sexual favors from him in several symbolically charged sites: at a wedding party, in a cemetery, in a convent, and in a chapel. In a self-reflexive mode, Zerón recalled one of those occasions: "Smiling, he [Zerón] took off his pants and he [Zepeda] touched with both hands his entire body and its parts with much longing [*con mucha ansia*] and in such a way that the said mulatto delighted in enticing his member in the extreme, and he [Zepeda] gave him [Zerón] many kisses on him and on his genitals . . . and this deponent spilled semen into the hands of the said mulatto, who took out a small cloth and cleaned this deponent, telling him that he should give him his semen whenever he asked for it."[13] Despite his explicit testimony and admitting to having ejaculated from mutual masturbation and fellatio with Zepeda, Zerón paradoxically told authorities that he had only "consented in order to figure out his [Zepeda's] intention, to report him to the law so that he would be punished, and to this end he made it known to your mercy, the said Governor."[14] This voyeuristic impulse, he tried to convince authorities, was at the heart of his consent and participation. Zerón, who was admonished by authorities for foolishly submitting to such base desires, was imprisoned along with his accomplice. Zerón's brother and other witnesses, who were questioned by authorities, professed that Zerón had exhibited the symptoms of dementia (*delirio*), a lack of judgment (*falta de juicio*), incapability (*incapaz*), and "profound melancholy" (*profunda melancholia*) in recent years. Nonetheless, the court fined him fifty pesos and sentenced him to two years of service in the Hospital of San Hipólito—a punishment that became increasingly common as the colonial period wore on. The comparative incoherence of Zepeda's testimonies was a decisive factor in determining his guilt. Zepeda initially denied all allegations against him, but in the careo, he admitted he had taken off Zerón's pants in the chapel— but only to help him get rid of lice or fleas. The court sentenced Zepeda to two years of forced labor in a textile mill, without pay for the first year. The sentences pronounced against both men at the close of the seventeenth century were comparatively lenient because neither had committed "perfect sodomy."

The numerous sodomy cases that were brought to light by eyewitness testimony attest to the importance of the observer and his or her credibility. As we saw in the previous chapter, many individuals who inadvertently stumbled across two men having sex in public or private would often call others to witness what they had seen: perhaps because they were in shock and needed independent verification, perhaps because they wanted to share in (or deride) the titillating moment with another, or perhaps in a more calculated effort to bolster their eventual claims. Though one person's testimony was needed to initiate a criminal sodomy case, at least in theory, the testimony of at least three adult witnesses was deemed necessary to secure a conviction for sodomy.[15] In 1723, in a small town near Colima, a young Nahua woman, passing by the hacienda Palmas de Aguacatitlán on her way home, saw two Nahua men lying on the ground under an avocado tree, "as if a man were hugging a woman lying on the ground."[16] She went and alerted the wife and son of the hacienda's superintendent, and news quickly spread among those living and working on the hacienda; many came to witness Flores on top of Montaño in the moonlight. Adding to the credibility of the witnesses, one man "saw that the buttocks and behind of he who had taken off his *calzones* were entirely moist."[17] Both men were tied up and whipped by the superintendent, and eventually sent to jail, where they awaited the decisions of the Real Audiencia in Guadalajara. The archival records are incomplete, and no further information is given.

It is clear that the plausibility of eyewitness testimony was enhanced by the number of witnesses who had observed the act. Sometimes, even more valuable were other types of corroborating evidence: the more tangible this evidence, the better. In these cases, a variety of physical details—such as wet clothing, bloody underwear, or money exchanged for sexual services—came into play and were used to determine the "truth." As we saw in the previous chapter, Pedro Quini's "white underwear wet with fresh blood" became a focal point of the testimony of the boy who initially discovered the two men having sex in the temascal. Wetness or moistness, which spoke to the immediate result of sexual activity, was another important sign that witnesses commented on. In the late 1600s aboard one of the galleons traveling between Cádiz, Spain, and the Americas, some witnesses in the sodomy case of the ten-year-old Juan Molé from Sicily observed that "the entire behind of the boy was wet."[18] One witness, the cabin boy Pedro Juan Bayarte, realized that, on coming closer to the boy who was lying face down in a hammock, his behind was "completely smeared, according to the smell and touch of semen."[19] Here, the ocular implicates the tactile: after seeing, Bayarte had to *touch* and *smell* the wetness to confirm that it was, in fact, semen. This evidence—coupled with confessions and the testimony of a surgeon who examined the boy—proved "without a doubt" that sodomy had been consummated aboard the ship. Three older Italians were implicated in the crime, one of whom was garroted in Spain, and the other two of whom were perpetually banished from Spain and its colonies. Because of his young age, the Spanish court sentenced Molé to be publicly shamed, forced him to watch the older man's execution, and was symbolically "passed through the flames," so as to dissuade him from ever again committing a similar crime.

These cases show that, on one level, colonial courts (and witnesses) privileged sight above all other senses. The centrality of that which was experienced *ocularmente*—ocularly—is pervasive in the archive, and can be found in nearly every case employed in this study. Yet, in reading "along the archival grain," we get a better sense of how all the senses mattered significantly in the adjudication, punishment, and reception of the crimes. The visual, the aural, the tactile, and the olfactory converged in ways that left (and still leave) archival traces. One need only imagine, for example, the largely unarchived reactions of bystanders who, through their own senses, witnessed the punishment of convicts one afternoon in the central plaza: did they react viscerally to the sound of a convict's screams, to the spectacle of him being tortured, to the smell of his charred flesh? For the courts, there was always far more eyewitness testimony than there was actual, physical evidence—a fact that points to the need for the judicial process to account for witness unreliability, equivocation, and even outright untruth. Yet this disparity also speaks to a hierarchy of legal value (and evidentiary weight) that different types of signs attained within the colonial courts.

False Accusations

What differentiates an act that is seen and then recorded from one that is seen and not recorded? Or, in the case of false accusations, from an act that is *recorded but not seen*? The cases above show the fallibility of eyewitness testimony in sodomy trials. Witnesses testified to the physical movements of the accused, the sounds that they made, the odors of their emissions, and the states of their bodies and clothing—all as proof that an act of sodomy had been committed. All statements involved some degree of assumption. Often, because of distance or occluded vision, it was impossible to tell if two men had actually consummated the act. Surely, some eyewitness testimony was entirely sincere, even if it was exaggerated, and even if the signs were misread. But sometimes, eyewitness testimony was purely fabricated.

I have found two intriguing, and intersecting, trends in sodomy trials over time. Throughout the seventeenth and eighteenth centuries, the severity of sodomy punishments declined; but alongside that decline, it became increasingly common to use the charge of sodomy to smear the reputation of one's personal or political rivals. As historian Geoffrey Spurling notes, "The pecado nefando served as a useful political tool in both the Old World and the New; a well-timed allegation could irrevocably stain the reputation of an adversary."[20] In the corpus of sodomy trials used for this study, there are at least six blatantly false sodomy accusations that all resulted in lengthy criminal trials. In each of these cases, which occurred between 1693 and 1818, lawyers and judges were able to prove that the charges levied against the men were fabricated and due to personal enmities, economic rivalries, or political motives. But the accused nonetheless spent between one and four years in prison as they awaited the outcome of the trial. In these six cases, the courts eventually absolved the men of their alleged crimes and sought to restore their honor. Those who levied false charges were also typically punished once the case was resolved—proof that lying could have a definite cost. There are dozens of other sodomy cases in which suspects who had been imprisoned for several years were finally absolved due to a lack of "definitive" proof.

In 1693 two local magistrates, or alcaldes, from the town of Texupa, Oaxaca, accused Domingo de Selís and Pascual de Santiago of sodomy.[21] The accused both admitted that they had frequently gone to the temascal together to bathe but denied all allegations of sodomy and successfully demonstrated that the two indigenous alcaldes who had levied the charges against them were old personal enemies of theirs. There is, of course, the possibility that the alcaldes believed their accusations even though they lacked definitive evidence, especially since their denunciations stemmed from rumors they had heard. Rumor, of course, is full of contradictions and, as Luise White notes, "may simply be poised between an explanation and an assertion: it is not events misinterpreted and deformed, but rather events analyzed and commented upon."[22] The court, however, eventually ruled that Selís and Santiago were innocent, and their "good credit and fame" were reinstated by the declarations made by a town crier in the central plaza. It is worth noting that the crier—the pregonero— could be used not only to shame and denounce but also to bolster someone's reputation.

Other motives could serve as an impetus for a denunciation. In 1715, near Hidalgo del Parral, the indigenous governor of the town of San Felipe, don Blas de Iriarte, was denounced for sodomy by four men who, upon investigation, had vengeful motives since they had all been severely punished by Iriarte for concubinage, the mistreatment of their wives, and other crimes.[23] Although the outcome of the case is not on file, Iriarte's defense lawyer sufficiently undermined the credibility of his accusers, and it seems likely that Iriarte was absolved. In a similarly incomplete 1728 case from Santa Fe, New Mexico, Miguel Martín convinced several individuals to falsely accuse the octogenarian Francisco Javier Romero of sodomy in exchange for money and livestock.[24] And in another example, from 1800, the court discovered that a false sodomy charge lodged against don Antonio Naredo, a public notary in Guadalajara, was the result of a campaign mounted by Isidro de Cueto, a boy of fourteen, who, for reasons unknown, pressured numerous boys to make false claims.[25] These charges were eventually linked back to personal and political enemies of Naredo. Given the lengthy duration of criminal trials and the extended periods that many men accused of sodomy spent in prison awaiting the outcome, it is easy to see how the charge of sodomy could be used as a weapon. These cases demonstrate the lengths to which some individuals would go to imprison an enemy and publicly stain their reputation. Just as important, they point to the unreliability of eyewitness accounts and to how reputation itself functioned as an important sign.

Importantly, colonial authorities did mete out punishments for false testimony. In 1818 don Vincente Ulloa, a wealthy Spaniard in Guadalajara, originally from the Peruvian city of Lima, was falsely accused by a number of his male servants of forced sodomy.[26] Andrés Luebano, a nineteen-year-old Spaniard, and Máximo Álvarez, an indigenous man of nineteen, detailed how they had been threatened and forcibly sodomized by Ulloa. As it turns out, the boys had been repeatedly hit and physically mistreated by their employer, and this was one reason they levied false testimony against him. Furthermore, the boys who denounced Ulloa for sodomy had stolen from him and wanted him imprisoned to prevent their being caught and punished. For calumny, both boys were sentenced to be whipped twenty-five times and to spend six months laboring on public works projects. Ulloa was absolved of the charge of sodomy (but, in an interesting turn, was punished for making and distributing contraband cigars in his house, the details of which came to light in his sodomy trial).

The final point that I want to distinguish here is between lack of proof and the conclusion that the accused was innocent. There are dozens of sodomy cases, which may or may not have been initiated by false accusations, in which suspects who had been imprisoned for years were finally absolved due to a lack of "definitive proof." In Puebla in 1714, for example, an indigenous man named Cristóbal de Contreras reported to authorities that one night another indigenous man, Antonio Pérez, had invited him to drink pulque. That evening, according to Contreras, Pérez tried to kiss him, hug him, and indecently touch him in an effort to incite him to commit sodomy. Pérez pleaded to Contreras, "Fuck me, man" (*hódame hombre*), but Contreras defended himself, telling him, "I am not of that type [a puto] and I do not want to do this. Now, I will take you to the house of the alguacil so that you will be punished."[27] At some point, prior to turning him over to authorities, Contreras personally whipped Pérez. Pérez adamantly maintained his innocence throughout the trial, blaming the accusation on the fact that Contreras was his enemy. Medical examinations, the topic of the following section, also proved inconclusive. Despite the fact that the only proof against Pérez was the word of Contreras, he spent four years in prison and was forced to pay the costs of the trial upon his release. In cases like this, it is virtually impossible to tease out the events as they actually took place.[28] Did Pérez attempt to have sex with Contreras? Or was Pérez wrongfully imprisoned for four years due to false charges levied against him? In this case, both parties agreed that "perfect sodomy" did not take place, but the court was more concerned with the *intent* to commit sodomy.

It appears that as the judicial punishments for sodomy and bestiality became increasingly lenient over time, false sodomy accusations became more common. This is clearly tied to the fact that sodomy in the later colonial period was typically punished less harshly (meaning that some people were more inclined to resort to sodomy as a means to tarnish another's reputation). More importantly, it is tied to the fact that people came to increasingly create and manipulate the signs of sodomy, many of which rested on stratified notions of social class and ethnic caste that are characteristic of the late colonial period. In these cases, we see not merely a reading of signs that already exist but also a making up—a fabrication and creation—of signs by the false accuser.[29]

Medical Expertise

Bodies themselves function as signs to be manipulated. Medical knowledge, in particular, offered a technical means to read the bodies of supposed sodomites, both externally and internally. As we have seen, eyewitness testimony often played a more central role than did physical evidence. Bodies, however, also became forms of legal evidence through interpretations offered by a range of medical experts, from university-trained physicians to unlicensed barber-surgeons. This was especially true in sodomy cases that purportedly involved violence or coercion. In such cases, medical expertise became central in assessing both the body and its physiological signs, especially for an individual who had been penetrated against his (or her) will.

After the initial fact-finding phase of a judicial inquiry had been completed and the sodomy suspects charged with a crime and imprisoned, the next step was typically the *reconocimiento del cirujano*. This "medical examination by a surgeon" was perhaps the most common way of determining whether anal penetration had been consummated. In the absence of a surgeon qualified by the Royal Protomedicato—the board of physicians in the Spanish Indies responsible for regulating medical practitioners and inspecting apothecary shops—a barber or another informal medical practitioner would sometimes be called to discern any irregularity in the colon, rectum, or anal canal. It is at this stage that the judicial proceedings become their most detailed (and voyeuristic), in content and form; the intimate inner workings of boys' and men's bodies were probed, and that information circulated to a wider network of witnesses, judges, and scribes. There is some overlap here with the common practice of examining female victims of *estupro*—a term that is somewhat analogous to our present-day concept of "rape" but refers more specifically to the act of forced intercourse with a virgin or a young, unmarried woman. Midwives (or, less frequently, male medics) meticulously examined these women, and the results of their findings were transcribed into the records of the court and eventually into the colonial archive.[30]

There were a few standard physiological signs that provided seemingly irrefutable proof of penetration. Alternately, the absence of such signs, as verified by surgeons, could also provide evidence to disprove sodomy allegations. This is what happened in the 1694 case of Zepeda and Zerón, who engaged in mutual masturbation, kissing, and fellatio in the late seventeenth century.[31] Both men denied having engaged in anal penetration, and the surgeon who examined them both duly noted: "there are no signs [*señales*] in the intestines or rectum, and the muscles so exceedingly strong that the introduction of an instrument confirmed the absence of any orifice other than the natural one, and that what they have stated is the truth."[32] The surgeon sought out clues internally—in the intestines, rectums, and anal sphincters of the men. He then searched for evidence that either one of the bodies had somehow deviated from nature in terms of their own physical constitutions, looking for "any orifice other than the natural one." The meaning here is vague, but it is likely that the surgeon was looking for major tears or ulcerations in the tissue, as well as for some "unnatural" orifice such as an inchoate vaginal opening that may have been present among ambiguously gendered (or intersex) individuals. In other words, he was to interpret, and make visible, the internal, physiological signs of the body in ways that could be meaningful for the colonial court. It was then the duty of the notary to faithfully transcribe those findings, which became part of the judicial proceedings. The relatively lenient sentences meted out to the two men—Zerón was fined fifty pesos and sentenced to two years of service in a hospital and Zepeda was sentenced to two years of labor in a bakery or textile mill—would have been harsher had perfect sodomy been demonstrated medically.

In one Guatemalan case from 1794, the absence of bodily signs shows the constructed and malleable nature of allegations and testimonies. That year Paulo Jiménez, a fifty-year-old mestizo, was accused of sodomy with José María Clemente, a boy of seven or eight. The boy's grandfather, who had been told by a relative that Jiménez "hugged and kissed" his grandson at night, filed the charges. The conflicting testimonies of the boy, who constantly changed his story, were deemed juridically unreliable: he repeatedly changed his mind about whether he had been hugged, kissed, or penetrated by Jiménez. Of equal importance, the surgeon who examined the boy found nothing abnormal internally or externally, and he declared that the boy experienced no pain or discomfort in his backside, thus further calling into question the alleged rape. The boy eventually admitted that the defendant had only fondled him, and that on several occasions, both in bed and on a nearby hillside, "the old man had put his *pajarito* [little bird] up against his," rubbing their penises against one another.[33] What cast the most doubt on his testimony, however, was his admission that his mother had persuaded him to tell authorities that Jiménez had penetrated him. We cannot know if, or why, she did so, though we can speculate that if the mother knew of her son's abuse, she may have wanted Jiménez punished to the full extent of the law. Instead, Jiménez was set free and absolved of the charges against him. In this case, we see how the medical examination became one of several forms of evidence that were considered by colonial courts. Furthermore, this case suggests that sexual abuse was sometimes seen as inconsequential so long as anal sex itself was not involved.

For perhaps obvious reasons, there were several problems associated with reliance on medical examinations to confirm or disprove sodomy. Common physical ailments or medical conditions—blisters, scars, lacerations, hemorrhoids, ulcers, intestinal irritation, or even a "loose" anus—could easily be misinterpreted as signs of anal intercourse (though evidence of such misinterpretation is difficult to find in the archival records that exist). Some doctors, however, were clearly aware of this possibility and sought to counteract it, as did the doctor cited in the incomplete 1780 sodomy case of the Spanish Leandro Hurtado de Mendoza and the indigenous Pedro Joseph Pinedo. Following both men being accused of sodomy, a medical doctor found irregularities in Pinedo's anus, which he nonetheless deemed insufficient to prove the crime. This doctor harshly critiqued the jurisprudential reliance on "very suspicious" physical evidence such as "bloodied sheets or a shirt stained with blood" to prove sodomy because, according to him, "in practice, innumerable ailments could be responsible for the corruption of the bodily humors."[34] On the other hand, for courts seeking to establish evidence of sodomy through physiological irregularities, sodomy simply did not always lead to the extreme irritation or other symptoms that courts and medics hoped to find in the body of one who had been penetrated. In addition, medical examinations could not offer immediate evidence, since days or even weeks or months had often elapsed between the alleged sodomitical act and assessment by a surgeon or physician.

In one remarkable case, the eighteenth-century trial of Antonio Pérez, the medical practitioner himself cast doubt on the very reliability of physiological signs. In an attempt to determine whether he had been anally penetrated, the surgeon filed a report stating that although he was lacking some folds of the anal skin and he had barely discernible fissures or minor "cracks" (*grietas*) in his lower intestines, his anal region was largely in its "natural state." This medic in particular noted that the interpretation of such physiological signs of sodomy was *materia tan dudosa*—a highly questionable matter—given that changes to the body may have occurred naturally due to diet, the consumption of acidic foods, disease, bowel irritation, or for several other reasons. Another doctor who examined Pérez asserted, "As long as the witnesses have not seen the blood of the nefarious act upon bed sheets or clothing, the crime cannot be proven."[35] In making such an assertion, this medic challenged physiological signs—irregularities of the anus and lower intestines—as reliable signifiers of sodomy. In doing so, the physician perhaps unwittingly undermined his own medical authority by challenging the legibility of bodily signs (that only he and other qualified medical experts could read), only then to turn to physical signs, like bloodied sheets, that could be even more arbitrary.[36]

As we already know from the 1604 trial in Michoacán, medical proof was by no means necessary to convict someone of sodomy. Yet even the intent to commit sodomy could be criminal, but only if it was proven that those involved had engaged in lesser acts, such as kissing or masturbation. In practice, the decision to punish someone for intent to commit sodomy depended greatly on the local court's interpretation of the evidence and of the law itself. The late eighteenth-century Guatemalan criminal case of Cristóbal Desiderio, a mulatto baker accused of sodomy, is a good example of insufficient medical evidence. Following the suspect's imprisonment, the criminal court called on the surgeon Nicolás de Montúfar "to find out if he had some lesion or other sign that would indicate the crime." The surgeon ultimately "could not find any lesion on the virile member or anus of the said patient," nor were there "stains of blood or semen on his clothing."[37] In this case, however, eyewitness testimony by a man who alleged to have seen an indigenous adolescent penetrating the forty-year-old mulatto on the side of the road was deemed sufficient evidence to convict both men. Yet, in the specific language of the court, it found the men guilty not of sodomy per se but rather of the *sodomia que parece pretendian cometer*—that is, "the sodomy that it seems they tried to commit."

To end this section, I want to highlight the ways that body and affect could converge, at least for the boys and men physically examined for evidence of sodomy, around the medical examination itself. As one might imagine, such examinations had the potential to provoke shame and, in rare cases, even elicit confessions. A 1764 Mexican legal treatise, the *Libro de los principales rudimentos tocante a todos juicios, criminal, civil y executivo*, for example, outlined that one mode of determining guilt in sodomy cases was to "examine [the suspect's posterior] with an instrument that surgeons carry with them, and, in its absence, with a hen's egg [*huebo de Gallina*] that is large and will be inserted in the posterior eye [*ojo de atras*, i.e., anus] to see if it disappears, and this examination will be related to the judge."[38] The use of an egg is particularly horrifying, and suggests a certain disregard for the well-being of suspects and victims. While the use of this recommended technique has yet to be documented in sodomy cases, medical practitioners did use special instruments to prod and penetrate the bodies of those who had allegedly been penetrated, sometimes against their will, by other men. Such was the case with the previously discussed ten-year-old Sicilian boy, Juan Molé, who, in 1697, was brought onboard a ship set to travel from Cádiz, Spain, to the Americas.[39] Eyewitness testimonies asserting that an older Italian sailor, Bartolomé Barres, had penetrated the boy were corroborated by the surgeon's examination. The surgeon noted that Molé, who was noticeably ashamed to be examined, confessed to him that Barres had penetrated him and that some other mariners had caught them in the act. Upon inspection, the surgeon found that "the external parts of the anus were completely lacerated with some sordid and callous ulcers— signs that they had committed the sin of sodomy many times with him."[40] This detail was crucial in convicting Molé and the men with whom he had had sex. Thus, one's own body could be used against him or her in the criminal courts.

Medical Voyeurism

Here, I focus on the textual circulation of an 1803 Guatemalan case of Juana Aguilar—a "suspected hermaphrodite," according to the doctor who assessed her—to argue that certain types of medical expertise were quintessentially voyeuristic. Indeed, science, medical voyeurism, and print culture became intimately interconnected in late colonial New Spain. Medical expertise was called on in a variety of situations to assess the bodies of ambiguously gendered individuals, and those who were literate seemed eager for information about anomalous bodies; this could even take the form of lurid journalism. The case of Aguilar, a mestiza in her thirties, shows us how medicalized readings of the body circulated simultaneously in the scientific, juridical, and popular spheres.

In 1803 Juana Aguilar was accused of the crime of "double concubinage" with a man and a woman in Guatemala City. Surgeon Narciso Esparragosa y Gallardo repeatedly examined Aguilar's body—probing her vagina, ovaries, and what he deemed a "prominent" clitoris—in order to determine her sex and see if she was indeed a hermaphrodite, all to resolve the allegations that she had committed sodomy with another woman. In essence, the surgeon needed to determine whether she was biologically capable of sodomy. While hermaphroditism itself was not criminalized, sodomy was; thus, the two categories overlap significantly in colonial thinking.

The bulk of what we know of Aguilar comes to us through late colonial newspapers: Esparragosa published excerpts of his medical reports on Juana Aguilar in two different issues of the *Gazeta de Guatemala*. Published on July 4, 1803, and July 11, 1803, the articles were both titled "HERMAFRODITAS" (fig. 3.1) and became, according to Martha Few, "a means to circulate information about Aguilar's exotic, exceptional body, both to the legal court and to the broader public."[41] Those documents do not shed light on Juana's age, race, ethnicity, or family (and indeed the original criminal trial has only recently been uncovered). As María Elena Martínez points out, Aguilar becomes material for historical study because of Esparragosa's report, "in which fragments of her life, and especially of her body, appear through different filters, among them colonial, misogynist, and homophobic."[42] Here we see how Esparragosa read the signs of Aguilar's body, circulating explicit knowledge about that body in late colonial Guatemala.

Esparragosa classified and taxonomized Aguilar, and he presented his opinions to the court in February 1803 along with a note offering to submit detailed illustrations of Aguilar's genitalia, which he had commissioned a local artist to draw (no trace of these illustrations exist).[43] Interpreting her body, Esparragosa concluded that Aguilar, "rare phenomenon" that she was, was not actually a hermaphrodite but rather someone whom, according to him, nature had denied the fully formed reproductive organs of either of the sexes. This

Num. 311   Tom. VII.   Fol. 177

GAZETA DE GUATEMALA

DEL LUNES 11. DE JULIO de 1803.

HERMAFRODITAS.

Informe del Cirujano de Camara honorario &c. (N. 310.)

A la primera vista se observan en la *Juana* los grandes labios, lo mismo que en qualquiera muger, con la diferencia que el *Clytoris* sale entre aquellos poco mas de media pulgada; lo que no es muy estraño, pues en algunas mugeres se advierte igual prominencia. Separados los dos labios, y reconocido el *Clytoris* desde su raiz, ya su longitud se advierte como de pulgada y media, su grueso como el dedo auricular ó pequeño de una mano de hombre, su configuracion exterior perfectamente parecida a la del miembro viril, con su cabeza glande y prepucio; pero le falta el conducto de la orina, con el que está perforado longitudinalmente el miembro del hombre. La consistencia de aquel *Clytoris* es tan floja, que por su propio peso está caido sobre las demas partes, sin que en los diferentes reconocimientos y manoseos le haya notado la mas ligera ereccion. Debajo de este organo se advierten las *ninfas*, aunque muy desvanecidas. Tambien se vé el conducto de la orina, aunque mas estrecho que lo regular, y este canal no solo ha servido para la espulsion de la orina, sino, como asegura la misma *Juana*, se han vertido por él las menstruaciones de una sangre aguada. Pero enteramente se halla cerrado, ó por mejor decir no aparece ni el mas ligero vestigio del orificio de la vagina; organo de los externos el mas esencial en las mugeres, pues sin él es imposible la generacion: y adelantando el escrutinio por asegurarme si solo el pellejo servia de cubierta á la vagina, para en este caso poder practicar la operacion conveniente, y franquear la entrada á aquel seno, me pareció muy juicioso la reflexion que el Dr. D. Josè Maria Guerra ha estampado en su informe precedente, conseqüente al dictamen de Mr. Levret, que asegura que las mugeres que se hallan con el conducto exterior de la vagina tapado, carecen en todo ó en parte de este organo, siendo puntualmente lo que yo he observado en la Juana, por que las partes que se hallan detras de la piel, en aquella region donde debe estar la vagina, están adherentes, y firmes, sin resquicio al-

demonstrated, to the doctor's satisfaction, that Aguilar could not have consummated sodomy with either men or women: "being neither man nor woman, Juana is incapable of incurring a crime that necessarily demands the existence of one of the two sexes."[44] Esparragosa, in his reports, made reference to Aguilar's enlarged clitoris of one and a half inches in size, which according to him was "recognizable when the labia are separated, [and] between them in the upper part is a small but somewhat prominent body, very similar to the virile member, called the *Clytoris*."[45] Esparragosa noted that Aguilar lacked a defined vaginal canal, that her "menstruations of watery blood" originated from the same orifice as her urine, and that despite his best efforts to "stimulate" the clitoris, it was, according to him, incapable of erection. As with the insertion of an egg into a man's anus, this stimulation of Aguilar's clitoris shows the horrific practices to which sodomy suspects were subjected in the name of science.

The doctor also documented the existence of "two glandular bodies, oval in shape, about the size of a cacao bean" inside her labia, which he posited were either inchoate testicles or malformed ovaries.[46]

In denying Juana Aguilar the status of man, woman, or hermaphrodite, Esparragosa intimates that she was what we, today, might term intersex. Importantly, his reading of her body likely played an important role in exonerating her from the charges of concubinage and sodomy (though the records of her trial are incomplete). As other scholars have demonstrated, writing about Aguilar was, for Esparragosa, also a means of bolstering his own credentials and demonstrating how his readings of Aguilar's body were informed by enlightened views and scientific inquiry. For she, in his own words, became the "object of my research and of this report." He publicly circulated knowledge of Aguilar—rendering Aguilar's body visible through its simultaneous lacks and excesses—in ways that served both science and voyeurism, boosting his own reputation and status.

It is worth reflecting on these two particular *Gazeta de Guatemala* articles, both as archival documents and as texts that circulated throughout New Spain. How did these two articles on Juana Aguilar, published in Guatemala City, end up in the national archive of Mexico, and why? Unlike Guatemala's Archivo General de Centro América, which has a complete set of the *Gazeta de Guatemala* issues, Mexico's Archivo General de la Nación holds only several complete issues of the Guatemalan newspaper from the year 1808, and they are classified simply in the archive's finding aid: "*Gazeta de Guatemala*, numbers 24, 25, 26, and 27." In contrast, the two stories from 1803 on Juana Aguilar are not labeled as such, and they have been excised from the newspapers. They are couched, instead, inside a very different archival classification: a one-page, handwritten formal complaint by Manuel Antonio Borjas against the newspaper, filed with the Mexican Inquisition on August 3, 1803, only a month following their publication. Borjas critiqued the *Gazeta* for "containing a report related to a certain Juana Larga, who is taken by some of the common people as a Hermaphrodite . . . for they [the articles] appear to me obscene and provocative, material far from that which should be [published] in the *Gazeta* in the hands of all, and they cannot be read without grave ruin to one's soul."[47] The cruel nickname "Juana la Larga," by which she was referred, pejoratively referenced her especially "long" clitoris.

The Mexican Inquisition, it appears, did not follow up on the complaint, yet the papers were archived among the files of the Inquisition. Nonetheless, the entry's framing of Esparragosa's writings on Juana Aguilar as both "obscene and provocative" show how some viewed the text—and, we can assume, the signs of sodomy that accompanied the text—as having a pornographic function when put into circulation. Here obscenity is defined not solely by the intent to sexually arouse or to provoke lust but rather by the potential to shock, to disgust, and to end up in the wrong hands. It appears from the language of the complaint that the problem was not solely the nature of Esparragosa's medical reports but also their wide circulation among commoners. Detailed medical descriptions of Juana Aguilar's body were, according to the petitioner, immoral and could lead to "grave ruin" if they ended up "in the hands of all." The recently uncovered court records of Juana Aguilar, Esparragosa's writing on Aguilar's body, and even the placement of Esparragosa's *Gazeta* articles within the files of the Mexican Inquisition show how the signs of the body—Aguilar's "Clytoris" and how it was read as not being stimulable by the surgeon—attained overlapping juridical, scientific, popular, and pornographic meanings when circulated among diverse audiences.

Ultimately, in Esparragosa's writings about Aguilar, the signs of sodomy (and hermaphroditism) point in multiple, contradictory directions. The criminal court required Esparragosa to examine Aguilar's body to determine whether she was biologically capable of committing sodomy. The doctor deemed that she was not but then circulated his reports in the public sphere, which seemed "obscene" to some. These interconnected readings of Juana Aguilar's body as "neither man nor woman" and of her genitalia as "obscene" are further illustrations of archival misinscription, though this time through the often-muddied lens of medicine and morality. From what we do know, Juana Aguilar chose to live as, and identify as, a woman.

Finally, as with other cases throughout this book, I myself and others before me are implicated in the continued circulation of Juana Aguilar's body. Historians of sexuality produce knowledge in ways that differ greatly from Esparragosa, though overlaps remain between the ways that bodies are displayed and exhibited textually in the archival and historiographic record. The criminal case of Juana Aguilar, the medical report it generated, the newspaper articles, and a series of historiographical inquiries into Aguilar's life (and even more recent satirical, and at times highly problematic, performances of Aguilar's body at academic conferences) are thus intimately connected, with each representing and circulating knowledge about the body of Aguilar to an audience far beyond those to whom she voluntarily chose to reveal herself.[48]

Nefarious Violence

The cases of Molé and Aguilar, and others like them, point to an epistemological issue at the heart of all sodomy trials. Simply put, it was often impossible for colonial courts (as for historians today) to determine one's level of agency, or its lack thereof, in sodomy. This section focuses on the decoding of violence in sodomy trials—violence that is often reflective of power relations between men and the dynamics of the spaces in which sodomy occurred. The coerced body—and even the social spaces through which that body moved—carried the potential to function as a sign, especially when narrated and medically examined.

William Monter appears right in his assertion that "power rather than eroticism" dominated most instances of "homosexual activity" in the early modern world.[49] As we know, the Spanish term *estupro*—often improperly translated as "rape"—referred in that era to "an illicit and forced carnal act or sexual intercourse with a virgin or maiden"; yet there is no corresponding term in the early modern Iberian Atlantic world that signified the male victim of a coercive carnal act.[50] I therefore use the term "nefarious violence" to refer to male-male sexual coercion, even though most involved would have simply referred to it as "sodomy." The important distinction here, however, is that if an individual could prove that he or she was forced into sodomy, he or she could be exonerated. For even in the thirteenth century, Alfonso X stipulated in the *Siete Partidas* that "any one of the people [from Iberian society] can accuse men who are guilty of the sin against nature, and this accusation can be brought before the judge of the district where the offense was committed. If it should be proved, both the party who commits, and the party who consents to it, must be put to death; except where one of them was compelled to perform the act by force, or is under fourteen years of age."[51] Of course, such exoneration was never a guarantee.

We see such potential for exoneration in the early nineteenth-century sodomy case of a Spanish soldier, Macedonio García. At three o'clock in the morning, another soldier caught García and a Mixtec servant of seventeen having sex in the corridor outside a Mexico City church.[52] Medical examinations of the boy, who swore that he had unsuccessfully tried to resist García's advances, showed that he had "a minor inflammation of the sphincter" and some internal secretions that, according to the surgeon, could only have been caused by the "introduction of a foreign body." In 1807 García was sentenced to four years of service in a hospital, and the lack of any other mention of the Mixtec boy in the trial transcripts suggests that he was exonerated. What does stand out in this case is the asymmetrical power relationship between a thirty-seven-year-old soldier and a seventeen-year-old indigenous servant, which in and of itself may have partly persuaded the court that this was indeed a case of forced sodomy.

Coercion—along with whippings, beatings, and other forms of physical violence—often loomed on the horizon of many sodomitical relationships, most often between older men and boys or adolescents, who could not fully defend themselves against the sexual advances of their aggressors. We must also remember that even when sexual relations were consensual, certain individuals may have strategically tried to portray sodomy as forced when telling their stories to authorities, casting themselves as innocent victims to evade the threat of punishment. Thus, witnesses and courts created, construed, and narrated the signs of bodily violence to prove either guilt or innocence.

Even in cases that involve extreme violence, medical readings of the body could be conspicuously absent. In 1633 an indigenous man named Alejo was imprisoned in Chiquimula, Guatemala, for having committed the nefarious sin with an indigenous boy named Gaspár, "from which his death resulted."[53] The boy's father brought charges against Alejo because "around the time that his son was close to dying, the boy declared that he was playing with the said Alejo near a cornfield . . . [when] Alejo negligently forced a large wooden stick or stake into his anus."[54] Alejo's defense lawyer asserted, however, that the crime was unproven and that "nefarious acts" were not known to provoke such quick deaths. It appears that there was no posthumous examination by a surgeon to confirm the cause of death (or it was not recorded in the trial records), and on March 18, 1634, the Real Audiencia absolved Alejo of any wrongdoing, thereby implicitly accepting the narrative created by the defense. It is possible that Gaspár's death was unrelated to his "playing" with Alejo, yet, at the same time, if he indeed forced a stick into the boy's rectum, it certainly could have caused a fatal infection or other internal damage. The audiencia did not pass any judgment on whether Alejo committed other sexual acts with the boy or if there were other reasons for some violent encounter between them. It is also unclear whether the boy was sick prior to the alleged encounter with Alejo. The case nonetheless reflects a power asymmetry between an older man and an adolescent, highlighting the complexities of reading the signs of sodomy and spinning historiographical narratives around them.

In nearly all instances of nefarious violence, victims were younger than their attackers. A representative sample of cases from the eighteenth and early nineteenth centuries shows a correlation between nonconsensual penetration and stark age differences between culprit and victim. It seems that the perpetrators of nefarious violence viewed their younger victims as relatively easy targets, perhaps physically weaker and less likely to tell or to be believed. In a 1786 case involving two shepherds, the thirteen-year-old Marcelo de la Cerda denounced Martín de los Reyes, age forty, for sodomizing him. The boy, who was suffering from a toothache, asserted that de los Reyes had cut some herbs to administer as an oral analgesic, when suddenly and unexpectedly the man began to force himself on the boy. In his own words, "because he was a boy he lacked the strength [to resist], and the said Martín grabbed him by the neck, half-choked him, and tore the strap off his pants, which fell down. And when he turned around, he saw that the said Martín was fornicating with him."[55] Martín admitted that while he was administering the analgesic, "Judas tempted him" and he had sex with the boy, who subsequently told his mother despite the fact that his assailant had threatened to kill him if he told anyone. The case is incomplete, and we have no information as to the fate of either. Such cases offer examples of older men who employed physical force to penetrate their victims and tried (unsuccessfully) to use fear as a tactic to prevent the boys from reporting the act. Significantly, a certain familiarity and geographic isolation created a context for some men to resort to nefarious violence. Because shepherds could often be out grazing the sheep for weeks at a time, it is easy to imagine a greater number of cases of sodomitical violence than we will ever have any archival record for.

While New Spain's criminal courts took allegations of coercive sodomy quite seriously, several documents show that the punishments meted out to the perpetrators of nefarious violence were no harsher than the sentences commonly pronounced in cases of consensual sodomy. In 1806 in Guatemala City, Catalina Rojas denounced José Victoriano Ambrosio, an indigenous man in his midtwenties, to secular authorities for having forced her son of fourteen, Joaquin Morales, to have sex. The boy related the following story to his mother. One morning, he was invited in the plaza by two indigenous men he had recently met to drink the alcoholic beverage *chiche* in a local tavern known as a *chichería*. He later accompanied one of them, Victoriano, to the outskirts of the city, where, out of nowhere, the man pushed him to the ground, stepped on his neck, and beat him, saying, "I will stop hitting you if we fornicate." Morales pleaded to be let go, but Victoriano forcibly stripped him, tied his hands behind his body, and violently sodomized him, "introducing his virile member into his posterior on three occasions."[56] When he finished, he tied the boy to a pole by the neck, his hands still bound behind him, so that he would not escape. Victoriano took all the boy's clothes (minus his hat) with him. It was not until nighttime that the boy wriggled himself free, and ran nude to the first house he found, where some women, seeing the marks on his body and his state, alerted the boy's mother. A medical examination confirmed that the boy had indeed been sodomized against his will. Victoriano, who denied everything, was sentenced to four years of forced labor on public works projects, both for sodomy and for several robberies in which he had been also implicated—a seemingly lenient punishment given the extreme violence of the act.

In a slightly later case from Zempoala, María Paulina de la Encarnación accused Lorenzo Aguirre, an indigenous man in his early thirties, of sodomizing her eighteen-year-old son, Mariano Marcos, from which he contracted an infection and died eight days later. Marcos, who confessed to having forced the boy into sex, and to having previously had sex with a donkey, was sentenced to ten years of forced labor.[57] One final example from Monterrey in 1829—less than a decade after Mexico gained its formal independence from Spain—shows that Reducindo Morillo was sentenced to merely five years of labor in Veracruz for violently sodomizing seven-year-old Matias Peña.[58] Early nineteenth-century cases that include sentences show that judges, when determining the appropriate punishment, distinguished between consensual and coercive sodomy only in order to declare that the person who had engaged in sodomy against his will was not guilty, but not to offer a harsher punishment for the sodomizer.

The final topic to discuss in relation to nefarious violence is the role of place, which, like the body, could also be read as a sign to be interpreted. Location played a key role in when, where, and how sexual encounters came about, and also in how (or whether) denunciations and testimonies made their way into the archive. Sodomy occurred in private, in public, and everywhere in between—personal residences, rented rooms, taverns, arcades and alleyways, public baths, pastures, at the edge of country roads, haciendas, slave quarters, prisons, ships and ports, schools, and churches all emerge in the archives. Many such places were male-dominated, and some lacked women entirely. Sometimes a place was selected to maximize privacy and at other times was chosen spontaneously, upon meeting someone with like desires. The spaces where sodomy occurred—be it partly occluded or openly visible—greatly influenced the chances of whether it would be seen as a crime, and thus the likelihood of it functioning as a sign and its being archived.

Of all the male-dominated spaces in the Iberian Atlantic world, some of the most notorious were in the prisons, both on the Iberian Peninsula and in the

Americas, and aboard ships that sailed across the Atlantic. These two spaces converge in the case of Gerónimo Juan Ponce, a mulatto sailor in his twenties, who, between the years of 1597 and 1603, was accused of repeatedly committing sodomy at sea and in the cities of San Juan de Ulúa (Mexico), Havana (Cuba), and Seville (Spain).[59] This case highlights the transatlantic nature of some sodomy trials, in which the official trial and punishment of the accused would vary between jurisdictions. Imprisoned in Havana for his alleged crimes, Ponce was transferred to the prisons of Seville for the duration of his trial, during which time he was accused of having committed sodomy with a mulatto prisoner, Domingo López. Other prisoners and a prison guard filed charges against the two men, after two witnesses, Tinoco and Pedro Sánchez, had caught them "on the ground together, with the said Domingo face down on the ground with his pants down and his shirt lifted up."[60] Among the prisoners and prison guards, news that the two men were "putos" spread quickly.

When interrogated, López said that Ponce had coaxed him into having sex, saying that in his prison cell, Ponce had grabbed him by the shoulders, and "the said Juan Ponze [sic] came to put his member inside of his ass [culo], and using force to insert it he got the tip inside because the rest of it was so thick that it would not fit, and having finished this confessant found his ass wet with the semen that the said Juan Ponze had spilled on him."[61] Ponce, however, steadfastly maintained his innocence despite his being repeatedly tortured at sea, in Havana while imprisoned, and in Seville. He maintained his silence through each ordeal. Nonetheless, the Casa de la Contratación in Seville sentenced the two men to be executed for their crimes. From the historical record, it appears that only Ponce was executed by garrote in 1605, with his body subsequently burned to ashes. This case, housed in Seville's Archivo General de Indias, shows that place mattered both in terms of how denunciations entered the archive and how such denunciations were dealt with, by which court, and under which jurisdiction. Prisons and ships were both highly charged social spaces. This case also would have been tried very differently, likely with another outcome for both men, had they been tried in either Havana or New Spain. Given that the death penalty for sodomy was employed more frequently in the Iberian Peninsula than it was in the Spanish colonies, geography and jurisdiction mattered as much as place and space in terms of how sodomy was dealt with and archived.

One major challenge, mentioned above, in assessing violence in sodomy cases is the difficulty of telling when the trope of sexual coercion was employed as a means of deflecting one's own guilt in the criminal act.[62] Was, for example,

Domingo López telling the truth or exaggerating his claims when he said that Ponce used force with him? The possibility of deceit adds yet another layer of archival misinscription. This time, however, the accuser and the accused create such misinscription rather than the translator, scribe, or archivist. Archives also contain several cases that appear to depict consensual, sometimes long-term, sodomitical relationships in which, in an effort to negate one's own agency and free will, one partner would tell the authorities that he had been coerced into the sexual act by the other (which may or may not have been true).[63] The archived body—read through physical signs and social space—is thus both unreliable and full of information.

Gender and Gesture

Everyday understandings of gender generated one particularly important set of rules that allowed for reading (and archiving) the signs of sodomy, some of which we have already seen through the "as if they were man and woman" understanding of sodomy. Sodomy was partly inferred from gesture and everyday performances of gender. All individuals in New Spain—just like all of us today—performed gender every day. If such performances, however, did not correspond to the gender assigned to one at the moment of birth, they tended to raise suspicions, both popular and official. Here I am interested in how gestures are enacted and gender is performed in ways that led outside observers to infer that a given individual had sodomitical tendencies. Part of this story is also gender ambiguity, which we saw in the case of Juana Aguilar. Importantly, however, while femininity in males or masculinity in females may have raised eyebrows, an implicit link between gender and sodomy was not necessarily replicated in court decisions.

Gestures are essentially movements of a part of the body that express an idea or a meaning. Like all signs, the ideas and meanings behind any given gesture depended partly on the observer, and were always open to a variety of interpretations; some of these interpretations held weight in criminal courts, and others did not. Cultural theorist Juana María Rodríguez notes how gesture "can signal both those defined movements that we make with our bodies and to which we assign meaning, and an action that extends beyond itself, that reaches, suggests, motions; an action that signals its desire to act, perhaps to touch. Gestures emphasize the mobile spaces of interpretation between actions and meaning."[64] Gestures are ephemeral, yet, as we will see later in this chapter, they are sometimes granted a textual permanence through the archival document. The ways that gender and gesture accrue to the body differs from the ways that the physiological signs of sodomy could accrue to the body. In the cases that follow, both gender and gesture become signs through which sex and desire made themselves known to (and also misunderstood by) a range of historical actors.

If, returning to Stuart Hall's definition, we take "sign" to mean that which is present as an implication of implied meaning, both gesture and performances of gender can function as signs of sexual desire. This is not to say that either masculinity or femininity in and of themselves are signs per se but rather that performances of masculinity (in women) and effeminacy (in males) served as cultural signs when they signaled one's sexual proclivities to an external observer. Individuals in New Spain who transgressed (or perhaps better said, reimagined) prevailing codes of gender—often as masculine women, effeminate men, or people of ambiguous genders—pervade the archival record, though in imbalanced ways. Here I turn to the figures of the *amujerado* (the "effeminate male") and the *mujer hombrada* (the "manly woman"), which are the most common instances of gender bending represented in colonial archives. Of these, the effeminate male appears most frequently in colonial archives, and reflects the presence in New Spain's urban centers of amujerados, who were sometimes gossiped about and documented. But, unlike full-fledged cross-dressing, effeminate gestures among males were not criminalized.

In the historiography on colonial Mexico, the most frequently referenced publicly effeminate man is Juan de la Vega, a *mulato afeminado*, popularly known as la Cotita, who was executed by fire with thirteen other men on November 6, 1658. The sexual activities between these men were not isolated cases; rather, as Gruzinski has shown, the documents reveal "the existence of a subculture with its own secret geography, its own network of information and informants, its own language and codes."[65] In the case of Juan de la Vega, colonial authorities duly noted the feminine dress and gestures of la Cotita: "the said mulatto would cinch his waist and on his forehead he would ordinarily wear a kerchief called a *melindre* that women use."[66] La Cotita would also sit on a small bench "in the manner of a woman" and customarily made tortillas, washed clothes, and cooked meals.[67] Obviously, la Cotita felt comfortable embodying their effeminacy in public, which implies a certain tolerance, however precarious, for effeminate men like Juan de la Vega who may or may not have lived and identified as women. Such archival references to everyday displays of male femininity are extraordinary, but they are not singular. Documents from a wide array of archives show that cross-dressing was not necessarily transgressive or even deemed worthy of punishment in colonial society. And while femininity in males might suggest to witnesses and to the court a person's sodomitical proclivities, they were not taken as proof.

In 1771 Mariano Rafael Puente denounced several *amujerados públicos*, "publicly effeminate men," to criminal authorities in Puebla for the crime of sodomy. Among those he denounced were Juan Pablo Suárez (mestizo, forty, alias "la Almoloya"), Pedro Joseph de Mesa (indigenous, thirty), and Fernando Sardo (mestizo, twenty-eight). Puente had inferred their criminal behavior from their effeminate appearances and mannerisms, and because they supposedly invited men to regularly "drink and dine" with them.[68] These gendered performances appeared to point toward the nefarious sin, yet as authorities began to investigate and interrogate witnesses, they found no evidence of sodomy, with the exception of isolated references to some of the amujerados trying to put their hands down the pants of other men. As authorities interrogated witnesses and suspects, references to other effeminate men in Puebla poured out. Miguel Antonio Vásquez, a married mestizo known as "la Golondrina" (the swallow); Pedro Palacios, a free mulatto known as "la Capulina" (the venomous cherry spider); Joseph Gabriel, known as "la Borrega" (the lamb); and Alberto Ramos de los Dolores were all imprisoned because their supposedly effeminate personae made them sodomy suspects.

A few of the men, such as Súarez, denied being effeminate, but some, including la Capulina and la Golondrina, admitted, in a fascinating self-referential use of the term, either that they were "amujerados" or that they were seen as such, but they refuted the idea that this was equivalent to being a sodomite. Alberto Ramos de los Dolores similarly stated, "Even though he is amujerado, this does not mean that he falls in love with men."[69] Beyond the crimes of public cross-dressing, or sodomy, the court had no law to apply to the amujerados; all were eventually set free. Sodomy, as we have seen, required a higher degree of proof, and could not legally be inferred from the apparent indications of femininity in males. This points to a significant gap between public assumptions and legal expectations around what constituted sufficient evidence of same-sex desire. In this vein, it appears that the defense lawyer of la Golondrina was convincing when he asserted, "in many ways a man can incur the touch of femininity . . . one can be effeminate [*afeminado*] in name, in appearance, by one's own inclination, and by the malicious use of one's sex."[70] The criminal court could not prove that final possibility, despite multiple interrogations, and therefore failed to demonstrably prove any inherent link between male femininity and sodomitical proclivities.

As in the case of la Cotita and his accomplices, it was common for sodomites to adopt female monikers when among friends, sexual partners, and, if prostitution was involved, potential clients. Another such example is provided by Juan Joseph Polverín, who was arrested with five other men for sodomy in 1722 and was known, likely in reference to sexual commerce, by the following feminine nicknames: "la Mora" (the blackberry), "la Mercadera" (the tradeswoman), and "la Francesa" (the Frenchwoman).[71] The adoption of effeminate nicknames both drew on and inverted the customs of male-female courtship practices and the world of sexual commerce.

Other references to male effeminacy are unevenly scattered throughout sodomy trials, as in the case of Manuel Gordillo, a Spaniard in his late fifties, who was denounced in 1765 in the city of Toluca, for repeated acts of sodomy, for offering money for sex, and for asserting that mutual masturbation between men "was not against the laws of God, the Virgin Mary, or the saints, nor was it the subject of heresy."[72] Gordillo was referred to by at least one witness, Cándido Agüero, in 1768 as an "amujerado," adding weight to the accusation.[73] Gordillo denied the fifteen formal charges against him and was tortured by inquisitors, after which he admitted to some of the charges but not to heretical statements. For his errant beliefs and unorthodox assertions, he was made to abjure *de vehementi* and was sentenced to read his punishment aloud in a church, whipped two hundred times, and exiled for a period of ten years, six of which were to be spent in a presidio in Havana.

We see a similar pattern—the sporadic archiving of male femininity—outside greater Mexico. In 1772 Cristóbal Desiderio, a forty-year-old mulatto, was accused in Guatemala of being penetrated by an indigenous boy named Juan Joseph Vivimos.[74] Investigators found Desiderio's protestations of innocence difficult to believe in the face of his "effeminate condition and behavior that the confessant demonstrates in manner."[75] Vivimos, on the other hand, who immediately fled the scene and was never caught, was still of "tender age." For "the sodomy that they aspired to commit," both Desiderio and Vivimos (in absentia) were sentenced to receive fifty lashes and undergo three hours of public shaming, on three separate days, in an iron collar.

In early nineteenth-century El Salvador, in the city of Metapán, Faustino Galdámez was sentenced to eight years of labor in a presidio.[76] Galdámez, who was described by his lawyer as "very effeminate, very sickly [*muy achacoso*], and of very little spirit," requested that the sentence be carried out in the city rather than on the presidio. His request was granted, and in 1814 he was sentenced to six years of public works in the city of San Salvador. As these scattered archival references to male femininity show, to be "effeminate" (afeminado) or "womanly" (amujerado) did not equate to being a sodomite in colonial courts. On the other hand, they hinted at sodomy and added to the plausibility of the accusation. The cases show that a number of men throughout New Spain felt bold enough to embrace a publicly effeminate persona, mannerisms, and, occasionally, dress, and that they did not live in fear for doing so.

Witnesses and officials also saw some women as betraying accepted modes of proper femininity because of their dress, mannerisms, and masculine personae. One late colonial case of a mujer hombrada—a masculinized or "manly" woman—is particularly fascinating not only for the contents of the case but for the way that it has entered the Mexican national archive's online catalog and digital finding aid. Archived cases of female transvestism are particularly rare in colonial archives, pointing to the singular nature of this case. In 1796 a woman named Gregoria Piedra, imprisoned by the Mexican Inquisition for having taken the Eucharist while "dressed as a man" and subsequently spitting it out of her mouth, was described by prison prefect Agustín José Montesano y Larreaga as such: "She is a manly Woman, ugly face, dark-skinned, curly hair, defeated, body and gait of a man . . . She is well known around here by [the name] Gregoria la Macho, her frequent pastime has been playing ball, picado, and hopscotch, accompanied more by women than by men."[77] The prison officer then mentioned that Gregoria had already been imprisoned four times for "having been found in man's clothes [en traje de hombre]" and for being involved in several fights and quarrels. The file makes a brief mention of Gregoria's inclinación a las mujeres—her "inclination toward women," without adding any more specificity and merely raising the unnamed specter of female same-sex desire. In the end, inquisitors found insufficient evidence against Piedra to convict her of sacrilege with the Eucharist and they exonerated her.[78]

Interestingly, in the catalog of the Mexican national archive, there is a repetition in the physical description of Gregoria la Macho, which is revealing. Montesano in 1796 opined, "She is a manly Woman, ugly face, dark-skinned" (Ella es una Muger hombrada, cara fea, trigueña), and the online archive catalog seems to confirm that description, as if it were objective—"This is a manly woman, ugly face, dark-skinned, body and gait of a man, in arms and more signs and paintings" (ESTA ES UNA MUJER HOMBRADA, CARA FEA, TRIGUEÑA, CUERPO Y ANDAR DE HOMBRE, EN BRAZOS Y DEMAS ROTULOS Y PINTURAS)—adding that Gregoria's arms and body were decorated with inscriptions and designs, most likely tattoos.[79] Can we detect a faint trace of twentieth-century disapproval for "manly" women in the archival descriptor?

The seemingly authoritative description leaves me wondering if this was perhaps a negative opinion of female masculinity *shared by* the individual responsible for entering the description of Gregoria Piedra's case into the online catalog and finding aid for the Archivo General de la Nación. Rather than assert that Gregoria Piedra is *described as such* by one witness, the archivist perhaps unwittingly legitimates the deprecating and racist description of her given by Montesano. In doing so, it subtly reveals the archival persistence of colonial hierarchies of race and gender into the present.

One final example from Guatemala City in the early nineteenth century demonstrates the criminality of female cross-dressing. One afternoon in 1806, on her way to the pharmacy, Remigia Ardón, a mulatta in her early twenties, passed some soldiers who were drinking near the national palace.[80] They drunkenly told her that she could only have their permission to pass by if she drank rum with them, sang, and exchanged clothes with one of the soldiers. She complied out of fear. That day, on her way home, colonial authorities, unsympathetic to her tale, imprisoned her for failing to comply with edicts that prohibited dressing in clothing that did not correspond to one's sex. Authorities paid no attention to the potentially coercive element of this case, and for this infraction, the court sentenced Ardón to six months of reclusion. Though the case is succinct and offers scarce detail, her punishment was also undoubtedly due to the fact that she was a dark-skinned mulatta civilian dressed in military uniform, and thus transgressed boundaries of both gender and caste.

As we have seen, gender and gesture could be read, on popular and official levels alike, as an inclination to sodomy, but rarely (if ever) were they alone taken to be juridical proof of sodomy. Witnesses and authorities nonetheless sometimes presumed sodomy from such behaviors, thereby setting in motion a chain of denunciations and testimonies that eventually archived several instances of such behavior. Both sodomy and gender crossing were irregularly denounced, prosecuted, and punished. Indeed, the social control of the sins against nature depended on the inherent inefficiencies of the colonial courts: a system of denunciations, testimonies shaped by the questions being asked, bureaucratic delays, confusion over jurisdiction, prosecutions that often lasted for long periods of time, and punishments that were often appealed, revoked, or modified. Although sodomy was technically always punishable by law, it was treated differently in rural and urban areas, among indigenous, black, and Spanish suspects, and when enacted by women, men, adolescents, or children. The gestures through which sodomy was read were far from absolute; so too are the ways that they narratively enter (and leave) the colonial archive.

Affect and Epistolary Traces

In colonial New Spain, just as today, the trappings of gender led to conflicted readings of bodies and to misinscriptions of those bodies in the archive. Writing itself can be a crucial gesture that, in the context of the colonial courts, could be interpreted to hint at certain forms of intimacy. This final section focuses on the archiving of affects associated with same-sex intimacy in New Spain. I am interested here in the archiving of affect on at least two different levels: spoken and written. First, I analyze how rumor and eyewitness accounts of intimacy could serve as evidence of sexual relations between men. Second, I explore how and why certain instances of same-sex intimacy entered the archival record. Given that no single unitary theory of affect exists, tracing the intersection of affect and the archive is, as we saw in chapter 1, particularly complicated. Marika Cifor offers a basic definition that allows us to link affect and archive in meaningful ways. Affect, for her, is key to how power is constituted and circulated, and is above all "a culturally, socially and historically constructed category that both encompasses and reaches beyond feelings and emotions."[81]

Affect thus points to those feelings and emotions that originate within the body but then exceed it. Affect points to that which is typically, though not always, unwritten and unspoken. Sodomy trials are valuable in that they are a rare place in which textual representations of same-sex intimacy sometimes appear; in the process, they offer clues as to how and why certain representations of emotion and feeling made their way into the archival record. As with gestures, traces of intimacy that were seen, heard, or read permitted witnesses and courts to read selectively into the bodies and behaviors of others. Thus, particular verbal utterances and written exchanges could function as evidence of intimacy (and therefore desire) between men, shedding light on how such evidence operated in a larger system of bodily and gestural signs. How do certain affective displays come to signify sodomitical proclivities in the popular sphere and within the court of law? How do such gestures—specifically, the performance of affect—come to be archived, and why? Lastly, how does affect attach itself to archival documents? As we will see, the realm of affect could be central to the workings of the sodomy trial, though not necessarily so. Just as with the hesitations of doctors, and the fragility of gestures, here too we see that the physical signs of the body seemed more reliable than the signs of emotion in judging the crime of sodomy, all of which points to hierarchies of legal evidence.

One of the earliest instances in which the signs of intimacy appear to have motivated the charge of sodomy is the 1542 case of two Italian mariners, Antonio Lipares and a young cabin boy, Cebrian, who worked onboard a ship near the island of Hispaniola. One sailor reported that he had seen "the two sleeping in one bed together" and that they "kissed each other with their mouths," which looked suspicious to him.[82] Cebrian, who was imprisoned and interrogated, asserted that Lipares was his father-in-law—thus, it was normal for them to share one mattress—and that when he was sick, Lipares had affectionately hugged him and kissed him on his cheek. For his part, Lipares referred to the "great and pure love" that he had for his son-in-law, Cebrian. For lack of proof, both Lipares and Cebrian were absolved and set free shortly after they were imprisoned in Santo Domingo. If we believe their testimonies, this case shows us how, especially in male-dominated spaces, intimacy between two men could easily be misunderstood and misconstrued by outside observers—as the sole witness in this case said, the two men kissing on the mouth "seemed immoral to him." The truth about the two men—whether they were lovers who successfully concealed their activities from authorities or whether they were in-laws—ultimately escapes us. The signs of affect could, of course, be seen as partial evidence of sodomy, as in the case of Juan de la Vega, who, as we know, was executed for sodomy in Mexico City in 1658 along with thirteen other men. According to witness testimony, de la Vega "was regularly visited by several boys who the abovesaid [de la Vega] would call 'my soul,' 'my life,' and 'my heart,' and the abovesaid [boys] would sit with him and would sleep with him in an inn."[83] Such verbal expressions of intimacy helped to sway the courts, but only when corroborated with other, more tangible forms of evidence.

In 1621 in Panama, for example, Francisco Hernández and a married couple spied Cristóbal Zamorano, a Spanish octogenarian, in his private abode sharing a hammock with his young Spanish servant, Moreno de Laguna.[84] According to their testimonies, they had previously witnessed the men hugging, kissing, and caressing each other; the two were frequently together, and had traveled together at least twice to a nearby island where Zamorano had invested in a fishing enterprise. Although an octogenarian traveling with his servant would not have been unusual, the court heard testimony from a number of slaves that Zamorano and his younger companion regularly slept together in the same bedroom. This case confirms Giraldo Botero's observation that men or women in lasting sexual and emotional relationships with members of the same sex "shared the spaces of everyday life like the home, the bed, [and] trips together," although this case has the additional master-servant dynamic.[85]

Both men denied any serious wrongdoing (aside from one occasion where Zamorano admitted to improperly touching Moreno), but the criminal court deemed the numerous eyewitness testimonies and hearsay evidence against them sufficient to convict them of sodomy. The judge sentenced Zamorano to be publicly shamed, to pay a fine of four thousand ducados and half the costs of the trial, and to be banished for a period of six years. Moreno was sentenced to two hundred lashes and two years on the galleys, though, in an appeal to lessen the sentence, the defense attempted to discredit the witnesses and highlighted Zamorano's repeated works of charity and generosity to the confraternities and petitioned that the sentence be lessened. The strategy partly worked, and, in the end, authorities from the higher court of the audiencia revoked Moreno's whipping and Zamorano's public shaming. Successful (and even partly successful) appeals such as this one demonstrate how interpreting the signs of sodomy at the level of local courts was always subject to reinterpretation at the level of the higher courts.

One affect inseparable from desire is jealousy, which functioned as another affective sign. For New Spain, references to jealousy among same-sex couples are rare, and the corpus of documents consulted for this study yielded only a few cases in which jealousy played even a minor role. One instance is an 1813 sodomy case from Guadalajara in which an indigenous soldier, Gabriel Meza, incarcerated for deserting his post, was accused of committing sodomy with several other prisoners, including a mulatto named José Guadalupe Silva. Witnesses confirmed that Silva was publicly affectionate with Meza and that he was also extremely jealous of him—a sign that pointed to his sodomitical proclivities. Despite the presence of hard evidence, the court sentenced Silva to labor on public works projects for a period of two years for trying to hug, kiss, and be overly affectionate with Meza.[86] This convoluted criminal case, like so many others, is replete with the unresolved—false accusations and vindictive denunciations that leave doubt as to what actually took place. That jealousy, commonly present in colonial Mexican archival records dealing with homicide, assault, and domestic abuse, is rarely archived in sodomy trials points to a disjuncture in terms of archiving and gender. Namely, the relatively clandestine nature of same-sex intimacies likely obscured the lived dynamics of jealousy in terms of which affects do (and do not) make their way into the historical record, and how they are interpreted when they do.

So far, we have seen examples of unwritten affect—that is, intimacies between men that were spoken or enacted, and only later written down, as part of an accusation or testimony. Even rarer than archival transcriptions of jealousy or other emotions are epistolary expressions of same-sex affection and love. We know from Luiz Mott's groundbreaking research that some eleven "letters of 'unspeakable' love," exchanged between friars in the second half of the seventeenth century, are preserved in Lisbon's historical archives.[87] Mott writes that many men "would avoid leaving behind written evidence that could be used as a formal declaration of guilt."[88] The same appears true for New Spain. While love letters were commonly exchanged between women and men in New Spain, those exchanged between men or between women are largely absent from historical archives.[89]

Thus far, I have found only one example, from Guadalajara in the early nineteenth century, that references *esquelas*—notes or short letters—exchanged between two men: the case of José Nabor de la Encarnación and Apolinario Salmón, who appear to have been lovers. Nabor's neighbors first denounced him in 1805 of being an *alcahuete*—a procurer who ran a house of prostitution and arranged meetings between female prostitutes and male clients. Central to the prosecution's case was the fact that some of the women who worked in that house had found letters in a box belonging to Nabor that were apparently written by Salmón, and were evidence of sodomy "according to their obscene and amatory expressions."[90] Such letters "unveil the world of small concerns, endearing terms, and chatty communications that have always been exchanged by lovers of all ages."[91] Authorities confiscated the two letters, both written by Salmón while he was in prison. To give a thorough idea of their content and their means of conveying affect in everyday life, I reproduce the two letters here in their entirety. The first letter reads:

> Señor don Nabor de la Encarnación, my dear and beloved friend of my greatest esteem and veneration, to whom I write with the utmost subordination that a captive heart desires with such a sovereign owner: My soul, will you do me the favor that if don Manuel asks to whom the blanket belongs, tell him that it was mine, and the bedspread too, I am also letting you know that I am separated in a dark room with a pair of shackles. About what you told me the night before last, I already had it to go see the bulls, but now consider how I will be without any discretion, only that you send me four ounces of thread, and one *real* of silver to make a pair of socks; I ask you to lend me this so that I can take off my rags to go out to the river, and send

me paper so that I can continue writing to you. Regarding that which I am requesting, don't go and mess it up; your response in this I, Polonio [Apolinario], await. And nothing more other than that God protect you for many years. Your *negro* that esteems you, Apolinario Salmon. [Postscript] I will not always be captive. I will have my liberty, all the pleasure you have had, pleasure that will return to you; with that I send you two dozen kisses and twenty hugs, that kiss your hand. o o o o o o o o o o o o o o o o o o o o o o o o o o x x x x x x x x x x x x x x x x x x x.[92]

The second note confiscated by authorities reads:

o o o o = Señor don Nabor de la Encarnacion, my very esteemed *negrito* [little black man] of my greatest estimation, I will be happy to find you with your health fulfilled as I desire, in the company of the garments to your liking. You, my soul for life, I beg you not to do anything indecent [*porquerías*] because I should know about it; of that which you tell me, that you already cannot wait for me to get out [of prison], you cannot have more desire than I do. My soul, don't think that that which I was requesting you send, it was not for me but rather to make you a pair of socks, since I am idle right now, since [I have] here your green silk, the blue and the black [but] this will not suffice to make them. Send it to me in the afternoon; also send me the thread that is perfectly round, and [I ask] no more than that God protect our life for many years. = Polinario Salmon. o o o o o o o o o o o o x x x x x x, there I sent you those kisses and hugs, receive them with much pleasure, I am already dying of desire for you to give me my little tongue and my little arms, I am with the abovesaid for not knowing what pimp would be biting my little tongue.[93]

As with all private letters that make their way into the archives, these notes are replete with terms and banter whose meanings are only partly decipherable. Many of the letters' details, which refer to everyday events and words exchanged between the two men prior to Salmón's incarceration, remain enigmatic to the outside reader, and would likely only have made sense to writer and recipient. The letters seem to point to a mundane domesticity, with their talk of bed coverings, blankets, and socks. Yet they point also to an intense intimacy. Salmón, for example, referred to Nabor as "you, my soul for life" (*mi alma por vida tú*), and he wrote of his own "captive heart." Salmón and Nabor, we gather, shared affective and sexual codes. The reference, in the possessive, to Nabor biting Salmón's tongue—*mi lenguita*—seems unmistakably sexual and charged with archived desires that fluctuate between ganas and deseos, yearnings and long-ings that are at once emotional and corporeal in nature. Finally, there is the seemingly unambiguous series of O's and X's at the end of each letter.

Upon interrogation, Salmón confessed that he was indeed the author of the letters, but there was a catch: Nabor was *not* the intended recipient. Instead, according to Salmón, Nabor was merely an intermediary to whom the notes were superficially addressed. Salmón explained to his interrogators that he had penned the letters at the request of another (presumably illiterate) inmate who addressed them to Nabor, who was to deliver them to a married woman named Mariquita. Salmón revealed as much when authorities asked him spe-cifically about the meaning behind the X's and O's embedded within the notes, to which he replied: "The written wheels at the end of the said notes signify kisses, and the X's hugs, which he was directing to the said woman [Mariquita] with whom Nabor has had no other business than a licit friendship, that they have kept since their tender youth."[94]

While Salmón's explanation may seem far-fetched, as it certainly did to Gua-dalajara's criminal court, it reminds us that the meanings behind any archi-val document are malleable and entirely dependent on the interpretation of signs. Here, we might also read Salmón's testimony for hidden transcripts and coded language: the word *mariquita* is the diminutive form of *marica*, a col-loquial term that according to the 1734 *Diccionario de las autoridades* referred to "an effeminate man of little spirit, who lets himself be dependent on and manipulated by even those who are inferior."[95] That the so-called Mariquita, with whom Nabor had close yet licit contact since his tender youth, was the connection between Salmón and Nabor is potentially revealing. Might the men have selected the name "Mariquita" to symbolize Nabor's own femininity, or the two men's shared desires? If so, would any inquiry into the whereabouts of this Mariquita have tipped off either Salmón or Nabor that their letters had been found, or that colonial authorities were poking around in their relation-ship? Or, is it possible that a woman (or an effeminate man) known by the name Mariquita actually was the intended recipient of the letters? At this point, other corporeal and gestural evidence—the body of Nabor and its gen-dered performances—became central to the case: "The public opinion is that José Nabor has always been an infamous pimp inclined toward his corrupt propensity to affect effeminate manners [*modales afeminados*] as much as pre-senting himself publicly dressed in women's garb."[96]

While the case against Salmón and Nabor was initiated in 1805, the records of an earlier criminal trial against Salmón are appended to the file. Investigations into Salmón's past further incriminated him by unveiling an 1801 criminal case against him in which he was tried and sentenced for "the sordid abuses of an obscene instrument."[97] At that time, Salmón was around seventeen years of age—and there are deliberations in the 1801 trial transcripts as to whether he should be tried as a minor or an adult—and he confessed to having supplemented his natural member with the "obscene instrument," though the surgeon who examined the stains on the dildo was unable to determine their origin or whether any act of penetration had been performed with it.[98] Nonetheless, judicial authorities sentenced Salmón to be publicly whipped, "with the instrument hanging from his neck" as a form of shaming, and to spend five years on public works projects. However, because Salmón was ill when sentenced, he was spared from being flogged and, so it seems, from being publicly shamed.

In 1807, despite hearsay evidence and Salmón's past criminal record, the court largely concurred with the defense lawyer that "the most pestilent correspondence" between Salmón and Nabor was inconclusive: "The amatory correspondence between those of the same sex is not an argument for the connate [nature] close to the crime with which we are dealing . . . and it is equally certain that the defendant cannot be condemned based only on his confession."[99] As a sign of "enlightened" beliefs about torture and the production of jurisprudential truth, the judge presiding over the case rejected the prosecutor's proposal to use torture on both Salmón and Nabor as a means of ascertaining the truth. In October 1807 Salmón was set free.

These letters, which gesture toward the romantic relationship between two men in the early nineteenth century, appear to be unique in terms of their status as archival documents for New Spain. Even so, they were deemed insufficient evidence of sodomy, and the personal and private meanings behind the letters escape us. The archiving of affect, as gleaned through these letters, raises epistemological questions similar to those of the archival documents that we have already seen. Namely, how (and why) do we—like other notaries and archivists before us—imbue such textual representations of same-sex affection with meaning? How can we tell the extent to which this epistolary exchange may or may not have intimated something more on the part of the writer and recipient? Ultimately these letters provide an impressive amount of information, and yet the meanings behind them remain partly occluded.

Affect resists archival representation in several senses. First and foremost, the emotive and the affective are defined in part by the fleeting and the gestural—by that which is not typically captured adequately in textual form. The traces of affect are confounded by and through multiple levels of transmission, reception, and interpretation. In terms of how affect, emotions, and feelings come into the colonial archive, we should not let ourselves get too distracted by these particular letters, fascinating as they are. The letters, no doubt, provide us with a phenomenal example of how affect comes to be textually recorded and subsequently read, though it is by no means the most common. The reading of affect (and its implications) in the context of the sodomy trial, as this chapter has shown, can only function within a larger system of signs pointing back to the body and its desires, gestures, and gendered performances.

The meanings of archival documents are, in and of themselves, never self-evident. Perhaps most significantly, this chapter has shown how the establishment of legal evidence of sodomy depended on overlapping and occasionally contradictory representations of the body, in its varied physical states and textual traces. The colonial court system needed to quite literally *produce* legal evidence—through the elicitation of witness and expert testimony—to prove or disprove discrete allegations of sodomy. In doing so, the court harnessed popular, medical, and even moralistic understandings of sodomy, even if legal evidence in these spheres required different levels of proof, some of which contradicted each other. Sex and the colonial archive thus intersect in ways that are as complex as they are ambivalent, at times pointing to the body as the most reliable indicator of sodomy (as in cases of coercive sodomy and when medical expertise was deemed reliable), and at others pointing toward the gestural (as in ephemeral performances of masculinity and femininity). The archival record relies on the body, and yet it also belies the body's instability and its inability to transmit certain forms of knowledge. In the end, the body itself remains an unreliable signifier of the signs that it did, and was supposed to, emit.

CHAPTER 4

To Deaden the Memory

Bestiality and Animal Erasure

In the port city of Seville, Spain, nestled between the Gothic Roman Catholic Cathedral of Saint Mary of the See and the Royal Alcázar of Seville—a royal palace created by Muslim rulers in the eleventh century—lies the Archivo General de Indias, one of imperial Spain's most important documentary repositories, inside the late sixteenth-century Casa de Lonja de Mercaderes that was once the old merchants' exchange. Housed within that archive is the earliest criminal case of bestiality from New Spain that I uncovered. The case, available to researchers only on microfilm, is unique in more ways than one. On January 12, 1563, in the city of Mérida, on Mexico's Yucatán Peninsula, Spanish authorities began a criminal investigation of Pedro Na, a fourteen-year-old Maya boy from a nearby village. His suspected crime: engaging in "carnal access" with a turkey.[1] The archival document from which we know this is unabashedly explicit. According to Juan Canuc, a witness from the town of San Cristóbal de Extramuros—whose testimony was translated from Yucatecan Maya to Spanish by a court-appointed interpreter—he was walking with his wife to a nearby *estancia* (a landed estate or ranch for livestock) on the outskirts of Mérida when they heard a number of chickens clucking loudly on the hillside, near a large cross. As they walked toward the commotion, they came upon the following scene: "The said Pedro Na had his underwear loose and was sitting on the ground with a turkey in between his legs . . . and saw that the said turkey had blood running out of its anus, and the said Pedro Na had his underwear untied and his reproductive member exposed."[2] A few hours later, Canuc denounced Na and local authorities imprisoned the boy. The unfortunate bird, which died within a few days as a result of the violence, was also "deposited" as evidence—that is, the court kept the rotting corpse of the bird—as was customary in bestiality cases.

Spanish authorities—under the administration of don Diego de Quijada, abusive alcalde mayor of the Yucatán Peninsula from 1560 to 1565—interrogated Pedro Na in an effort to elicit a confession. The boy began by stating that he had been baptized and was Christian, and that he had left his village for Mérida some five weeks prior to his arrest. Although he was unsure of his age, the scribe noted that he looked about fourteen years old. When asked about Canuc's testimony, he confessed (like Canuc, in his native Yucatecan Maya, which was translated and recorded only in Spanish): "It is true that yesterday afternoon in the said road, he came across some turkeys and chickens, and he took the said turkey and went to the hillside with it and with the carnal alteration [alteración carnal] he felt, he took his reproductive member in his hand and put it into the anus [sieso] of the said turkey. He had carnal access with it and from this he made blood run from the bird's anus, when the two Indians arrived."[3] Here, the use of alteración carnal—a "carnal alteration," a common description of the process of becoming carnal—nicely illustrates the crossing of the human-animal boundary that resulted from lust.

Although Na denied having had sex with other animals, he later confessed to having committed the same act with another bird a year earlier. In response to further questioning, Na asserted that he had never seen it being performed, nor did anyone else teach it to him. He gave no further indication of the reasons behind his acts or of how he came to learn of them. As with all bestiality cases, what started with a seemingly harmless act of looking at a given animal spiraled into something entirely different, following Na's "carnal alteration." Characteristic of so many other cases, and just as importantly, was the fact that Canuc and his wife happened to see the scene. These overlapping acts of observation and voyeurism—Na watching the turkey as well as Juan Canuc and his wife watching Na with the bird—are central events in the recording, archiving, and punishing of any act of bestiality. Furthermore, as we have already seen, the archivist, the historian, and the reader of this book are similarly implicated in these overlapping observations.

For this infraction, Spanish criminal authorities sentenced Na to be publicly shamed, spectacularly punished, and then permanently exiled. The court pronounced that Pedro Na "be taken from prison on the back of a saddled animal, his hands and feet tied, and with the voice of a town crier manifesting his crime. The justice commands that he [then] be brought through the public streets of this city and taken to the ground that is in the city's plaza, and there he be castrated and his genitals be cut, and [he shall be] in perpetual banishment from these provinces of Yucatán."[4] It seems that Quijada, the governor of Yucatán, wanted to make a blatant and gruesome public example, not only for the recently colonized and converted native population in and around Mérida but also for Spanish colonists and the African slaves they had brought with them to the Americas. While castration itself was not an uncommon punishment for sodomy in Christian Iberia in the Middle Ages, within New Spain, Na's sentence appears to have been unique.[5] The court's sentence also shows the extent to which ritualized spectacles of punishment both relied on and effaced animal presence in the staging and recording of the event.

Animals, especially beasts of burden, as this example shows, played a significant role in punishing crimes like bestiality: it was a mule or donkey that carried convicts throughout the city during processions of public shame. The juxtaposition of humans and animals was symbolic: condemned criminals were stripped from the waist up or occasionally arrayed in penitential garments, and placed on the backs of saddled horses or mules, to be further shamed and denigrated. But the beast of burden was not alone; even more significant was the defiled animal itself. On February 14, 1563, after an appeal by Na's defense attorney had been rejected, authorities further stipulated that because "the turkey with which the said Pedro Na committed the said crime is dead and has been saved, it was ordered that for the said sentence to be carried out it be hung from the neck of the said Pedro Na, and he be brought with it through the accustomed streets of this city and after the said sentence is carried out, the abovesaid ordered that the said turkey be burned in live flames and be made into dust."[6] Yet again, the juxtaposition of human and animal bodies, in this instance the rotting corpse of the turkey, had symbolic ends: it was meant to add to the shame and grotesquery of this ritualized spectacle. The "real," material animal—the physical evidence and memory incarnate of the crime— was quite literally erased, rendered absent, and turned into ashes not unlike some of the unlucky sodomites throughout the Iberian Atlantic world.

The details of the case are both troubling and fascinating. The case begs us to think through the ways that animals and animal bodies became legal forms of evidence, serving as a particular type of "document" in the eyes of colonial legal systems. The textual trace of the turkey reminds us of the sexual violence it suffered at the hands of Na. Yet the physical trace of the turkey—its defiled corpse, which colonial authorities ritualistically burned—served not only as a warning to colonizers and colonized but also as a way of symbolically eradicating both memory and tangible evidence of the nefarious act. The turkey then marks the colonial historical record in at least two overlapping ways, as does the disfigured body of Na, who, through the very act of castration, was negated any future reproductive potential. This case shows not only that the Spanish colonial state did punish those sexual acts, such as sodomy and bestiality, that it deemed "against nature" but also that it manipulated nature—rendering, in this instance, Na's body permanently unnatural—in the service of viscerally exercising power over the bodies and minds of New Spain's colonial subjects, especially indigenous peoples.

Though the case of Pedro Na is unique, it serves as a guide to my corpus of bestiality cases in New Spain. The first uniqueness is that it is the earliest case of bestiality that I uncovered in the archives, and its outcome for Na should perhaps be seen as an outlier due to the grotesque punishment that was enacted on his body. The second uncommon detail is this is one of only two cases in my corpus that unambiguously involved an animal native to Mesoamerica—the *gallina de la tierra*, otherwise known as the turkey.[7] This fact will become crucial to understanding a long-standing Spanish notion that bestiality was primarily an indigenous crime—and to understanding how that notion falls apart on closer examination. That said, the role and place of the turkey in this 1563 case is illustrative of the ways that colonial authorities dealt with animal bodies in criminal cases of bestiality.

Within my corpus, I have documented 144 archival references to bestiality. These consist of 111 criminal cases of bestiality (which are composed of complete criminal trials, fragments of cases, judicial summaries, appeals to higher courts, and relevant correspondence between the lower courts and the Real Sala del Crimen in Mexico City); 25 denunciations that were lodged with the Inquisition but ignored; and 8 cases of bestiality that were tried by ecclesiastical courts in Valladolid, Michoacán. Like sodomy, bestiality in New Spain was, at least in theory, to be tried by secular and not ecclesiastical courts or by the Inquisition in New Spain unless a member of the clergy or some overt heresy was involved. This corpus of cases, however, shows a more complicated jurisdictional picture.

Through the lens of bestiality, as it came to be archived in colonial New Spain, this chapter invites us to explore the murky terrain of animal absence and presence within historical archives, and asks us to pay attention to the textual traces of animal bodies in the documents themselves. Doing so allows us to reconsider the ways in which animals, human or otherwise, do (or do not) become the subjects of the histories we write. This corpus shows us how archival animals are constituted by and through the historical record, always mediated by the archives and their catalogs and descriptors. The narratives about Pedro Na and the unfortunate turkey with whom he fornicated serve as a prime example of the myriad ways that nonhuman animals simultaneously appear and disappear from the physical world, from historical documents, and from the archive itself.

Animal Histories

Rather than (incorrectly) view bestiality marginal to the historical past, I suggest that archival narratives of this particular act and its judicial outcomes are central to the intimate workings of colonialism in New Spain. I propose that through bestiality trials, recorded and preserved in colonial archives, we can articulate how and why animal bodies came to function as forms of evidence—as corporeal and metaphorical signs to be interpreted, and through which public and private memory could be both produced and eradicated. As Etienne Benson notes, "All history is animal history in a sense—that is, history written by, for, and about animals. The only question is which."[8] This seemingly simple yet profound statement reminds us that humanity itself is a historically fragile and labile concept. For in the end all humans are essentially animals too, though this was not a belief shared by theologians and jurists in the Iberian Atlantic world.

The very slipperiness with which dozens of bestiality cases are archived is telling in and of itself. Many bestiality cases are classified under the term *bestialidad* or *bestialismo* in finding aids and card catalogs that were created in the nineteenth and twentieth centuries; yet many more are cataloged and classified within the archives of New Spain under less precise terminology: *sodomía* (sodomy), *pecado nefando* (nefarious sin), *cópula carnal* (carnal copulation), *actos carnales* (carnal acts), *delicto bestial* (bestial crime), and *acto torpe* (lewd act). Beyond these I have also found a few euphemistic phrases: *asseso bestial como dentro se expresa* (bestial access as is expressed inside, fig. 4.1) and even *maltrato a una vaca* (mistreatment of a cow). This variety reveals that witnesses, lawyers, and judges alike often used the similar or identical linguistic constructions and evasions to refer to both same-sex desire and to human-animal sex. Sodomy and bestiality were, at least in theory, not equivalent but intimately related. Among the sins against nature, according to the hierarchy of sins provided by Thomas Aquinas, bestiality was the gravest sin, masturbation the least serious, and sodomy fell somewhere in between. The conceptual linking of sodomy

Fig 4.1 Title page of an 1807 criminal case of bestiality from the town of Atitalaquía, Hidalgo, "against Jose María Maturana for Bestial access as is expressed inside." Courtesy of the Archivo General del Estado de Hidalgo, Pachuca, Mexico. AGEH, Tula Justicia, caja 52, exp. 12.

and bestiality since the early days of Christianity helps overturn the idea that bestiality was perceived as a marginal act. Rather, it was presumed to exist along a spectrum of acts that were, to varying degrees, "against nature." That spectrum, in turn, exposes the instability of both "human" and "animal" in the past, as well as the historical anxieties that rose up around these slippery categories.

Here, as throughout this book, I believe that all animals—human and non-human alike—are inherently *archival animals*, whose historical meanings are partly constituted by and through the historical record. All animals, humans included, figure into historical archives in multiple and contradictory ways. Nonhuman animals, for example, are ordinarily recorded in the archival documentation, and they often make up the very documentation about which we speak. They have historically become the raw materials—the vellum, leather, parchment, glues and adhesives—of the archival document itself. The very production of European-style paper, made from wood pulp or linen rags, historically relied entirely on animal bodies: "When ready, the [paper] sheet is 'sized' by lowering it into an animal glue made from boiling scraps of vellum or other [animal] offcuts."[9] As did the quills, inks, adhesives, and bindings that were used to produce much of the documentation that eventually ended up in historical archives. Animality, in other words, is inseparable from textuality.

This chapter takes seriously Benson's call for historians to be more attentive to the "embodied traces of past animal lives," both within and beyond the archive.[10] With respect to my corpus of bestiality cases, how does Benson's notion of embodied traces of animal bodies and lives—that go beyond mere representation—push our conceptualization and writing of animal histories? What might it mean for an archival trace to be embodied by nonhumans? Finally, how does the notion that the archive contains the embodied traces of animals intersect with the phenomena of animal erasure? The very notion of animal history—of writing histories that seek to center animals as active agents and co-creators of history—is a vexed one. For many scholars, it seems that the desire to recover lost historical subjects and speak for the subaltern has become grafted onto the very notion of writing animal histories and conferring agency on animals. There is, to be certain, an activist bent to this type of thinking, which can be traced to the desire to speak for and lobby on behalf of animals that have been historically abused, exploited, and otherwise mistreated. Yet as Benson notes, "One may use the techniques to look for the traces of nonhuman animals in human archives that are superficially similar to those one uses to look for the traces of subaltern, poor, or disenfranchised humans in the archives of the powerful, but there seems to be a deeper divide."[11] This divide is both epistemological and ontological. Neil L. Whitehead echoes similar concerns about the project of "centering animals" within historical narratives: "the perceived lack of opportunity or inability to 'speak for oneself' invites the rescuing discourse of inherent 'rights' to supplant this silence."[12] My own work here emerges partly from the tension between my own desire to advance the project of animal history and my reluctance to speak of animal "agency" in the past.

We can perhaps best understand the animals that feature in bestiality cases as disappearing animals. The notion of animal erasure has several provocations, each of which points to a different type of disappearance. At the most literal level, these animals were literally erased: the animals implicated in bestiality cases were regularly killed "so as to deaden the memory of the act." Through this notion, we also see how corporeal desire metaphorically transformed one particular animal—man—into another type of animal, erasing his or her "humanity." Animal erasure also has an archival resonance: it refers to the ways in which nonhuman animals disappear from the historical record. The implicated animal in all these bestiality cases is referred to merely as private property and legal evidence. In contrast to the ways that humans come to be archived, animals attain their archival meanings primarily through the economic value with which humans have imbued them. Thus, what also disappears from the archive is a concern or compassion for the animal's own welfare.

Nonhuman animals both appear and disappear from colonial archives in ways that differ drastically from humans. Thus far, we have seen several examples of how people and cases disappear from the archives, because records are lost, court proceedings are not documented, or testimonies are not faithfully transcribed. Given that nonhumans have no "voice" (in an anthropocentric sense) and had no legal rights, their potential for erasure within the archives overshadows that of even the most marginalized humans. Ultimately this chapter examines how animals come to be archived, textually and physically, by the humans who seek to preserve and eradicate select aspects of the past through the manipulation and erasure of animal bodies. We can better grasp the profundity of bestiality in the past by first exploring other human-animal crossings; for it is here that we see how the human is constantly under threat of becoming less human—descending into animality—by and through the loss of reason.

The 1726 *Diccionario de autoridades* offers two entries for the term *bestial*, the first of which is, simply, "that pertaining to beasts" (*lo perteneciente à las béstias*). Offering further clarification, the first dictionary entry provides this example of the word in context: "They are comprised of brutes and birds, accomplices in their lascivious and bestial sexual intercourses." The second entry is as follows: "Metaphorically it is taken as that which, in some way, is external to the reason and understanding of man himself, being of the violence of the passions and bodily feelings: as in 'bestial desire,' 'bestial appetite,' etc." These definitions presume that the human is unique and quintessentially distinct from that which pertains to "brutes" and "beasts."[13] Yet they also hint at the tenuous boundary between the human and the animal. Furthermore, they illustrate how animality and desire are intimately related in Latin and its derivative Romance languages. The insinuation here is that man can symbolically descend to the level of brute beasts through his senses, passions, and desires—a possibility expounded on and articulated by theologians, judges, and the like in the early modern Iberian Atlantic world. I suggest that these human-animal transformations are not limited to the metaphorical, as the above dictionary entries lead us to believe. Rather, wayward passions and desires such as lust challenged the presumed foundation of humanness: reason.

One remarkable example from New Spain comes to us through a sermon given by Jesuit priest Juan Martínez de la Parra in 1691, which is documented in his *Luz de verdades católicas y explicación de la doctrina christiana*. Martínez de la Parra illustrates how the sin of lust—*luxuria*, which he personified as a monstrous, Medusa-like creature—could transform men into beasts.[14] The priest shared the following image with his congregation: "I would give lust twisted snakes for hair, the forehead of a goat, the eyes of a toad, the ears of an ass, the nose of a simian, the mouth of a dragon, the teeth of a crocodile, the neck of a camel, the tightest chest of a greyhound, the belly of a giant pig, the hands of a bear, the feet of a horse, the tail of a snake, the spots of a tiger, the foul-smelling breath of a lion. And its entire figure would be that of a demon, and of man, nothing: all of man being this way because of lust."[15] Given the differences between humans and "brutes" as laid out in theological treatises, it is no mere coincidence that Martínez de la Parra employed this hybrid animal to represent the monstrous, diabolical, and dehumanizing effects of this sin. Lust symbolically destroys the very humanity of the human, leaving behind only disparate and scattered nonhuman body parts in its wake.

Such beliefs, of course, can be traced historically. This comparison to animal sexuality has its historical roots in the writings of theologians, including Saint Augustine and Saint Thomas Aquinas, who accepted animals as inherently lustful beings. Both Augustine and Aquinas tried to understand how animals copulated, and subsequently argued that humans differentiated themselves on the scale of being through proper intercourse, which (naturally) excluded nonprocreative acts like masturbation, fellatio, sodomy, and bestiality.[16] Joyce Salisbury explains that "medieval thinkers believed that animals by and large exhibited more lust than humans did. This idea, of course, derives from the belief that lust is the opposite of reason, so as animals lacked reason, they expressed more lust."[17] From Augustine to Aquinas to Martínez de la Parra, the human could indeed, metaphorically, become animal, and in doing so becomes a monstrosity that destroys the rules that are binding on both humans and animals. According to most Europeans and Creoles in New Spain, the perceived potential for monstrous transformation was even greater for New Spain's indigenous, African, and racially mixed inhabitants. In this sense, race itself is an index of animality.

Such anxieties are laid bare in a short two-folio criminal denunciation from 1701, written in both Nahuatl and Spanish, preserved in the historical archive of the state of Tlaxcala. In the file, two indigenous men from central Mexico accused another indigenous man, Francisco Martín, of witchcraft, *nahualli* shapeshifting, cannibalism, and sexual excess. In the Nahuatl-speaking regions of central Mesoamerica, a nahualli was an individual said to have the ability to physically shift into the form of an animal or other natural phenomena—according to Alfredo López Austin, a "being who can transform itself into another."[18] Hernando Ruiz de Alarcón, in his 1629 *Treatise on the Heathen Superstitions That Today Live among the Indians Native to This New Spain*, referred to the nahualli as "a sorcerer who has the power to transform himself into an animal" and "a sorcerer who has an animal as an alter ego."[19]

In the first of two criminal denunciations, Diego Felipe complained in Nahuatl that once, when he was sick, "I was watching Francisco Martín and, on many occasions, he frightened me. I saw him in the form of a goat, and other occasions I saw him in the form of a bull with his hands and feet all hairy. And one night he went to my wife with whom I have a son, and he said to my wife, 'you will give me your son so that I may eat him because he is mine, although you may do whatever you might.'"[20] While the nahualli discussed by Ruiz de Alarcón turned into crocodiles, bats, foxes, jaguars, eagles, and snakes—animals autochthonous to Mesoamerica—the animal forms adopted by Francisco Martín are tied to early modern European iconic representations of the Devil. According to his detractor, Martín had appeared in the forms of a bull and a goat, animals that were brought from Europe and rapidly incorporated into the changing agricultural economy of Mexico. This denunciation, replete with images of Francisco Martín's "hands and feet all hairy," shows the extent to which indigenous narratives of shapeshifting could be recast in Christian terms, and the extent to which European animals made their way into archival narratives.[21] This denunciation of Martín presents an exemplary case of the meeting of two ideas about species crossing. One the one hand, Mesoamerican nahualli shapeshifting is premised on the porousness of the boundary between humans and animals. On the other hand, as we have seen, European Christian discourse on nature premises a metaphoric erasure of that boundary through the embodiment of lust that did, quite literally, strip the humanity away from the human.

Finally, Martín's transformations alluded to sodomy. In his denunciation, Juan Domingo claimed that one day when the two men were together in a temascal, Martín slapped his buttocks, thereby causing his thighs and lower body to become "sick," as if he had ants crawling up and down his body. Martín was also said to have suddenly appeared naked one night in Domingo's bed: "And one night I saw him enter [the bedroom] naked and coming up under the blankets, he came up to my genitals, and then he grabbed me and he wanted to take me out."[22] The account is vague, and the reference to same-sex desire oblique. Yet the narrative deliberately links nahualli shapeshifting to witchcraft, cannibalism, and sodomy. In doing so, the denouncers render Martín unnatural in overlapping yet contradictory ways. By his taking on the physical forms of European animals, Francisco Martín is portrayed as a creature outside the order of nature—that is, he is not a nahualli in the traditional Mesoamerican sense but rather a diabolical figure who morphs into the European bull and goat.

Francisco Martín's monstrosity is expressed by his wanting to eat Diego Felipe's son, casting spells, and desiring human flesh (in many senses). He is thus represented as being outside of the natural order, organized partly by procreation. Unfortunately, we have no further information about Francisco Martín or his denouncers. As far as we know, this Nahuatl-language denunciation, though translated into Spanish and presented to judicial authorities, never culminated in a criminal trial against him, indicating that by the early eighteenth century, denunciations of witchcraft and shapeshifting were only of marginal interest to colonial authorities, who likely saw them in terms of superstition rather than heresy or criminality per se.

The above examples deal not with the sin and crime of bestiality but with the types of human-animal crossings—metaphorical, literal, and chimerical—that are inseparable from archival narratives of bestiality, and from the colonial archive itself. Animals percolate the historical record in contradictory ways, highlighting the divide between real and discursive, or merely representational, animals. Not unlike the Spanish dictionary definitions of the term *bestial* and Martínez de la Parra's illustration of lust, the accusations against Francisco Martín's share something in common with the case of Pedro Na: excessive lust challenged the very status of the human. Yet, as we will see, the way New Spain's colonial courts made sense of and punished bestiality actually served to reify, not disintegrate, the "human."

Domestication and Desire

Bestiality cases provide historians with a surprising amount of information about the colonial past—everything from rural mores and environmental change to legal traditions. Why then has bestiality not been the focus of more serious scholarly attention? As Piers Beirne observes, in the humanities and social sciences scholars often treat bestiality as a "disturbing form of sexual practice that invites hurried bewilderment rather than sustained intellectual inquiry."[23] This section therefore elaborates the dual themes of animal domestication and the demographics of bestiality in New Spain to show how—in spite of increasing archival references to the act throughout the seventeenth, eighteenth, and early nineteenth centuries—historians of New Spain have, perhaps unwittingly, silenced such narratives.

In *Silencing the Past*, Michel-Rolph Trouillot tells us that silences enter the process of historical production at four separate stages: "the moment of fact creation (the making of *sources*); the moment of fact assembly (the making of *archives*); the moment of fact retrieval (the making of *narratives*); and the moment of retrospective significance (the making of *history* in the final instance)."[24] In the case of bestiality, these varied forms of silencing converge unequally. Bestiality itself was not uncommon in New Spain, especially in rural areas, yet the dearth of scholarship on the topic would lead one to believe otherwise. Indeed, in the face of hundreds of cases of bestiality preserved in historical archives throughout Mexico and Guatemala, to date only a handful of academic works on the topic exist, none of which theoretically analyze the animal in question.[25]

According to Virginia DeJohn Anderson, in colonial North America no act "threatened to erase the boundary between people and animals quite so thoroughly as bestiality."[26] Similarly, Erica Fudge writes, "Bestiality is a crime which results not merely in the destruction of a human institution—marriage—but in the destruction of the human self."[27] While these assertions are partly correct, it is also true, as we will see, that bestiality could simultaneously reify the boundary between humans and other animals. Such was the case with Pedro Na and the turkey. Certainly, in legal and theological discourse, Na's act and his misguided lust lowered him to the status of "brute beast." The turkey, on the other hand, had it not died a brutal death due to the sexual act, would have been killed by authorities who, following injunctions set forth in the Book of Leviticus, typically burned, hanged, or beat to death (with blows to the head) those animals implicated in bestiality cases. In New Spain, most animals involved in cases of bestiality were put to death, whereas the humans involved were not. Humanity, in this sense, was rhetorically destroyed, though ultimately humanity was safeguarded by the very decision not to kill the human convicted of the crime.

For colonial New Spain, in both legal documents and prescriptive literature, we find ample references to bestiality. The act figured centrally into bilingual confessional manuals—guides written by priests in both Spanish and indigenous languages such as Nahuatl, Purépecha, Zapotec, Mixtec, or Yucatecan Maya—which assisted priests who were not yet fluent in native languages to catechize indigenous peoples and administer the sacraments in their own tongues. Bartolomé de Alva's 1634 *Confessionario mayor*, for example, provided priests with Nahuatl translations for a variety of topics that were to be discussed with native penitents. Prominent among them: "perhaps you were responsible for the frightful sin, unworthy of being done, of having sexual relations with a four-legged animal or a beast."[28] Although Bartolomé de Alva failed to mention animals by species or name, he employed the Nahuatl term *yolcatl* (beast), which in the colonial period was used primarily to refer to horses and other large European domesticated animals. The joining of *yolcatl* with "the frightful sin" is no surprise, and reflects the strong associations between the constitution of the crime and colonialism itself.

The eventual ubiquity of European donkeys, mares, dogs, mules, cows, goats, and sheep in rural areas, scattered among innumerable farms, haciendas, and hillsides, reflects the changing human-animal terrain, evidenced by shifts toward new agricultural systems and the steady growth of pastoral farming among indigenous peoples. In the 119 criminal and ecclesiastical cases of bestiality, we find that the 1563 criminal trial of Pedro Na represents one of only two bestiality cases in which the sexual act involved an animal—a turkey, described in Spanish as a *gallina de la tierra*—completely indigenous to Mesoamerica. The available data (on 135 animals) shows that 42.2 percent of the animals implicated in bestiality cases were female donkeys (*burras*). Mares accounted for nearly 20 percent of the cases, followed by female dogs and mules (each at 7.48 percent), cows (5.2 percent), female goats (3.7 percent), female sheep (2.9 percent), and turkeys (1.5 percent). The high proportion of donkeys can be partly explained by their ubiquity throughout rural and urban New Spain, and by the versatile uses to which humans put them. As the colonial period progressed, donkeys were increasingly used as draft animals on farms. On haciendas, donkeys were used for transport, and in mines they were used to carry ore and to operate heavy machinery like the water wheel. On the outskirts of cities and large towns, they were used to pull carts and transport everything from produce and pulque to textiles into the city for sale.

As with all statistics, these numbers are partly misleading due to several factors. First, some perpetrators confessed to having sex with an unspecified number of animals—a fact that already distorts the percentages above. In 1738, for example, Juan Lázaro, a mulatto shepherd, confessed that he had sex once

TABLE 4.1 Dates of Criminal and Ecclesiastical Cases of Bestiality in New Spain, 1563–1821

	1500S	1600S	1700S	EARLY 1800S	TOTAL
Number	1	6	71	41	119
Percentage	0.84	5.04	59.66	34.45	100

with a sheep, while a fellow shepherd, José Domingo, had intercourse with "at least" three sheep and one goat.[29] In the early nineteenth century, Perfecto Galván, an eighteen-year-old mulatto in Suchitlán, confessed to having sex with five mares over the course of six years.[30] Second, there is no possible way to ascertain the actual number of offenses that any given individual committed. Most of the adolescents and men who were caught in the act vehemently declared that it was their only time. In actuality, many may have been repeat offenders. Another evident pattern in this corpus is that male perpetrators seem to have invariably chosen female animals for sex. In his study on bestiality in modern Sweden, Jens Rydström notes, "The male perpetrators of bestiality, with few exceptions, chose female animals, making bestiality in reality a heterosexual, 'heterospecial' endeavor."[31] Similarly, in New Spain, given that no cases of sex with male animals have surfaced, bestiality also appears to have been "heterospecial," raising the possibility that adolescents mimicked—and learned from—the male animals that they watched copulating with female animals. Boys raised in rural environments inevitably became accustomed to the sight of domesticated animals mounting each other openly, and some of them, it seems, imitated what they had seen.

Demographic details help elucidate the contours of the crime and its frequency of being recorded. First, regarding the chronological breakdown of the criminal cases of bestiality employed in this chapter (summarized in table 4.1), the majority of cases come from the eighteenth century (seventy-one cases) and the first two decades of the nineteenth century (forty-one cases). This chronology is reflective of several phenomena. The surge in the late colonial period has to do with the increase in the human population and domesticated animals, and with improved (or at least more prominent) recordkeeping practices. This rise also has to do with the passing of the Bourbon Reforms in the early eighteenth century, which sought to increase taxation and control of the Spanish American colonies. With these reforms, colonial authorities escalated their efforts to regulate and punish crime, which had significant effects on the ways that crime came to be documented and archived in eighteenth-century

TABLE 4.2 Ages of Males Implicated in Criminal and Ecclesiastical Bestiality Cases in New Spain, 1563–1821

	11–19	20–29	30–39	40–49	50–59	60–69	TOTAL
Number	45	20	4	2	0	1	72
Percentage	62.5	27.8	5.5	2.8	0	1.4	100

New Spain. In this record set, I was able to locate six criminal cases from the seventeenth century and only one—that of Pedro Na—from the sixteenth.

Using these 119 criminal cases, we can discern some other important patterns of this crime in the colonial period. Bartolomé Bennassar, in his study of the "abominable sins" in early modern Aragón, Spain, noted that bestiality was most frequent among poorer rural males who spent many hours alone due to their jobs in agriculture, animal husbandry, and animal caretaking.[32] William Monter observes that a pastoral economy in Spain, where livestock outnumbered human inhabitants, "produced a pastoral sexual deviation."[33] Similarly, in New Spain the frequency of bestiality cases in rural areas greatly surpassed those in urban centers.

For those charged with bestiality between the years 1563 and 1821 (summarized in table 4.2), the crime was most common among the young, rural working class. This suggests that bestiality became a viable option among those—especially shepherds, farmhands, and cowboys who spent extended periods of time away from friends, family, and the company of women—who were in the sexually exploratory phases of their adolescent lives. As Penyak has observed, those convicted of bestiality in late colonial Mexico "tended to be young, single males who worked on *haciendas*."[34] Nearly a third of the cases do not note the age of the accused. But for those seventy-two individuals whose ages were recorded, the majority fell between the ages of eleven and nineteen (62.5 percent), while twenty individuals were in their twenties, and only a small percentage of men were in their thirties or older. The recorded age of the youngest perpetrator was eleven years old, the oldest was sixty, and the overall average age of those accused of bestiality in criminal courts was just over nineteen. As we will see, especially for those boys aged fifteen and under (who accounted for approximately 38 percent of the total), youth and the "ignorance" that went alongside it could be important mitigating factors in the sentences meted out by criminal courts.

The young age of most of the perpetrators can be partially explained by the fact that bestiality, for many, was a means of accruing sexual experience. In

Hidalgo del Parral in 1718, Lorenzo Benítez, a twenty-eight-year-old mulatto farmhand and cowboy, was caught by his employer, Juan Saenz, having sex with a cow in the corrals.[35] When Benítez, who admitted his crime, was asked about his motive behind such an "ugly and unnatural act," he replied that he had committed the act "in order to gain experience and to see if he would feel pleasure by having sex with the cow, as if he were doing it with a woman."[36] He later stated that "his work was so excessive and unending that he had neither holidays nor outings, for which reason he never had the opportunity to satisfy the appetite of nature."[37] In a rare application of the death penalty for the crime of bestiality, in 1719 the governor of Parral sentenced Benítez to be garroted and his corpse burned. This sentence was carried out at eleven o'clock in the morning on November 11, 1719. The court also mandated that the owner of the cow was to kill the animal in his possession (possibly without compensation). Benítez's impulse to "satisfy the appetite of nature" with an animal became fatal for both him and the cow from his herd.

A century later, explanations remain quite similar: bestiality was frequently framed as a temporary substitute for customary sexual activity between a man and a woman. This explanation suggests that, in contrast to the views of theologians and jurists, most perpetrators of the crime may not have seen their acts as challenging the natural order but rather as temporarily substituting it. In 1818, in the town of Teocaltiche, when two men came upon Tomás Amador, a twenty-four-year-old mestizo, having sex with a mule, they interrupted the act and, confronting him, asked him why he did not have sex with women.[38] To this he replied that he had tried to have sex with women, but without success. In other cases, bestiality suspects refuted accusations and defended themselves by stressing their own natural sexual desires. In the Tlaxcalan town of San Agustín Tlaxco, Justo Rufino, a young indigenous man accused of having sex with a donkey in the early nineteenth century, denied the charges against him and asserted that were his temptation ever so strong, rather than pursue a brute beast, "he would seek out a rational woman with whom to satisfy himself."[39] Reason, in a sense, thus becomes the very object of his desire—embodied by the hypothetical "rational woman," who shields him from the accusation of bestiality. After spending nearly four years in prison, however, Rufino was freed due to the inconclusive evidence against him.

A certain level of voyeurism, as we saw in the case of Na, was central to the act of bestiality. We see this in the case of Miguel Maldonado, a Spanish boy who confessed that he became sexually excited while caring for a sick young mare, and watching her closely, on a farm in 1768.[40] Similarly, in 1782, in the town of Hacienda del Rincón in Michoacán, Francisco Neri, an indigenous *ladino* in his thirties, admitted that "as a weak man, and deceived by the Devil, he was unable to resist the temptations of the flesh, and looking at the donkey he was provoked, and he consented in his miserable state to cohabit with her."[41] Given Neri's confession, the local ecclesiastical judge remitted the case to the bishop of Valladolid, but no further information is recorded in the files. Close proximity to domesticated animals, and the potential for privacy, thus gave rise to ample opportunities for boys to experiment sexually with animals.

While most instances of bestiality were solitary, occasionally boys performed such acts in the company of another, to show someone how to perform— perhaps not unlike Lázaro Martínez's learning of sex with the dead from his friend Miguel. This was the case with two young shepherds in Santa María de las Parras, José Domingo and Juan Lázaro, who were caught having sex with a sheep by a hacienda employee in 1738.[42] Domingo successfully fled, but Lázaro, who was turned over to authorities, confessed that he had committed bestiality only once, after watching his friend have sex with several goats and sheep. For his crimes, Domingo was sentenced in absentia to die. The court, on the other hand, sentenced Lázaro to be paraded through the streets, publicly shamed, and "violently passed through the flames of a bonfire two or three times, [but] in a way so that he does not burn," though upon appeal his sentence was suspended.[43] There is no information about the punishment he eventually received, although the passing through the flames was meant to be a symbolic version of burning the violated animal. In the Iberian Peninsula, passing one "through the flames," as opposed to burning them, was a punishment occasionally reserved for boys and adolescents convicted of sodomy or bestiality. The tactic was meant to terrify youths to change their ways, or—the threat went—they too would end up in the fire.

Although the vast majority of perpetrators were *solteros*—single, unmarried males—married men occasionally committed bestiality. In 1749, in Querétaro, several women accused Lázaro de Herrera of having sex with a female dog, which he had tied up by its neck in the kitchen of a home where he was spending the night.[44] Although Herrera maintained his innocence, his wife, Gertrudis, testified that her husband had previously been caught by the owner and two employees of the hacienda where he worked having sex with two donkeys and a mare. The criminal court in Querétaro sentenced Lázaro de Herrera to be garroted for his crimes, with his corpse burned alongside the dog. Herrera's defense lawyer appealed the sentence; the records of the case are incomplete and no information on the final outcome is recorded. In another example, from

TABLE 4.3 Ethnic Makeup of Men Implicated in Bestiality Cases in New Spain, 1563–1821

	INDIGENOUS	MESTIZO	MULATTO	SPANISH	NEGRO	LOBO	CASTIZO	UNKNOWN	TOTAL
Number	48	13	11	10	2	2	1	32	119
Percentage	40.33	10.92	9.24	8.40	1.68	1.68	0.84	26.89	100

the town of Sololá, Guatemala, in 1785, Bernabé Camey, an indigenous man who had been accused of sodomy with a mule and was languishing in prison awaiting a trial, appealed to the king that either he be quickly punished for his crime or set free to return home to live with his wife.[45] His petition read: "I beseech Your Majesty, I have asked the alcalde mayor don Domingo Salgado why, if I am guilty, they do not punish my sin and then let me go to my town to live with my wife because I have been suffering so long [in prison]. I am always asking the alcalde mayor whenever he comes to the prison, and he replies, 'I am not at fault' . . . if I am guilty, I will pay [for my sin], and if not, I will go to live with my wife."[46] It was not until December 1786 that Camey was sentenced to be whipped two hundred times and to spend four years laboring in a presidio. The mule with which he was caught was killed.

One final example, from 1804, is especially interesting in that a married woman denounced her own spouse. In Colima, María Nicolasa Aguilar accused her husband, Juan José Albersuna, of having sex with a donkey because, according to her, she had denied him sex because he was suffering from *mal de gálico*—syphilis. According to Albersuna, some four years earlier, "when his mouth, nose, eyes, and other humid parts on his body, including his genitals, had erupted in lesions, his wife had resisted when he wanted to have sex with her."[47] For this reason, according to what he had told a neighbor, he sought sex with the donkey. The records of the case are incomplete, and we do not know the fates of either Albersuna or the donkey. For his wife, however, such an act was unacceptable and required the intervention of criminal authorities.

Another important demographic component in these records is ethnicity. Table 4.3 depicts the ethnic and racial makeup of the accused. The ethnicity of thirty-two of the men is unknown or not recorded; of the remainder, forty-four individuals (just over 40 percent) were indigenous males. They were followed by mestizos, mulattos, Spaniards, blacks, and then by the members of the racially mixed *castas*—that is, *lobos*, who were of indigenous and African parentage, and *castizos*, who had one mestizo parent and one Spanish parent. The fact that most of the men convicted of bestiality were indigenous males can be partly explained by the rural nature of the crime and the simple fact that indigenous inhabitants comprised the highest percentage of peoples living in rural areas, an explanation far more plausible than the colonial tropes that native peoples were more disposed to unnatural desires.[48] That said, sodomy and bestiality trials and punishments in New Spain simultaneously functioned as a means of exerting colonial control over all segments of the population, including Spaniards. Still, accusations of bestiality were most likely to be levied against indigenous peoples as a manifestation of bias toward them. As we have already seen, members of the upper echelons of colonial society were rarely tried for the sins against nature, and when they were, they received punishments that were less harsh (and less public) then the masses.

Gender is the final demographic component that we can glimpse from the corpus. Only three of the 144 bestiality cases examined here involve female perpetrators, and each of the documents is exceedingly vague. It is therefore impossible to tell whether the women were penetrated by the animals in question, or if there was some other type of physical contact between them. Of those three women, it appears that only one—María Bárbara López, in 1772—was actually tried by secular authorities for "for bestial sodomy."[49] The original criminal case is missing; all that remains is a fragment of judicial correspondence. In parts of early modern Europe, there are indications that women were occasionally, though rarely, sentenced to death for the crime of bestiality; there are no such indications for New Spain. Keith Thomas mentions one case from Tyburn, England, in which a woman and her dog were hanged for bestiality in 1679.[50] Rydström discusses a 1782 case from Sweden in which a forty-three-year-old maid was convicted of "intercourse with a bull," for which she was sentenced to die.[51] On appeal, she was reprieved and sentenced instead to a prison in Stockholm, where she labored for six years. Two of the three colonial Mexican cases dealing with female perpetrators come to us from the files of the Inquisition. In a self-denunciation to inquisitors in the town of Zinguilucan, Ana María de Leyba, an eighteen-year-old Spanish woman (discussed at length in the final chapter), confessed in 1752 that "for about one year, she frequently had lewd contact with an image of the Virgin Mary. Furthermore, on these occasions, she would first have [carnal] access with beasts, and would then come up to the image and attempt to get that very animal to have access with the image."[52] The records of her case are incomplete, and we have no information on how, or even if, she was punished.

In 1762 a Mexico City priest, Nuño Nuñez de Villavicencio, requested permission from the Inquisition to absolve an unidentified woman who confessed to him that on three separate occasions she had "lewd contact with an animal." According to the priest, she confessed that the first two times she felt no pleasure and, therefore, on her third attempt, she "vehemently desired that the Devil were inside of the animal, so that she could attain pleasure."[53] The priest, unsure as to whether the penitent, in invoking the Devil, had engaged in "heretical sorcery," denounced her to the Inquisition. Inquisitors, however, succinctly replied: "So far as the Holy Office is concerned, there is no impediment to absolving the penitent."[54]

The final archival reference to female bestiality is the 1772 criminal case of María Bárbara López, of which only a fragment of judicial correspondence remains. López was "tried in that [criminal] tribunal for bestial sodomy," and Simón de los Santos Losada, the witness, was remitted, along with his wife and son, to the royal jail of the court, most likely to testify against her.[55] No traces of María Bárbara López in Mexico's national archive have been found, and we do not know how, or if, she was punished. The corpus points to the ways that the bestial act itself was highly gendered, in terms of both the embodiment and the recording of the act. Through these three archival fragments involving women we can speculate that, for some, illicit contact with animals may have been more about religious doubt and desecration than sexual desire per se, which is certainly not the case for most adolescent boys and men who engaged in bestiality. However, in the absence of the only criminal case of a woman tried for bestiality by a secular court, we cannot get a sense of how María Bárbara López, as well as those around her, perceived of her act.

The transcripts of bestiality trials point to the ways in which humans and animals disappear from the colonial archive in very different ways. The dearth of bestiality cases involving women shows how the act, much like sodomy, was understood principally through gender. The ample presence of bestiality cases in colonial archives throughout the Iberian Atlantic world has not been afforded the historiographical attention or analysis that it deserves—a vivid demonstration of Trouillot's argument about how silencing factors into historical production. Bestiality has been silenced primarily by historians' depriveleging of archival narratives rather than by the colonial archive itself—yet another form of animal erasure. This is especially true when we compare the historiographical negation of bestiality to the ways that scholars have written (and indeed championed) histories of same-sex sexuality in the early modern world. With regard to bestiality, the colonial archive itself is abundant; the problem is that most scholars have been largely blind to that abundance, or they, for one reason or another, have simply not wanted to deal with it.

Explaining Bestiality

In the previous chapter, we saw how people inferred sodomy from a range of signs, from the body's physiology and gestures to everyday performances of gender and morality. Now, we turn to some of the most common explanations behind bestiality accusations, paying particular attention to the signs through which witnesses and courts tried to make sense of the act. We find remarkable similarities and significant differences in how individuals read the bodies of sodomy or bestiality suspects. In both, medics were called on to physically examine the bodies in question, to see if penetration had taken place. Yet, because the animal in question could not be verbally interrogated, courts turned to a series of other explanations—from the suspect's ignorance and "rusticity" to his moral character and perhaps inebriated state—to explain what happened.

To begin, the tropes of ignorance and *rusticidad*—rusticity—play a more central role in bestiality accusations than in those of sodomy, in part because the crime was largely limited to New Spain's rural areas. According to the 1737 *Diccionario de autoridades*, the word *rusticidad* is defined primarily as the "simplicity, naturalness, and lack of artifice that rustic things [and people] have." In the second definition, rusticity refers to "the crudeness, roughness, and brutishness of rustic things."[56] In New Spain, as we will see, rusticity was coded as much in terms of race and ethnicity—Indianness, to be exact—as it was through proximity to the rustic. One criminal case from Tulancingo in 1801 tells the story of an eighteen-year-old mestizo, Ysidro Bonifacio, who was caught in a drunken state having "carnal access" with a female donkey. Bonifacio was caught red-handed by Antonio de Nicolás, a fifty-five-year-old Spaniard who euphemistically asserted that he had "found him materially introduced in the base of the said donkey, and then when the witness saw him, he separated himself from the donkey, which went to the street, spilling liquid and pissing, as the boy attempted to cover himself."[57]

When authorities interrogated Bonifacio, he admitted his crime, asserting that "possessed by the fires of concupiscence, and not having any means to extinguish them, he came up to a brown donkey that belonged to his father, and he consummated the carnal act with it."[58] The prosecution, emphasizing the unnaturalness of this act, pressed that "he be charged with the gravity of the crime, hateful to nature itself . . . [for] cohabiting with a dissimilar [being]."[59] In a seemingly successful effort to mitigate the severity of his crime, Bonifacio's defense lawyer pejoratively asserted, "He had the level of reason of a little shepherd among the animals, and that, incited with brutal concupiscence, he neither recognized nor reflected upon the gravity of the sin and detestable crime."[60] Though Bonifacio was a racially mixed mestizo, the stereotypes of "Indian" ignorance and rusticity—as well as his pastoral proximity to animals—became key to his defense. Indeed, they seem part of an argument made from habit, both popularly and judicially. For his transgressions, Bonifacio was sentenced to three years of confinement in a presidio, but without hard labor.

Men of all ethnic backgrounds in colonial Mexico, as we have seen, were accused of this crime. This did little in the eyes of many, however, who typically associated bestiality with "Indians" and with a lack of Christian teachings and mores. In a slightly later criminal case from central Mexico, in 1809, a young indigenous man named José de los Reyes was caught having sex with a female donkey on the hacienda of Santa María by a man, Cornelio Acamapichi, who was out hunting. Upon arriving at a clearing at the end of a small road on the hacienda, he discovered "the said defendant stopped in the highest part, and the animal in the lowest part with its buttocks pressed against the thighs of the defendant, who was moving himself in a way that left not the slightest doubt as to the bestial access that he was consummating."[61] Indicating that the act was initially seen as un-Christian rather than unnatural, the witness exclaimed: "Fuck! [*Carajo*] What are you doing? Are you not Christian?"[62] Despite José de los Reyes suffering from some mental problems—he was repeatedly referred to as *asimplado*, a simpleton—and from the early stages of elephantiasis, he was prosecuted and sentenced to two years of labor on public works projects. That both of these men, caught having sex with animals in the early nineteenth century, were sentenced to relatively short periods of confinement or forced labor was, as we will see, characteristic of the late colonial period.

In each of these cases, signs and explanations converged, pointing to the consummation of bestiality. Spanish witnesses in particular assumed that being indigenous and, to varying degrees, being mestizo went hand-in-hand with ignorance, rusticity, heathenism, and animality—with all the potential for criminality these qualities implied. The presumption here is that if a Spaniard were to commit bestiality, he would have to have been rendered temporarily irrational—through impaired judgment, drunkenness, or a momentary lapse of reason—whereas natives and mixed-race individuals had an inherent propensity for bestial desire. Indeed, suspects themselves occasionally resorted to some of these same stereotypes when trying to explain their actions. As Mílada Bazant notes, two of the most common claims utilized by suspects and their defense lawyers in the late colonial period in an attempt to mitigate the severity of punishment for bestiality were ignorance and drunkenness.[63] Indeed, the further one descended to animality, the greater the propensity to commit bestiality.

The documents provide us with copious examples of individuals who claimed they simply did not know bestiality was a sin. In 1809 Perfecto Galván, an eighteen-year-old mulatto shepherd from Suchitlán who confessed that he had sex with some five mares over six years, told authorities that "he did not know it was bad" and that "it did not appear to him to be a sin."[64] He did, nonetheless, admit that "it was true that when he confessed, he felt ashamed to tell the priest."[65] Some individuals may have genuinely been telling the truth when they claimed ignorance about bestiality's sinfulness, especially if we consider Bazant's suggestion that bestiality may have been "an established custom in the rural setting."[66]

Alcohol, cited repeatedly by witnesses and suspects, also played a crucial role in interpreting and rationalizing acts of bestiality. In 1626 an indigenous man named Alonso admitted to being drunk when caught fornicating with a sow.[67] As William B. Taylor notes, "Although trial records can exaggerate attitudes about alcohol as a cause of crime, it still appears that Indians, especially in central Mexico, were beginning to adopt the Spanish view that alcohol could dissolve one's natural judgment and good sense and could, alone, cause crime."[68] In 1722 when Jacinto Mascorro was discovered having sex with a donkey, witnesses referred to him as being "more dead than alive" from the stupefying effects of alcohol.[69] In 1780 José Resendis, a Spaniard in his mid-twenties, drank so much pulque that he claimed he forgot having had sex with a donkey in a corn field.[70] Although he remembered being tied up and turned in to authorities, he did not know why. In 1805 Domingo Antonio, a mulatto in his early twenties, admitted that the idea of "sinning with the donkey" came to him only after drinking pulque. Blaming alcohol and ignorance, Antonio said that he merely rubbed against the donkey's backside, though he was careful to note that his semen "fell to the ground, not inside of the donkey . . . [and] afterwards he remained a while, looking at his member next to the donkey's ass."[71] In 1807 José María Maturana, a mulatto in his early twenties, confessed that he "had bad thoughts" about a donkey only after imbibing pulque.[72]

In popular narrations of bestiality, alcohol—distorter of both good judgment and free will—frequently merged with diabolical temptation. In 1797 Felipe Nari, an indigenous boy of fifteen who was arrested for having sex with a mare, said that because of his drinking pulque, "the Devil had deceived him" into wanting to sin with the animal, though he denied committing the act.[73] In 1803 Joseph Florentino from Ixmiquilpan confessed to authorities that he had had "bad thoughts," after which he tied up a donkey and stood on a large stone in order to penetrate the animal, and "only the Devil could have inspired him that day."[74] When those accused of bestiality did mention the Devil, they appear to have done so either as an attempt to deflect their own agency in the act or to mitigate the punishment. A number of men in New Spain who confessed their bestial acts mentioned the malign influence of the Devil; yet, such references did not make judges more sympathetic to them. Thus, while the accused regularly invoked the Devil, prosecutors and judges in New Spain did so rarely, if ever. Diabolical influence thus functioned as an explanation of bestiality, but largely on the part of suspects and their legal defense.

As with the crime of sodomy, bestiality in New Spain did not fall under the jurisdiction of the Inquisition because it did not invoke or imply heresy. Despite this, as evidenced by twenty-five denunciations of bestiality to the Inquisition over the course of the colonial period, some witnesses saw bestiality first as a sinful and potentially heretical act. In none of these instances, however, did the Inquisition follow up on the denunciations. One interesting outlier is the eight bestiality cases that diocesan courts in Valladolid, Michoacán, tried in the eighteenth century. These are the only examples I have found thus far of ecclesiastical courts adjudicating bestiality. The cases occurred over a long period of time—between 1703 and 1783—and were tried by different ecclesiastical judges, bishops, and priests. Furthermore, none of the cases involved the clergy as suspects, which would have justified diocesan intervention. These may simply be instances of overzealous bishops or ecclesiastical judges deciding that these *should* be cases for the diocesan courts, and no alcalde or secular judge stopped them. These cases may merely be a legal aberration, or part of protracted struggles over jurisdiction between civic and diocesan courts in Michoacán. For it was not normal for the church in New Spain to get involved in bestiality.[75]

The physical signs through which bestiality was interpreted and explained were both physiological and tangible, pointing to certain similarities with sodomy trials. Criminal investigations relied on medical examinations, in which doctors tried to determine if the animals deposited as evidence had been penetrated by a human, and other physical evidence—anything from semen spilling from an animal's genitals, ropes used by the suspect to tie up the animal's front or hind legs, or the strategic placement of a rock, grindstone, or makeshift step on which to stand in order to reach the animal's backside. These signs all pointed back to the body of the animal in question. In one fascinating example of an animal medical examination, after a fellow soldier caught José Beltrán allegedly having sex with a female dog in 1816, medical inspectors examined the dog and concluded "that the animal in question could not have tolerated penetration."[76] Doctors reasoned that Beltrán had probably intended intercourse, but that he "ejaculated between the legs of the animal and not in the vagina."[77] Here, the medical examination actually served to exculpate the suspect by disproving that penetration had taken place. Beltrán, who retracted his initial confession, eventually declared that he had only actually masturbated near the animal, and subsequently cleaned himself on the dog. After spending some four years in prison, he was absolved.

As far as criminal courts were concerned, proof of ejaculation inside an animal was the surest sign that bestiality had been consummated. Yet such proof was rare; far more common, and more problematic, was the reliance on eyewitness testimony about the animal in question. In the 1801 trial of José Antonio Rodríguez, the sole witness, Santiago Terán, asserted that he had seen the suspect standing on a wooden beam and penetrating a mare that he had tied up. The animal, according to Terán, died eight days later. Terán also asserted that he had seen "semen spilling immediately from the vagina of the mare."[78] The defense, however, argued that ejaculation never took place; the fluid seen by the witness spilling from the animal was merely urine. For the fact that "the configuration of seminal fluid does not vary in its color, glutinous texture, and quantity removes any doubt" that it was urine, not semen.[79] Four years later, in 1805, the criminal court nonetheless sentenced José Antonio Rodríguez to two years of labor in a presidio in Havana, Cuba. In 1806, however, given the long time he had already spent in prison, he was freed.

In another example, taken from an 1812 case from Sacatepéquez, Guatemala, Pio Moreira caught Juan Hernández, an indigenous boy of sixteen, having sex with a sheep on a hacienda.[80] Hernández, who often "played with the sheep," admitted that although he intended to have sex with the animal, he never consummated the act. The witness's observation, that "the sheep's parts were inflamed and red ... and the sheep was very hot because it was caressed by the person enticing it," contradicted the boy's account.[81] Taking all the evidence into account, the criminal court sentenced Hernández to receive fifty lashes inside the prison and to labor for four years on public works projects, showing that proof of ejaculation was far from necessary to convict someone of bestiality. The sheep was to be killed, but it died of natural causes beforehand.

The two common technical problems that men attempting to commit bestiality with large domesticated animals encountered—how to reach the physical height of the animal's genitals and how to make the animal stand still—also became important signs that could indicate both intent and guilt. Numerous witnesses commented on the fact that male perpetrators typically tied up the front and hind legs of the animals in order to get them to stand still, and also to minimize the possibility of being kicked or otherwise physically harmed by the animal. In the 1818 trial of Tomás Amador, who had tied up a mule and covered its eyes, he confessed that although his intention was to fornicate with the animal, "he got to unbuttoning his underwear, but he did not sin [with the animal] because the mule resisted [*se resistió*], kicking him in the shin."[82] This is one rare instance in which an animal, if the story is true, may have succeeded in "resisting" human sexual advances. In our cases, we see that perpetrators used a variety of means to restrain an animal—covering their eyes, tying them up by their necks, and binding their legs—and such preparations were read by witnesses, lawyers, and judges as indicative of intent. Many a suspect, when faced with the evidence that he had tied up the animal, or had placed an object behind it on which to stand, claimed that he was merely trying to saddle the creature, mount it, or load it with cargo to be transported into town. The witnesses, they asserted, must have misinterpreted the scene. Ultimately, archived representations of bestiality rely on an assemblage of imperfect explanations and ambivalent signs, which were spun into narratives for the court to assess blame.

Declining Severity

So far, we have encountered a range of punishments for bestiality—death sentence, castration, passing through the flames, whipping, public shaming, exile, forced labor, and spiritual penance. The particular punishments, and their severity, varied greatly across the colonial period. These punishments, of course, have a history, which, in New Spain, can be traced back to the first few decades of Spanish colonial presence in the sixteenth century, and in Europe, much further. Throughout the colonial period, harsh corporeal punishments—especially public whipping—were the most common, though they were applied irregularly. In 1563, as we have seen, a fourteen-year-old Maya boy, Pedro Na, was paraded to the town's central plaza, with the corpse of the turkey hanging around his neck, and was publicly castrated and perpetually banished from Yucatán. Were it not for his age, the boy might have been executed. In 1656 Lorenzo Vidales, a thirteen-year-old indigenous boy from Monterrey, was caught having "carnal access" with a goat, which was subsequently killed by its owner.[83] Vidales was tied to the gallows and received one hundred lashes, was perpetually banished, and his labor for a period of six years was "sold" to a man who vowed to keep him away from livestock. The same harsh punishments, meted out irregularly, are also seen in the eighteenth century. In 1709, for example, a mestizo boy of seventeen, Salvador de Cuenca, was convicted of bestiality with a female dog. The dog was burned in his presence, and he was given one hundred lashes in the public plaza and subsequently banished from Hidalgo for four years.[84] In 1724, in San Luis Potosí, Francisco Xavier, an indigenous fifteen-year-old boy who was caught having sex with a donkey, was sentenced to "be taken from prison, on a pack animal, through the public streets and given one hundred lashes until he arrives at the *quemadero* [the place where convicts were burned], where he will be passed through the flames, and the donkey converted into ashes."[85] He was also sentenced to five years of labor in a textile mill.

Our corpus shows that courts sentenced at least twelve bestiality convicts to be publicly whipped, usually receiving one hundred lashes and, on occasion, two hundred. The cases began in the following years and locales: 1614 (Guadalajara), 1656 (Monterrey), 1709 (Meztitlán, Hidalgo), 1711 (San Luis Potosí), 1713 (San Luis Potosí—this sentence was revoked), 1724 (San Luis Potosí), 1747 (Xantetelco, Morelos), 1755 (Valladolid, Michoacán), 1755 (Huipustla, Mexico), 1775 (Taos, New Mexico), 1785 (Sololá, Guatemala), and 1812 (Sacatepéquez, Guatemala). In all but two of the cases—that of the seventeen-year-old mestizo punished in 1709, and a nineteen-year-old lobo, of African and indigenous parentage, in 1755—the individuals sentenced to be whipped were indigenous. A secular court in Guatemala sentenced Juan Hernández to be whipped fifty times in prison, in 1812; it is possible that others were whipped even more recently for the same crime, but documents have yet to surface.

The vicious nature of these punishments, however, obscures a larger trend. The frequency of documented trials steadily increases throughout the eighteenth and early nineteenth centuries, indicating that, relative to the total number of bestiality cases that were tried by secular courts, the percentage of whipping sentences actually decreased over time. We also see that, as the colonial period progressed, an increasing number of men convicted of bestiality were punished with temporary banishment and specified periods of forced labor on public works projects (usually between two and ten years). Banishment and mandatory labor became characteristic punishments of the late colonial period, and in general, punishments for bestiality grew less severe over time. That said, individual punishments varied widely, and depended entirely on the particular court, the judge, and the appeals process.

As we know, criminal and ecclesiastical authorities differentiated sodomy from bestiality, despite biblical argument that those accused of either should be executed. Regarding bestiality, Leviticus 20:15–16 states, "And if a man lie with a beast, he shall surely be put to death; and ye shall slay the beast. And if a woman approach unto any beast, and lie down thereto, thou shalt kill the woman and the beast: they shall surely be put to death; their blood shall be upon them." While men convicted of "perfect sodomy"—anal penetration with ejaculation—were put to death routinely as late as 1691, those convicted of bestiality in New Spain were rarely put to death for their crimes. Between the years of 1563 and 1821, there is evidence that courts in New Spain sentenced at least a dozen individuals to be executed for the crime of bestiality. Only three of these death sentences, however, were actually carried out—all, surprisingly, in the first half of the eighteenth century. Most of the remaining nine cases were, between 1711 and 1820, appealed and the sentences subsequently revoked by higher courts. Yet these three deaths must be reckoned with since their relatively late occurrence seems to contradict the assertion that the severity of punishments lessened over time. Extant archival documents show that the death penalty was used later for bestiality than for sodomy, which, in part, may be an indication of decreasing communal intolerance for same-sex acts in comparison with human-animal sex. Bestiality, especially among older men and recidivists, was treated more harshly than among young adolescents, as the cases below demonstrate. Though speculative, this may also have had to do with increasingly medicalized notions of the body, crime, and sin over the course of the eighteenth century. Perhaps jurists (and doctors) came to view offenders of bestiality as "deviant" in ways that, by the eighteenth century, differed from how they then largely viewed sodomites. The sample of bestiality death sentences is too small to be able to draw definitive conclusions, though the difference in death penalty dates is striking.

The earliest execution, from 1704, is that of Juan Thomas, a free black condemned to death for the crime of bestiality *and* for having robbed clerics with weapons.[86] From the case fragment it is impossible to determine if the death penalty was pronounced primarily for the crime of bestiality or for the collective crimes he committed. The second case is that of Lorenzo Benítez, a mulatto in his late twenties, discussed above, who was garroted in 1719, with his corpse subsequently burned to ashes.[87] The final death sentence for bestiality, pronounced by the alcalde mayor of San Luis Potosí, was meted out to Joseph de la Cruz, a free mulatto of thirty-four, who was garroted and then burned in 1723, alongside the mare he had been caught having sex with.[88] On January 9, 1726, de la Cruz was paraded through San Luis Potosí to the outskirts of town, where "by the hand of Agustín de Castillo, executor of royal justice, he [Joseph de la Cruz] was garroted, from which he died naturally, and the mare was killed with a blow from a stick and thrown upon the body of the said Joseph. That same executioner set up a bonfire with abundant firewood, and another, with the mare, at some distance from the first. He lit both, and in this manner both Joseph and the mare were converted into ashes."[89] The corpses of the man and the mare were briefly united, thrown on top of one another, then burned separately. All three men, coincidentally, were mulattos, and their skin color certainly played a role in their excessively harsh punishments.

These records show that as late as 1726—nearly four decades after documents indicate that the last individual in New Spain was executed for sodomy—secular courts executed a man for the crime of bestiality, a fact that appears to demonstrate that, at least in the eighteenth century, bestiality was deemed more egregious than sodomy. We find two other pronouncements even later, though we do not know if they were carried out. In 1738 José Domingo was sentenced to death in absentia, but, as far as we know, judicial officials in Nueva Galicia never captured him.[90] Lastly, in 1749 in Querétaro, Lázaro de Herrera was sentenced to be executed for bestiality with a female dog.[91] His lawyer appealed this case, but since the records are incomplete, we do not know if his appeal was granted.

As we have seen, the death sentence was not uncommonly pronounced on men convicted of bestiality by local courts, but documents show that higher judicial courts typically revoked these sentences. Such was the case with one Pedro Joseph. In July 1755 the mayor of Valladolid condemned this indigenous man to death for "sexual congress" with a female donkey. While the details presented in this five-folio case are scant, it is clear that the mayor's sentence was revoked when the accused appealed to a *procurador de indios*, a legal representative of native peoples, for the review of his case.[92] In October of that year, prosecutors of the Audiencia Real of New Spain, after revoking the death penalty, imposed the severe punishment of two hundred lashes and ten years of service in a textile mill.[93] In one other example, from 1789, the Audiencia Real of Guadalajara revoked Juan de los Santos de Luna's death penalty for bestiality, instead sentencing him to work on an overseas fort for a period of ten years.[94] According to Bazant, the judicial authorities who tried bestiality cases in colonial Mexico always cited the laws requiring the death penalty for both human and animal partners in this crime—specifically, title XXI of book XIII of the *Recopilación de Leyes*—but then attenuated the punishments for the human upon sentencing.

We are left with a complicated, though perhaps not contradictory, portrait of bestiality and its punishments in New Spain: it seems to be seen as an increasingly illicit act, especially when committed by adults, over the colonial period, and yet the punishments on the whole—with some noticeable exceptions—grew less severe. It also suggests that higher judicial courts in the eighteenth and early nineteenth centuries dealt harshly with the crime, but not as severely as at the local level. Those men who were ultimately executed for the crime may have been especially unlucky in that their death sentences were either never appealed, or the appeals themselves were unsuccessful. Again, the fragmentary nature of the documents makes definitive conclusions difficult.

Ultimately, there was much variation over time in the ways humans were punished for bestiality, and even if the human perpetrators were typically spared death, the animals were not. The certainty that the violated animal had to die reflects the ways that human memory is symbolically grafted onto the animal, rendering a second violation—the killing of the animal—necessary to ritualistically purify the human offender and the community. Most importantly, these cases reflect a subtle shift in the ways that some types of unnatural sex were viewed over the colonial era, with the distinction between (an increasingly tolerable) same-sex desire and (an increasingly pathologized) human-animal desire slowly distilling out over time.

Animal Bodies, Animal Traces

After analyzing the contours of bestiality in New Spain, I am left with lingering questions: How do humans and animals appear within, and disappear from, historical archives? How do human and animal erasures differ in the archival process? Animals clearly mark the historical record, but do so in quite different ways from humans. As each testimony is assiduously transcribed by a court notary for the purposes of the judicial process, bureaucratic correspondence, and (eventual) archiving, most humans are likely cognizant of the fact that their statements are being recorded for a particular purpose that will, in some senses, determine their fates. Thus, humans appear in the historical record, in the context of sodomy and bestiality trials, aware that they are being transcribed onto paper, and that such transcription holds significant meaning, even if they were unfamiliar with, or perhaps terrified by, the very judicial process through which they were being put. Animals, on the other hand, mark the (human) historical record without necessarily knowing that they are doing so—at least not in ways that are intelligible, or even noticeable, to humans.

This final section focuses on the intimate connections between the archive, the animal, and the human. To put it bluntly, the archive only exists because of the human need to document. That is to say, the archive is fundamentally anthropocentric. Here, I am interested in how, and why, the animals implicated in bestiality cases were killed. What purpose did such deaths serve, and what was the logic behind them? Who killed the animals, and how? If the archiving of our (human) past is part of some central aspect of *being human*, does that require destroying the vestiges of other species, both for our own benefit and for the propagation of our own human-centered memory projects?[95] Our corpus of bestiality cases certainly seems to fit this interpretation, especially in terms of the physical, symbolic, and mnemonic erasure of animal bodies. Animal traces come into archival being, at least partly, through animal death.

Throughout this chapter, I have alluded to animal erasure, reminding us how animal subjectivity disappears—and never really appears in the first place—from the colonial archive. This is not to say, of course, that human subjectivity can necessarily be found in the archive; all the archive contains, as we have seen again and again, are fragmented traces—archival flickers—of what it documents. Nonetheless, the archived animal will always be less legible than the archived human, perhaps simply because humans (presume to) share a capacity for language in ways that negate the very capacity for animal communication. The archived human thus disappears—and is erased—with less frequency than the archived animal.

The human who falls prey to excessive lust is also a disappearing animal— one that hides behind the conceptual cloak of humanity. We saw this, on the one hand, in Martínez de la Parra's late seventeenth-century monstrous illustration of lust, which metaphorically deprives the human of all his or her humanity. On the other hand, we see this in the ways that sodomy and bestiality were discursively framed as practices more inherent to non-Spaniards: the Indians, blacks, mestizos, mulattos, and the racially mixed castas. The very fact that throughout the colonial period Spaniards and American-born Creoles were referred to (by themselves, of course) as *gente de razón*—"people of reason"—in comparison to the presumably more unreasonable, racialized inhabitants of New Spain, illustrates the colonizer's tendency to deny the humanity of the colonized other. As the next chapter, on solicitation in the confessional, shows, Spaniards and Creoles were often found guilty of sodomy, but by and large their racial and social status protected them in ways that were not afforded to the vast majority of New Spain's population. The same is true of bestiality, though less so. "Humanity" in this sense is tied not to the human form but rather to the ways that colonized peoples were denied their humanity by the fundamental workings of colonialism, and exacerbated by allegations of sodomy and bestiality among those to whom Spaniards rhetorically denied reason, whether because of their "rusticity," their "ignorance," their racial status, or their unfamiliarity with the precepts of Christianity.

Here, I want to return to Benson's call for historians to be more attentive to the "embodied traces" of animal lives (and bodies) in the historical past. The archival presence of the animals involved in bestiality cases, and the violence done to them, must not be overlooked. In his analysis of bestiality in the early North American colonies, John Murrin describes "the inability of contemporaries to see animals as victims in bestiality cases."[96] In bestiality cases, animals were victims in two ways: victims of human sexual coercion and of judicial processes. This corpus offers us numerous examples of animals that were coerced, violently (and sometimes fatally), into sex acts with humans. The fact that most men trying to engage in sexual intercourse with large farm animals had to physically restrain them or cover their eyes signals that the animals often tried to "resist." Furthermore, the insertion of a man's penis into a smaller animal could cause injury or death, as in the case of Na and the turkey in 1563. Criminologist Piers Beirne, for one, asserts that "while researchers have seldom examined the physiological consequences of bestiality for humans, they have paid almost no attention whatsoever to the internal bleeding, the ruptured anal passages, the bruised vaginas, and the battered cloacae of animals, let alone to animals' psychological and emotional trauma."[97] None of my archival examples, however, even hint at whatever other nonphysical forms of distress the animals endured.

There are few, if any, indications in the documents that humans paid much attention to animal suffering, either when bestiality was enacted or when the animals were killed. Nonetheless, the colonial archive mediates the spectacles of animal suffering and death. Secular and ecclesiastical courts, following biblical injunctions, regularly mandated that the animal in question should be killed—some of them publicly burned in front of *or even by* the men convicted of the crime. In 1775, for example, José Antonio, a thirteen-year-old indigenous boy, was forced to burn the calf with which he was caught "with his own hands" at a stake erected on the outskirts of a city in New Mexico.[98] In the 1768 case against a young mulatto, José Nicolás, in the town of Acámbaro, Michoacán, the cow with which he confessed to fornicating "was to have its throat slit and then completely burned" while the boy was publicly shamed.[99] Owners, and sometimes witnesses, took matters into their own hands by killing the defiled animal. In 1656 the man who caught Lorenzo Vidales with a goat took it upon himself to kill the animal.[100] In the 1784 case of Simón de Torres, the sole witness, Juan José de Luna, strangled the dog in question—*ahorcó la perra*—with his own hands.[101] In analyzing these deaths, we must also look at the archival implications of the treatment of animals in bestiality cases.

In the rare moment when contemporaries did pay attention to an animal's emotional state, it was not out of concern for the animal but rather to use its behavior as evidence. In Atitaliquía in 1675, witnesses presumed to be able to read the signs of distress in a mare as evidence that the alleged sexual act between the animal and Juan de la Cruz, a mulatto of sixteen, did or did not take place.[102] Although the fly of the boy's pants was "covered with the hairs of the mare," the defense demonstrated that when taken back to the same place where the sexual act allegedly took place, the mare was "very tame, very quiet, and calm, without being agitated."[103] According to the defense, these signs pointed to the animal's well-being, thereby demonstrating the suspect's innocence. In a 1796 example from Zacatecas, Juan de Rentería and his wife testified that they saw Manuel Morales having sex with a female dog. Having previously heard that "the animal was crying"—*el animal lloraba*—most likely out of pain, they concluded that it was not the first time that he had engaged in carnal access with that animal.[104] Humans thus read the signs of animal distress—or lack thereof—as evidence.

We will, of course, never be able to know the animals' thoughts or experiences regarding the carnal acts that were forced on them. As Erica Fudge has noted, animals appear in historical archives "as absent presences: there, but not speaking."[105] But we can consciously confront anthropocentrism by centering individual animals (as opposed to a generic reference to the whole species), and critiquing their treatment, within historical narratives. Beirne, showcasing such an approach, states that "seldom, either in past times or now, do popular images of social control include recognition of the terror and the pain that judicial examination and execution inflict on animals convicted of sexual relations with humans."[106] Although the records for New Spain stipulate that over two dozen animals implicated in bestiality cases were killed during the colonial period, we can be certain that dozens, if not hundreds, more were killed. Their deaths, however, were either too mundane to be recorded in the criminal proceedings, or they were documented, but in cases for which we do not have complete records.

But why this mandate of animal death in the first place? An official in a 1614 criminal case noted that "the mare with which Bartolomé Juan committed the said sin was to be killed and buried beneath the earth *so that no memory of this sin remains*."[107] Two centuries later, in the 1801 case of Isidro Bonifacio Peña, the court stipulated that the donkey be killed, "*so that in this way the memory of the act will be deadened*."[108] The language and concept here show a remarkable continuity enduring for over five centuries; in the thirteenth century, Alfonso X promulgated his massive legal code, the *Siete Partidas* (1251–65), in which he proclaimed that in cases of bestiality, "the animal must also be killed, *in order to blot out the remembrance of the act*."[109] Judges in New Spain utilized parallel language to describe their rationale for killing defiled animals—to erase the very memory of the crime through the eradication of the animal body in question. We see similar attacks on memory in the burning of sodomites, but animal bodies were, as always, more vehemently targeted for erasure.

While in early modern Castile, it was common to hang or burn the animals implicated in bestiality cases, in New Spain, it was more typical to kill the animal with a blow to the head or a swift cut to the throat, and to subsequently burn the corpse.[110] The practice of hanging animals in early modern Europe for bestiality is one that, so far as I am aware, was not transposed to New Spain. I speculate this had to do with changing legal practices between medieval and early modern Europe around the late fifteenth century. The hanging of animals seems to be a vestige of medieval animal trials, found all over Europe, in which pigs, donkeys, and other animals were tortured and publicly hanged, sometimes dressed in human clothing, for "crimes" such as having eaten a child or maimed a human.[111] In New Spain, the animals were killed not because they were seen legally as a culpable party but because they had been defiled.

Keith Thomas argues that bestiality was ultimately a "sin of confusion; it was immoral to mix the categories."[112] It was inherently unclean as well because, as Murrin notes, "bestiality lowered a man to the level of a beast, but it also left something human in the animal."[113] None of the bestiality cases analyzed for this study mentioned the possibility of monstrous offspring or hybrid creatures, as has been documented in some European bestiality trials. In the 1783 trial of Julián Viveros, a young cattle herder in the town of Apatzingán—who admitted to having had sex with a mare only after the vicar and ecclesiastical judge used "smooth words" to convince him to tell the truth—there is a vague yet fascinating reference to the *muleto* or "young mule" the mare gave birth to after the fact. The judge mentions that "the beast with which he [carnally] mixed gave birth to a young mule," and orders that the creature be sent to the court by the day that the sentence was to be carried out. The case, however, is incomplete, and there is no information on what that sentence was, or why the offspring of the mare was to be present, though I presume it was so that both the mare and the young mule could be publicly killed, just in case.[114] Authorities recognized, and perhaps feared, the uncleanliness—embodied by the animal, and perhaps even its offspring—that resulted from this confusion of categories.

Punishing the animals was not the reason—at least officially—for killing them. Animal eradication had more to do with a need felt in the community at large for cleansing, a need codified in Leviticus and Deuteronomy about ritual uncleanliness, pollution, and limiting contact with "abominable things."[115] Jonas Liliequist's observation regarding the slaughter of animals implicated in early modern Swedish bestiality trials appears to hold true for New Spain: "Behind the legal terms and arrangements, it is not difficult to discern a sense of the bodily corruption of the animal, especially obvious as an aversion to unclean food."[116] To be certain, when witnesses, animal owners, and secular courts made the decision to kill a violated animal, they were not punishing the animal for the offense to nature but attempting to obliterate the remembrance of the act and to prevent the inadvertent human consumption of the meat, milk, or eggs that came from the tainted creature. The killing and immolation of defiled animals in New Spain ultimately speaks to the human need to eradicate animal bodies that functioned literally and symbolically as the memory of the crime, the legal evidence and physical body on which the crime itself had been enacted.

There is a fascinating archival paradox at work here—one that we will also see in the following chapter, on the Church's "archives of negligence." The ultimate goal of effacing animals implicated in bestiality cases was to "deaden the memory of the act." Many of those very memories, however, came to be archived—permanently in some cases (especially with the increased efforts to digitize archival documents), and less so in others—precisely *because of* the very efforts of colonial authorities to suppress such iterations of sex and de-

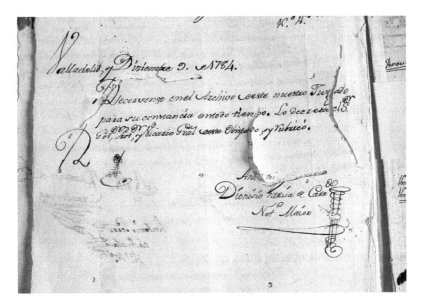

Fig 4.2 Final page of the 1783 bestiality trial of Sebastián Martín. Courtesy of the Archivo Histórico Casa de Morelos, Morelia, Mexico. AHCM, caja 832, exp. 5, fol. 22.

sire. A wonderful example of this archival paradox comes from the 1783 trial of a fifteen-year-old indigenous boy from Almoloyan, Sebastián Martín, who was convicted of sex with a donkey by an ecclesiastical court in Valladolid, Michoacán. The priest and ecclesiastical judge, Manuel José Laso, sentenced the boy to be paraded around town on horseback, nude from the waist up, with a *coroza*—a cone-shaped hat made of paper that was typically used by the Inquisition to shame heretics—on his head, "and on it painted [images of] a man and a donkey."[117] With a town crier publicly proclaiming the boy's crimes, he and the donkey were led to a giant bonfire, with throngs of people following them, where "the donkey's throat was slit and it was thrown into the fire until it was reduced to ashes, which were thrown into the wind."[118]

The boy was subsequently returned to prison, and one week later, it being a holiday and holy day, the judge "commanded that . . . he be placed in the main door of the parochial church, at the time of the largest Mass, standing with his hair loose, his face exposed, a noose around his neck, a crucifix in his hands, and a crown of thorns in his head, and that he be allowed to kneel only between the liturgical preface [the Eucharistic prayer] and the ablutions [when the priest rinses his hands in wine and then in water following the Communion]."[119] Afterward, he was given over to a Spanish resident of the town, who, because of his "God-fearing conscience and well-known virtue," was to take care that the boy be properly raised and fulfill his spiritual penances until he became of legal age. The two-part punishment itself is astonishing, especially as it is one of the few cases in this corpus of documents in which an ecclesiastical court adjudicated bestiality. The symbolic shaming in the entryway of a church for the crime of bestiality is itself unique in our corpus. Particularly intriguing, in light of the donkey's being "reduced to ashes" to erase the memory, is the legal language on the final page of the case file, dated December 9, 1784, which reads: "Reserve [these files] in the Archive of this, our tribunal as evidence *for all time*"—*en todo tiempo* (fig. 4.2).

The animal thus disappears from the archival record, but does so in contradictory ways that leave behind textual traces that are to be preserved "for all time" to come. These records offer us examples of how "the animal emerged as humanity's other," both in the historical past and in the colonial archive itself.[120] Historically, theological discourse has framed bestiality, even more so than sodomy and perhaps even cannibalism, as the epitome of that which contravened "natural law," but scholars of the Iberian Atlantic world have remained largely silent about this act. These cases thus invite us to think through the types of interspecies gazing that characterized everyday human-animal interactions in colonial New Spain—a gazing that involved multiple desires in the very act of seeing animals, and rendering them visible through spectacular deaths. The animals, of course, looked back, though the archives are largely silent on how they did so. Seeing animals archivally—that is, tracing the ways that animal bodies figure into archival documents through chains of witnessing—exposes the epistemological limits of representing (other) animals in the past.

CHAPTER 5

Archives of Negligence

Solicitation in the Confessional

Preserved in the Archivo General de la Nación's Indiferente Virreinal—which gave us several of the sodomy cases discussed earlier—is an extraordinary case of a violation of religious norms. The case revolves around sodomy by a priest, and is, by far, the most extensive case of priestly sodomy that has thus far surfaced in New Spain. Unfortunately for historians, the seventy-seven-folio case does not include a final sentence, but the records that do exist are no less impressive for it. In the early eighteenth century, Father Juan Vallejo Hermosillo voluntarily admitted to several hundred sodomitical encounters, with at least some 115 men, in and around Mexico City. That revelation, however, came with a caveat: all these encounters, he insisted, took place *outside* of the act of confession, which meant that technically he had not committed an act of heresy by defiling the sacrament. As we know, when it came to the other sins against nature, New Spain's secular courts had jurisdiction over the act, whereas the Mexican Inquisition was primarily interested in the theological implications of heretical thoughts.

The case began in an ecclesiastical court in 1712, when Diego Magdaleno, one of Vallejo's mulatto slaves, denounced him for regularly "committing the abominable, obscene, and foul sin of sodomy."[1] Magdaleno testified that during the eleven years he had been working for the priest, he had seen Vallejo lock himself in his private quarters on innumerable occasions with individual men; he had kept his secret for so long because he was afraid of being punished by the priest for denouncing him. According to Magdaleno, among the men were a servant named Juan, a painter named Miguel, and a mulatto named Tibursio. In yet another stunning example of voyeurism, spying through a crack in the unlocked door, Magdaleno said, he had seen with his own eyes

Tibursio, and another man on a different occasion, serve both "as man" and "as woman" with the priest.

Magdaleno himself had resisted the priest's advances, which he also made to a number of boys, including Andrés González and Juan Francisco. As the ecclesiastical judge called forth witnesses for interrogation, they heard initial testimonies from five young men, each with a similar story: Vallejo would offer them food and clothing to enter his bedroom, then he put his hands inside their pants and attempted to commit the nefarious sin with them. One witness had also seen a number of *hombres agembrados*—womanly men—frequently accompany the priest in public, implying that his reputation was not one he sought to conceal.

After corroborating these accounts, on September 5, 1712, the ecclesiastical judge imprisoned Vallejo, sequestered his goods, and took a statement, in which he was initially reticent—at least in comparison to what would come. He first confessed "as a fragile, wretched man, to having committed the said sin of sodomy."[2] Vallejo, who was thirty-seven, originally from Mexico City, and had been ordained as a priest three years prior to his arrest, confessed to having had sex with six men, both before and after ordainment. These men—none of whom he had met in church or during confession—included Tibursio, a mulatto slave named Manuel, a painter named Miguel, a "little black boy" named Nicolás, a mestizo named Miguel, and a light-skinned mulatto named Nicolás, who was coincidentally also in prison for an unrelated sodomy charge. Vallejo also referenced a drunken party he once attended in Mexico City, where he witnessed some seventy men drinking pulque, flirting, hugging, and kissing. He also told the judge that he knew of an inn in which many men, including a light-skinned mulatto nicknamed "Luna," frequently met for sex. It appears Vallejo wanted to leverage the politics of denunciation in his favor by denouncing others.

In his second confession, taken on September 12, 1712, Vallejo radically altered his story. He recounted how he first committed sodomy, at age thirteen, as a bottom to an older slave named Juan de Dios. This happened some seven or eight times, but Vallejo stopped the relationship because the act was physically "hurting him." Those experiences, we might speculate, may have influenced Vallejo to later pursue sexual relationships with boys younger than he was. Far beyond the six men with whom Vallejo initially admitted to having sex, his revised confession was so lengthy and detailed that it took him several days to confess his sins. In this extraordinary confession, Vallejo admitted to having sex with those 115 men, a group that he classified with phenomenal racial specificity: six black men and boys (referred to respectively as *negros* or *negrillos*), fifty-two mulattos, fifteen young indigenous men, nineteen mestizos, two lobos, one Spaniard, one redheaded boy, two *chinos* (Filipinos or their descendants), and seventeen men of unknown identity. Vallejo, in what perhaps amounted to a racial fetish, exhibited a clear preference for dark-skinned mulattos. We are left to wonder how he remembered such details.

While still in prison and awaiting the outcome of his trial, in 1715, Vallejo died of unspecified causes. He received no sentence while alive, and the case against him records nothing more about him after his death. Is it possible that Vallejo, in prison, could have remembered all those individuals with such detail? In dozens of pages of recorded testimony, he gives long lists of the men with whom he had sex, and their frequency: a free mulatto named Juan Manuel (between twelve and fourteen times); a dark-skinned mestizo boy with "an unattractive face" (over forty times); a young indigenous boy who made rosaries (over forty times); Joseph, a mulatto servant who worked on the street of San Bernardo (over thirty times); and an indigenous man named Domingo, who always assumed the bottom (five or six times), among dozens of other men.

Vallejo classified these men by three different categories: their names, their racial designations or skin color, and the number of times he had sex with them. Might Vallejo have kept a private archive, documenting and cataloging each and every one of his sexual encounters? Did he fetishize the very act of documenting these sexual encounters, which perhaps helps explain the sheer volume of detail he was able to recall? And, though it seems unlikely, could he have memorized the details about his sexual encounters with all 115 men? Or, perhaps a better question: how many of these acts were real, how many were fabricated or exaggerated, and how many were a combination of both, improvised or elaborated on as he was giving his testimony? Did he experience some pleasure by recounting these acts to his interrogators? The documents, of course, raise more questions than they answer.

I begin this exploration of solicitation in the confessional with the case of a priest who claimed that his sex life had nothing to do with his duties to perform the sacraments, nor did the encounters take place during confession. Why? Several reasons. First, Vallejo reminds us of the various ways priests forged relationships—emotional, or physical, or both—with laypersons. By *not* soliciting sex in confession, he was in fact protecting himself from serious charges of heresy. The ecclesiastical records of Vallejo's case are likely filed in Indiferente

Virreinal, and not within the files of the Inquisition, for this very reason: Vallejo was tried by an ecclesiastical court, and not by the Inquisition. The case thus illustrates how priests, regardless of their vaunted status in colonial society, could, in theory, be punished for sodomy. Yet we can be assured that Vallejo, unlike a layperson, would not have been sentenced to death, corporeally punished, publicly shamed, or been made to perform labor for extended periods of time. Indeed, there is no archival evidence that *any* priest in New Spain was sentenced to death for sodomy, though in contemporaneous Spain several were. As the first page of Vallejo's case file tells us, were he to have been found guilty of all the allegations against him, the most severe penalty he might have received would have been spiritual: excommunication. That is, he could have been permanently denied membership in the Catholic Church, thereby depriving him of the Eucharist, the other sacraments, and the blessings of ecclesiastical society. For sure this would be a damning punishment for the faithful, but far less so for a priest who harbored doubts about his profession or his faith.

I begin with Vallejo because he introduces us to the vast world of priestly sex but does so in a way that uncomfortably blurs the lines between the worldly and the sacred, between the layperson and the priest. Vallejo and his brethren were seen as God-ordained mediators between humanity and the divine; thus, when priests had sex, they blurred the boundaries of religion. Vallejo, so far as we know, was never accused of heresy. The same, however, cannot be said for many priests who sexually, spiritually, and emotionally abused their female and male parishioners during confession in New Spain. Vallejo too, despite his claims to the contrary, was manipulative, abusive, and vicious according to his denouncers. Magdaleno, who first denounced him on August 17, 1712, ratified his statement a few weeks later to say that he had recently been locked in the priest's quarters against his will. Vallejo made Magdaleno undress, violently spanking and biting him. He then forced Magdaleno to insert his thumb and fingers into the priest's "posterior vessel" and made Magdaleno have sex with him (as a top, because Magdaleno would not consent to being penetrated).[3]

This chapter thus moves us from Vallejo's sexual encounters beyond the church's walls to the tangled reality of priestly sex within sacred space. The Catholic Church has, for centuries, been inattentive in dealing with the sexual abuse of children, adolescents, and adults. This is true whether such acts took place during confession and whether priests or parishioners depicted them as "consensual." The fundamentally unequal relationship between a priest and his parishioner thus distorts the very conditions under which mutual consent is possible (though there are scattered archival cases in which a priest's sexual advances seem to be welcome). By and large, however, as with recently unearthed cases in Ireland and the United States and elsewhere, solicitation cases from New Spain trace long and willfully obscured histories of negligence and cover-ups by church administrators across the three centuries of Spanish colonial rule in New Spain. Together these cases make up what I call an *archives of negligence*—that is, a repository of historical records (created and maintained by the Catholic Church and, more specifically, by the Holy Office of the Mexican Inquisition) that reveal the imbalance of power between priests and their denouncers, and the selective interpretations that inquisitors and other agents of the Catholic Church used to shift the balance of blame away from the Church.

Archives of Abuse

In 1215 the Fourth Lateran Council changed the nature of the interaction between the priest and his congregation by requiring that every Catholic who had attained "the age of reason" confess his or her sins to a qualified priest at least once a year. This precept gave priests an unprecedented opportunity to abuse their positions. The Church had already struggled for centuries with such abuses, as priests committed a wide variety of infractions, from breaking their vows of celibacy and soliciting sex from nuns or parishioners to drinking, gambling, and absenteeism. Another problem that plagued the early Church was sodomy, which several theologians—including Peter Damian (ca. 1007–70), Albert the Great (1200–1280), and Thomas Aquinas (1225–74)—tried to find solutions to.

Catholicism spread, and evolved, and reckoned with the massive challenge of the Protestant Reformation, but the problem of priestly abuses only grew. By 1559 confessional abuse had become so pervasive in Spain that Pope Paul IV issued a briefing to the inquisitors of Granada asserting that priests who sexually abused their confessants were suspected of heresy, and should therefore be subject to the Holy Office of Granada. Subsequently, the task of prosecuting solicitation fell to inquisitors (as opposed to a broader body of ecclesiastical courts) in Spain; these inquisitors were instructed to hand over egregious offenders to secular authorities for execution by fire.[4] The shifting definitions of solicitation in Europe, in turn, influenced the nature and quantity of solicitation cases tried (and archived) by the various tribunals of the Inquisition that Spain and Portugal eventually established in their colonies in Asia, Africa, and the Americas. A papal bull issued on April 14, 1561, authorized the various Inquisitions in Spain and its colonies to investigate and punish priests who solicited women. Yet this bull limited the activities that fell within the purview of solicitation, restricting the crime of solicitation only to women and only to those advances that had taken place during the act of confession itself. It was not until Pope Gregory XV issued the *Universi Dominici Gregis* on August 30, 1622, that solicitation came to encompass all indecent conversations and acts, with women or men, that took place before, after, or during confession in Europe and its colonies.[5] Thus, we see a certain degree of clarity in New Spain: the Mexican Inquisition, established in 1571, determined that the sexual solicitation of both men and women was a crime.

From Vallejo's 1712 case, I want to step back exactly one century to outline a different scene of priestly manipulation. In 1612 don Cristóbal Barrosio de Palacios denounced fray Hernando Ruiz, a Spanish priest living in Oaxaca, to the Mexican Inquisition for making unwanted advances on an adolescent boy.[6] According to Barrosio de Palacios, his neighbor's nephew, a fourteen-year-old Spanish boy named Francisco Sánchez, had been solicited for sexual favors. The story told by Barrosio's neighbor went like this: A few months prior, her nephew, who was then studying with the Jesuits, was making preparations in church for the local Festival of the Cross. There he was met by Ruiz, who took him by the hand and led him to an isolated part of the church, at which time the priest "told him that he wanted to sin with him."[7] Sánchez naïvely asked Ruiz why he would want to sin with him, not being a woman. The priest assured the boy that this made no difference, but this instance did not result in any physical or sexual contact. Rather, it began Ruiz's dogged campaign to tempt the boy. The priest then asked him "if he wanted to go to his house, where he would give him gifts and sleep with him."[8] He provocatively touched the hands and face of the boy, who forcibly pushed the priest away from him. At this point, Sánchez told his aunt, who consulted her neighbor, Barrosio, who in turn denounced Ruiz to the Inquisition. Five other boys (or their family members) told similar stories about Ruiz; he had earned the nickname *siete cabezas*—seven heads—referring to the seven-headed dragon in the Book of Revelations. Ruiz allegedly took the hands of one boy and began to tickle him, told another boy that he was beautiful, and showered yet another boy with amorous words, promising him new clothes and an *agnus dei*, a blessed disc of wax impressed with the figure of a lamb that was used as a protective object of devotion, if he would submit his body to the priest.[9] Ironically, the agnus dei symbolized the virgin flesh of Christ, and the cross that was associated with the lamb suggests the idea of a victim offered in sacrifice. While all these boys resisted Ruiz's attempts, many other boys (solicited by other priests) accepted such "gifts"—the archives mention everything from food, chocolate, candy, clothing, cigarettes, scapulars, romance novels, a place to sleep, absolution for sins, and money—either with enthusiasm or ambivalence or, more likely, some combination of both.

The Holy Office of the Mexican Inquisition, the primary purpose of which was to combat heresy within the Catholic Church, as best as we can tell, conducted a perfunctory investigation into these claims. Once inquisitors were assured that no sexual acts had taken place between Ruiz and the boys, and that he had not solicited anyone in the confessional, he was let off and, as far as we know, was neither punished nor reprimanded. We will encounter this scene—a priest surrounded by numerous young boys, amid rumors, family concern, and inquisitors' prying eyes—again and again. And we will find that, in spite of suspicious circumstantial evidence, or even more shockingly, explicit evidence, Penyak's claim holds true: "Inquisitors frequently neglected to prosecute clerics who solicited other males, a policy that suggests an active cover-up of deviant priestly activity."[10] That cover-up, needless to say, happens partly through the archive, bleeding all too painfully into the present. Anthony Petro, analyzing a twentieth-century archive of Catholic sexual abuse—BishopAccountability .org—tells us that this archive "powerfully demonstrates how sex becomes imbricated in, and produced through, relations of piety, power, and coercion."[11] That murky blend of piety and power is, of course, nothing new; the intimate nature of confession between priest and parishioner in New Spain could, as we will see, incite the very sinful desires that it sought to extirpate.

This chapter builds on an assemblage of forty-one Inquisition cases of clerical sexual (and spiritual) misconduct in which variations on the Vallejo and Ruiz scenarios were played out—largely on boys and male adolescents, though sometimes on females as well. Of those, only a handful were convicted, most often to abjure *de levi*, which meant that they had been found guilty of light suspicion of heresy (see tables 4.1 and 4.2). In the archives of colonial New Spain, there are hundreds, if not thousands, of cases of priests soliciting sexual favors from women during confession. And while the solicitation of female penitents by priests in the Iberian Atlantic world has received ample historiographical attention, little scholarship has been devoted to the solicitation of males in the confessional—a fact that is partly a reflection of the colonial archive itself.

We know about these solicitation cases and other instances of priestly sex because, at some point, a denunciation was made and recorded in the files of the Inquisition (or some other ecclesiastical court with a wider purview). Such denunciations had to be documented, but they did not necessarily lead to action by the inquisitorial authorities. Inquisitorial organization and procedure are important here. The Mexican Inquisition itself was normally staffed by two general inquisitors in Mexico City, along with dozens of secretaries, *alguaciles* (bailiffs), *fiscales* (prosecutors), *calificadores* (members of the secular clergy who served as theological evaluators and often influenced whether a denunciation would develop into a case), and *consultores* (theologians who offered counsel). The Inquisition also relied on a vast network of *comisarios* (locally appointed judges who were able to hear trials outside of Mexico City), *familiares* (anonymous informants who reported on the potentially deviant practices of the population at large), and a number of notaries, lawyers (*procuradores*), doctors, and jailers, among others.

It was the job of the *promotor fiscal*—the public prosecutor—to examine recorded denunciations in order to decide whether there were grounds for filing a formal charge against the accused.[12] As in the case of Ruiz, the administrative apparatus of the Holy Office did not charge the vast majority of those who were denounced to the Inquisition with heresy or any other crime. Of the tens of thousands of denunciations that came before inquisitors between the years 1522 and 1820—divided among 1,759 volumes in Mexico's national archive—most were not worth pursuing or prosecuting. In some cases, the denunciations were for crimes over which the Inquisition had no jurisdiction—as in the case of sodomy and bestiality, so long as there were no signs of heresy. Many more may have not been given the attention they deserved by an overworked and underfunded inquisitorial administration. Others were not corroborated, and still others were willfully ignored.

Sifting through these records of solicitation, we get a unique glimpse at the alleged actions of priests but also occasionally at what everyday women and men were actually confessing to their priests. Inquisitors, for example, encouraged testimony about the types of questions that the accused priests had asked and, more importantly, the penitent's reactions to those questions. The Inquisition's records, in this sense, contain a privileged view of when and how parishioners—be they Spanish, indigenous, black, mestizo, or mulatto—

¶ Dixi confitebor aduerſum me iniuſtitiam
meam Domino :

Et tu remiſiſti impietatem peccati mei.
Pſal. 31.

Fig 5.1 Woodcut from Juan Bautista's *Confessionario en lengua mexicana y castellana* (1599), depicting the ideal confession, with an angel guiding the priest's line of questioning, and a devil guiding the parishioner's answers. Courtesy of the Lilly Library, Indiana University, Bloomington, Indiana.

thought that their modesty, or honor, or privacy, or some combination of all three, had been breached by the words or actions of unscrupulous priests. These records thus allow historians to probe the ordinary life of the community, as gossip, rumor, and scandal so often played a part in accusations lodged against priests; from these cases thus emerge the anxieties of the era, around everything from the Catholic principles of sacerdotal celibacy to the unequal power relationships that unfolded within the confessional.

The relationship between a priest and his parishioners, as we will see, could evolve in any number of ways (fig. 5.1). A priest and his penitent occasionally embarked on a relationship that was both sexual and consensual (there is ample documentation of torrid love affairs, for example, between priests and women, be they nuns or laypersons). More commonly, however, there was some degree of coercion on the part of the priest. The priest could be successful or could be refused, as in the case of Ruiz (if the allegations against him were true, that is). If the priest was successful, the solicited parishioner could choose to keep quiet about what had happened, or tell friends, family, another priest, or formally denounce the priest to the Inquisition. If the act happened in the confessional, thus profaning the sacrament, or if a priest uttered heretical or blasphemous statements during the act, or in an attempt to incite the act, inquisitors and the prosecutor would be more likely to take the accusation seriously.

Often, however, the Inquisition only launched a serious investigation into a priest if there were repeated denunciations of sex in the confessional, from different individuals in multiple parishes, over a long period of time. These many possibilities created a complex archival landscape of denunciation, prosecution, and concealment. To map that landscape, we begin by exploring the world of confessional confusion, and then move on to denunciations that were exaggerated, those that were ignored, and, finally, those that were followed and prosecuted. The further we delve into this paper trail, the more evidence we find of negligence and abuse on the part of priests, local church officials, inquisitors, and bishops. These archives of abuse elucidate how confession in New Spain was, for many confessants, a concurrent space of intimacy, expiation, and confusion.

Confessional Confusions

Among Catholics, confession is one of the most private, intimate, and potent aspects of religious life. Given the ideal of confession as a private conversation between priest and penitent, sitting side by side—the Council of Trent (1545–63) explicitly called it the "secret sacramental confession"—it is difficult to know what goes on in confessional exchanges, past and present. There is, however, another facet of confession that is quite the opposite, and is often based on real-life questions that priests did, and were counseled to, ask their penitents. The confessional manual is a genre of writing that spread from Spain to its colonies in the Americas and the Philippines with Catholic missionaries, and which proliferated immensely under colonialism. Whereas confessional manuals in Spain and Portugal were written in Latin or in the vernacular, in New Spain they were frequently bilingual, as we have seen, written in Spanish and an indig-

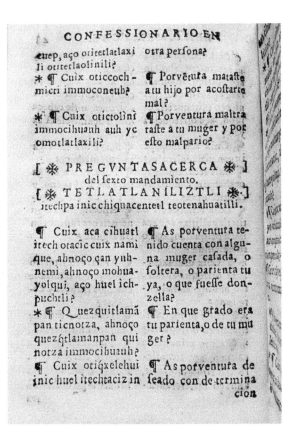

Fig 5.2 Folio 48v from Juan Bautista's *Confessionario en lengua mexicana y castellana* (1599), on which the questions on the Sixth Commandment, in both Spanish and Nahuatl, begin. Courtesy of the John Carter Brown Library at Brown University, Providence, Rhode Island.

enous language. They were typically penned with the Spanish in one column and the indigenous translation in the other, as in Franciscan fray Juan Bautista's 1599 *Confessionario en lengua mexicana y castellana*, written in Nahuatl and Spanish (fig. 5.2). Spanish-Nahuatl confessional manuals were most common in New Spain; also popular were those printed in Spanish and Purépecha, Yucatecan Maya, Mixe, Zapotec, Tagalog (in the Philippines), and other native languages. The manuals themselves consisted of admonitory speeches and of lists of questions, with hypothetical answers, specific to each of the Ten Commandments, and were used by priests who needed to hear confessions from native peoples in their own tongue.

As a genre, confessional manuals from New Spain are a rich set of texts, full of detail and description. Missionaries, who dedicated years or even decades of study to attain fluency in one or more native languages, penned the vast majority of confessional manuals, partly based on their own experiences catechizing and confessing native peoples. The manuals themselves occasionally have lurid interests lurking behind their structure and content, especially in relation to the Sixth Commandment, "Thou shalt not commit adultery." Bartolomé de Alva's 1634 Nahuatl-Spanish *Confessionario mayor* is one of many that explicitly phrases questions to native parishioners about a litany of lustful sins, including sodomy, bestiality, masturbation, incest, witchcraft, rape, prostitution, pimping, and drunkenness. Alva offers the following questions to guide priests' confessional encounters with Nahua parishioners:

> Have you had concubines? Have you licentiously enjoyed yourself? Have you given yourself over to earthly sin and lust? Or did you have sexual relations and sin with one [woman] or a few? Married women? Widows? Single women? Or completely virgin maidens? Is one of them your relative or relation or your older sister, your sister-in-law, your niece or your relative or offspring within the first, second [or] third degree [of consanguinity?] When you had sexual relations with your relatives, were you drunk or not? Did you repeatedly force her? Did you have sexual relations with her by means of fear and terror? How many times did you have sexual relations with each one of the women you mentioned? How many married women have you had sexual relations with, and how many times? Perhaps when you got drunk and lost your sense you fell into the abominable sin of sodomy, having something to do with another man? Perhaps you were responsible for the frightful sin, unworthy of being done, of having sexual relations with a four-legged animal or a beast? Did you sometimes touch your body thinking of some woman? Did you then spill your semen, you thinking that it was just as if you had really had sexual relations with that person? Did you deceive some woman? And if it is a woman, she will be asked: did you deceive some man, putting something on your body so that he caught some illness when you had sexual relations with him or he had sexual relations with you? When you had sexual relations with your wife or some other woman: was she menstruating? Was she with her monthly periods? Answer. Yes/no.

> Here is what the women will be asked. Were you menstruating sometime when your husband or some other man had sexual relations with you? Did you repeatedly feel your body, thinking of a man, and wanting him to sin with you? Did you do it to yourself with your hands, bringing to a conclusion your lust? When your husband was drunk: did he have sex with you

where you are a woman, or sometimes did he do the disgusting sin to you [sodomy]? Did you restrain him? Were you responsible for dirty words with which you provoked and excited women? When you cohabited with some woman: did you show and reveal what was bad in front of those who had not yet seen the sin? Did you ever pimp for someone? On account of you, did they know themselves through sin, you yourself provoking a woman for whom you had summoned someone? Did you know the failings of your mother or your father, your children and your relatives, your household dependents, that they were cohabiting, and you did not restrain them? When they were drunk and intoxicated in your home, there committing before you sins unworthy of doing: didn't you restrain them? Did you just look at them?[13]

These excerpts should not be seen as guides to what individual Nahua women and men were actually doing in private; rather, they lay out the Church's concerns—embedded within the personal interests and apprehensions of the author—with the broad sweep of sexual conduct that fell under the purview of the Sixth Commandment. Not surprisingly, however, generations of scholars have latched onto these manuals to try to uncover the intimate dynamics of confession between priest and penitent, especially under colonial rule. The result is that we have a distorted vision of what confession did, and how it functioned in practice. Henry Charles Lea, in his 1867 *History of Sacerdotal Celibacy in the Christian Church*, posited: "The power of the confessional, one of the most effective instrumentalities invented by the ingenuity of man for enslaving the human mind, was peculiarly liable to abuse in sexual matters."[14] Lea's language reflects centuries of Protestant propaganda about confession, but his remark also reflects a theme that Michel Foucault, over a century later, theorized in the first volume of *The History of Sexuality*: "One does not confess without the presence of a partner who is not simply the interlocutor but the authority who requires the confession, prescribes and appreciates it, and intervenes in order to judge, punish, forgive, console, and reconcile."[15]

These formulations come a century apart but overlap, offering a particular view of confession—seen as a mechanism of social control performed and administered by a mediating agent between humans and God—in which the power of the priest can be reified, complicated, and even subverted through the act of confessing. Colonial confession is even more vexed, especially as the manuals *appear* to offer evidence that confession in New Spain functioned, as one scholar asserts, as a "refined tool of ideological subjection and of domination over the individual."[16] Other scholars echo similar claims, writing of "control mechanisms" bound up in the penitential discipline of native peoples, or seeing confession as an "instrument of spiritual conquest."[17] Here, confession becomes the privileged site of sexual encounter between colonizers and colonized. Such interpretations, however, are built on the assumption that priests perfectly transcribed confessional manuals into practice.

Beyond these theories, the intended meanings of the Christian sacrament of confession were inevitably altered in translation. The Nahuatl term that missionaries selected to signify the Catholic sacrament of confession, *neyolmelahualiztli*, literally translated to "straightening one's heart."[18] By rendering confession as such, Louise Burkhart notes, confession appears to have presented Nahuas with a unique opportunity to cure internal disruptions and all types of ills, both moral and material, in ways that may have differed from what priests and friars had in mind. Much to the dismay of some missionaries, if we are to believe their reports, many native peoples evaded questions during confession, gave equivocal answers, feigned contrition, and failed to fully grasp the Church's intended meaning behind confession: to obtain absolution for sins committed and to reconcile oneself with the community of the faithful.

Missionaries' frustrations with native misunderstandings of confession are evident in the very pages of confessional manuals. Fray Bartolomé de Alva, for instance, lamented, "You natives, even though you are cohabiting for two [or] three years already with a woman and sinning with her every day and every night, when the priest and confessor questions you about how many times you have sinned with her, you just reply: 'Two times, three times.' And you all make the same statement, and with this you really damage your confession."[19] Even after a greater number of priests gained proficiency in Nahuatl, the persistence of linguistic and conceptual barriers "dramatically heightened the flaws in communication between friars and Indians," especially in the realm of confession.[20]

Confession had still other practical limits in the Spanish colonies. Indigenous communities, for example, often complained that there were not enough priests to administer the sacrament. Given the relative scarcity of priests in many corners of New Spain, it would be an error to assume that confession served primarily as a tool for spiritual domination (or that it was an effective one). In the Philippines, for example, by the first half of the seventeenth century, fewer than three hundred priests had converted over half a million Filipinos, making the systematic administration of confession virtually impossible. Thus, it is safe to say that many colonized peoples simply did not, or could not, go to confession. Reports also mention the long distances to outlying indigenous towns that many priests had to travel to administer the sacraments.[21] The scarcity of priests adequately trained in indigenous languages further limited the administration of sacraments.[22] It is thus unrealistic to assume that the voluminous questions in the bilingual confessional guides were regularly posed, in anywhere near their comprehensive wording, to a significant segment of New Spain's population, indigenous or otherwise.

Ultimately, confession was less an efficient tool of domination than a "confused discourse in which priests and penitents negotiated meaning through their different interpretations of language and symbols."[23] We see as much in that priests were sometimes seduced by the line of questioning they themselves incited. Some confessional manual authors were aware of the effects questions regarding lust could have on confessors. Martín de Azpilcueta, a Jesuit missionary from the Iberian Peninsula, was adamant in his 1556 *Manual de confessores y penitentes* that priests should avoid asking unnecessary questions regarding the Sixth Commandment, so not to incite concupiscence or provoke "involuntary pollutions" in their minds and bodies.[24] These are instances in which "the intensity of the confession renewed the questioner's curiosity; the pleasure discovered fed back to the power that encircled it."[25] We see this at work when priests solicited male penitents *after* becoming sexually excited by the confessional exchange. In 1659, for example, an unidentified mulatto man in Mexico City confessed to his priest that he had committed sodomy, expecting to be subject to some appropriate penance. Instead, he was surprised to find himself being propositioned by the priest (a solicitation he accepted), who no doubt took the man's confession as a sign that his advances might succeed.[26]

Another Inquisition case tells the story of Gerónimo Calbo, whom criminal courts sentenced to death in 1658, along with la Cotita and thirteen others.[27] The night prior to his execution, inquisitors questioned Calbo about his relationship with a Jesuit priest named Father Matheo (for whom inquisitors were still searching). Calbo recalled how three years earlier, when he was sixteen and sick with typhus, he "lost his judgment" due to fever and confessed to a priest that he had previously committed the nefarious sin with an Indian. The priest, likely interpreting Calbo's confession as an opportunity, touched the boy's arms, face, chest, and then his "shameful parts," fondling the boy.[28] On two subsequent occasions Calbo said he visited the priest in his cell and, accepting chocolates and money, repeatedly had sex. Inquisitors never located

Father Matheo, and Calbo was executed in Mexico City. Other documents tell similar tales, including the 1799 Inquisition case of José Gregorio Zebrian, who initiated over forty sexual encounters with males after voyeuristically hearing their confessions and becoming excited by their sins of lust.[29] Women, with even greater frequency, denounced priests for having asked excessive questions about masturbation, menstruation, conjugal life, their undergarments, and other intimate matters.[30]

These archival narratives, and those that follow, illustrate the abundant opportunities for confessional confusions, prior to, during, and after the ritualized exchange between priest and penitent. If the confessional manuals represent one realm in which confusion could arise, the real-world interactions between priest and penitent offered many more. Moving from the confessional manuals to archived cases of solicitation, we see not only how the practice of confession entered the historical record but also how allegations of priestly misconduct elicited contradictory responses, individually and institutionally. Both exaggerated accounts and more accurate representations of priestly abuse could be filed away and institutionally ignored, followed with a certain disinterest, or corroborated and prosecuted. The difference depended partly on the particulars of the case, and even more so on the goals of a religious institution that had long buried such cases deep within its own archives. These archived records of solicitation hold invaluable clues to the ways that religion and spirituality were experienced by the inhabitants of New Spain, and they repeatedly reveal how that experience unfolds at the intersections of the private, the civic, and the sacred.

Native Tongues in New Spain

One of the more remarkable (and heretical) cases of priestly abuse to be found in the archives is that of fray Esteban Rodríguez, a Franciscan who was tried by the Mexican Inquisition in the first half of the sixteenth century for the "solicitation of boys in the act of confession" (fig. 5.3). Nearly all the cases I analyze in this chapter come from Mexico's Archivo General de la Nación, but this particular case is now part of the "Mexican Inquisition Papers" at the Huntington Library in San Marino, California. This collection, which spans 1525 to 1822, is made up of ninety-three trials that were once part of the archives of the Holy Office of the Mexican Inquisition (although there is no information on how or why they were taken from those archives).[31]

Fig 5.3 Title page of the 1622 Inquisition trial against Franciscan friar Esteban Rodríguez for soliciting boys in the confessional. Courtesy of the Huntington Library, San Marino, California. HUNT, vol. 15, HM 35109, Mexican Inquisition Papers.

In this section I focus on native tongues and the distortion of dogma in the Inquisition case of Rodríguez, one of hundreds of priests who was tried for solicitation in the confessional (though the vast majority were guilty of soliciting women). In its metonymic sense, "tongue" is a figure of speech that is used to signify a language or a body of languages. The tongue is the linguistic means through which European missionaries translated the tenets of Catholicism into dozens of languages. Indeed, Rodríguez's proficiency in multiple Mesoamerican languages was central to the eventual outcome of the Inquisition case against him. In its more literal sense, of course, "tongue" refers to the primary organ through which he elicited the boys' confessions that excited him so, and through which he verbally distorted dogma to coax them into sexual situations. The boys' tongues—desired by the priest linguistically and, perhaps with even more fervor, corporeally—mediated the dialogue with their priest. Rodríguez's file, made up of several accusations, ratified testimonies, confessions, and petitions, begins in 1620 and ends in 1640—another reminder of the vast expanse of time over which some Inquisition cases took shape. The themes that emerge here articulate the pervasive relationship between the demands of priestly celibacy, the colonial impulse to catechize, and the (coercive) erotics of confession.

To best understand the case of fray Esteban Rodríguez, I turn first to New Spain's complex linguistic landscape, and to the priests and missionaries who proselytized in native tongues. Catholic missionaries were greatly aided in their efforts to preach throughout New Spain by a growing body of native-language dictionaries, grammars, and catechisms penned largely by priests and grammarians—many of whom identified as Franciscan, Dominican, or Jesuit— throughout the colonial period. While proficiency in indigenous languages varied greatly among Spanish priests throughout New Spain, Francisco Moya de Contreras, the third archbishop of Mexico, made it a requirement for rural priests to possess knowledge of indigenous languages when he implemented the *Ordenanza del Patronazgo* in 1574.[32]

When his Inquisition trial began in 1626, Rodríguez was a Franciscan friar, confessor, and local superior of the convent of Tlaxcalilla in the northern silver-mining province of Zacatecas.[33] It was customary, for the solicitation cases that the Inquisition prosecuted, for several denunciations to be lodged locally with priests or commissaries of the Inquisition in diverse parishes, often from several towns and provinces over the span of many years. If inquisitors found grounds to charge a priest with crimes, these denunciations were corroborated and centralized in the archives of the Holy Office in Mexico City. The case of Rodríguez fits this pattern, though it is uncertain exactly when the case preserved at the Huntington Library was compiled into one file. Interestingly, the solicitation trial of Rodríguez is (literally) affixed to the Inquisition case of another Rodríguez—Domingo Díaz, alias Domingo Rodríguez, from Portugal (mistakenly referred to as "Esteban Rodríguez" in some of the documents)— who was tried from 1620 to 1625 for practicing and spreading Judaism in New Spain. The file itself is chronologically out of order, and it appears inquisitors or scribes, at one point confusing these two individuals for the same person, merged the records of their cases into one file. The two trials are stitched together as one *expediente*, or file, with the 1620 date written by another hand.

On April 15, 1622, during Lent, a Purépecha man from the town of Uruapan in Michoacán, Antonio Juan Apatzi—a widowed mineworker in his midtwenties—made the first documented denunciation against Rodríguez. Apatzi said that one year earlier, on the second week of Lent, he had gone to confess his sins to the priest, who spoke both Purépecha and Nahuatl, in the convent of Tlaxcalilla, where he had been working in the mines. According to his testimony, one afternoon Rodríguez had been confessing Indians in church. When Apatzi knelt down and confessed his sins, which included "drunkenness and sensualities," in his native Purépecha (though he also spoke Nahuatl and Spanish), the priest told him his penance, absolved him of his sins, and requested that he wait for him to finish confessing three others. Later the priest led Apatzi to his cell, latched the door, told him to get on his knees, and asked him "if he had committed any other sins with women in front of any images of Our Lady."[34] The fact that no confessional manual advised that priests ask their parishioners such questions suggests that the priest likely experienced some excitement inquiring about the pollution of religious icons.

Perplexed, Apatzi replied that he had already confessed his sins and had nothing else to say, whereupon "still kneeling down, the priest told him (urging and persuading him in the Purépecha language) to take out his shameful parts. Perturbed, fearful, and confused, he always replied that he would not." Then Rodríguez "put his left hand inside the fly of his pants and took out his member, stimulating and rubbing it with his palm closed, in order to make him fall into pollution."[35] The priest asked him repeatedly if he wanted to "spill his seed," and Apatzi repeatedly replied in the negative. At this point, Rodríguez told Apatzi that he "wanted to say a prayer for him" and, still masturbating him with his left hand, he took the cord of his religious habit in his right, and with it made the sign of the cross over Apatzi's genitals, "moving his lips as if he were praying, for about the time it took to say the Ave María."[36] After this, Rodríguez abruptly sent Apatzi on his way.

Certain spaces, like the priest's cell, took on legal and theological significance in the Inquisition's investigations of solicitation. The question of when and where individuals were solicited, and whether such acts occurred before, during, or after confession, was one of the determining factors in the prosecution of the alleged offender. The Catholic Church introduced the confessional box in Europe, with its partition physically dividing priest and penitent (often through a side grille or wooden window), in the sixteenth century as a result of the Counter-Reformation's attempt to limit and control priestly abuses of their penitents. Even when the confessional box was used, there were ample opportunities for physical contact with the priest in question. Ideally, the priest sat in the seat, the penitent sat outside, and a small wooden window (just barely

Fig 5.4 Colonial confessional box (*penitenciario*) in Mexico City's main cathedral, the Catedral Metropolitana. The penitent would sit outside the box, on one side, and would speak with the priest through the small grille. Photo by the author, 2016.

visible in fig. 5.4) would lift up, through which the two would communicate. The adoption of the confessional box was slow, gradual, and uneven throughout Spain and its colonies. Henry Charles Lea discovered that even as late as the eighteenth century, the Spanish tribunals of the Inquisition were still trying to enforce the use of the confessional during confession, suggesting the ingrained habit of priests hearing confession anywhere in the church that happened to be convenient.[37]

In New Spain, although it was required that women be confessed in the confessional, as far as we know, the Mexican Inquisition never issued any edicts asserting that male penitents were only to be confessed in the confessional. Priests were therefore technically allowed to confess male penitents in any part of the church or convent, which ultimately led to a number of abuses, as in the case of Rodríguez.[38] Some four years after Apatzi lodged his denunciation in Michoacán, which inquisitors did not initially look into, priests in Zacatecas received new denunciations of Rodríguez. In 1626 Francisco de Arévalo, a Spaniard in his early twenties, denounced Rodríguez for events that had taken place three years earlier in the same convent of Tlaxcalilla. Rodríguez asked him to take out his "shameful parts" shortly after he had confessed "many sins that he had committed with diverse women." The priest touched the boy, who could not get an erection, at which point Rodríguez said it was necessary for him to utter a special prayer. In the end, the boy did not receive the said prayer, saying, "Father, there is no way that I can get excited, even if I wanted to."[39] That same year, two other boys, Diego Balça and Alonso Gómez Montesinos, came forth with parallel stories of the priest masturbating them in his cell. Rodríguez's cell seemed to be, in the words of Mark Jordan, a "site of extraordinary trials for the flesh . . . [and] extraordinary intimacy between men."[40] In the end a total of nine individuals denounced the priest, all of whom Rodríguez solicited in Tlaxcalilla or in the nearby province of San Luis Potosí between 1620 and 1626.

Several other denunciations were lodged *after* the Inquisition imprisoned Rodríguez in June 1626, all from when the priest was serving in Tlaxcalilla and Zacatecas. One such denunciation was lodged in 1627 by thirty-year-old Juan Alonso in the town of Querétaro, just east of Mexico City. Some seven years earlier, Alonso had gone to church with another boy to confess their sins. At one point, the priest asked "if he had been sodomitical [*somético*] and if he had incurred any sins from behind?"[41] Alonso said that he had not, but that as a young boy he "often played [by] taking out his member, and the other boys theirs, and when they became excited, they would rub their members against one another."[42] This was a sin that, according to Rodríguez, could only be absolved by Alonso exposing his genitals and allowing the cord of the priest's habit to be placed on it. Then Rodríguez caressed him "until he came to pollution and spilled his seed in the said fray Esteban's hand, and the said seed fell from it onto the said priest's habit."[43] Afterward, Alonso expressed his confusion at the course of events, asking the priest if he was going to be accused of the sin he had just incurred. Rodríguez replied that God would forgive the boy if he carried out his penance. Afterward, Alonso went to the patio where his friend was waiting for him, and entered the church one more time to pray before leaving.

In August 1626 Rodríguez was placed in the Inquisition's secret prisons; his personal belongings were confiscated and documented. In his first hearing,

Rodríguez, who was originally from the town of San Felipe in Michoacán, voluntarily confessed that his unorthodox prayers for men began fourteen years earlier, in 1612, when a man confessed to bestiality "with all types of animals." Rodríguez told inquisitors that, having read how Saint Francis performed miracles with the cord of his religious attire, he believed that his cord might have the same effect. He absolved the man of his sins, and then touched his genitals three times with the cord of his habit while reciting the prayer of Saint Anthony of Padua—a measure that apparently turned out to be effective since the man later affirmed that the prayers were beneficial; he never again committed bestiality or incest with his sister.[44] Thus convinced that his method worked, Rodríguez told inquisitors that he continued administering these penile prayers to a number of men, including a certain Father Juan de Mora (who had committed several sexual sins), on whom his ritual ministrations also miraculously worked. It was not until some seven years later that Rodríguez began to caress his male parishioners alongside his prayers, though according to him he never did this out of pleasure but only to help them.

Needless to say, scandalized inquisitors admonished Rodríguez, clarifying that they had never heard of any confessional manual that described how one should uncover their "dishonest parts" to be absolved of sins related to the Sixth Commandment. Begging for mercy, Rodríguez remorsefully acknowledged the severity of his sins. In several hearings with inquisitors over the course of two months, Rodríguez "remembered" other occasions in which he had administered his prayers, including to a mestizo who confessed to incest and "bestial acts," and to one man who confessed to having had sex with a woman in church. Whether these men the priest remembered were the same as those who denounced him is uncertain. It is clear that Rodríguez used the confessional manual questions about the Sixth Commandment as a means of learning which of his male parishioners had committed sins of lust and gauging their potential to receive his prayers, blessing his spiritual sons' penises with his cord in the form of the cross. Rodríguez also said that he was a priest who was "ignorant" in several matters and that he could barely understand Latin, but that he could confess parishioners in several native languages.

Though prosecutor and inquisitors believed Rodríguez to have committed sodomy and other related sins (including masturbation) with several men, the priest never confessed to as much in the multiple interrogations over the course of 1626 and the first half of 1627. The prosecutor, in a unique request, demanded the priest be tortured to tell the truth and then punished to the full extent of the law, but the Inquisition treated Rodríguez leniently and never subjected him to torture—yet another example of the favoritism shown to priests in comparison to laypersons. On July 15, 1627, the Inquisition sentenced Rodríguez to abjure de levi—of light suspicion of heresy—and to four years of confinement in a convent. They also exiled him from Tlaxcalilla and San Luis Potosí for a period of ten years, and they stripped him of his privilege to administer confession. We will never know the sincerity of Rodríguez's remorse, the meanings behind his acts, or the extent to which he (or others) may have believed that the cord from his habit was actually imbued with ritual or fetishistic powers.

The paper trail, however, does not end there. In 1630 a priest from the monastery where he spent four years in reclusion requested that he, once again, be granted the privilege to administer confession in Zacatecas because of his fluency in several native tongues. A 1631 correspondence, included in his file and penned by a priest, states that for many years Rodríguez was an example for all in the monastery, exhibiting suffering, patience, and humility without fail. Finally, almost a decade later, on August 1, 1640, church officials, citing the dire need for priests fluent in native tongues, reinstated Rodríguez's license to administer confession, oddly enough, only to men. Perhaps this is an example of an effort, both conscious and unconscious, on the part of ecclesiastics to ignore or deny sodomy among the clergy. Or, maybe officials responsible for this decision never actually read Rodríguez's case, merely glancing at the phrase "solicitation in the confessional," and assumed the victims were women. In any case, such a decision is difficult to understand given the many boys and men Rodríguez had abused.

Rodríguez's own plea, which appears in an unnumbered folio in the middle of the case, most likely out of chronological order, gives some sense of the logic behind the Church's decision to reinstate his right to administer confession. After years of confinement in the convent, Rodríguez stated: "I am an elderly friar, son of good parents [i.e., with *limpieza de sangre* and no Jewish, Indian, or black relatives], and I confess my crimes with true repentance of them, and I will naturally live few more years, now that I am already a minister so necessary for the new conversions [of Indians] because I speak four languages, some of the most difficult that there are in this said province [Zacatecas], which are Nahuatl, Otomi, Purépecha, and Guachichil, in which I have administered for a period of thirty years."[45] Simply put, there was an urgent need in the mid-seventeenth century to continue proselytizing, which this case shows could come very much at the expense of native peoples.

Fluency and Leniency

We see similar patterns of negligence as far as the Philippines, a Spanish colonial possession from 1521 to 1898. The late eighteenth-century Inquisition case of fray Agustín María—an Augustinian missionary who lived in the Philippine Islands and was fluent in one or more local languages—resonates with that of Rodríguez, but with crucial differences. María's Inquisition file, which spans from 1771 to 1796, was initiated when Manuel Martín, an "Indian" from the town of Bezeña in the province of Oton, denounced him. In 1771 Martín accused the priest, who was then in his midforties and living in Manila, of requiring him to perform unorthodox penance.[46] Immediately following the confession of his sins, which he likely recounted in his native Hiligaynon (colloquially known as Ilongo) or possibly in Tagalog, the priest asked him "if he was willing to receive a penance of lashes," to which he responded that he would do whatever was required of him to make a good confession.[47]

The priest then led Martín to his cell, where, in the accuser's words, "he made him take off his underwear and kneel down, during which he was pinching and touching the upper part of his body down to the lower part, trying to uncover his shameful parts, which he was hiding with his hands."[48] The confessant resisted these advances, and told María that God would see all his actions on Judgment Day. The priest refused to absolve Martín of his sins, and commanded that he return the following Saturday (after he more fully "examined his conscience"), which he reluctantly did. Martín returned to the priest's private cell, where he encountered another Filipino man whose sins had also not been absolved by the priest because "his confession was also *tiao tiao*, that is, halfhearted [*de cosa de poco mas o menos*]."[49] Here, Martín's denunciation concludes, and we do not find out if the priests ever absolved either of their sins.

The very presence of the term *tiao tiao* in the court records is telling: the term itself appears to be neither Hiligaynon (spoken in the western Visayas, where the town of Oton is located) nor Tagalog (spoken in central and southern Luzon, where Manila is located) but rather Chinese, or, more precisely, a Hokkien or a Hakka word that was likely introduced to the Philippines by diverse communities of Chinese traders.[50] The presence of the term is one rare instance where indigenous words seep into the archival document: in doing so, it evinces some of the cultural and linguistic complexity of diverse diasporic communities in the Spanish colonial Philippines. Its presence subtly challenges the very process of misinscription; *tiao tiao* also hints at the possibility that the parishioners could be deliberately evasive in their confessions, as so many Spanish priests complained.

Between 1775 and 1784, another three Filipino men from diverse towns denounced the same priest, Agustín María, for privately whipping them and for explicit acts of masturbation and sodomy, sometimes ejaculating on the buttocks of the men. In one case, María made the penitent whip and masturbate him. One man responded to these advances, telling the priest "in the language of this land that the doctrine of the catechism told that such sins were very serious, and Father María responded that that was a lie."[51] One Filipina woman also denounced him for similar acts of solicitation and whipping. In each instance, the priest's unorthodox penance was levied in exchange for the absolution of sins that penitents had revealed.

María was imprisoned in July 1784, after years of sporadic denunciations, pointing again to the Church's protection of priests who were fluent in native languages throughout New Spain. The records of María's case are incomplete, though part of his confession is documented. Asking for forgiveness from God and the Holy Office, María admitted to habitually "giving confessants their penance with his own hand, and that with the pain of the whip, they writhed and uncovered their own flesh [*descubrian sus carnes*]; he would dishonestly touch them under the pretense of making them stay in one place and not squirm, and in this was his sin."[52] In total, he confessed to soliciting twenty-three men and four women in the colonial Philippines, and though he did not specify their identities, we can assume that most, if not all, made their confessions to the priest in one or more of the native languages in which María had gained proficiency. He was sentenced in 1786.

Though the Inquisition case is incomplete, a crucial document exists in the archives, which reveals both the priest's punishment and his ultimate fate.[53] The consequences for María were analogous to Rodríguez's punishments: banishment from Manila, reclusion in a monastery for ten years, spiritual penances, and loss of the privilege to administer confession. The document references a 1792 letter written by fray Gergorio Gallego, provincial superior of the Augustinian order in the Philippines, stating that as a result of having spent many years in reclusion and exhibiting good behavior, María was reinstated as a priest in a convent some twenty leagues from Manila, where he was, after some eight years, once again allowed to preach and administer confession to native Filipinos. The Inquisition cases of fray Esteban Rodríguez in Mexico and fray Agustín María in the Philippines are exemplary of how archives of negligence took shape over long periods of time.

Abuse and Its Exaggerations

Priests throughout New Spain were denounced for any number of alleged crimes: charging exorbitant fees for services, violently punishing parishioners or sexually abusing them, getting drunk and acting violently, maintaining mistresses and fathering children, and profaning the sacraments. Historians have rightly warned against using criminal and Inquisition cases to reconstruct historical realities. Kevin Terraciano, for one, tells us that not all the testimonies in any given Inquisition case "are entirely credible, especially considering how both Spaniards and native peoples used the inquisitorial process to defame their enemies."[54] Indeed, in the solicitation cases I examine here, there is ample evidence that allegations were sometimes exaggerated or the truth simply not told. Yet rather than discredit the validity of claims that are documented in the archive's files of the Inquisition, we should analyze the complex reasons behind why individuals and communities may have produced certain narratives of "truth," blurring the lines between fact and fiction.

Accusations of solicitation were especially prone to distortion; yet it is also true that many priests did eventually admit to at least some of their infractions. So, while we might want to believe that most priests in New Spain properly performed their duties and fulfilled their sacerdotal obligations, we know that many did not. With this in mind, I turn to two extensive seventeenth-century cases of priests, one from Oaxaca and the other from New Mexico, whose indigenous parishioners accused them of sodomy, solicitation, and other abuses. Rather than fetishize the representation of "truth" in the accusations, I focus on the calculated tendency to exaggerate charges against priests who were perceived as being abusive in more ways than one. As solicitation denunciations went hand in hand with accusations of other abuses, rumors and partial truths about the lascivious desires of certain priests rapidly circulated throughout local communities in New Spain.

In 1609 dozens of Maya parishioners from the largely indigenous towns of Hocabá, Sanlahcat, Yaxcabá, and Hoctún, all in the Yucatán Peninsula, denounced a Spanish priest named Cristóbal de Valencia for solicitation, attempted sodomy, oral sex, and heretical statements. One allegation was particularly damning: that he had told numerous male parishioners in Yucatecan Maya that fellatio was one sure path to sainthood, adding that Saint Peter and the apostles had all practiced it in order to enter Heaven.[55] A sixteen-year-old Maya youth, Pedro Couch, told inquisitors that while decorating the church on the eve of a religious festival, he reluctantly complied with the priest's invitation to his cell. There, the priest performed fellatio on him, swallowed his semen, and assured him that "it was a Christian act, a work of the angels, and in the service of God. In this manner, they too would get into Heaven and become angels."[56] As the case unfolded, some nineteen Yucatecan Maya young men and women, including Clemente Ek, Juan Couch, Francisco Che, Cristóbal Chan, Ana Çimá, and Clara Pot, came forth to denounce Valencia for similar heretical statements and sexual improprieties. Furthermore, dozens of other natives denounced him for violence and maltreatment, sacramental abuse, drunkenness, and breaking fast during Lent. Several young cantors and sacristans in the church also complained that the priest occasionally beat them—a fact testified to by other priests who had also observed Valencia's poor treatment of his parishioners and nonobservance of fasting days.

Valencia denied all allegations of heretical statements and sought to discredit his indigenous detractors by asserting that they were all "bad Christians," drunks, and sinners who did not believe in God; each of them, he claimed, was unable to distinguish reality from dreams.[57] Such assertions appealed to common Spanish prejudices about Mexico's indigenous inhabitants. Complicating matters, in the course of the trial it became apparent that some of the Maya men and women who denounced the priest likely fabricated or exaggerated their accounts. Historian John Chuchiak writes that Valencia's own denial of the allegations against him "leaves the historian with the question of whom to believe, the Mayas or the priest. The overwhelming number of Mayas who testified against the priest suggests either a high level of sexual depravity on the part of the clergyman or an impressive ability of the Maya to conspire to remove their priest."[58] In reality, this seems to have been a case of both sexual misconduct on the part of the priest and some collusion on the part of Maya parishioners. While we may never know with certainty if Valencia uttered heretical statements, the priest's claim of innocence was riddled with inconsistencies.

In his first interrogation, on July 10, 1610, Valencia, then forty-five years old, whose father was a Spanish conquistador in the Yucatán Peninsula, admitted that although he did indeed have sex repeatedly with Clara Pot, he did not recall having solicited anyone during confession. As his interrogation progressed, Valencia, still denying the more serious charges against him, admitted how "as a wretched being, he had engaged in some caresses and pollutions [i.e., masturbation] with some men in the manner described in the charges against him," but did nothing else.[59] He swore that "as a good Christian" he had never uttered heretical statements about oral sex, but he had nonetheless given in to "sins of the flesh," rarely fasted during Lent, and beat several sacristans for their sins.[60] Valencia begged that inquisitors show him mercy on the grounds that fray Fernando de Nava had previously punished him for many of his sins (although he did not elaborate). At a later date, however, he unsuccessfully attempted to retract this confession. The Inquisition was unsympathetic to this change of heart and, on February 16, 1612, found Valencia guilty of solicitation. He was sentenced to abjure de levi—of light suspicion of heresy—and was exiled for six years and deprived of the right to administer confession (to women), but only for two years. He was also fined one hundred pesos for the costs of his trial.[61]

Given Valencia's 1610 confession—in which he admitted to repeated sex with Clara Pot, having touched several boys, and having been previously disciplined by a priest for his sins—it is clear that this is not simply a case of local Maya communities fabricating accusations against an unacceptable priest to evict him from his parish. That said, native peoples recognized that allegations of heretical statements—whether true or false—would have merited inquisitorial attention in ways that mere accusations of priestly abuse and sex would not. Valencia had a tendency to be violent with his parishioners, and his confession of sexual misconduct with men and women is more credible than his retraction two years later. His purported acts formed the center around which Maya communities, through gossip and rumor, wove more exaggerated claims—sometimes true, sometimes embellished, and sometimes fabricated—in order to rid themselves of an abusive and greatly disliked priest. Valencia may have expected that the Inquisition would not take claims of indigenous youths against him very seriously. Whether he uttered heretical statements about fellatio being the path to sainthood (a remarkably strategic lie, if it was one, in order to interest the Inquisition) is entirely another story, and one for which we have no satisfactory answer. In the end, Valencia was only made to abjure de levi and not *de vehementi*—of light, rather than serious, suspicion of heresy. The latter would have had more severe consequences for the priest, though in the end it appears that inquisitors partly bought into the priest's rhetoric that his detractors were all Indian, and were therefore ignorant, idolatrous, and given to drink and untruths.

In an archival turn that is not particularly surprising, this is not the only paper trail that leads to Cristóbal de Valencia. There is another, even more extensive Inquisition case against him, also from 1609, in which many of the same individuals who initially denounced him appear once again. This case, analyzed in detail by Chuchiak, documents *hundreds* of allegations against the priest, all of which outline his abusive behavior and his penchant to solicit sex in confession.[62] Here, Valencia admitted to having sex with many of his parishioners but again denied uttering heretical statements. Inquisitors ultimately protected a man who, despite voluminous allegations of abuse and misconduct against him, posed no major threat to orthodoxy that could be proven in an inquisitorial court.

This same dynamic—of rumors, partial truths, and community mobilization against priestly abuse—are at play in several other documents, including the 1637 denunciations against the brutality and salacity of fray Nicolás Hidalgo in the northern province of New Mexico.[63] In a letter to inquisitors in Mexico City, don Luis de Rosas, governor of New Mexico, accused Hidalgo of sodomy, rape, siring children, and acts of extreme violence. These reports came to Rosas from several indigenous men in Taos, who complained of Hidalgo's attempts to commit the nefarious sin with them. There were also reports that the priest had castrated some of the indigenous men with whom he had committed acts of sodomy, and that he drove one man to commit suicide with his harsh punishments, only to later engage in an illicit relationship with the wife of the deceased.[64] In 1639 fray Nicolás Hidalgo—who likely spoke Taos or some other Tiwa language—was removed from his post in Taos, though this is perhaps no surprise because, as Robert Haskett reminds us, "reprimands, removal, or even jail terms were meted out to clergy found to be guilty of excessive corporal abuse."[65] In Hidalgo's place, the Church instated fray Pedro de Miranda, who proceeded to admonish the congregation for maligning their former cleric. On December 28, 1639, events unfolded in a grisly manner for the new priest: the Taos Indians killed Miranda along with two Spanish soldiers, and subsequently destroyed the church and convent, profaning the Eucharist in the process.[66] These acts, carried out against Hidalgo's replacement (rather than Hidalgo himself), register the intense level of anger, frustration, and disillusionment that the Taos mission community experienced. The Taos community's defiant reactions aimed to curb the abuses of their immediate circumstances but made a larger statement about how they came to view the Spanish agents of spiritual and colonial domination.

There is no way to ascertain the veracity of all the allegations against fray Nicolás Hidalgo, but if he was indeed guilty of committing sodomy with (and castrating) some of his parishioners, news spread quickly to other members of the Taos Pueblo community. As in the case of Valencia, it matters less whether Hidalgo was actually guilty of what he was accused of. What does matter are the ways that native communities throughout New Spain verbally disseminated information about, and eventually confronted, particularly egregious forms of priestly abuse. In both cases, the accusations that eventually made it into the archival record were likely embellished as they circulated from person to person but were not entirely unfounded. Both cases point to a particular type of negligence on the part of the Catholic Church: Valencia was minimally punished for his acts, as was Hidalgo, who was simply removed from the Taos mission. Though speculative, patterns in the archives suggest that both priests—after a short period of some restrictions, which may have included confinement to a monastery, temporary exile, and spiritual penances—would likely have been reinstated as priests elsewhere in the Spanish Empire. Again, furthering the spiritual conquest of the New World was the most important objective. While native peoples regularly mobilized, corroborated their claims, and succeeded in ousting abusive priests from their communities, the Church protected those same priests one way or another.

Fabrication and Negligent Favoritism

If hyperbole is one important facet of how abusive priests came to be documented in the archives of the Inquisition, then fabrication and "negligent favoritism" are equally so.[67] There is ample documentation of seemingly false accusations being lodged against priests throughout the colonial period. This seems to have been the case with Pedro de Heredia, the mulatto slave of clergyman don Carlos Jiménez Mondragón, who denounced him in 1716 for mutual masturbation, attempted sodomy, and for stating such acts were not sinful.[68] Mondragón declared the accusation a lie, and, over the course of the trial, it was discovered that Heredia suspected the priest of having an affair with his wife. Other witnesses also cast doubt on Heredia's accusations. Although the records in the case are incomplete, the charges against Mondragón were dropped. Another case involves a (seemingly) false accusation made by Francisco Mariano Suárez against fray Romualdo Velasco y Vargas for sexually soliciting him in Oaxaca in 1780. After inquisitors learned from Mariano Suárez that this same priest had forced his sister to marry a man with whom she had engaged in premarital sex, they determined the allegations "very doubtful" and did not pursue the matter further.[69]

Mexico's Inquisition archives hold hundreds of denunciations of priests for solicitation that, for one reason or another, inquisitors deemed not worth pursuing. I have thus far uncovered fifteen denunciations made by boys and young men that, as far as we can tell, were not discounted by inquisitors as false or calumnious but nonetheless received little attention. The archival presence of these accusations points to cover-ups by inquisitors or bishops or bureaucrats, and more likely to disinterest. The denunciations made against fray Hernando Ruiz, discussed earlier, were unworthy of inquisitorial attention because no sexual acts had taken place, and because the priest's advances occurred outside of confession. When a priest was accused of heresy, inquisitors and the prosecutor were, in theory, to review the seriousness of the allegations to determine if there were grounds for filing charges. In reality, unless the priest was a repeat offender, had uttered blasphemous statements, or committed some grave heresy, the Inquisition typically took no action.

Such was the case with a certain fray Pedro de San Francisco, denounced in 1604 by Gaspar de los Reyes, a twenty-year-old Spanish page; having invited the young man into the convent of Cachula, offering him food, clothing, and gifts, the priest put his hand inside de los Reyes's pants.[70] Given that de los Reyes did not even know the name of the priest, it seems that he had little reason to fabricate the story. In a 1614 denunciation that was never followed up, a Spanish boy accused Father Patricio de Arcaya of luring him into his cell, where the priest stripped the boy and inappropriately touched him.[71] In 1625 a Nahua man in Huehuetoca, Juan Sebastián, denounced a Father Betema for "touching his shameful parts" in confession one year earlier during Lent.[72] In 1694 a student denounced Father Felipe de Monroy in Santiago de Guatemala for having placed the boy's hands on his genitals during confession, after which the priest ejaculated and then absolved the boy of his sins.[73] In 1716 the mother of a thirteen-year-old mulatto servant in Mexico City's convent of San Diego denounced fray Joseph Jiménez for hugging her son, kissing him, and taking off his pants, asserting it was a sin for a man and woman to engage in the "carnal act" but not for two men to do so.[74] The list goes on. Despite there being little reason for inquisitors and the promotor fiscal to ignore these allegations, they were not a priority. In deprioritizing allegations of priestly sexual abuse—whether made by women or men—inquisitors exhibited favoritism for priests over the parishioners they allegedly abused. The Inquisition also punished laypersons more severely than priests for seemingly equivalent blasphemies and heresies; laypersons were not uncommonly subjected to torture, public shaming, and corporeal punishment while priests rarely were.

Several cases are characterized by overt negligent favoritism on the part of inquisitors. In 1747, for example, Agustín de Rojas told inquisitors he had engaged in mutual masturbation with a Jesuit priest, Father Alberto Zarzoza, following confession.[75] Inquisitors did not follow up until 1758 (over ten years later), and only after compiling denunciations across time and place. These included, among others, two accusations made by women in the 1730s (ten years prior to Rojas's claim) in a different parish from the rest. Despite mounting allegations, inquisitors did not file charges; perhaps they viewed Zarzoza as a minor threat to his parishioners (and a handful of infractions over the course of several decades left little reason for concern).

In a 1794 example, a married eighteen-year-old Yucatecan Maya, Francisco Xavier Vicab, denounced fray Julian Quijano, priest of Bacalar, for sodomy and heretical propositions.[76] Vicab was a stranger to that parish, there only to deliver images to the church when Quijano lured him into his cell. Vicab initially resisted, saying touching each other was sinful, but the priest replied, "*Do not think like that, because it is not a sin, and since I am a priest, I know this.*"[77] Quijano then offered Vicab one peso to penetrate him, and he consented. The priest, however, only paid Vicab three reales, which impelled the latter to denounce him. Not surprisingly, the Inquisition paid little attention. It was only four years later, in 1798, when the priest (who died later that year) was denounced for repeated drunkenness and illicit relationships with numerous women, that he was imprisoned.[78] Vicab's denunciation highlights the transient nature of sexual relationships with priests; if Vicab was telling the truth, Quijano likely chose a stranger to his parish to diminish his chances of being caught.

These cases intimate that perhaps the most expedient solution for inquisitors and church officials, in terms of both economic resources and public reputation, was simply to not make a big deal out of them. That solution, of course, has awful resonance with twentieth- and twenty-first-century cases of sexual abuse by priests (and of Church cover-ups). That is, priests were shuffled around from parish to parish or temporarily secluded in convents until their crimes had been sufficiently forgotten. However, to prove this through New Spain's archival record is difficult, especially given that Catholic priests typically moved from one parish to another as a normal part of clerical life. The vast files of the Mexican Inquisition, however, when pried open, reveal well-hidden patterns of negligence on the part of inquisitors, church officials, and bishops.

The two tables in the appendix to this book offer us a macrohistorical sense of how, especially in comparison to cases examined in previous chapters, the Church dealt with priests who were convicted of solicitation and sodomy, and with those who denounced themselves for such acts. More often than not, priests who denounced themselves to the Inquisition for having solicited men and women in the confessional went unpunished. Such, for example, was the case with fray Francisco Pulido, who remorsefully confessed to inquisitors in 1761 that he had committed sodomy some five times with an indigenous servant of his.[79] Inquisitors specifically noted that no action should be taken against Pulido; the acts did not take place during confession so "it is not a concern of the Holy Office."[80] In this sense, the incomplete case of Vallejo at the beginning of the chapter would have been exemplary had the ecclesiastical court actually excommunicated him for having had sex with over one hundred men (though, having delved deeply into these archives, my suspicions are he would not have been had he lived to the end of his trial).

Inquisitors did not convict any of the priests whose files I consulted for this chapter of serious suspicion of heresy, in which case they would have been required to abjure de vehementi. Archives show that the Catholic Church in New Spain did not regard those priests convicted of solicitation and sodomy as serious heretics—as they did bigamists, blasphemists, crypto-Jews, and Lutherans (some of the Inquisition's primary targets in New Spain). Furthermore, they never executed priests for sodomy, tortured them, or subjected them to public shaming or corporal punishment, unlike laypersons convicted of the same crime by the secular courts. Higher-ranking church officials thus ultimately protected priests who solicited sex from men or women, even if they had uttered heretical of blasphemous statements in the process.

These *solicitantes contra naturam*—to use a phrase sometimes employed in the documents—were shielded from the public eye, and perhaps the harshest punishment they received was the embargo of their private goods. One priest's interaction with the Inquisition shows this. Fray Ángel María Quesa was accused of soliciting sex from women and men in the confessional throughout the 1760s, among different parishes in Mexico City and Guadalajara, and in November 1773 the Inquisition imprisoned him, embargoed his goods, and expelled him from his religious order.[81] A year later, he was convicted of solicitation and was made to abjure de levi, with his right to administer confession permanently revoked. A 1785 petition requesting that Quesa's right to administer confession be reinstated also made clear that, unlike fray Esteban Rodríguez and fray Agustín María, Quesa was perhaps not as contrite as he should have been. He once brazenly complained to another cleric that the Inquisition had "treated him with injustice, sentenced him without cause, and had embargoed one thousand and seven hundred pesos from him."[82] The petition, which was almost certainly not granted by church officials, shows that the economic consequences of a solicitation conviction could indeed be severe.

One common tactic of abusive priests, as we have seen, was to handpick those they thought least likely to turn to the Inquisition or be seen as credible witnesses. This was often youths, regardless of their ethnic backgrounds, and indigenous peoples who did not speak fluent Spanish. When a priest thought that, at least for the time being, he had been able to get away with soliciting one person in the confessional—unless he was riddled with the guilt and self-doubt that led some priests to denounce themselves—he became more likely to make repeated attempts at soliciting other penitents, often divided by intervals of time and between different towns and parishes. There, too, is the geographical dispersal of denunciations in some cases, reflecting the priest's ordinary routine—which often took him to different places in his parish, particularly to towns in the countryside. Priests like fray José María García—who denounced himself in 1793 for soliciting thirty-two men and at least two women in over ten towns on the outskirts of Zacatecas, Puebla, and Guanajuato over the course of a decade—in his own words, "always searched for rustic and ignorant people in whom there was the least danger that they denounce or defame him."[83]

One final characteristic that I want to pull from the cases is the tragic time lag between when certain events took place and when they were reported to inquisitors. This interval may factor into why the Inquisition did not go after some errant priests, and it certainly points to the emotional pain of abuse (because it took some victims so long to come forward, and many never did). In one such case, from 1719, Antonio Joseph Navarro denounced a Spanish Carmelite priest, fray Antonio de San Joseph, for having solicited him and spoken "amorous words" some ten years earlier, when he was nineteen and living in Andalucía, Spain.[84] Because the alleged event took place in Spain, Mexican inquisitors remitted the denunciation to Spanish inquisitors, but unless the priest had more serious charges against him, it would have been ignored. In a denunciation from 1739, fray Esteban Morales, who was by then a priest, denounced Father Ignacio María Napoli for pressuring him into lewd acts some fourteen years earlier. Napoli had invited Morales, who at the time was studying for the priesthood, into his cell, where he took off both of their clothes and ejaculated on the young man's legs and genitals.[85] Napoli then led the boy to the confessional and absolved him of his sins. Baring his conscience and years of misgivings to inquisitors, Morales admitted he never knew if he had an obligation to denounce the priest. In one final example, from Teotitlán, Pedro

Donantes, who was fifty-seven and married when he reported his experience to the Inquisition in 1784, denounced a Father Serafín for an event that took place decades earlier. Internalizing his abuse for over forty years, Donantes said that when he was fourteen, the priest repeatedly invited him into his cell, offered him fruits and sweets, improperly touched him, and penetrated him once.[86]

Significant delays such as these can be partly explained by the guilt and embarrassment on the part of the victims, who may have also felt some other societal pressure not to tell. As far as we know, none of these denunciations culminated in formal charges against any of these accused priests. This, however, may have had less to do with negligence and more with the fact that significant chronological gaps made it hard to find witnesses and obtain testimonies. The fact that none of these abuses took place during confession meant that they were of little interest to inquisitors. It is possible, though unlikely, that one or more of these priests was eventually tried for sodomy or solicitation, but that the documents no longer exist. It is also possible that denunciations sent to Mexico City inquisitors from the peripheries of New Spain did receive attention, and that inquisitors sent back instructions to local commissaries to exact some punishment. Such correspondences may have become lost or destroyed over the years, or may not have been preserved or centralized in archives. Such explanations, plausible as they are, do little to undermine the Church's long legacy of sexual abuse, and the Church's tendency to confront it only when the crime was a heretical theological violation, or when it could not be swept under the rug.

Historian William B. Taylor notes that priests who committed sodomy were "under considerable pressure to suppress or hide such relations, and the pecado nefando may have been so threatening to the church that the Inquisition suppressed most rumors and poorly established accusations of it against priests."[87] This matrix of suppression, negligent favoritism, and archival politics leaves us with a jarring image of the Catholic Church valuing the services and reputations of priests more than the well-being of individual parishioners (or the opportunity to redress the perennial problem of sexual abuse by the clergy). Given the large number of accusations against priests that were not followed up by inquisitors, we too are left with the impression that the Church simply did not worry much about those priests who had only solicited a few individuals as opposed to dozens or more. Even then, action on the part of the Church of the Inquisition was not guaranteed. All of this points to an even greater impulse to cover up such acts, burying them deep within the archives.

In *Archive Fever*, Derrida famously asserts that one of the impulses behind memory is destruction: our "silent vocation is to burn the archive and to incite amnesia."[88] The Church's treatment of solicitation is an awful instance of how the archive can be mobilized to hide, ignore, and forget. Yet, as the present-day church scandals that have come to light partly through archival research show us, the archive is also a place to expose, reveal, and remember. That archive, as this book shows, bends to our own will and desires.

CHAPTER 6

Desiring the Divine

Pollution and Pleasure

The files of the Mexican Inquisition in the Archivo General de la Nación hold dozens of cases that attest to intense desires for the divine. In the late spring of 1690, Juan Esteban Pérez, a literate fifty-year-old unmarried Spaniard who had been living in the city of Puebla for two and a half years, confessed his sins to a Jesuit priest, who advised that he denounce himself to the Holy Office of the Inquisition. A few weeks later, on May 23, 1690, Pérez voluntarily appeared before don Francisco Flores de Valdes, priest and commissary of the Inquisition in Puebla, seeking forgiveness and absolution. The narrative of Pérez's self-denunciation tells the following:

> Fifteen days after arriving at this part [New Spain], forgetting about God and believing the temptations and persuasions of the Devil, he began to commit sin [*delinquir*] on the occasion of having repeatedly kissed a bronze engraving of [Our] Holy Christ, affixed to a cross made of the same metal, which he wears around his neck, [and passing it over] all the natural parts of his body, in front and back, thinking them licit. And from these acts, it came about that he also kissed the feet of Our Lady the Most Virgin under the devotion of the rosary; and then he passed [the rosary with the Virgin] over his hands, mouth, eyes, and his natural parts [i.e., his genitals], the Most Holy Virgin being [represented] on a painted canvas and on a medallion that he wears around his neck.[1]

Flores de Valdes, in his denunciation, painted a picture of a man who was immensely conflicted, occasionally lashing out at the Devil who tempted him. According to the inquisitor, "as a fragile man, he fell [into temptation], carrying into his imagination two thousand errors, that those natural parts of the Virgin represented the Most Holy Trinity and the gates of Ezekiel."[2] Furthermore, Pérez seemed to be unaware of some of the things he said, for he occasionally heard voices, and he was firm in his belief that one day at daybreak, the Holy Trinity "married him to the Virgin," after which he went to bed and "had a pollution, believing that he was married to the Virgin."[3]

I begin this chapter with an archived act of "pollution," incurred (repeatedly) by Pérez in his desire for the divine, a fascinating manifestation of the remorseful pleasures of profanation. In this context, the term *polución*— pollution—could refer to the act of masturbation by a woman or a man, or to any emission of "semen" outside of the so-called proper or improper vessel, respectively the vagina or the anus (the latter of which constituted sodomy instead of mere pollution). Historically the term itself has vague and shifting meanings: a 1620 Spanish-Italian dictionary defined *polución* as "corruption in the venereal act"; a 1705 Spanish dictionary specified that it was "the loss of the seed of the man when he sleeps"; the 1737 *Diccionario de autoridades* defined it as "the effusion of semen, voluntarily or in dreams." In its entry, the *Diccionario de autoridades* referenced the Latin *mollities*, which translated into Spanish as *molicie* (and was defined in the same dictionary as the "sordid sin against nature").[4] Thus, these diverse terms and concepts—pollution, molicie, and masturbation—commingle with (and partly comprise) the sins against nature. But they do so in partial tension with one another, and without fully overlapping conceptually, theologically, or juridically. These terms are central to the cases that I discuss and analyze in this chapter, though for several reasons the archiving of pollution takes center stage.

In the archives of the Inquisition, "pollution" refers to its primary meaning, but often in ways that necessarily invoke its other (more lustful and corporeal) definitions. The primary definition of *polución* provided by the 1737 *Diccionario de autoridades* is a "bodily stain that makes [one] ugly"—some kind of mark that disfigures and renders someone (or something) defective.[5] In this sense it can be seen, both figuratively and metaphorically, as some type of "impurity" of the body or the soul. A late eighteenth-century definition more purposefully relates pollution to the sacred: Esteban de Terreros y Pando, author of the *Diccionario castellano con las voces de ciencias y artes*, defines the term as the "profanation of a temple or holy place."[6] We see these many definitions (imperfectly) converge in the case of Pérez. Of course, kissing the rosary was accepted practice for Catholics, but experiencing lust in doing so was not. Pérez polluted holy images as he rapturously kissed a bronze engraving of Jesus and the feet of the Virgin on his rosary. He passed these objects over those body parts through which he could best sense their divine (and erotic) power—skin, eyes, mouth, genitals. He longed for the image of the Virgin Mary, as she appeared both on the painted piece of canvas and on the pendant he wore around his neck. He also polluted himself—that is, he came to experience bodily pleasures that resulted in seminal emission—as he encountered the divine through the sensory, in embodied (and visceral) ways.

In touching, feeling, and experiencing the divine, Pérez mixed categories that, according to the Catholic Church, were not supposed to commingle (at least so explicitly). This is a mixing of categories—sacred and profane—that we have seen throughout the book: in the late eighteenth-century Inquisition trial of Manuel Arroyo for "counseling that sucking semen from men was not a sin"; in the early nineteenth-century criminal case of José Lázaro Martínez for "profanation of cadaver"; and in the seventeenth-century solicitation trial of fray Esteban Rodríguez for passing the cord of his religious habit over his Nahua parishioners' penises and "moving his lips as if he were praying." If we return briefly to the case of Rodríguez, we see just how thin the line between the sacred and the profane was. According to the inquisitors who evaluated Rodríguez's transgressions, he had "committed the very grave sin of mixing sacred and blessed things that our Holy Mother Church uses, such as the prayers of Saint Anthony of Padua and the blessed cord [of the habit of] Saint Francis with the sordid and despicable nature of his sensualities, profaning and violating the purity of the holy sacrament of penitence with his abominations and *torpezas* [impurities]."[7] Here, the gravity of the sin lies not solely in the heretical belief or blasphemous statement per se but rather in the very "mixing"— *mesclando*—of sacred and sordid, of blessed and sensual. For the Holy Office of the Mexican Inquisition, herein lies the unacceptable transgression: not the act itself, but thoughts behind it, which assimilated categories that were meant to be inherently separate from one another. Yet the reality was more complex: the desires to venerate the divine and to pollute the divine were not necessarily in opposition but rather existed along an intimate spectrum of religious devotions, desires, and doubts.

This chapter focuses on desire for the divine—everything from "pollution" to "obscene acts," from "claiming sexual intercourse with saints" to "other errors"—and on how these desires came to be archived in colonial New Spain. Many such desires were experienced viscerally, and manifested themselves through a longing to pollute or profane the divine. Just as the very definitions of polución shift subtly, or drastically, depending on who is doing the defining, personal understandings of (and interactions with) the divine vary just as widely depending on who is doing the devotion. Although the Church took a strong position against the "impure" and "polluting" beliefs and acts of individuals who blasphemed and profaned the sacraments (like Juan Esteban Pérez, Manuel Arroyo, fray Esteban Rodríguez, and many other protagonists), the Catholic Church itself sponsored much of the baroque religious iconography that inspired these desires. This chapter argues that the Catholic Church in New Spain (as in the Iberian Peninsula) contributed greatly, though perhaps unwittingly, to a devotional climate that humanized Jesus, the Virgin, and the saints, and thus that fostered "polluting" beliefs about them. These intimate experiences of the divine, even when eroticized, were not necessarily at odds with religious dogma. Many of those who desired the divine struggled to make sense of their own religious experiences, and they had difficulty relating the nature and intensity of their experiences to inquisitors. This intersection points to the ineffable—to that which cannot be adequately described by words—and thereby analyzes the archivable partly through that which remains unarchivable due to the limits of language: spiritual ecstasy, rapture, and union with the divine.

This chapter thus frames these individuals' relations to the divine in terms of desire but also in terms of the ineffable, inexplicable, and archivally unknowable. The archives of the Mexican Inquisition offer an unrivaled glimpse at the ways that certain priests, nuns, and laypersons in New Spain interpreted and experienced the divine through desires of both body and spirit that intersected with communal religious beliefs and practices. These Inquisition cases point to a relatively unknown world of religious devotions, some of which were deemed to be desecrations, and all of which manifested themselves through the body of the devotee (and occasionally through the body of Christ).

The archives of the Mexican Inquisition, to be sure, house dozens of known cases in which individuals eroticized the divine, and there are undoubtedly many more to be found. But the colonial archive itself complicates the very process of uncovering these eroticized devotions and desecrations in New Spain. For most instances of eroticized religiosity are couched within more salient crimes—heresy, blasphemy, and solicitation—under which the acts themselves were subsumed. Many more, as in the case of Esteban Pérez, are obscured by the vague language with which the cases were first documented and entered into the archive of the Inquisition. The Mexican Inquisition cases analyzed in this chapter insinuate a larger realm of human experience with the divine, despite the fact that on the surface the archives themselves do not seem to hold much material on the topic.

By articulating the connections between colonial archives and intimate experiences of religious devotion, this chapter ultimately argues that when priests, nuns, and laypersons desired the divine, they simultaneously expanded their own devotional and erotic imaginary as well as that of the archive. This is not to say that all bodily longings for the divine were experienced as "sexual" per se—either by those who experienced them or by inquisitors presiding over the cases—but rather that desires coagulate around the divine in ways that complicate our very understanding of how spiritual devotion was seen, felt, and experienced in the past. I propose that despite the seeming scarcity of cases such as those that follow, the experience of eroticizing the divine was far more common in New Spain than, say, instances of "carnal congress" with a corpse (though it is impossible to compare quantitatively with sodomy and bestiality). However, because these cases deal with interior desires of body and spirit— pointing to masturbatory acts that were carried out in private and to emotions and thoughts that were not typically archived—we can never know the extent to which a much larger segment of the population may have eroticized some aspect of their relationship to divine objects, images, and personae.

As we delve into these rare cases, it is important to acknowledge that the bodily act of "pollution" is often tangential to the cases themselves. For what concerned inquisitors—as we saw in the previous chapter—was not the act of masturbation itself but rather the heretical beliefs and desecrating acts that went alongside it. Scholars of colonial Latin America have uncovered several Inquisition records of nuns and laywomen who were implicated in solitary (and sometimes mutual) acts of "pollution," typically brought to light only because of an accompanying unorthodox belief or blasphemous statement. Jacqueline Holler, for instance, has examined the 1598 Inquisition trial of a Mexico City *beata*, or a local holy woman, Marina de San Miguel, who was convicted of prophesying and *alumbradismo* (claiming to have been personally and spiritually illuminated by the Holy Spirit), and who also confessed to erotic visions, masturbation, and sexual relations with priests and other holy women.[8] Nora Jaffary has discussed a late colonial nun, Ana Rodríguez de Castro y Aramburu, who used her menstrual blood to fake stigmata, who did with another woman "what a man can do in this manner with a woman and giving her kisses during the night," and who masturbated with the Eucharist, putting it in her "private parts."[9] Jaffary theorizes the concept of "sexual desecration" through the eighteenth-century Inquisition case of María Gertrudis Arévalo, who, alongside other heretical beliefs and sinful acts, applied the rosary and the holy cross to the "indecent parts" of her body, at times inserting engravings of the saints and other holy objects into her "unclean vessel."[10] Lee Penyak has uncovered a one-folio reference to a 1796 criminal case, which is lost, in which a twenty-eight-year-old mestiza, María Ramona Sánchez, was sentenced to six years of seclusion "for masturbation and other dishonesties."[11] Unfortunately the vague reference gives no other information. This is the only case among the group that has no connection to the eroticization or desecration of the divine. These scattered cases give a sense of how rarely female masturbation enters the colonial archive, and when it does, it is almost always only in conjunction with more serious sins and crimes.

Below we will dig deeper into the unusual corners of this archival corpus, focusing on a handful of exceptional Inquisition cases that center on pollution of the body and of the sacred. The cases gesture toward the ways that religious devotion merged with the erotic, the profane, and the archival in New Spain. In three of the cases, women are the main protagonists. Jesus, the Virgin Mary, and several Catholic saints—with whom the accused communicated verbally, physically, and spiritually—also take on central roles as protagonists in these archival narratives. The acts and desires depicted in the Inquisition files stem from the intimately personal endeavors of those who sought to experience and feel the divine in ways that pushed the very boundaries of orthodoxy. Here we find several individuals who creatively built upon church dogma and imagined new possibilities for the divine, either overtly or unknowingly challenging orthodoxy along the way. Many questioned some aspect of the supremacy of the sacred and the power of the divine, and simultaneously reaffirmed certain aspects of their faith. Through the archives of the Mexican Inquisition, the two underlying conceptual definitions of "pollution"—relating to the body and the sacred, to emissions and desecrations—converge and intersect with individual notions of purity and pleasure. The women and men who so desired, and desecrated, the divine expanded the devotional, erotic, and archival imaginary in the very process.

Archiving the Obscene

As with so many cases in my corpus, I would never have encountered these documents had my terminology and research methodologies not expanded over the course of archival digging. Just as the criminal case of Lázaro Martínez for "carnally mixing" with a corpse only came to me sideways, while researching the history of suicide, it was another project that led me to Pérez. In the summer of 2015, I began research at Mexico's Archivo General de la Nación on a

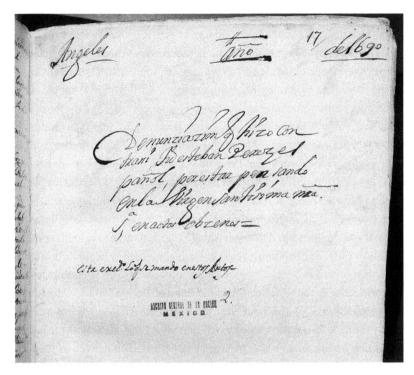

Fig 6.1 Title page of the 1690 Inquisition file for José Esteban Pérez, tried "for thinking about the Holiest Virgin, Our Lady, in obscene acts." Courtesy of the Archivo General de la Nación, Mexico City, Mexico. AGN, Inquisición 680, exp. 2, fol. 17.

new project, analyzing the relationship between historical archives, pornography, and censorship in late nineteenth- and early twentieth-century Mexico. It was only then that I began to search for terms like "pornographic," "obscene," and "immoral" in the archive's online database. On a whim, I searched for those same terms in the archive's database of colonial documents. My hopes were not high. The terms *pornografía* and *pornográfico* offered nothing, and *inmoral* mostly brought up references to "immoral" literature from Europe that was increasingly censored by the Inquisition into the early nineteenth century. Searching for *obsceno* (and its cognates), in contrast, produced some unexpected and fascinating results, one of which was the case of Pérez. Indeed, it is the terminology of obscenity that makes this document stand out. The original title page of Pérez's Inquisition file states simply: "[Puebla de los] Angeles. Year of 1690. Denunciation that Juan Esteban Peres [*sic*], Spaniard, made against himself, for thinking about the Holiest Virgin, Our Lady, in obscene acts" (fig. 6.1).[12]

What is especially unique in the case of Pérez is exactly how this archiving of the "obscene" came about. In an odd turn of events, extremely rare within the procedural norms of criminal and Inquisition cases, the archival file includes a short five-folio letter written by Pérez himself. This is literally the only case (of the more than three hundred that I consulted for this study) that includes something written firsthand by a suspect. This switch from the third-person voice to the first is exceptional, and invites us to inquire into the conditions under which Pérez archived himself, verbally, textually, and affectively. That said, we should not assume that Pérez necessarily archived himself (or his desires) entirely of his own volition, or that his writings offer us direct access to him as a historical subject. Although it seems that he wrote the letter willingly, the letter itself is mediated by the very expectations for confession through which it was produced, and through which Pérez first came to verbally confess his sins in early 1690 to a Jesuit priest in Puebla. In essence, he wrote the letter of his own accord to be read by inquisitors, most likely in an attempt to prove his cognizance of the sinful nature of his acts and desires (and thereby minimalize inquisitorial wrath). To be clear, inquisitors never requested this writing from Pérez. Of course, this is not to say that what he wrote was not true but rather that it was crafted with a particular audience in mind. Even so, the fact that Pérez voluntarily denounced himself to the Inquisition, at the urging of his confessor, shows that he wanted to reconcile the sinful nature of his religious fervor with the norms of Christian behavior.

Mary Louise Pratt uses the phrase "authoethnographic expression" to refer to "instances in which colonized subjects undertake to represent themselves in ways which engage with the colonizer's own terms."[13] I suggest that the letter written by Pérez is an *autoarchival expression*: through it, the author documented himself in ways that engage archivally with the recorded transcriptions that inquisitors and notaries had already produced from his own verbal self-denunciation and confession. In the letter directed to inquisitors (fig. 6.2), Pérez relates several of his intimate acts with sacred objects and divine figures, though he does so haphazardly. The narrative is confusing and written without much sense of chronological order. Pérez begins by saying that one day, as he was walking through a plaza "feeling unsettled and with a broken body," he began to kiss an image of Jesus and the hands and feet of the Virgin Mary on his rosary. Shortly thereafter, acknowledging the diabolical nature of such acts, he writes, "this Devil that solicited these bad things was pretending to be my Lord."[14]

Pérez told of how getting intimate with the divine—in particular, the kissing of a statue of Jesus—left him in a state of desire and love: "I found myself

Fig 6.2 Two folios of a 1690 letter that José Esteban Pérez wrote to his inquisitors, detailing the corporeal and spiritual nature of his religious devotions and acknowledging their sinfulness. Courtesy of the Archivo General de la Nación, Mexico City, Mexico. AGN, Inquisición 680, exp. 2, fols. 21v and 22.

with heart enamored and my pollution [semen] spilled, and I was sweating."[15] Pérez then spoke of several instances at some point in the coming months when he kissed the "natural parts" of Jesus and the Virgin, which also culminated in pollution. He wrote: "I had fornicated with my Lady as if she were my beloved wife, for that was what she called for, appearing to me in my imagination." He also said that through the canvas painting of Mary, "I believed that I was fornicating with her, kissing her face and mouth as I sweated." We never learn what the "fornication" consisted of, though he likely masturbated while watching the image, possibly rubbing his penis against it. He similarly described how one time, taking hold of an image of Our Lady, he "felt such harmony with her eye watching me wherever I went in the house, and it seemed to me a miraculous thing; and when it seemed to me that I was fornicating with her as if she were my wife, I would put this image in front of me, alongside five others [of the Virgin], and with this effort so that I would fornicate with she that appeared to me and chose me."[16] The letter repeats several other instances of similar acts, often with great detail, and with a clear sense of the "as if she were my wife" justification, evidence of how Pérez framed his acts to inquisitors.

His first-person letter, in concert with his verbal testimony (documented in the third person by a notary), offers an archival glimpse of an individual whose fantasies were fueled by religious iconography, and who was intensely conflicted over his own thoughts, desires, and actions. But Pérez also (reluctantly) resisted the erotic manifestations of his religious devotion and spiritual desire. The notary recorded that Pérez, in response to inquisitors' questions, deeply regretted "having had diverse obscene and lascivious thoughts," going so far as to say that "he places hope in God that he will be forgiven, and even if the Inquisition were to burn him [at the stake] he is prepared to obey."[17]

Beyond this testimony—both verbal and written, documented in the first person and the third—Pérez's body became central to the case, and to how inquisitors assessed the sincerity of his repentance. At one point, inquisitors commanded him to "state the sickness or sicknesses that you presently have and [that you] have had."[18] Pérez, recognizing the dangers of mixing self-pleasure and devotion, responded partly by telling inquisitors that he had "taken the utmost diligence to extinguish the fire of sensuality—with fire and burning fat he seared his natural parts, which are still injured to this day." Pérez even offered to *hacer demonstración*—to demonstrate his wounded genitals to inquisitors—but the "commissary [of the Inquisition] impeded him."[19] Imagining this impeding of Pérez, we can almost sense the visceral reaction of the inquisitor who declined Pérez's invitation. In doing so, inquisitors refused to witness the bodily evidence of atonement for his sins (simply taking his word for it). Pérez's act of genital mortification gestures toward the intersections of pleasure, punishment, and pain. While Pérez certainly experienced agony searing his "natural parts" with scorching fat, we cannot know if he too might have experienced some pleasure at the very act of mortification. Similarly, Pérez might have also experienced some form of sinful pleasure in the (autoarchival) writing down of his experiences for inquisitors to read, or in recounting the details of his sins to confessors and inquisitors.

Pérez's case is one of a handful in colonial archives in which women and men disfigured their bodies to punish themselves and prevent sin. Perhaps the most extreme case I uncovered is a 1767 criminal case from Querétaro, in which reports surfaced that Juan Chrisodomo, a mulatto journeyman in his late thirties who worked at a sugar mill, had been brutally and forcibly castrated.[20] Chrisodomo initially accused two men, one indigenous and the other mulatto, of accosting him in the mill's corrals and perpetrating the heinous act, from which he fainted due to blood loss. Only later, upon local officials' inability to corroborate his story, did Chrisodomo confess that "it was he who by his own hand had cut off his testicles with a knife he had borrowed that morning from a man named Pedro Arévalo who worked at the sugar mill."[21] Arévalo confirmed having lent him the knife that day. The motive behind Chrisodomo's self-castration leads us into the realm of the spiritual: "because he was going to offend God [with his genitals], he executed this act without having told anyone about it."[22] Two months later, after questioning several witnesses, secular authorities concluded that foul play was not involved, and Chrisodomo had voluntarily castrated himself—an act for which there was no punishment. This act, we might speculate, stemmed from a visceral craving to impede the sins of the flesh. These archival traces of voluntarily mortified, disfigured bodies illustrate the extremes to which some individuals could go to comply with the precepts of the Church. Though unusual, they are undeniably part of a much longer religious tradition of mortifying the body through both ascetic practices and castigatory disciplines, common among priests, nuns, and Catholic societies and approved of by the Church. Mortification, most commonly flagellation, was thus considered an important accessory to the spiritual relief and penance offered by confession.

Pérez's act of mortification, coupled with his verbal and textual statements, paints a picture of a man—who regularly fasted during Lent and on Fridays and Saturdays—engaged in a profound religious and moral struggle with his own desires, which were directly shaped by the religious iconography with which he surrounded himself. Given his own declaration that for some time he "believed his acts and pollutions to be licit," we might ask how he could have held this belief.[23] Alison Weber, writing about the raptures and ecstasies of the Spanish nun Teresa of Ávila, has pointed out that in Europe and its colonies the Counter-Reformation began to insist on a clearer distinction between the sacred and the erotic.[24] In the early years of Spanish colonial presence in the Americas, it was not uncommon for the Catholic Church to represent divine figures in baroque, overly humanized, and subtly erotic ways. Nuns, priests, and laypersons alike were inevitably influenced by the Catholic Church's presentation of the divine. Thus, by fantasizing about intimate, sexual encounters with Jesus and the Virgin, Pérez incorporated and creatively altered the theological lexicon of devotion into his own bodily and spiritual practice—humanizing and eroticizing the divine in the process.

Pérez's reinterpretation of the sacred also appears to have been as much a result of his distressed mental state as it was of his desire for love, affection, and divine recognition. Inquisitors evaluating Pérez viewed his acts as fundamentally "obscene and lascivious," and were convinced that his treatment of holy objects and images counted as profane. They also concluded that he had suffered severely from "melancholy," he was "fatuous," and he suffered from unspecified "sicknesses."[25] This was partly brought on by his having been struck in the head by several black men at the sugar mill of Santa Inés, after which, in Pérez's own words, "his judgment was agitated."[26] Inquisitors were ultimately convinced that his repentance was heartfelt and treated him leniently. Inquisitors let Pérez off with a warning: in the future, he was to guard against "similar mistakes," to perform "beneficial penitence," and to confess with the priest assigned to him, who would "console him and try to calm the abovesaid thoughts and scruples."[27] A few months later, on August 11, 1690, Pérez was called before inquisitors who again questioned him and concluded that he had been set morally right; he was "no longer deceived."[28] The leniency of the Inquisition regarding Pérez's eroticized desire for the divine is indicative of how the Church did not necessarily view such acts as threatening to the tenets of faith, especially in contrast to more egregious heresies. As transgressive as Pérez's archived thoughts and acts might seem to us today, inquisitors were not substantially threatened by his "obscene acts" and they reacted sympathetically to his demonstrative contrition. "Obscene acts" were thus not necessarily disruptive, in either the lived past or in archived form, so long as they were carried out in private and caused only internal turmoil.

Loving Jesus and the Virgin

On January 23, 1621, a Spanish priest and commissary in Querétaro, fray Manuel de Santo Tomás, denounced a young mestiza woman, Agustina Ruiz, to the Mexican Inquisition. The twenty-year-old Ruiz, according to him, never finished confessing her sins with him, which she began on the eve of Pascua de Reyes, the Feast of the Three Kings, several weeks earlier in the Carmelite convent of Santa Teresa. He sent for her at home, urging her to return to church to complete her confession. When she failed to do so, especially given the gravity and heretical nature of what she had told him, the priest had no choice but to denounce her to the Inquisition. According to that denunciation, Ruiz had committed the sin of "pollution" nearly every day since the age of eleven, exchanging "dishonest words" with Saint Nicholas of Tolentine, Saint Diego, Jesus Christ, and the Virgin. Perhaps most seriously of all, "she believed that they [in turn] join themselves with her in different ways, with her underneath them, and from the side, and her on top of them, and also with her lying face down while they conjoin themselves with her through both of her dishonest parts," meaning both vaginally and anally.[29] What equally perturbed the priest was Ruiz's assertion that sometimes at Mass, as the priest raised the Eucharist, she would see Jesus Christ with his "thing exposed" and would experience "carnal alteration," sinning with herself right there in the church.[30]

This is the beginning of a unique and elaborately detailed Inquisition case—preserved in the Bancroft Library and archived and described as a case of "claiming sexual intercourse with saints" in the catalog—in which one young woman was charged with a variety of seemingly heretical sins all manifested through her visions, her actions, and her body. At 69 folios—that is, nearly 140 single-sided handwritten manuscript pages, recorded on the recto and verso sides of each folio—this is one of the more extensive cases of our corpus. The Inquisition file of José Esteban Pérez, by contrast, consists of only thirteen folios (including the five-folio handwritten letter). The Inquisition trial of Ana María de Leyba, which follows, is only nineteen folios. The archival narrative of Ruiz and her life is thus more extensive than many Inquisition cases I consulted for this study, nearly rivaling the Inquisition case of fray Esteban Rodríguez, analyzed in the previous chapter, at eighty-two folios. What makes this case unique are its explicit and meticulous archival depictions of the largely unarchived world of female "pollution" and accompanying autoerotic fantasies. This level of detail is particularly valuable because the overwhelming majority of sodomy and bestiality cases found in colonial archives (and discussed throughout this book) involve only men.

In broaching masturbation among women in colonial Mexico, Lavrin asserts that in theological discourse, "masturbation, always described as a masculine problem, deeply concerned the church."[31] This case demonstrates that pollution was not seen solely as a masculine problem. The act itself, despite its ample presence in colonial confessional manuals, did not concern the Church on any practical or enforceable level. Even in Europe during the later Middle Ages, when theologians began to associate masturbation more closely with the sins against nature of sodomy and bestiality, it "was decidedly the most innocent of the bunch and in fact received far less attention in the succeeding ages than its essential wickedness would lead us to expect."[32] Masturbation thus played a minor role in the hierarchical drama of sexual sins. It is not that women did not commit the sins against nature but rather that they were prosecuted far less frequently than men for sodomy, bestiality, pollution, and molicies in New Spain. Women like Agustina Ruiz become more central figures in archival narratives of unnatural desire primarily in the ambit of religious unorthodoxy. It remains a challenge to locate cases of female pollution (and same-sex intimacy), as the cases that reference such acts usually do so tangentially, and typically only in relation to other, more legible crimes. Such was the case with Ruiz: her crime was not the act of pollution but believing that she had engaged sexually and exchanged "dishonest words" with Jesus, Mary, and the saints.

When the commissary of the Inquisition made his formal charge against her in 1621, she was twenty and unmarried, living with her seven-year-old son, Francisco, in the house of Alonso de Garibaldi and his wife, María Meneque. After her parents' death, the young Ruiz lived with a neighbor in Puebla until she was "tricked" into going to Mexico City by a certain Diego Sánchez Solano, the eventual father of her son.[33] According to her testimony, after three years in Mexico City—still an unmarried virgin—Sánchez Solano convinced her that they should get married, after which they engaged in sexual relations and she became pregnant. As was common in Mexico of the time, the two never did marry and lived together in the state of concubinage. It was only after the unexpected death of Sánchez Solano, a few years later, that she moved to San Luis Potosí for three years before ending up in Querétaro. Ruiz related how, two months earlier, her "brother," Cristóbal Felipe (who might have been a lover whom she planned to marry, rather than her brother), had sent her and her son from San Luis Potosí to the home of Alonso de Garibaldi, where they were to remain until he came for them.[34] Her involuntary placement in this house by a close male relative was likely meant to punish, protect, and separate the young and unmarried Ruiz from the outside world and its sinful influences, to which she had already showed herself to be especially vulnerable.

During the Inquisition's first hearing on February 6, 1621, Ruiz, like so many brought before the Holy Office, stated she did not know why she was being interrogated. She said she knew nothing when inquisitors formulaically asked if she or anyone close to her had said, done, or committed anything that seemed contrary to either the Holy Catholic faith or the evangelical law of the Church. Only when asked about previous conversations between her and her confessor did she admit to having had "bad thoughts and bad images" of Jesus, the Virgin, and saints for years.[35] She denied having told her confessor that she saw Jesus with his natural parts exposed during the consecration of the Eucharist (though this she later admitted). She also rejected the suggestion that she ever masturbated in church; rather, it was in her own bed. Inquisitors asked for more details, to which she replied: "Since the said age of eleven until some six months ago she made use of the said sin of achieving [pollution] with her hand, touching her dishonest parts, realizing that she was with the said saints [Saint Nicholas and Saint Diego], Jesus, and the Virgin; and she carnally achieved [pollution] with them, and they with her; and this has been more or less three times per day for the entire time [some nine years]."[36] Inquisitors then asked Ruiz if she had ever used any "instruments" aside from her hands, to which she replied that she had not. She then affirmed that no one had even seen or heard her in the act of pollution, nor had she mentioned this to anyone except her confessor.

Inquisitors euphemistically asked her if the "dishonest words" she exchanged with Jesus, Mary, and the saints were used to describe the "dishonest parts" of man and woman in an act of fornication. She said that they were. Here, once again, we are confronted with archival misinscription: Ruiz, in her own words, seems to repeatedly refer to "dishonest words" and "dishonest parts," though, especially in light of the more colloquial and vulgar terms she would later use to describe the body and copulation, it is very likely that this is an instance of the notary paraphrasing her responses. In doing so, he employed the lexicon of the confessional manuals like Franciscan fray Juan Bautista's 1599 *Confessionario en lengua mexicana y castellana*, written in Spanish and Nahuatl, which phrases several questions around "dishonest" words, acts, and body parts: "Did you deceive yourself and say dishonest words to provoke another into sin? When you join with your wife, do you guard the natural order, or perhaps you joined her from behind, or perhaps in that act you had other ways, dishonest and unworthy of being named here?"[37] The implication is that the corrupt utterance of such words, or the illicit pleasure derived from such body parts, was effectively a multilayered form of deceiving oneself, God, and the Church. While Ruiz admitted to most of these accusations, she asserted that she had stopped touching herself some six months earlier, though she never mentioned why.

In this first hearing, inquisitors produced some twenty-one charges for Ruiz to respond to. Her responses piqued their interest, but they felt that she was not telling all. Part of her prevarication is due to the semantic slippage around the words Ruiz used to describe her visions in such realistic terms that inquisitors seemed baffled. She regularly employed the Spanish phrase *hacer cuenta*, meaning "to realize" or "to become fully aware of (something)," in reference to her physical encounters with the divine. In one of many examples, we see this in her statement about touching herself "and realizing that she was [carnally] with the said saints, Jesus, and the Virgin." Did Ruiz merely fantasize that Jesus,

Mary, and the saints came to her to exchange "dishonest" words, kisses, and embraces? Did she believe the reality of her visions, sure that these holy figures had appeared in the flesh? Or some mix of the two? In articulating her encounters with the divine, Ruiz repeatedly used similar language, going into such vivid detail that it became impossible to distinguish reality from fantasy. Indeed, that inability to separate the real from the imagined seemed to be the experience not just of Ruiz but also for the Bancroft Library archivist who described the case as one of "claiming" sex with the divine, and even for me as I read through the trial transcripts in the archive.

Here we find an intriguing point of comparison between how Pérez and Ruiz portrayed the reality, or lack thereof, of their encounters with the divine. From the beginning of his trial, Pérez articulated his pollutions primarily in terms of the chimerical, invoking the ways that sinful visions entered his *imaginación*—his "imagination." His pollutions, in his own words, resulted from his *imaginativa*—from his very capacity to envisage the fantastical. Early in his trial, Pérez confessed that he "believed" he was married to the Virgin, that he heard voices, and that his pollutions were "licit," but never that he had physically encountered her. Rather, he thought about her in "obscene" acts through the mediums of the rosary and the painted canvas. Some of his pollutions, too, were nocturnal, brought on by dreams. This contrasts with Ruiz's language of "realizing" or "recalling" her verbal and physical interactions with the divine. It was not until her subsequent inquisitorial hearings, as we will see, that Ruiz invoked the language of the imaginary. Yet even then she told inquisitors how, in the absence of her divine lovers, "when she was alone and she touched herself she would carnally fulfill [her desire] with her memory of them," though she always "had the desire to have them present and pleasure herself [*holgarse*] with them."[38] The comparison is telling, and speaks to the different ways that fragments of interior thoughts, and the murky realities to which they point, enter the colonial archive.

In her second declaration, taken shortly after the first, we glimpse some of the intense pressures and fears that Ruiz must have felt once she realized that her case was not going to be taken lightly by the inquisitors. Ruiz abruptly retracted all her previous confessions, and alleged to suffer from *mal de corazón*, or "illness of the heart." The invocation of mal de corazón was ubiquitous in the early modern Iberian world, and could refer to a variety of physical, spiritual, and emotional maladies, everything from vertigo, swooning, and spasms to heart troubles, loss of consciousness, apoplexy, and melancholy; thus, it is difficult to determine exactly from what Ruiz suffered.[39] Ruiz unsuccessfully tried to convince the inquisitors that because of her malady she could not re-member her first declaration. Inquisitors were skeptical, and shortly thereaf-ter they removed her from the home of Garibaldi and Meneque, placing her under the care of Andrés de Montoro, the head of the textile factory, who put her in a home that was presumably more trustworthy than her previous residence. There, Ruiz—described as "small in body and skinny, with brown skin . . . with a small birthmark above her right eyebrow"—was to remain "in the good company of women" and was not permitted to leave or to speak with any man unless given permission by the commissary of the Inquisition.[40]

Following Ruiz's relocation, inquisitors took a third confession from her on April 1, 1621. This confession—referred to by Ruiz as her "true confession"—not only confirmed much of her first confession but also went into much greater detail. In what is only a short excerpt, Ruiz described Jesus, the Virgin, and the saints appearing to her in the following manner:

> They came with their dishonest parts altered [i.e., excited], and each one made it understood that now they wanted to see her loved, and they de-sired her; they came down from Heaven to Earth to fulfill her desire, but afterward, hugging and kissing her, they became inflamed in their passions, and they engaged in even more dishonest acts and words, like a man has with a woman, actually engaging in carnal copulation with her; and that with the Virgin, she would kiss her and hug her in the bed, and they would place their dishonest parts, one against the other, and that, of the rest, Jesus Christ was the one who most showed that he cherished her and who treated her well with the abovesaid acts, dishonest copulation, deeds, and dishonest words; and that he told her that he had made her to be so lovely and beautiful, and to his liking, so that she would be his whore [*puta*], and to enjoy her, and enjoy himself with her, and that he was her *puto* and her *rufian* [pimp].[41]

It was immediately following this statement that inquisitors clarified, "It is the Catholic truth that the saints from Heaven and Jesus Christ and the Virgin Mary do not sin, they cannot, nor could they have come down from Heaven to Earth to do and say the things that this declarant [Ruiz] has confessed that they have done and said to her; and that it was the Devil instead."[42] According to inquisitors, the Devil, taking on the guise of Jesus, Mary, and the saints, tricked Ruiz into believing what she did. Immediately after hearing this explanation, Ruiz admitted her guilt, acknowledging that all along the Devil had tricked her: she knew "in her soul that had been wrong and had offended God, the saints, and the Virgin with lewdness and dirty things [*suziedades*] and that she committed offenses against God and the saint, and she asks him for forgiveness."[43]

What becomes evident over the course of Ruiz's inquisitorial hearings is the profound intensity of her religiosity and devotion. She framed her relationships with Jesus, the Virgin, and the saints in erotic terms but also through divine sanction and gratitude: "They showed her their gratitude with the dishonest and amorous words they spoke to her, which corresponded to those that she said, and they named the dishonest parts of men and women."[44] Here, we catch possible glimpses of formulaic language embedded in her responses (such as her use of "dishonest" words), but she also complicated such terminology, asserting that such words could be both dishonest *and* amorous in nature. The words directly spoken to her by her divine visitors signaled the love that they had for her, and that which she had for them. Through her confessions, Ruiz painted a picture of sincere and even singular devotion between herself and the divine figures she encountered.

A central component of Ruiz's devotional expression is its simultaneous embrace of the sacred and the vulgar. When speaking in her third confession of her experiences, she said that Jesus explained why he fornicated with her: "You are my soul, my life, and my most beloved of all, and you have a sweet and delicious *coño* for me."[45] Agustina Ruiz also stated that "before having carnal copulation and having her, he would tell her, and she would respond, 'I put you in my soul,' and she would say, 'My eyes, your *carajo*, I put your *carajazo* in me,' and he would ask, 'In where?' And she would reply 'In my *coño*, which is yours,' and he would say 'And what do I do to you?' And she said, 'Fuck me, you are fucking me.'"[46] The terms Ruiz employs, *carajo* and *carajazo*, are vulgar terms for the penis, whereas *coño*, like *crica* below, colloquially refer to the vagina. Similarly, *hoder*, for which the modernized spelling is *joder*, is a crude and popular shorthand for the "carnal copulation" of which she previously spoke; it is most closely linked to our own use of "fucking." Ruiz also spoke of receiving Jesus and the saints *en quatro pies*—on all fours. These graphic colloquialisms seem proof that the notary transcribing her testimony did not alter a good portion of Ruiz's lexical choice.

This mixing of the sacred and the profane is equally central to the narration of her relationship with the Virgin Mary. Diverse acts of "pollution" and manual penetration between the two women, one mortal and the other divine, were the climax of an involved relationship between these two, which involved exchanging amorous words, hugging, kissing, and sitting next to one other with their "dishonest parts" exposed. In her third confession to inquisitors, Ruiz offered the most detail about this particular friendship, saying:

> That with the Virgin, with the kisses and hugs, they referred to each other as "*tú*" ["you," informal] and "*vos*" ["you," formal], and as "my soul," "my life," and "my love," and they would tempt each other's dishonest parts, asking each other "What of yours do I arouse?" and "What of mine do you arouse?" and they would reply to each other, "the *coño*," for you to rub, and "the *crica*," and in saying this to each other, they realized that one was the man for the other, and that the finger and the hand was the *carajo*, and they would each put it inside of the other, and from this they received pleasure [*recibían el gusto*] as if a man were fucking them; and they called each other "fucking strolling whores" and they spoke of that which could give the most pleasure, but they did not get one on top of the other, nor did they join their dishonest parts; and that these acts with the saints, Christ, and the Virgin took place in her bed, and their words sounded in a clear voice, as if talking with these men and woman in such a manner that if someone had been present, that person would have heard and understood them . . . and that each one of the said persons, the saints, Christ, and the Virgin, told her and made it understood that to repay her for her love and friendship that they enjoyed with her in this life, afterward in Heaven this declarant [Ruiz] would become a great saint.[47]

These excerpts provide a glimpse at how Ruiz attained an intimacy with the divine that was part physical, part spiritual, and part affective. Ruiz, in these narratives, repeatedly used the word *meter*—to "put" one thing inside another—when referring to her putting Jesus in her soul, to him putting his *carajazo* inside her *coño*, and to she and the Virgin putting their fingers inside each other. For Ruiz, the devotional metaphor of "putting" herself in the souls of Jesus and Mary, and they in hers, seems inseparable from the physical act of penetration. These metaphors resonate too with the sweetness of God's love—Bartolomé de Alva's 1634 confessional manual, for instance, characterizes the law of God as "being so sweet, so gentle and pleasant [*sabrosa*]"—and of Ruiz's "sweet and delicious [*sabroso*]" coño.[48]

Ruiz, it seems, consciously or not, drew heavily from hagiographies and autobiographies of early modern female mystics and saints, as well as from colonial Mexican religious imagery. The exchanging of hearts between Jesus and the mystic, the metaphor of marriage with Christ the bridegroom, and the

Fig 6.3 Late colonial drawing of Jesus nailed to the cross behind a
nun, subtly depicting the erotics of religious devotion. The inscribed
prayer reads "Sweet nails you have / Crucified my Love / Fix me
to the cross with him / Because with Him I die." Courtesy of the
Archivo General de la Nación, Mexico City, Mexico. AGN, Mapas,
Planos e Ilustraciones 280, "Cristo y monja" (1804, Querétaro).

sublimation of carnal desire into spiritual desire are all dominant themes within
Catholic traditions of female mysticism, rapture, and ecstasy (fig. 6.3). We cannot
be sure of the extent to which Agustina Ruiz may, or may not, have been influenced
by widely publicized mystics such as Saint Catherine of Siena (d. 1380), Saint
Teresa of Ávila (d. 1582), or the recently deceased Peruvian mystic Saint Rose
of Lima (d. 1617), but there are many similarities and overlaps.[49] We see this in
the highly erotic language used by mystics to describe the ineffable nature of
religious ecstasy and the mystical experience. Ruiz lacked a convent education
and likely had scant exposure to the rhetoric of the mystics aside from what she

may have heard in Mass or on the street, so she used vulgar street language to describe her spiritual and physical union with the divine.

Perhaps not entirely unlike Ruiz using the language of physical and spiritual penetration in describing her experiences, Saint Teresa of Ávila, in her autobiography, told of how a beautiful angel with his great golden spear "plunged [it] into my heart several times so that it penetrated to my entrails. When he pulled it out, I felt that he took them with it, and left me utterly consumed by the great love of God. The pain was so severe that it made me utter several moans. The sweetness caused by this intense pain is so extreme that one cannot possibly wish it to cease, nor is one's soul content with anything but God."[50] It is through the idiom of sexual pleasure that the ineffable nature and intensity of physical and spiritual union with Jesus is most closely approximated.[51] For Ruiz, it was ultimately her desire for spiritual salvation that manifested itself through physical intimacy with the divine.

Given the gravity of the case, on April 22, 1621, inquisitors decided to send Ruiz to Mexico City to be imprisoned in the Inquisition's secret jails. While her son, Francisco, remained in Querétaro, Ruiz was transported to Mexico City, allowed to bring only white clothing and, if she had any money, one hundred pesos to cover the costs of transport and food while in prison. It was there, in the prisons of the Inquisition, that Ruiz gave her final confession, in which she candidly discussed the origins of her erotic visions, and where we finally can see the importance of her life experiences.

Ruiz's earliest pollutions occurred shortly after the unexpected and violent death of her husband-to-be, Diego Sánchez Solano, in a fire while she was pregnant with their son. In search of solace, she went to visit a neighbor who had a painting of Saint Nicholas of Tolentine mounted on a small altar. The painting was so beautiful that she fell instantly and intensely in love. Afterward, she explained, "with this imagination, she went to her house and lying in bed that same night, touching her shameful parts in order to achieve pollution, the image of the abovesaid image of Saint Nicholas presented itself to her, bringing him from her memory for the said act, and in effect, she consummated [copulation] as if she were sinning with him."[52] The next morning, in bed and touching herself, she saw Saint Nicholas suddenly enter through the door of the house, donning his priest's robe, "which was full of resplendent stars."[53] He touched her face with his hand, and "tender endearments and flatteries" ensued. Saint Diego, Jesus, and the Virgin appeared to her in the days that immediately followed, also to console her in a similar manner.

The document thus hints at the painful experiences of a young girl whose parents died when she was young, who was compelled to move around between Puebla, Mexico City, San Luis Potosí, and Querétaro, who got pregnant around age twelve (possibly through coercion or violence), and who survived the ultimately tragic death of her child's father while still pregnant. Perhaps it was that the "pleasure" she experienced with her divine lovers mitigated sadness or other negative emotions, and it is very possible that they were more compassionate lovers than those that she had previously known. Indeed, her narratives depict (and archive) overlapping types of pleasure, expressed through a number of several different terms. The 1734 *Diccionario de autoridades* provides the following definitions of some of those that she used most commonly: *gusto* ("indulgence, pleasure, or desire for something"); *deleite* ("delight, pleasure, recreation, special *gusto*, happiness" or "carnal and venereal *gusto*"); *gozar* ("to have, possess, and achieve something" or "to have carnal congress"); and *holgarse* ("to have *gusto*, joy, and pleasure from some thing, to content oneself with it").[54] For Ruiz, divine love offered solace and affection, pollution and pleasure. Ruiz ultimately knew, and eventually acknowledged, that some of her actions and visions contravened religious dogma, but she nonetheless continued to experience the pleasures they brought her. Her willingness to evade dogma indicates that her very human desires were not so unnatural after all.

Agustina Ruiz ultimately pleaded that inquisitors show her mercy, expressing a wholehearted desire to put an end to her sinful acts and visions. Inquisitors, for their part, expressed their desires for Ruiz—to punish her, absolve her, and reconcile her with the Church—through a determination to interrogate and document her. The Holy Office of the Mexican Inquisition eventually sentenced Ruiz to spend three years of reclusion in Mexico City's Convent of the Conception of Nuns—a perhaps ironic punishment for someone whose crime was to eroticize the very religious iconography and language of devotion that would be ubiquitous within the convent's walls. In addition, she was brought before a medical doctor of the Holy Office to determine whether she was pregnant (she was not) and was made to receive the sacrament of confirmation, thereby strengthening her relationship with God and with the Catholic Church.[55] As with the Inquisition's sentencing of Esteban Pérez, and in spite of the seemingly transgressive nature of Ruiz's pollutions, inquisitors accepted her desire for absolution, and were ultimately more concerned with rectifying her than punishing her for her errant ways. Ruiz committed grave sins, but she always saw herself as a devout Catholic who never set out to contravene religious dogma or offend the Church.[56]

Desecrating the Divine

In the central Mexican town of Singuilucan, over the course of several days in the spring of 1752, Ana María de Leyba, an eighteen-year-old Spanish woman, confessed an egregious litany of sins and heretical acts of profanation to her priest, Father Juan Francisco Domínguez. The priest feared for her soul, but so too did she. In May of that same year, the priest denounced her to the Inquisition, but he did so at her request. In the archived denunciation of Leyba, the priest gave a highly detailed account of her sins, rendering her words in the first person, precisely as they would have been spoken to him. It is unclear, however, whether he reproduced her confession verbatim or paraphrased it. Given the highly uncommon framing of the denunciation—written by him without altering her first-person confession into the third-person voice, as was customary in inquisitorial denunciations—he most likely based his account on his own assiduously handwritten notes, jotted down with her knowledge and consent either during or immediately after her spoken confession.[57]

Among her many sins, the priest wrote, Leyba confessed to having "first made a pact with the Devil, who appeared to me in the visible figure of a man, obliging me, through this pact, not to conduct any exercise of virtue nor to wear a Rosary around my neck from then on; and I confirmed this pact with three documents [*sedulas*] that the Devil himself wrote up, and, among other things, it required that I give him my soul."[58] Leyba also admitted that she frequently encountered the Devil, "and I maintained a sordid friendship with him for a period of two years, during which I had sordid access [*accesos torpes*], with copulation consummated, on seven occasions, more or less."[59] Thus begins the Inquisition record of Ana María de Leyba, and its remarkable convergence of archival documents and documentary practices, from Leyba herself, the Devil who tempted her, the priest who documented her confession, and the Inquisition that judged her. It was the diabolical pact penned by the Devil on a *cédula* (document), and archived in her memory, that bound Leyba's soul to him. And it was the denunciation penned by the priest, and archived in the files of the Inquisition, that bound her to the Holy Office and its assessment. These diverse documents—the demonic pact, the priest's handwritten notes, the inquisitorial denunciation, and the notary's transcripts—both chimerical and real, paint a complicated picture of how and why Leyba, her doubts, and her desires came to enter (and disappear from) the colonial archive.

The archival case itself is woefully incomplete; it contains neither the full transcripts of the trial nor a final sentence (assuming the Inquisition tried Leyba in full, which it appears they did). The nineteen-folio document that is archived in Mexico's Archivo General de la Nación consists primarily of several letters (and copies of letters) by Domínguez to the Inquisition, brief information on her family background and her youth, and mundane inquisitorial correspondence attesting to the difficulties of finding her baptismal records and corroborating statements about her upbringing. We learn, for example, that Leyba, who was born in Mexico City and whose mother died while giving birth to her, lived in the Convent of San Juan between the ages of three and thirteen. At thirteen, she left and went to live with her father, but "after one year, her downfall began." Unfortunately, the document, with the exception of Domínguez's three-page denunciation of her, contains little else spoken by Ana María de Leyba herself. In contrast to the complete Inquisition trials of Pérez and Ruiz, these records contain no information on inquisitorial hearings with the suspect, if indeed she did undergo them. Yet even Leyba's short confession, which committed her to the archival record, is rich with detail about her desires and desecrations.

The reality of diabolical pacts, like the one Leyba described in her confession, would not have surprised eighteenth-century inquisitors. Neither, for the most part, would the great lengths to which Leyba had gone to profane the sacred. Many of her acts were intimately related to religious doubt: "On three occasions speaking with the Devil, I told him from my heart that I did not believe in God, although shortly thereafter I regretted having felt and professed this."[60] As her confession progressed, Leyba described some of the many ways that she polluted her body, the body of Christ, and the image of the Virgin Mary: "For about one year, I frequently had sordid accesses with an image of Our Lady, the Virgin Mary; and it should be known that on these occasions, I first had these accesses with beasts, and afterward I would come up to the image and try to get that same beast to have access with the image."[61] The image itself was most likely a painting or an engraving of the Virgin Mary, but the vague excerpt is silent on many details.

Elsewhere in our corpus, *acceso carnal*—carnal access—refers to sexual penetration; here, it seems to refer to the rubbing of one's genitalia against an image. It is still not entirely clear how she had "sordid accesses" with the image, though we can speculate that she somehow willfully defiled it with her body, possibly with saliva, menstrual blood, urine, vaginal secretions, or other bodily fluids. It is equally unclear what these "*accesos* with beasts" actually consisted of, or how she would subsequently encourage animals to have "access" with the image. Given the specific language she uses, it seems that she would have had some type of sexual contact with the animal in question, be it manual, oral, vaginal, or something else. It seems she would then, upon having excited the beast, quite possibly to the point of "pollution," get the animal's bodily emissions to come into contact with the image of the Virgin. Regarding the type of animal, we can speculate that Leyba was speaking either of domesticated dogs or of European domesticated farm animals—the very same that were implicated in criminal cases of bestiality throughout New Spain. Interestingly, this is one of the few archival references to a woman engaging in acts of bestiality. The details are scant, and because records of her inquisitorial hearings are not included, we cannot know whether inquisitors asked her to elaborate. Leyba also confessed that "three times she had impure *accesos* with the image of Christ, and many more times with the image of the *Señor niño* [baby Jesus]," and she also had unspecified "sordid accesses with various images of the saints."[62]

Leyba profaned the body of Christ in multiple and overlapping ways, reinterpreting the Holy Eucharist in a reversal, of sorts, of the Eucharist's typical aim of incorporating the divine through digestion. Leyba confessed that once when receiving Communion, instead of swallowing the Eucharist she waited until she left the church to spit out the partially digested body of Christ, and gave it to an indigenous woman, Teresa López, who had requested it. Accordingly, López "tore it into bits and mixed the pieces [of Eucharist] with some herbs, and said that the virtue of that mixture was to provoke men to obscene things."[63] López then added the herbal concoction of Leyba's expelled Eucharist into the food, drink, and clothing of the men she wanted to inflame with passion. This passing of the Eucharist between many mouths and hands, with the aim of inciting desire, was one of Leyba's many misuses of Christ's body. She too sacrilegiously took Communion many times only to "offend God," says the priest's denunciation. On another occasion, she took the Eucharist from church and guarded it in a small chest in her home, believing that it would alleviate her poverty. Most offensive, however, was how "on another occasion she had impure touches with the same Consecrated Host."[64] Here, she is being euphemistic, but the implication is that she had carnal access with the (symbolic) body of Christ, most likely by masturbating with the consecrated wafer, by inserting it into her vagina, or by rubbing it on her "dishonest" parts.

Like many in New Spain, Leyba was riddled with religious doubt, which was partly the result of daily hardships she faced. She struggled to reconcile religious tenets with her own feelings of skepticism. Her compulsion to profane holy images stemmed from her own deeply conflicted relationship with the divine. Viscerality plays a crucial role here, evidenced of course by the physical intensity of her actions, but perhaps just as important, by the uncontrollable anger she felt at times toward Jesus and the saints. Leyba, for example, would have "sordid accesses" with the saints when she asked something of them, but if her requests were not granted, she would rail against the saints, "spitting on the floor in the presence of their images, in a display of ire, and telling myself that the saints do not have the power to achieve from God that which I asked of them."[65] Leyba, it seems, sincerely wanted to believe, but in light of the fact that so few of her prayers were answered, her doubts continually grew and she increasingly exacted revenge on God, Jesus, the Virgin, and the saints by polluting them—spitting out the Eucharist, having accesos with holy images, and the like. Perhaps given the Church's misogynistic and depreciatory views on female sexuality, she saw her body and bodily emissions as the most effective means through which to exact retribution.

Leyba's wrath toward the divine was certainly visceral, but so too were those unshakable feelings that drove her to expose her inner thoughts to her priest in the first place: guilt, remorse, shame. In this, she shared something in common with others, including Esteban Pérez and Agustina Ruiz, whose relationships—physical and affective alike—with God, Jesus, the Virgin, and the saints were, in one way or another, tortured. According to Massumi, "The felt quality of guilt has its own affective ambience, which can transmute into a number of specific emotions: hatred, resentment, disgust, distrust."[66] Indeed, it appears that Leyba's guilt manifested itself through intensely conflicted emotions, which she expressed in numerous ways—through her devotion and supplication, as well as through doubt and anger. Leyba mentions that on several occasions she had confessed many of her sins to other priests, who absolved her of them. Jaffary writes that women and men in colonial Mexico who polluted the sacraments often experienced ritualized "cycles of desecration followed by guilt, repentance, and confession."[67] Indeed, Leyba seems to fit this pattern perfectly— starting as early as age thirteen to pollute herself, desecrate the divine, and experience a mix of ire, remorse, and doubt, confessing these acts to her priest only, we may assume, to engage in increasingly sinful acts related to her body, the Devil, animals, and holy images.

Father Juan Francisco Domínguez, who denounced Leyba to the Inquisition, was initially convinced that she was sincere in her remorse and contrition. In the first of several letters, in May 1752, he wrote to inquisitors that she severely suffered from "sicknesses of spirit and body," occasionally vomiting blood, but that she was willing to do whatever penance was necessary of her.[68] The priest begged that inquisitors treat "this poor woman" with kindness and leniency. Leyba herself explicitly asked forgiveness from God and the Inquisition both for the sins she had willingly disclosed as well as those that did not "come to her memory." In a second letter to the Inquisition, dated June 1752, the priest wrote that he sensed in her "a genuine contrition and a sincere intent to rectify her life," and requested that the Inquisition be prudent and merciful in its decision.[69] These early letters also make reference to Leyba suffering from mal de corazón—the same sickness Agustina Ruiz was said to have. On August 19, Domínguez wrote back to inquisitors in Mexico City, who could find no records of her birth certificate and no evidence in the convent's archive that she ever lived there. The priest reexamined her, and reported that her answers were true. Now, however, Domínguez also concluded, "this woman is possessed by the Devil, from one month ago up to today," and that she was harboring from an occult, malignant spirit, and battling her greatest temptations yet.[70] This final letter is followed by some mundane correspondence about Leyba's family, and with this the archival record abruptly ends.

The eighteenth-century title page to Leyba's 1752 Inquisition file makes only vague reference to the sins themselves, reading, "Against Ana María de Leyba. For the crime of pact with the Devil and other errors" (fig. 6.4).[71] Couched within these *otros errores*—other errors—are acts and desires that seem to be of even more concern to inquisitors, though in the archival description (both the original description penned in the eighteenth century, as in the various ways the phrase is used up to the present) there is an emphasis on the diabolical pact as if *it* were the more serious sin that Leyba had committed. Archival description, as we have seen repeatedly, can "serve to create (or occlude) conceptual categories that inscribe significance and meaning, and hence condition the ways the pasts they evidence are understood."[72] This is certainly the case with Leyba, as well as for people such as Lázaro Martínez (for "profanation of cadaver") and Manuel Arroyo (for "counseling that sucking semen from men was not a sin"). Archival documents such as these assemble—but more often, disperse—a fascinating array of criminal acts and heretical thoughts, which are subsumed under the occasionally unclassifiable "other errors" in the lexicon of notaries' terminology and archivists' descriptors.

I conclude this discussion of the archival, erotic, and devotional imaginary with one final case from the files of the Mexican Inquisition. Archived in the

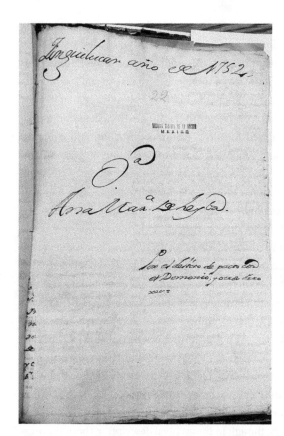

Fig 6.4 Title page of the 1752 Inquisition case "against Ana María de Leyba. For the crime of pact with the Devil, and other errors." Courtesy of the Archivo General de la Nación, Mexico City, Mexico. AGN, Inquisición 981, exp. 22, fol. 327.

online database of Mexico's Archivo General de la Nación is the 1790 "spontaneous denunciation of Ramón Sánchez de la Baquera [*sic*], Spaniard, of single status, unemployed, of thirty years of age, who lives in the street named De La Estación, for having accesses with sacred images, invoking the Devil, and superstitions."[73] The archival database entry notes that the commissary of the Inquisition in the town of San Juan del Río in the state of Querétaro informed the Holy Office that according to his thoughts, comportment, and manner, he was "a dumb man, and simpleton, and of those crazies [*locos*] who are tolerated."[74] This case merges several components of the cases of Pérez, Ruiz, and Leyba, introducing new expressions of eroticized religiosity, as well as the relationship between guilt and the suspect's own mental capacity.

The case itself helps us make sense of possible motives behind Leyba's repeated, ritualistic pollutions of the divine but also of the fetishistic qualities that some suspects, such as Pérez and Ruiz, imbued certain religious objects and images. Vaquera's Inquisition file is short—only thirteen folios—and is chronologically out of order, which poses challenges to piecing together the narrative. Vaquera made his first self-denunciation to inquisitors on November 12, 1789, admitting to "having had access with two images of Our Lady the Virgin Mary, which are venerated in the church of the Dominican convent of the said town" on three occasions.[75] He was purportedly absolved of this sin, in its first occurrence, by an unidentified priest who, according to inquisitors, because of his ignorance "did not recognize the gravity of this crime."[76] The second priest to whom he confessed suggested that he should denounce himself to the Inquisition, yet it was not until the third time he confessed his sins to a priest that he then took the initiative to denounce himself.

Months later, in January 1790, upon being imprisoned by the Holy Office, Vaquera went into greater detail about the nature of his crimes: "He equally declared having executed the same (*cum efusione seminis*) that he had expressed having done to the Images of the Virgin to the martyr Saint Peter over the course of a year."[77] Inquisitors' use of Latin here—"with seminal effusion"—is yet another example of the insertion of formulaic language by the notary, or perhaps inquisitors themselves, into the testimony of the declarant. Vaquera specified exactly how he had "access" with the Virgin: "with the image of Our Lady of the Rosary that is venerated in the church of the convent of Our Father Saint Dominic, in whose sacred place he has committed [accesses] by having rubbed [*confricando*] his virile member against the robes of the sacred image, and that over the course of eight years, or perhaps more, there he committed this crime so many times that he cannot estimate the number."[78]

Having polluted the robes of the image of Mary with such frequency, Vaquera told inquisitors that he could not remember the number of times that he had done so. He did, however, claim to recall the specific number of times, or close to it, that he had pollutions or "seminal effusions" with other holy images, especially when they took place inside a church or a convent. His pollutions on the image of the baby Jesus, for example, took place on "four to six occasions, sometimes in the day, and others at night, without being able to verify the days or hours."[79] Vaquera recounted the following pollutions to his inquisitors: six times in church with a small image of Our Lady of the Rosary; about eight times in church with an even smaller image of Our Lady; fifteen times in a Dominican convent with an image of Saint Mary of Magdalene at Calvary; twelve times with an image of Our Lady on the church's alms box; seven times in church on the glass case that protected a painted image of Saint Anne; and, among several other examples, ten times each, at home, with two different medallions with images of Our Lady of the Rosary. Vaquera's enumeration of his "accesses" with particular images (as well as with the glass case enclosing that of Saint Anne) is fascinating, and points back to the emphasis in the confessional manuals on memorizing the exact number of times one committed a sin, so as ensure a "good" confession.

When inquisitors asked Vaquera about his having committed other, similar crimes, "he said that he was so habituated to the sin of lasciviousness, and so impassioned by this manner of objects [*tan apasionado a esta calidad de objetos*] to which his declared sins refer that never satisfied with the horrendous accesses he has expressed, on many occasions he would end up having them [pollutions] on the mouths and hands of the sacred images . . . considering those images the object of his sordidness."[80] The grammar of Vaquera's peculiar "fetishes" (if we can call them that) and religious desires was determined by an atmosphere of extreme veneration for holy images and iconography. In solely desiring the tangible sacred *objects* themselves, rather than divine figures that they represented, Vaquera differentiated himself from Pérez, Ruiz, and Leyba but shares something inherently visceral, and intimately related to the divine, with them. Very much in contrast to the desecrations that Leyba engaged in with the sacred, Vaquera avowed that he "had never felt negatively toward Our Lady the Virgin and her saints, and that guided by his natural simplicity he directed [his acts] more [toward] the cult and veneration that he had for the Holiest Virgin."[81] In the narrative Vaquera constructs for his inquisitorial audience, he never meant to profane or desecrate the sacrosanct but simply could not contain his passion for sacred objects, especially when he found himself alone in a church or convent.

Finally, Ramón Sánchez de la Vaquera admitted that on several occasions he had invoked the Devil, but mainly "so that he would take away the stultifying simplicity and craziness that he has, and to sin with the images and women of the world."[82] As such, he carried with him a miniature image of the Devil, painted for him by an indigenous *brujo* (or "witch") named either José or Vicente Resendis. He told inquisitors that he regularly kissed this image, offering up fasts for the Devil. He also carried with him "some bones and fingers of the dead" that an Indian woman named Micaela had given him. Such "superstitions" could have exacerbated the wrath of the Inquisition, though here they did not.

Vaquera's acts were apparently unsuspected, until he denounced himself. From details found in the historical record, he evidently felt conflicted about the sinful nature of his acts and the compulsion to pollute venerated religious objects. Though he obviously succumbed to the temptation to continue these acts over the course of many years, by the time he had denounced himself to the Inquisition, Vaquera was repentant. Having voluntarily admitted his sins, Vaquera told inquisitors how "to fulfill this, his declaration [of repentance], he wished to be hanged and burned [by the Inquisition] to God's satisfaction."[83] Inquisitors, acknowledging his contrition, noted as well, "the delinquent [Vaquera] is apparently a fatuous man, reputed to be demented and harmless by the townspeople."[84] In contrast to Manuel de Arroyo, who was severely punished and publicly shamed for expressing the belief that "it is not a sin to suck human semen," Vaquera was punished minimally. Inquisitors sentenced him to work in a convent under the close supervision of priests for an unspecified number of years. The leniency of his punishment derived partly from the inquisitors' perceptions that he was unsound of mind and that his acts were the direct result of "craziness," which, as well, likely eroded inquisitors' confidence in the veracity of his account.

Glaringly absent from the archival documents—and in seemingly drastic contrast to how criminal courts dealt with the polluted bodies of animals in bestiality trials—is any mention of the fate of the sacred images, adorning robes, glass encasings, and engraved alms boxes that Vaquera had polluted with his "voluntary emissions" of semen. Inquisitors, we might assume, would have been concerned with their very existence and with their continued use in churches and convents. There is, however, no archival evidence that points to any need on the part of church officials to locate, cleanse or purify, or eradicate them. As such, archival pollutions persist textually, in the rich transcriptions found within the files of the Inquisition, and maybe even physically, in the potential existence of polluted sacred images and objects themselves. It seems that the social memory of bodily pollution did not live on in holy objects and images in quite the same way that it did through the body of the defiled animal in bestiality cases.

These colonial Mexican Inquisition cases of desiring (and polluting) the divine are also meaningfully connected through the court's suggestions that each individual was, in his or her own way, unsound of mind or emotionally agitated. Everyone discussed in this chapter was said to suffer immensely from one or more of the following ailments: mal de corazón or "illness of heart," melancholy, dementia, fatuousness, locura or "craziness," and other unspecified "sicknesses" of body and soul. While spiritual and physical illness was nothing new to inquisitors, we do see a subtle yet significant shift, from the seventeenth century to the eighteenth, in terms of inquisitors' increasing willingness to interpret unorthodox religious desires through humoral models of excess desire rather than through heresy or sacrilege.

We see this in the Inquisition case of Francisco Xavier de la Vega, a Spaniard in his midthirties who voluntarily denounced himself to the Inquisition in 1700 for having committed sodomy with a priest, for wanting to "commit the same sin of sodomy with the images of Christ" that he had encountered in a church, and for being consumed by *tan perbersas pensamientos*, "such perverse thoughts."[85] The inquisitor who interrogated Xavier de la Vega acknowledged the gravity of his sins but concluded that he was suffering from "what medics call 'satyriasis' in men, and 'uterine furor' in women, originating from the excessive and acrimonious heat in the genital humor and salts of such activity, which reduce the patient to such an extreme of libidinous impetus, that they, like brute beasts, lose their natural sense of modesty, as the medics I have read, and some moralists and jurists, propose."[86] The lexicon of *perversion*, employed by Xavier de la Vega and transcribed as such by the notary, and of the medical *patient*, used by the inquisitor, is illustrative of a shift in language and attitudes at the onset of the eighteenth century. Indeed, the Spanish word *perversión* has no entry in dictionaries prior to the eighteenth century. Inquisitors, interpreting the signs of Xavier de la Vega's desires through medical rather than religious signs, interned him in the Hospital de Jesus, where he could be more thoroughly examined and treated by medical doctors. No further information about de la Vega is included in the Inquisition files, yet given the trends that have emerged in this chapter, we can safely assume that the Inquisition did not punish him with any severity, despite the ostensibly egregious sin of sodomy with a priest and his longing to commit sodomy with images of Christ. Thus, by the late colonial period, we find increasing evidence of a shift in the attitudes of the Church and the Inquisition toward sacred pollution and its causes, which correspondingly altered the grounds on which such acts entered the colonial archive.

Archiving Guilt

Asunción Lavrin is correct in her assertion that voluntary pollution "contravened the church's view that seminal emission must be carried into the female vagina (*intra vas naturale*) for the purpose of procreation." Yet, as this chapter has shown, the conceptual category of pollution encompassed much more than masturbation, and was not limited to the emission of male semen outside the "proper vessel" of the vagina. Women too fell into pollution, largely through the acts of solitary or mutual masturbation, and in the medieval and early modern worlds, women's emission of "semen" (though different from the semen produced by male testes) was a central component to the act. Pollution—but one of the many sins against nature, as it came to be archived in these and other cases—bridges the human, the animal, and the divine, at times calling into question the discrete coherence of each of these categories, and at others reifying them in ways that benefited one at the expense of the other. Pollution, and the desires that invariably accompany it, expands the boundaries of the archival imaginary and indeed the very limits of bodies and souls, both human and divine.

The spiritual and bodily interactions of these individuals—José Esteban Pérez, Agustina Ruiz, Ana María de Leyba, Ramón Sánchez de la Vaquera, and Francisco Xavier de la Vega—with the divine are each nuanced and slightly different, pointing to the terminological and conceptual limits of framing these desires through the category of "sex" (or through that of the "unnatural"). These narratives highlight the epistemological limits of the colonial archive but also illustrate the wealth of information that can be both accessed in, and reimagined through, archival documents. These archival traces of divine desiring radically expand our possibilities for thinking through and engaging with the desires of the past. The archived desires analyzed in this chapter are not automatically "sexual" in terms of how we understand the word today. Certainly, we find various elements of the erotic—the stories here variously refer to the obscene, lascivious, sensual, sordid, and perverse—all tied to the sin of pollution, but each of these archival cases is organized not around desires that are explicitly "sexual" but rather around real and imagined intimacies with the divine. These desires transgressed, and were simultaneously modeled on, Church dogma in ways that for these individuals were positive and negative.

Desires for the divine manifested themselves through bodies, thoughts, devotions, and acts of profanation that were meant to test, provoke, and retaliate against the divine. These cases are exceptional in that they represent certain corporeal and eroticized configurations with the divine that are not found in any other archival documents of which I am aware. The narratives that emerge in these cases hint at a level of interiority—intimating the innermost thoughts of a suspect—far more so than the majority of sodomy and bestiality cases. As such, we retrospectively (and archivally) gather glimpses of the intermittent pangs of guilt, and traces of shame, that these already fragmented historical subjects appear to have felt and experienced viscerally and profoundly.

Amid these rare, sometimes shocking moments of insight, we are also witnessing guilt as a cultural and historical construct. We cannot discount the possibility that these suspects may have experienced both guilt and shame formulaically at times, perhaps *performing* remorse, on occasion, for themselves as for their confessors and inquisitors and even for God. Here, I understand guilt to be a frenzied affective state—fluctuating between (and disrupting) pleasure and regret—that is experienced both emotionally and physically, through the body. Some manifestation of guilt, in each of these cases, served as a primary impetus to confess one's sins to a local priest and, on occasion, to voluntarily denounce oneself to the Holy Office, sometimes only at the urging of a priest who was unable to absolve the penitent of potentially heretical sins. Whatever performances we glimpse in these archives, however, do not detract from the sheer humanness that, in all its messiness, emerges from these cases.

Here we find an important difference between how pollution and the other sins against nature typically came to be documented, and eventually entered colonial archives. Sodomy, bestiality, and solicitation in the confessional— of which there are hundreds of extant cases, and many more denunciations, scattered throughout archives in Mexico, Guatemala, Spain, and the United States—usually came to be recorded by means of the denunciation of another person. This individual may have witnessed, been the victim of, or simply heard about the unnatural act from the mouth of another. The same, however, cannot be said for archival references to pollution, perhaps because of the private, solitary nature of masturbation and its accompanying fantasies. Yet we should be wary of any assertion that pollution was an inherently private or solitary act. As the cases here show, pollution was often imagined and believed to be communal in nature, something to be engaged in with an individual and the many manifestations of the sacred: divine figures, holy images, religious objects, many of which accrued a further erotic charge with the possibility of committing the act in sacred (and communal) space such as a church or a convent. Pollution—as articulated in confession with a priest or in a self-denunciation to the Inquisition—entered the colonial archive through a person's ritualized disclosure of their own sin, through the demonstration of contrition, and through the affective experience of guilt.

Ever since I first read through the Inquisition file of Agustina Ruiz at the Bancroft Library in 2006, I have wondered what that particular image of Saint Nicholas of Tolentine—from which her earliest erotic visions of the saint partly originated—might have looked like. We know it was mounted on a small altar in the house of Ruiz's neighbor in the early decades of the seventeenth century, but we know next to nothing about the image itself. All we know is that some confluence of affect, circumstance, and representation—intense sadness at the death of her husband-to-be, longing for spiritual and physical solace, proximity to the religious painting, its striking visual details—made this particular painting of Saint Nicholas stand out in a way that it may not have on any other day, at any other moment of time. More than a decade has ensued since I encountered that image in Ruiz's transcribed confession; and still every time I come across a religious painting of Saint Nicholas—be it in an art museum, colonial church or convent, in printed books, or on the Internet—I wonder if the image might share something in common with that one. Was the image Ruiz gazed upon copied from a painting endorsed by the church, painted by a talented artist in exquisite detail, or one of many created by a local street artist who peddled religious images to make ends meet? Did the image depict the saint's face, body, hands, and feet, or a halo around his head? How might his eyes have followed hers, in ways that made his countenance legible and meaningful?

There are, of course, no satisfactory answers to such questions. Yet the very impossibility of answering them says something important about the nature of the colonial archive and about our relation to it. We will never know what those holy images—so desired by the women and men in this chapter, along with so many others in New Spain and the wider Iberian Atlantic world—actually looked like, or why they were chosen over others that were equally accessible. Most of the actual images referred to in these cases are probably long gone, lost or destroyed by the ravages of time. It is also possible, though perhaps unlikely, that some were purposely eradicated either by the protagonists of these Inquisition trials or by church officials who sought to take them out of spiritual circulation. Ultimately, the visual archives of sainthood that partly inspired Ruiz's visions are forever lost to history. So too are the religious images and objects that Pérez, Leyba, and Vaquera passed over their bodies, both deliberately and unintentionally polluting them (and themselves) in the process. These archival documents, read in the present, point again to these overlapping absences—a point that I elaborate further in the conclusion.

These instances of eroticized religiosity are revealing of our archival engagement in another way: the relationship between the concept of the archive and the divine, especially in Judeo-Christianity. Any and all desires for the divine exist in relation to the implicit archives of the divine. That is to say, the archive of colonial New Spain, like every archive, bears partial witness to the sinful acts and desires of the past. But for many people, these earthly archives pale in comparison to the "records" kept by God, who knows and sees all. It was thus God's vast (unwritten) archive of the sins of humanity that really troubled sinners and believers in New Spain. For it was this ethereal archive of the sinner's faith and contrition—not the bureaucratic, mundane criminal or ecclesiastical archives—that would ultimately determine one's fate in the afterlife, that would make the difference between the everlasting bliss of Heaven and the perennial torments of Hell. The very notion of an all-encompassing, all-knowing archive, which records all facets of human experience, is just a further reminder of just how limited the human potential for archiving really is.

Those who desired the divine a bit too much, not unlike all we have encountered throughout this book, come to us through an uneven arrangement of oral, textual, visual, and corporeal archives. They exist on a continuum, constantly traversing the presumed gaps between devotion and desecration, discretion and revelation, pleasure and remorse. The archived subjects about whom we read and write, perhaps not unlike ourselves, inhabit multiple points along the vast spectrum of human desires, between what is "natural" and what is "unnatural," uneasily posited between archival presence and archival absence in the past and in the present.

Conclusion

Accessing Absence, Surveying Seduction

Students are told about the many types and varieties of repository and record office, and the fragmentary, incomplete material they contain; they are told about "the cult of archive" among certain historians and those sad creatures who fetishise them; they are warned about the seductions of the archive, the "entrancing stories" that they contain, which do the work of the seducer.

—CAROLYN STEEDMAN, *Dust: The Archive and Cultural History*

Sins against Nature has surveyed a range of archival narratives about "unnatural" bodies, desires, and devotions in New Spain. We have, in the process, worked through some of the many glaring gaps and absences of the colonial archive—historiographical silences, visceral reactions, missing native-language testimonies, lost or incomplete trial records, incinerated human and animal bodies, ritualistically burned dildos, disregarded female same-sex desire. Here, partly though my own archive stories, I turn to the question of archival access, and to how we, as researchers, access the archival absences that we do. I turn, as well, to the "seduction of the archives" of which Carol Steedman wistfully speaks in *Dust: The Archive and Cultural History*. To do so, I articulate how and why I, like Steedman, let myself be seduced by the archives—by the many fragmented memories it promises to give up, and by those it holds back. The answers to why, of course, are professional, personal, and political. Anjali Arondekar asks an important question, based on her research on sodomy and sexuality in the archives of British colonial India: "Put simply, can an empty archive also be full?"[1] In some senses, my problem is quite the opposite: the archives of colonial New Spain are teeming with documents related to the sins against nature. Still, the question of archival absences—and how we access them—remains central to my research and writing of history.

Every archival encounter is partly determined by the granting of, and limitations to, access. In late 2016, the Comité Mexicano de Ciencias Históricas—an association of institutions and historians dedicated to the protection and stimulation of historical inquiry in Mexico—published a petition harshly critiquing the earlier 2016 Ley General de Archivos (General Law of Archives), which, among other things, restricted the Mexican public's access to its own archives. One part of that petition—titled "Por el derecho a la memoria," that is, *for the right to memory*—reads: "We—the [archival] researchers who dedicate our efforts to better comprehend the historical development of our country [Mexico], as well as its current problems, so that we can contribute to the creation of a better future—express our profound preoccupation with the initiative known as the Ley General de Archivos that on November 17, 2016, was put forth for Senate debate. The Law, which could be an opportunity to improve Mexican archives and support transparency, in its current state will provoke precisely the contrary."[2] The petition itself—published in the press and online in November 2016—was directed to the Mexican people, to the Mexican government, and, specifically, to the director of the Archivo General de la Nación (AGN). For as "Por el derecho a la memoria" reminds us, accessing the past is always an intimately personal and intensely political issue, and it is one that Mexicans continue to struggle for legally, politically, and historiographically.

When I first walked toward Mexico's AGN (fig. C.1) from the San Lázaro metro station in the summer of 2003—smack in the middle of Mexico City, less than two miles northeast of the capital's frenetic central plaza, the Zócalo—it was with all the excitement and trepidation of a young researcher. For the very first time, I was coming into contact with historical archives. I was anxious and ready to be drawn in but also unnerved—both by the towering complex of penitentiary buildings in which the documents were preserved and by the sixteenth- and seventeenth-century Spanish handwriting that was then barely legible to me. The national archive was housed in Mexico's infamous penitentiary, the Palacio de Lecumberri (more colloquially known as the *Palacio Negro*, or the "Black Palace"), which was in operation from 1900 to 1976. The prison was decommissioned and repurposed in 1980, and the AGN opened its doors in 1982. The prison was inaugurated under the auspices of Porfirio Díaz, who served seven terms as president, from 1876 to 1910, and is best known for the period of Mexican history known as the Porfiriato, which was characterized by remarkable economic growth and an abundance of in-

Fig C.1 Photograph of the main entrance of the Archivo General de la Nación, Mexico City, Mexico. Photo by the author, 2015.

vestment and modernization, and an equal amount of political and social repression.

The Palacio de Lecumberri is perhaps most notorious for having held thousands of left-wing political prisoners, many of whom were tortured and killed, in the aftermath of the Mexican student movement and the Tlatelolco massacre of 1968, on the eve of Mexico City's Olympic Games, and throughout Mexico's Dirty War of the 1970s and early 1980s—its *guerra sucia*. The Mexican government has never fully acknowledged the vicious things that occurred within these walls. Throughout its existence, Lecumberri functioned, at least in theory, as a correctional and preventative institution, aspiring to rehabilitate prisoners by shaping them into law-abiding citizens. A database of many of the prisoners interned between 1920 and 1976—10,111 pages long, based on documents held at the Archivo Histórico del Distrito Federal—suggests that the prison sought to punish and rehabilitate convicts for the most ordinary crimes, from the awful to the mundane: rape, homicide, spousal abandonment, adultery, fraud,

Fig C.2 Undated postcard with an aerial photograph of the Lecumberri penitentiary, now Mexico's national archive. Photo courtesy of Silvia Mejía of Rozana Montiel Estudio de Arquitectura, Mexico City, Mexico.

forgery, falsification of documents, breaking and entering, carrying concealed weapons, and *malvivencia* (literally "bad living," which implied loitering and vagrancy).[3]

We know, however, that this list is not exhaustive. Homosexuals, for example, were imprisoned at Lecumberri, though not necessarily because of their homosexuality, which was decriminalized in 1871, but rather because of "immorality" and other conveniently vague crimes. There is no explicit mention of homosexuals in this particular database. Neither is there mention of left-wing students and political prisoners. Their traces lie elsewhere, such as in the partly deteriorated twentieth-century acetate negatives of those jailed *jotos (maricones)* homosexuales—or "~~fags (queers)~~ homosexuals"—the partly crossed-out labels used in the thematic index of the Inventario Henrique Díaz, stored in the AGN's Fototeca, its photographic library. If we look closely enough, we can begin to locate these gaps and absences. Both homosexuality and sodomy can thus be found in the traces, but only if we acknowledge their own illegibility, if we recognize how these fragments of past lives confound the archival present with the historical past.

Especially striking is the architectural structure of the prison (fig. C.2), in which several massive corridors housing all the jail cells emanate from a central watchtower, the embodiment of the Panopticon, designed in the late eighteenth

Fig C.3 "Corredor E completed" of the Lecumberri Prison, taken shortly after construction. Courtesy of the Archivo General de la Nación, Mexico City, Mexico. AGN, Fototeca, Álbum de obras de ampliación de la penitenciaria del Distrito Federal, Obras Ampliación Penitenciaría 83 (February 25, 1910): "Crujía E completa."

century by English philosopher and social theorist Jeremy Bentham. His Panopticon directly inspired the Lecumberri, in which "all the cells, organized in corridors that formed the seven arms of a star, could be easily watched over from a central point."[4] The patio that once surrounded the Lecumberri's watchtower (visible in figs. C.2 and C.3) has long since been redesigned as the central foyer of the AGN, through which researchers and archivists must pass in order to enter the archive's reading room. The lookout tower has long since been replaced by a massive central dome, with a large Mexican flag emblazoned on its eastern side. The flag hangs directly in front of Gallery 4, which, until late 2016, held the vast majority of colonial documents (and long served as a reading room for researchers). The adjacent galleries—previously the wings that held prison cells—until 2016, housed photographs, maps, documents, and administrative papers from the colonial period through the twentieth century.

The historical origins of the current archive can be traced back to 1790, when Juan Vicente Güemes Pacheco y Padilla, Second Count of Revillagigedo and Viceroy of New Spain, proposed that the Spanish government's Ministerio de Gracia y Justicia establish the Archivo General de la Nueva España (General

Archive of New Spain). The purpose was to centralize and reorganize the vice-regal papers and bureaucratic correspondence pertaining to the viceroyalty of New Spain. That archival project has, in the more than two centuries since, undergone several iterations and relocations including its move to the Lecumberri in 1980. Its most recent major shift took place in late 2016, when the AGN transferred nearly all its documents (from the colonial period to the late twentieth century) into a newly constructed building just behind the Lecumberri, which has a greater capacity to permanently store and preserve the massive quantity of papers. These massive legal and structural changes were tied, in part, to the November 17, 2016, Ley General de Archivos, which is harshly (and rightly) critiqued by the Comité Mexicano de Ciencias Históricas and other concerned citizens.

As with every archive, the protocols of the AGN, just like its purpose, have shifted dramatically over the years; such changes have been both positive and negative. When I began my research at the AGN in 2003, researchers were prohibited from taking photographs of the documents (nor were they required to wear latex or cloth gloves, which they now are). Instead, researchers had to request and pay for photocopies—occasionally illegible or cut-off on the margins—of the original documents, which undoubtedly contributed to the gradual deterioration of each photocopied page. One can easily imagine the "dust" (to return to Steedman's evocative title) from all the accumulated documents that had to be brushed from the copy machine at the end of the day. Fortunately, sometime in my final years of research, the director of the AGN altered this policy, allowing researchers to take photographs (without flash) of any document, at no cost.

Such long-awaited changes are frustratingly at odds, however, with the 2016 Ley General de Archivos—critiqued in "Por el derecho a la memoria"—which brought about several unwelcome modifications in terms of archival access: shorter hours for researchers and archivists; necessary appointments, which must be scheduled days or weeks in advance, in order to enter the reading room and access the documents; stringent restrictions on the files of the Mexican Inquisition (only low-quality digital scans are currently available to researchers, not the original documents themselves as they previously had been); limitations in terms of who can access archival documents; and caps on the number of documents researchers can access per day. Part of this law even intimates that unspecified documents at the AGN may be under threat of destruction; Article 14 of the Ley General de Archivos specifies that all documents should be reappraised within two years, which could mean that several documents will be transferred to other archives or simply destroyed.

These new archival restrictions are, of course, not without precedent. Though Article 6 of the 1977 Mexican Constitution guarantees "the right to information," laws relating to information access have undergone changes both subtle and significant across the early twenty-first century. On January 23, 2012, for example, in a move that has been excoriated by human rights activists, the Mexican government silently blocked access to archival documents dealing with Mexico's Dirty War.[5] It is easy to see why researchers, historians, and even archivists are frustrated with these policy changes and limitations on access to information. In the words of the Comité Mexicano de Ciencias Históricas, such changes put at risk the very "possibility of constructing a collective memory" in Mexico.[6] Here, we discover an uncanny resonance between how the Catholic Church hides sexual abuse by priests (within the Inquisition's vast archives) and how the Mexican government hides its own complicity in violent acts of state terror (within its own vast national and state archives, increasingly off-limits to the Mexican public).

Despite these major changes in the organization and operation of the AGN, the traces of the Lecumberri's past still abound throughout the building—both in the archive's holdings and in its very architecture. The history of the Lecumberri, and its transformation into the AGN, embodies a fundamental archival reality: the physical space of any given archive directly influences its status as a memory space, affecting how we do (or do not) access particular pasts. While there are no longer any prisoners held within the walls of the Lecumberri, the old jail cells that once housed inmates served, from 1982 to 2016, as a storage facility for the documents for a significant portion of some fifty-two linear kilometers of documents, an equivalent of approximately 375 million folios (figs. C.3 and C.4). Up until the end of 2016, if a researcher in any of the eight individual galleries requested one of these documents, the archivist would walk to the back of the corridor, or up the stairs to the second floor, and retrieve it from within one of the old jail cells.[7] In this sense, the physical structure of the Lecumberri directly impacted how archivists, staff, and researchers engage with the documents housed there. It is the physical space of the archive, alongside the content of that archive, that seduces our readings of the present through the past, and vice versa.

Achille Mbembe tells us that "the archive has neither status nor power without an architectural dimension, which encompasses the physical space of the

Fig C.4 Galería 4 (Gallery 4) of Mexico's Archivo General de la Nación, with the old jail cells being used for document storage (in 2015), which long functioned as the AGN's reading room. Photo by the author, 2015.

site of the building, its motifs and columns, the arrangement of the rooms, the organisation of the 'files,' the labyrinth of corridors, and that degree of discipline, half-light and austerity that gives the place something of the nature of a temple and a cemetery."[8] The Lecumberri seems to embody Mbembe's claim, as its "status" and "power" derive partly from this entanglement of building and document, place and page. This entanglement is part of what is so seductive (and troubling) about this particular place; it is an architectural space, a historical monument—a kind of "document" in and of itself. Given the peculiar history of the Lecumberri, Mexico's national archive—even more so than most archives, which are kept in buildings (like the new AGN building) designed and constructed specifically for the purpose of storing documents—abounds with archival absences that are always partly present yet constantly evasive.

Archives—with their dusty boxes, crumbling pages, and computer notations—harbor an incredible potential to seduce. And, in turn, each of us who uses them, organizes them, and otherwise comes into contact with them has the potential to be seduced. We in the humanities seem to be obsessed with the archives and all that they can do to us. In recent years, we have seen a virtual explosion of monographs, special issues, anthologies, journal articles, conferences, and symposia dedicated to the theorization of archives and their "material and absent presence."[9] Interestingly, much of the recent work on archives is interdisciplinary, and comes from fields other than archival science, library and information studies, and history—the disciplines within which our nuanced conceptualizations of the archive and its classificatory systems first originated. Especially with the "archival turn" in the humanities, which largely followed the publication of Michel Foucault's genealogical approach in *The Archaeology of Knowledge* (1976) and Jacques Derrida's deconstructive approach in *Archive Fever* (1996), archivists and scholars in an ever-widening diversity of disciplines have deepened our understanding of archives. Many of these voices have also cautioned against being seduced by the archives.

The notion of seduction intimates the archive as a source of temptation, both dangerous and disingenuous. From the "seductions of access" and "seductions of historical recovery" to the "epistemological seduction" of the archive and the archive's penchant for "seducing us by its appearance of the real," archival seduction comes off largely as something that we must guard ourselves against—at least, if we want to be good, methodologically rigorous historians.[10] I, however, believe that there is something theoretically and methodologically productive in occasionally letting ourselves give in to archival seduction. Kathryn Burns, working through the archives of colonial Peru as "murky, clouded windows" on the past, tells her readers that at times "we let our mind's ear enjoy the seduction of the archival first person, the 'I' created through notarial mediation."[11] Yet the admission that one might *enjoy* the seductions of the colonial archive, at least in the context of colonial Latin American historiography, is neither owned up to nor theorized with much frequency (with some exceptions, like Burns). The very idea of the "archival first person" might also refer to those scholars, like myself, who affectively engage with archives (in the first person), admitting to being seduced by them and to giving in to their allure.

Seduction is a meta-theme that has emerged in each of the chapters of this book, sometimes subtly, sometimes explicitly. We should resist the simple admonition against being seduced and instead explore the nature of that seduction. But what about the archives, aside from the "entrancing stories" found within, is seductive? How, and why, do archives seduce? And, returning to the epigraph, what exactly is this "work of the seducer" of which Steedman speaks? Why do we so often seem to believe that researchers in the archive must be on guard, warily looking out for the surreptitious ways that the archives suck us in and induce attraction—whether for the archives themselves, or the documents they house, or the narratives held within? It is easy to take such seduction for granted; far more challenging is to examine the visceral reality of this seduction. Archival seduction—as I hope this book has demonstrated through its many enticing and often troubling stories of desire, viscerality, misinscription, voyeurism, animality, and eroticized religiosity—is most valuable when it causes us to articulate our own desires in relation to the archive as an institution, as a system of classification, and as a physical space, each with its own peculiar history. Archival seduction thus should force us to examine and analyze the ways we understand the past, as well as our relationship to it. It is my hope that *Sins against Nature* has harnessed and conveyed some of the seductive potential of the archive, and has perhaps seduced you, the reader, into the fascinating and complex worlds of the colonial archives of New Spain.

Here, I take us through archival seduction—accessing absence partly through a close reading of one outstanding eighteenth-century archival fragment of female sodomy from Mexico City. Archives of colonial rule, as we have seen throughout the book, become meaningful sites of historical inquiry partly by creating an intimate connection between bodies and documents. As the archive draws us in, it opens up the possibility for exploring how our desires intersect with those of the past. This, of course, happens within the walls of the archive only if we are willing to trace our own affective engagements with the documents and the historical subjects they represent. Each and every archived subject—not unlike the archivists and researchers who encounter them years, decades, or centuries after the fact—is fractured along multiple axes. Like light passing through a prism, unavoidably bent and refracted, the archived desires of historical subjects—when put on paper, thrust into an archive, classified, cataloged, and interpreted by archivists and historians alike—separate out, opening themselves up to multiple and often contradictory readings and interpretations. Despite our efforts to create narratives about the desires and experiences of people in the past, they will always remain partly (if not mostly) illegible to us.

I turn first to that particularly seductive archival fragment found in Mexico's AGN: a brief five- or six-line reference to a 1732 criminal case against a woman named Josepha de Garfias "for the crime of sodomy she perpetrated with other women."[12] The topic of same-sex desire among women in New Spain, readers will have no doubt noted, is—with the notable exception of Agustina Ruiz's fantasized relationship with the Virgin—woefully underrepresented in this book. This is not because I did not search for sodomy trials involving women. I did, extensively. With the exception of colonial Brazil, accusations and prosecutions of female sodomy are exceedingly rare for all of colonial Latin America.[13] In the hundreds of cases read, I was able to locate only one unambiguous archival reference in the records of New Spain to a woman who was tried for and convicted of the crime of sodomy. Traces of female same-sex desire, as we saw in the previous chapter, do exist, but archival references are either vague or entirely absent. Yet it is not simply that female sodomy is *missing* from the colonial archives. Rather, its rare and checkered archival presence intimates an absence—one predicated on our own perceptions, and specifically on the gaps between colonial and modern-day taxonomies of female same-sex desire.

The scant facts of this (now lost) criminal case are presented within an efficient ten-folio judicial summary titled "Case Documents against Diverse Persons for the Sin of Bestiality and Sodomies," which includes minimal information on twenty-two separate criminal cases that implicate some thirty-six individuals—all men, with the exception of Garfias—in these crimes between 1709 and 1769. In this document, the sole paragraph dedicated to Garfias and her crime tells us that the case was initiated in an ecclesiastical court but was transferred to secular criminal courts and prosecuted by Juan Carrillo Moreno, judge of Mexico City's Real Sala del Crimen, the highest-ranking criminal judicial institution in the city and its vicinities, in 1732. The summary registers that the court "substantiated the case" against her and pronounced a "definitive sentence": that she serve the sick for a period of two years in the Hospital of San Juan de Dios in Mexico City and fulfill a series of "medicinal penances." In the sole mention of the implement with which Garfias committed her crimes—itself a significant archival absence—the court "mandated that among other things certain instruments which she used for her sordid crime were to be burned."

To be clear, original documentation of the criminal case—that is, the original trial transcripts—to which this judicial summary refers, so far as we know, no longer exists. Perhaps the files were lost or damaged or otherwise destroyed sometime in the previous three hundred years. Or perhaps it is simply misplaced, miscategorized, or unprocessed, sitting in an unfiled box right under our noses. Perhaps one day the case will be located in the archives, just like the criminal trial of Juana Aguilar—the suspected hermaphrodite maliciously nicknamed "Juana la Larga," discussed in chapter 3—which was previously thought to have been lost. Yet in 2012, historian Sylvia Sellers-García came across

Aguilar's trial transcripts in the Guatemalan archives when a card catalog description—one that previous scholars, myself included, failed to see in that very same archive—piqued her interest. Based on this exciting find, new histories of Aguilar will soon be written; perhaps, one day, new histories will also be written of the historical subjects we have encountered throughout *Sins against Nature*. Ultimately, Garfias's judicial summary thus provides a particular type of archival absence: an indexical one that reveals some of the details and then thwarts our own desires to learn more about the life, narrative, and confession of Garfias herself—all of which the missing original transcript of the case against her would have contained.

If indexing is speaking in the present about the past through particular signs, then the very notion of indexical absence here also takes on heightened meanings. If smoke can be regarded as an index of fire, or a dried-up river basin an index of water, then the "certain instruments" with which Garfias committed her crime function as an (absent) index of desire. Absences here coalesce in multiple and overlapping ways. The missing transcripts of the criminal case represent one level of archival absence; the missing instruments represent another. Just as the garroted corpses of sodomites in the early modern Iberian Atlantic world were sometimes burned so as to eradicate any memory or physical evidence of the crime, here the instruments—dildos or artificial phalluses that likely would have been made from leather, vellum, or cloth, as they were in early modern Europe—used to penetrate the bodies of other women were sometimes similarly annihilated. The ritualistic burning served to eradicate bodies, physical evidence, and the very memory of the "sordid crime."

The absent presence of those "certain instruments" Garfias supposedly used to penetrate another woman (or other women) functions, in the words of Anjali Arondekar, as an "archival figuration": that absent presence mediates the relationship between our finding and what is found (both within the archive and within the historical record). For, according to Arondekar's analysis of the India-rubber dildo's place within Victorian pornography, it "(as both material and absent presence) captures a central representational paradox at the heart of our archival labors."[14] The material dildo is missing—burned to ashes like the bodies of many convicted sodomites throughout the Iberian Atlantic world—but traces of desire remain nonetheless, though they are shaped and mediated by our own. In the end, we are left merely with a faint textual trace of Garfias's desires, which are gleaned through the very indexical absences that can seduce us into wanting to know more. Ultimately, the specificity of her desires remains illegible.

In the end, the questions that remain eclipse the facts that are established. What exactly did Garfias do with the "instruments"? With whom had her crimes been "perpetrated"? Did she regularly engage in sexual contact with other women, or was this a unique occurrence? How did the politics of denunciation play themselves out, and who initially denounced her? Was she caught in flagrante delicto, or did rumors about her merely circulate until they reached the ears of colonial authorities? Did witnesses actually *see* the crime with their own eyes? Or might Garfias have confessed to a priest in an attempt to absolve her sins, only to be directed initially to an ecclesiastical court and eventually to secular justices? Finally, how did the "instruments" make their way into the hands of authorities? Was their burning done in public so as to shame Garfias, or did authorities not want to disseminate the details of such a crime to the masses? These questions are unanswerable, but they help us speculate about—and reckon with the sheer vastness of—the unarchivable aspects of desire.

These questions also help examine how Garfias does, and does not, fit into existing histories of "homosexuality," and of gay and lesbian pasts. Just as the archival traces of her have the potential to seduce us, we too have the potential to seduce her into our historiographical narratives. After all, from the very nature of the archival fragment, we might be tempted to classify her— perhaps as a "sodomite," a "lesbian," as someone with "homosexual" tendencies. Yet what we ultimately have is a mere fragment—an "archival sliver"—of an otherwise absent historical subjectivity, which is mediated by and through absence at multiple levels. Archivist Verne Harris asserts that "if archival records reflect reality, they do so complicitly, they do so in a deeply fractured and shifting way"; for the window through which we view the past is responsible for "transposing images from 'this side' and disturbing images from the 'other side.' "[15] Garfias's desires are thus similarly fractured when we read the register (and the larger indexical absence) "along the archival grain," to return to Ann Stoler's apt expression, and even against it. Perhaps Josepha de Garfias was indeed a "sodomite" or a "lesbian." Or perhaps her own desires escape the very classificatory regimes we could impose on her from the "other side" of the murky window between the past and the present.

Archives and their classifications, as we have seen, undergo subtle changes and radical shifts over time; any and all archival research is thus subject to these vagaries. The archive is a reflection not necessarily of reality but of how certain individuals at any given point in time have sorted and categorized that reality. Early on in my research, I learned that to locate the documents I cared about, I first had to peruse catalogs, finding aids, and unprocessed archival boxes for a very particular vocabulary: obscure and antiquated Spanish-language terms such as *contra natura* (against nature), *pecado nefando* (nefarious sin), *sodomía* (sodomy), *sodomita* (sodomite), *somético* (sodomitical), *sodomítico* (sodomitical), *bujarrón* (penetrative partner), and the like. Yet in contrast to this terminology, some special collections libraries in the United States (and elsewhere) read more "modern" desires onto the past, not unlike several scholars of gay and lesbian history. Paradoxically, in an effort to make legible the desires of the past, sometimes the exact opposite can take place. That is, the categories of sexual identity that we have fought so hard to make historically visible—lesbian, gay, bisexual, transgender, transsexual, intersex—have, ironically, the potential to produce new possibilities of archival absence.

When I first encountered the archival holdings of the Latin American Library at Tulane University in 2010, I remember searching through the card catalog for the usual suspects, though now in English: "sodomy," "sodomite," "against nature," "bestiality," and "nefarious." Yet my searches turned up no results. When I inquired, the archivist asked if I had checked under the letter *H* in the card catalog. I had not, but it took a second for me to make sense of the archivist's query. I was, once again, looking in the wrong places. The archivist was, of course, speaking of "homosexuality." The term, as we have seen, did not even come into existence until the end of the nineteenth century, well after Mexico's independence from Spain in 1821. Upon looking, I was thrilled to come across one entry of "HOMOSEXUALITY (MEXICO)" (fig. C.5). The catalog entry referenced the incomplete pecado nefando trial from 1725 in which a thirty-year-old lay brother, Beato Juan de la Asumpción, and a fifteen-year-old "light-skinned little mulatto," Francisco Servando, were caught by some indigenous villagers committing sodomy in a chapel in the town of Tecpán. Faced with the damning allegations of the witnesses, the lay brother eventually admitted that he had let the mulatto boy "put his member inside a little . . . but it was very little."[16] The testimonies are fascinating, but once again the archival document is incomplete and no sentence is recorded for the crime. More important, however, "homosexuality" itself is arguably irrelevant to the case itself, or at least to the lives of Asumpción and the unidentified mulatto with whom he had sex.

Here, the language of archival classification is anachronistic (or, perhaps, deliberately counterchronistic). Our contemporary language of homosexuality has

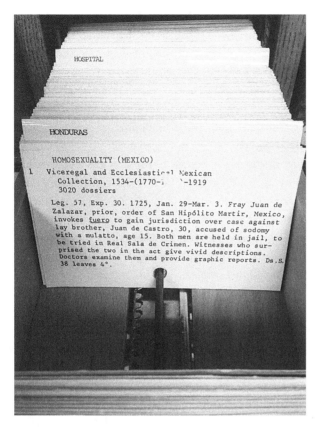

Fig C.5 Manuscript card catalog entry for "HOMOSEXUALITY (MEXICO)" at the Latin American Library at Tulane University, New Orleans, Louisiana. Photo by the author, 2014.

unintentionally created new archival absences—counterabsences, perhaps—for those (like me) who otherwise would never have thought of looking under the letter *H* to find colonial cases of sodomía and the pecado nefando. The very notion of the archival counterabsence points to an archival presence that I would have otherwise experienced as an absence had I not purposefully engaged in the counterchronistic exercise, at the suggestion of the Latin American Library's archivist, of employing terms that subverted and countered the very terms that the colonial archives chronologically set out to capture. Thus, perhaps archival presence and absence exist only in gradations. Archival absences come in many forms, always in relation to a certain archival presence:

textual, physical, digital, and taxonomic. They point to material missing from the archives—incomplete dossiers, misclassified documents, stolen records, files in transit, and absent archival referents—but they always allude to the seductive hope of one day being found.

Those of us who have conducted extensive research in the archives know what it is like to be seduced by them. Many of us have sensed punctuated moments of elation, often scattered among weeks or months or years of research that can border on the monotonous. The juicy details of the cases seduced me, but so too did that which was not revealed—the gaps and absences that mark the colonial archive, as in the archival trace of Josepha de Garfias. Archival seduction, access, and absence will be forever intertwined; for they are at the center of every experience in the archive.

The archive's empty spaces allow us to fill in the gaps partly with our own hopes, fantasies, and desires for the subjects of the past. I, for one, want to think of Garfias as embodying a past that satisfied, even in some marginal way, her own desires—even after her public punishment and shaming. I want to believe that she was part of a now illegible network of women, however small, who knew when and where to seek out and engage in sex, to explore intimacies, with other women in eighteenth-century Mexico City. For this is what I would have liked to find in the original criminal trial, had it not been lost, misclassified, or destroyed. It is also possible, however, that the case may represent something radically different: perhaps it was a case of violence and sexual abuse, whereby one woman wielded power over a younger girl, who may have been marginalized in terms of race, class, and social status. To speculate about Josepha de Garfias, whatever direction that may be, is to allow our own imaginations to intertwine with the archival imaginary about her.

———————

Over the course of the last decade and a half, during which I conceptualized this project and carried out the archival research, dozens of individuals—archivists, colleagues, students, friends, and family members—have asked me what led me to this project. They did so in informal conversations, conference panels, academic job interviews, archival trips, and classroom settings. Their queries were usually curious and genuine, though others were critical or even came with a hint of cynicism. Sometimes their questions were anticipated, and other times they took me completely by surprise, pushing me to rethink more explicitly my own political goals, my past, and my desires in relation to the archived subjects about whom I was writing. At times my inquirers projected their guesses on me: some asked if I had been abused by a priest in my youth, if I was sexually attracted to animals, or if something had happened in my past that got me into such "perverse" topics. I candidly answered in the negative, and always articulated something along the lines of my being absolutely fascinated by the intersections of sex and colonialism. Rarely did I share some of the many origin stories that, at least in part, did lead me to this project.

Indeed, there was one profoundly personal experience that I had long ago, sometime between the ages of nine and eleven, that pushed me toward this project. I will never forget the night in my early adolescence that I masturbated for (what I remember to be) the first time. Since I was raised Catholic and attended Catholic primary and secondary school, the topic was not broached explicitly in my formal education. I remember being intensely conflicted that night, knowing that what I was doing was a sin, but not entirely sure why. I had already heard about sex and about "making babies," but nothing had mentally prepared me for that intensely pleasurable and absolutely shocking moment of my first orgasm and ejaculation. The deeply visceral sense of guilt that I experienced both during and immediately afterward was distressing to me as a young Catholic boy; I wholeheartedly believed that I had just killed what would otherwise have been my firstborn children. I feared that I would incur the wrath of God. I remember crying, looking into the toilet bowl (where I hoped that the sperm could somehow swim to safety and survive!) in a state of panic and disbelief. Unsurprisingly, in my youth I never shared that experience with anyone, despite the fact that I was supposed to when I went to confession several times a year. Pangs of guilt and shame remained—that is, at least until I came to terms with the fact that masturbation was absolutely worth the risk of eternal damnation. The priests at St. Patrick Catholic School, fortunately, never asked me any explicit questions about "pollution" (perhaps they had never read fray Bartolomé de Alva's 1634 *Confessionario mayor*!), and I never divulged as much when I confessed my more venial sins.

I offer my (almost unarchived) memory of masturbation as a way of working through questions of historical recollection and archival absence. For the absences of the archive intersect with my own checkered memories of desire; absence is thus always part of both us and the archive. Linking that masturbatory experience to my own archival research—and to the very impetus to study the history of sexuality—shows me how my own impulses, both affective and corporeal, are thus inseparable from the archives I go to in order to better understand the documenting of desire. Antoinette Burton recounts how many of the archive stories scholars divulged to her "have been framed by confessions of archive pleasure—what one historian has called 'the thrill of the archival "pay dirt" moment'—or alternately, confessions of archive aversion."[17] This is perhaps my own "pay dirt" moment, which I share here not to absolve myself of my "sins" but rather to illustrate how intensely personal this project has been for me, intellectually, politically, and sexually.

I concluded the previous chapter with a reflection on the nature and significance of archiving guilt—something that is intimately and personally bound up with one of several events in my life that, then unbeknownst to me, would contribute greatly to the shaping of this book and to my entire intellectual trajectory. That experience—alongside my memory of the confirmation teacher telling our class that homosexuals were, sadly, going to Hell—decades later made me want to understand how both religion and the invention of sin could have such a profound influence on the beliefs, thoughts, and experiences of a person. The older I got, the more I came to terms with my own messy and flickering sexual desires, and the more I came to relate myself and my own past to those that I began to research in the archives (archiving my own body in the process). Catholic confessional discourse has thus been absolutely central in more ways than one to this project and to my own intellectual development. At least for me, this entire book (and the archival research that went into it) is inextricable from my memories of that night, from my subsequent confessions, or from my confirmation teacher's religiously sanctioned homophobia. As you may have guessed, I never did receive the sacrament of confirmation.

Here and throughout the book, we have seen how archival absence—that of Josepha Garfias just the most glaring in a long list—is produced in the documents themselves, in the classificatory system of the archive, and in our own engagements with those records, catalogs, and descriptors. As I hope this book has shown, the interplay of archival absence, access, and seduction is not abstract—this intertwining happens not merely in our own bodies and memories but also in the very buildings in which we do our research. And, as the Comité Mexicano de Ciencias Históricas's 2016 petition to the Mexican government and the director of the AGN remind us, accessing the past—having "the right to memory," the right to different versions and interpretations of the past—is always an intensely political issue. Standing at the entrance to the AGN, the façade—not to mention every corridor and every former jail cell—reminded me of looking at an archival fragment; initially we only see the surface, but the further we dig, the more we find (and the more we realize we will never be privy to).

The more I uncovered about the historical subjects of this book, the more glimpses I got of myself as someone who was seduced by the archives for a reason, and as someone who engaged the archives for so much more than to write this book. To delve into my own personal experiences of sex and desire is to acknowledge that my own past has inevitably colored my approach to the colonial archive and my engagement with what it contains. The more I researched the history of male and female "sodomites" in the colonial period, the more I learned about the material and architectonic history of the Lecumberri and about its transformation into the AGN. The more I, too, learned about the twentieth-century political prisoners and "homosexuals" who had previously inhabited the very same walls that the archival documents did, the more explicit connections I began to draw between myself, my own desire to write particular versions of the past, and the representations of history that the archive (and its card catalogs and finding aids) put forth.

Rather than fear, malign, or warn against archival seduction, we should analyze that which is productive—theoretically, affectively, methodologically—and problematic in sometimes letting ourselves give in. As I initially began the research for this book, I found myself being seduced by the narratives and the stories I encountered in these diverse archives, spread across Mexico, Guatemala, Spain, and the United States. The pleasures of historical research were, at times, diminished by certain archives' increasingly complicated security protocols—bureaucratic rules of access, complicated guidelines for registering, limitations on the number of files or expedientes that one could see in any given day, documents removed from circulation, and the like. And, almost always, the archivists who helped me along the way made the pleasures of research all the more fulfilling. These facts made even more explicit the interconnectedness of archival access, seduction, and absence. In terms of my own imagination of the colonial past, I ultimately came to be seduced by narratives of erotic religious visions of Jesus and the Virgin Mary, of sodomy and sex with animals, of gendered violence and sodomitical coercion, and of priests who reinterpreted the discourse of the Church for their own erotic gratification. At the same time, as Arondekar so carefully articulates, we must also be wary of our own desires for access to the archive, and should be forever critical of any suggestion that the "truth" (of sexuality, or of anything else) can be found definitively in the archive.

This book has taken seriously calls by Ann Stoler, Nicholas Dirks, Durba Ghosh, Kathryn Burns, and others who have emphasized the importance of taking ethnographic approaches to the colonial archive.[18] As Stoler notes, "Ethnography in and of the colonial archives attends to processes of production, relations of power in which archives are created, sequestered, and rearranged."[19] *Sins against Nature* attends to such processes, and even seeks to go beyond them. As we have seen, an ethnography of these processes is supplemented by a critical analysis of our own hopes and desires in the archives—and *for* the archives—by paying attention to our own subjectivities and our stakes in the archival projects we carry out. This book has also taken seriously calls by gender, sexuality, and queer studies scholars to be attuned to the impulses and pleasures of archival research. My own intellectual pleasures at (and struggles with) recounting the intimate details of past lives and desires—embodied pleasures and pains in the colonial past—will always be a necessary part of this story. To write about or engage with an archival document, physically and affectively, is to already be in the archive, and to become part of that particular document's opaque history. Furthermore, the very impulses to watch and witness, to denounce or transcribe, to read about and write of the sexual desires of another can never be disentangled from the archived desires of the past and our own archival desires (and ethical responsibilities) in the present. The archive itself—that is, its physicality, its subject headings, descriptors, and classifications—becomes a sign of the desiring body, just as the textual representation of the desiring body within the archive becomes a sign that opens itself up to multiple readings and interpretations across time.

It is in this sense that we might speak of what Carolyn Dinshaw calls the "queer historical impulse" or what Elizabeth Freeman calls the "visceral encounter between past and present"—that is, the impulse to make connections across time between the lives, texts, and cultural phenomena that have typically been excluded from sexual categories of the past and the present.[20] *Sins against Nature* itself—as an object and artifact—is an archive, a mere flicker of desire, and a constant reminder of archival absence. As with any archive, seduction is, I believe, an enticing possibility, and such seductions may operate on concurrent intellectual, corporeal, and emotional strata. There are, however, competing archival seductions at play, and the trick here is to allow the seductions of the archive to influence us in ways that allure us intellectually and politically but at the same time counter "the seductions of recovery and the occlusions of such retrieval measures."[21] In this vein, it is my hope that this book—and the archival thrills and "pay dirt" moments represented within— has seduced you and touched you, stimulated you and discomfited you. It is only by acknowledging the visceral reality of the past that we can reimagine the very contours and boundaries of the archive, as well as our intimate relationship and ethical responsibilities to it.

APPENDIX

TABLE A.I Inquisition and Ecclesiastical Trials of Priests for Sodomy and for the Solicitation of Males

DATE*/PLACE	PRIEST/LANGUAGE†	ACCUSERS/CRIME
1609–12 Mérida, Hocabá, Sanlahcat, Yaxcabá, and Hoctún	Cristóbal de Valencia Spanish and Maya	19 Maya women and men denounced him for solicitation, oral sex, masturbation, and heresy
1622–27 Tlaxcalilla and San Luis Potosí	Esteban Rodríguez (Franciscan) Spanish, Nahuatl, Purépecha, Otomi, and Guachichil	5 indigenous, Spanish, and mestizo boys and young men denounced him for mutual masturbation and solicitation during confession
1637–39 Taos, New Mexico	Nicolás Hidalgo Spanish and possibly Taos and/or Tiwa	2 indigenous men denounced him for sodomy and castration, others for illicit sex with women and violence
1658 Mexico City	Father Matheo Spanish	Gerónimo Calbo (who was executed for sodomy) was questioned about the times he had committed sodomy with the priest
1659–63 Mexico City, Zacatecas, Oaxaca, Puebla, and Veracruz	Nicolás de Chaide (Jesuit) Spanish	Ramón Zerón, mulatto, denounced him for solicitation and sodomy. Denounced for *mala amistad* with Ana, *china*
1712–15‡ Mexico City	Juan Vallejo Hermosillo Spanish	The priest's mulatto slave Diego Magdaleno denounced him for sodomy with a number of men, himself included
1713–14 Valladolid, Oaxaca, and Toluca	Antonio de Asunción (Carmelite) Spanish	3 men (mulattos and a mestizo) denounced him for solicitation and masturbation

* Dates between first recorded solicitation and the end of trial or interrogation

† Languages spoken by the priest in confession

‡ This is the only case tried by an ecclesiastical court rather than the Inquisition.

CONFESSION	SENTENCE
He admitted to "sins of the flesh," having sex with 1 woman, and having masturbated "some men"	Abjure de levi; exiled for 6 years; lost right to confess women for 2 years; 100 peso fine (trial costs)
He admitted to masturbating numerous men while praying for them during confession	Abjure de levi; confined to a convent for 4 years; exiled for 10 years; lost right to confess, which was reinstated in 1640
No information given	Relieved from his post as a priest in New Mexico No other information given
The Inquisition was unable to find the priest (he may have fled to Guatemala)	No sentence
He admitted to soliciting, masturbating, and/or having sex (without penetration) with some 12 males and to *mala amistad* with Ana	Abjure de levi; confined to a convent for 4 years; perma-nently lost right to confess
He admitted to having sex with at least 115 men (mestizos, mulattos, blacks, indigenous, and Spanish) before and after being ordained	Died in prison in 1715 Some of his accomplices imprisoned No further information
He admitted to soliciting at least 6 men, and penetrating 1 mestizo. His confession is incomplete.	Incomplete case No sentence is recorded in the document

TABLE A.I *(continued)*

DATE*/PLACE	PRIEST/LANGUAGE†	ACCUSERS/CRIME
1716 Celaya	Carlos Jiménez Mondragón Spanish	Mondragón's slave Pedro de Heredia accused him of masturbation and attempted sodomy
1718 Oaxaca	Marcial de Melo (Jesuit) Spanish	Novice Pedro Arias was called forth to testify against the priest, stating they had sex repeatedly
1732–50 Mexico City, Atlisco, Puebla, Toluca, San Luis Potosí	Anastacio de San Joseph Spanish	7 boys denounced him for solicitation and masturbation between 1732 and 1750
1765–74 Mexico City and Guadalajara	Ángel María Quesa Spanish	Denounced by Francisco Xavier de la Vega for "sodomitical acts" and later by 2 women for solicitation
1771–86 Manila, Philippines	Agustín María Spanish and Tagalog	4 indigenous Filipinos and 1 Filipina denounced him for whipping, masturbation, and sodomy
1784–1800 Calimaya and numerous other towns	José Gregorio Zebrian Spanish	Starting in 1797, he was denounced by some 5 boys for solicitation and mutual masturbation

CONFESSION	SENTENCE
He denied the charges. Heredia held animosity toward the priest.	Incomplete case The charges were dropped and Mondragón was absolved
No known confession	We have no records of a trial against him
He admitted to soliciting 20 boys and 1 woman	Abjure de levi; exiled from Mexico City, Toluca, and San Luis Potosí for 6 years; confined to a convent for 4 years; permanently stripped of the privilege to confess
Incomplete case He was tried in 1774, but his confession does not exist	Abjure de levi; goods embargoed; stripped of the privilege to confess. In 1785 he petitioned that it be reinstated.
He admitted to soliciting 23 men, 4 women, and becoming excited while whipping them	Abjure de levi; exiled for a period of ten years; stripped of the privilege to confess In 1796 he was reinstated as a priest in a convent in the Philippines
He admitted to soliciting over 40 boys and men between 1784 and 1799	Abjure de levi; exiled from Mexico City and Calimaya for 10 years; permanently stripped of the privilege to confess

TABLE A.2 Self-Denunciations and Resulting Inquisition Trials for Sodomy and for the Solicitation of Males

DATE/PLACE	PRIEST/LANGUAGE	SELF-CONFESSION	SENTENCE
1696–1709 Tenantzingo	Francisco de Zavela Spanish and Nahuatl	In 1705 he denounced himself for having solicited indigenous and Spanish boys. He admitted to having sex with 2 Spanish boys and paying indigenous boys for sex (In 1696 he was denounced by Melchor Rodríguez Lucío. The denunciation was ignored)	In 1709 Abjure de levi; permanently exiled from Tenantzingo; lost right to confess; sentenced to serve the poor for a short period in a Mexico City hospital
1716 Oaxaca	Ignacio de la Madre de Dios (Carmelite) Spanish	He denounced himself for having touched and attempted sodomy with 2 boys and for having solicited 2 women (In 1717 he was denounced by a woman for solicitation)	Incomplete case Inquisitors held a formal hearing but no final sentence is recorded
1761 Ciudad Real	Francisco Pulido Spanish	He denounced himself for having committed sodomy 4 or 5 times with an indigenous male servant	No action was taken because sodomy was not under the jurisdiction of the Inquisition and because his acts did not take place in the context of confession
1782–95 Zacatecas, Puebla, Guanajuato, and numerous towns	José María García Spanish	In 1789 he denounced himself for soliciting 1 man. In 1793 he eventually admitted to soliciting at least 32 men and 2 women (In 1785 he was denounced by a mulatto in Zacatecas. The denunciation was ignored)	Abjure de levi; permanently stripped of the privilege to administer confession except to members of the clergy; spiritual exercises for 1 month
1802 Guanajuato	Joaquín Luciano de la Cruz Spanish	He denounced himself for having committed sodomy with an indigenous boy raised by him since infancy	No action taken because sodomy was not under the jurisdiction of the Inquisition and because his acts did not take place in the context of confession

ARCHIVES

AGCA	Archivo General de Centro América (Guatemala City, Guatemala)
AGEH	Archivo General del Estado de Hidalgo (Pachuca, Mexico)
AGI	Archivo General de Indias (Seville, Spain)
AGN	Archivo General de la Nación (Mexico City, Mexico)
AGNP	Archivo General de Notarías de Puebla (Puebla, Mexico)
AHCM	Archivo Histórico Casa de Morelos (Morelia, Mexico)
AHEA	Archivo Histórico del Estado de Aguascalientes (Aguascalientes, Mexico)
AHESLP	Archivo Histórico del Estado de San Luis Potosí (San Luis Potosí, Mexico)
AHET	Archivo Histórico del Estado de Tlaxcala (San Pablo Apetatitlán, Mexico)
AHEZ	Archivo Histórico del Estado de Zacatecas (Zacatecas, Mexico)
AHJO	Archivo Histórico Judicial de Oaxaca (Oaxaca, Mexico)
AHMC	Archivo Histórico del Municipio de Colima (Colima, Mexico)
AHMM	Archivo Histórico Municipal de Morelia (Morelia, Mexico)
AHPJQ	Archivo Histórico del Poder Judicial del Estado de Querétaro (Querétaro, Mexico)
AMHP	Archivo Municipal de Hidalgo del Parral (Hidalgo del Parral, Mexico)
AMMNL	Archivo Municipal de Monterrey, Nuevo León (Monterrey, Mexico)
BANC	Bancroft Library, University of California at Berkeley (Berkeley, California)
BNAH	Biblioteca Nacional de Antropología e Historia (Mexico City, Mexico)

BPEJ-FE	Biblioteca Pública del Estado de Jalisco, Fondos Especiales (Guadalajara, Mexico)
DAFH-UG	Dirección de Archivos y Fondos Históricos, Universidad de Guanajuato (Guanajuato, Mexico)
HUNT	Huntington Library (San Marino, California)
SANM	Spanish Archives of New Mexico (microfilmed at the University of Texas at El Paso)
VEMC	Latin American Library at Tulane University, Viceregal and Ecclesiastical Mexican Collection (New Orleans, Louisiana)

NOTES

Introduction

1. AMMNL, Criminal 8, exp. 104, fol. 1: "la d[ic]ha cabra entre las piernas." Unless otherwise noted, all translations are my own.

2. AMMNL, Criminal 8, exp. 104, fol. 1: "teniendola por los cuernos la fornico doz vezes."

3. AMMNL, Criminal 8, exp. 104, fol. 6: "que sea dado cien azotes colgado por la sinctura en la horca pública de la d[ic]ha ciudad cuya pena se le da por su menor edad."

4. Stoler, *Along the Archival Grain*, 44.

5. Sellers-García, *Distance and Documents at the Spanish Empire's Periphery*, 17.

6. Brown, *Immodest Acts*, 15.

7. Horswell, *Decolonizing the Sodomite*, 33.

8. Wiesner-Hanks, *Sexuality and Christianity in the Early Modern World*, 3.

9. Covarrubias, *Tesoro de la lengua castellana o española*, 308.

10. Covarrubias, *Tesoro de la lengua castellana o española*, 427.

11. *Diccionario de autoridades*, vol. 3.

12. *Diccionario de autoridades*, vol. 1.

13. Pratt, *Imperial Eyes*, 6–7.

14. Burton, *Archive Stories*, 11.

15. Martínez, "Archives, Bodies, and Imagination," 160.

16. Freccero, "Archives in the Fiction"; Dubois, "Maroons in the Archives," 295.

17. For the online appendix, which contains archival references and summaries of each of the cases I researched for this book, see https://archive.nyu.edu/handle /2451/40720. I will periodically update this, adding new archival references as I come across them.

18. K. Burns, *Into the Archive*, 124.

19. Mirow, *Latin American Law*, 47.

20. Cutter, *The Legal Culture of Northern New Spain*, 125.

21. K. Burns, *Into the Archive*, 34.

22. Arondekar, *For the Record*, ix.

23. Farge, *The Allure of the Archives*, 42; Dinshaw, *How Soon Is Now?*, 29.

24. Freeman, *Time Binds*, xi.

25. Freccero, *Queer/Early/Modern*, 18.

26. Harris, "A Shaft of Darkness," 75.

27. Freccero, *Queer/Early/Modern*, 18; Muñoz, *Cruising Utopia*, 65.

28. Steedman, *Dust*, 45.

29. Schwartz and Cook, "Archives, Records, and Power," 12.

30. Arondekar, *For the Record*, 3.

31. Farge, *The Allure of the Archives*, 69.

32. Holland, Ochoa, and Tompkins, "On the Visceral," 399.

33. Mbembe, "The Power of the Archive and Its Limits," 21.

34. Petro, "Beyond Accountability."

35. D. Taylor, *The Archive and the Repertoire*, 21.

1. Viscerality in the Archives

1. AGN, Criminal 705, exp. 24, fol. 242: "lo encontraron dos mugeres en el campo santo de San Juan de Dios sobre una muerta a quien estaba fornicando que esto lo hiso porque se lo aconsejó Miguel el moso del Padre Lastra sacristan del mismo conbento a quien por dos ocasiones vio que se encerró en el campo santo y le dijo que iba a fornicar a las muertas, porque alli estaba enterrada su amasia que habia muerta preñada en el proprio hospital que dicho Miguel le aconsejó tambien que le hiciera un agujero en las enaguas a la difunta para poderla fornicar."

2. AGN, Criminal 705, exp. 24, fol. 246: "Dixo que esta preso por q[ue] vino de San Juan de Dios, por que lo [h]allaron en el campo santo sobre una muerta, pero que el no se acuerda por que estava vorracho, y responde."

3. Aggrawal, *Necrophilia*, 235.

4. Gómez, *Compendio de los comentarios extendidos*, 336: "El delito *contra naturam* se castiga con la pena ordinaria, aunque no sea perfecto y consumado, sino solo intentado y preparado, por razon de su gravedad tan singular."

5. Gómez, *Compendio de los comentarios extendidos*, 336: "solo merece un castigo abitrario el acceso con otro, no *per vas exterius*, sino por otra parte del cuerpo, ó si solo hubiere tocamiento de manos con derramamientos de semen."

6. AGN, Inquisición 125, exp. 19, fol. 1.

7. AGN, Criminal 705, exp. 24, fol. 247: "del castigo que considera sele deve imponer por un [h]echo tan escandaloso, y [h]orrible repugnante a la misma naturaleza y aun hasta los brutos, y mucho mas haviendolo verificado en un lugar santificado, y dedicado, para cepultura de los cadáveres que fallecen en aquel Hospital."

8. Tortorici, "Reading the (Dead) Body."

9. AGN, Criminal 705, exp. 24, fols. 237–50, accessed October 15, 2017, http://www.agn.gob.mx/guiageneral/contenido.php?CodigoReferencia=MX09017AGNCL01FO007RASE010CUI705UC024.

10. AGN, Criminal 705, exp. 24, fol. 237: "Mexico, Año de 1810. Contra José Lázaro Martínez por haberse encontrado mesclando carnalm[en]te con una difunta."

11. Massumi, "The Bleed," 32–33.

12. Holland, Ochoa, and Tompkins, "On the Visceral," 394.

13. Farge, *The Allure of the Archives*, 6.

14. Martínez-San Miguel, *From Lack to Excess*.

15. Ligorio [Liguori], *Theologia moralis*, 1:467: "Quale vero peccarum fit coire cum foemina mortua? Dicendum cum *Holz. n. 720. Salm. n. 74. Spor. n. 639. cum Tamb. &c.* communiter, non esse fornicationem, quia fit cum cadavere; nec bestialitatem, ut quidam volunt; sed esse pollutionem, & fornicationem affectivam."

16. Gómez, *Compendio de los comentarios extendidos*, 336.

17. Ahmed, *The Cultural Politics of Emotion*, 94.

18. Holland, Ochoa, and Tompkins, "On the Visceral," 395.

19. Massumi, "The Bleed," 33.

20. AGN, Criminal 705, exp. 24, fol. 240: "vieron que aunq[ue] la difunta no tenia levantadas las enaguas, pero si un ahugero en ellas asi a las partes pudendas."

21. "Inquiring about the Inquisition?"

22. "Survey of Mexican Inquisition Documents," Bancroft Library, accessed October 9, 2017, bancroft.berkeley.edu/collections/latinamericana/inquisitionsurvey.html.

23. Blouin and Rosenberg, *Processing the Past*, 55.

24. AGN, Inquisición 1167, exp. 6, fols. 76–79: "por averse egercitado en tocam[ient]ᵒˢ obscenos, y defender que son licitos y buenos."

25. See also AGN, Inquisición 1179, exp. 30, fols. 287–89: "Publicación de los testigos que han depuesto en la causa que en este tribunal sigue el señor fiscal, contra Manuel Arroyo, mestizo o mulato, sobre hechos observados, y haber defendido ser lícitos y cristianos, México."

26. BANC MSS 96/95, 13:1, fol. 5: "no es pecado chuparle con la voca a los hombres el semen humano por rrazon de la salud . . . y que es buena esta obra para quitarse de los malos pensamientos con las mugeres, y para quitarse de andar pecando con ellas . . . *que es pecado no dejarse chupar el semen.*"

27. BANC MSS 96/95, 13:1, fol. 7: "que por caridad le daba un bocado."

28. BANC MSS 96/95, 13:1, fol. 7: "le aseguró q[ue] una noche le havia tocado tambien sus partes pero que no lo havia sentido, y q[ue] la causa de hazerlo era porque conocia q[ue] este declarante tenia una enfermedad oculta, q[ue] solo él se le havia de curar, y que esto lo haria en caridad de Dios: que con esto persuadio al q[ue] declara, y aquella misma noche le hizo el remedio de esta suerte: luego q[ue] se acostaron empezó a tocarle y jugarle las partes con las manos y asi q[ue] se alteró la naturaleza, y comenzó el derramamiento, se lo chupó con la boca y diciendole que no sabia el beneficio q[ue] con ello le hacia, porque no pensaria en malos pensamientos, ni pecaria con las mugeres."

29. Farge, *The Allure of the Archives*, 7.

30. BANC MSS 96/95, 13:1, fol. 16: "tenia el capullo lleno de granos."

31. BANC MSS 96/95, 13:1, fol. 16: "con aguardiente alcanforado tomado una bocarada de el y al mismo tiempo meterse el capullo en la boca con el fin de labarselo y este labatorio estubo executado lo unas catorze vezes."

32. Tortorici, "Visceral Archives of the Body," 422.

33. BANC MSS 96/95, 13:1, fol. 33: "de estatua regular, de color trigueño, ojos pardos, nariz chata no mui cerrado, barba, pelo negro y tambien trayo al cuello un rosario."

34. BANC MSS 96/95, 13:1, fols. 45 and 19: "medicina tan obscena y repugnante a la naturaleza" and "la accion asquerosisima de chupar el derramamiento, mas parecen caninas que humanas, y son tan vergonzosas y agena de los racionales que no aun de los gentiles romanos, artefactos de maldades obscenas se veen."

35. Boswell, *Christianity, Social Tolerance, and Homosexuality*, 328.

36. Chen, *Animacies*, 89.

37. Miller, *The Anatomy of Disgust*, 44.

38. Ahmed, *The Cultural Politics of Emotion*, 83.

39. Stoler, *Along the Archival Grain*, 33.

40. Stoler, *Along the Archival Grain*, 19.

41. Farge, *The Allure of the Archives*, 8 and 131.

42. Berco, *Sexual Hierarchies, Public Status*, 3.

43. Steedman, *Dust*, 17.

44. Steedman, *Dust*, 27.

45. Steedman, *Dust*, 27.

46. McLellan and Baker, "Incidence of Allergy in Archival Work."

47. Jeanneret, *A Feast of Worlds*, 136.

48. Steedman, *Dust*, 18.

49. Freeman, *Time Binds*, 110.

50. Freeman, *Time Binds*, 123.

51. Hillman, "Visceral Knowledge," 96.

52. Holland, Ochoa, and Tompkins, "On the Visceral," 395.

2. Impulses of the Archive

1. For more on the archive, see http://www.morelia.gob.mx/archivohistorico/.

2. AHMM, caja 30, exp. 20, fols. 1–76.

3. AHMM, caja 30, exp. 20, fol. 4: "el uno ensima del otro desatacados los calzones como si fueran hombre y muger."

4. AHMM, caja 30, exp. 20, fol. 3: "entendio que heran hombre y muger y que estavan alli cometiendo algo carnal porque oyo los asesidos del yndio que estava ensima y le vio que estava dando rrempuzones como si estubiera ensima de alguna muger."

5. Stoler, *Along the Archival Grain*, 35.

6. Blouin and Rosenberg, *Archives, Documentation, and Institutions of Social Memory*, 1.

7. Fuentes, *Dispossessed Lives*, 16.

8. Steedman, *Dust*, 150.

9. AHMM, caja 30, exp. 20, fol. 3: "tiene por cierto que ambos a dos estavan cometiendo el dicho pecado y de mas de lo que tiene dicho, vido al dicho yndio q[ue] primero deprendio que tenia unos calzones blancos mojados de sangre fresca y que lo que tiene dicho es la verdad."

10. AHMM, caja 30, exp. 20, fol. 9: "Se fue con el al dicho temascal y este testigo entro del primero y se le echo al suelo para dormir y luego el dicho yndio que era preso que no save como se llama se llego a este testigo y le comenzo a abrasar y a besar y le metio la mano que [h]abia puesta en la bragueta."

11. AHMM, caja 30, exp. 20, fol. 10: "le dixo a este t[estig]° que el tenia mucho deseo que se lo hiziese y que le daria la rropilla a este t[estig]°."

12. AHMM, caja 30, exp. 20, fol. 10: "el dicho yndio quito a este confesante la sinta de los calzones y los desataco y se desataco ellos suyos y se tendio en el suelo y estando arremangado este testigo se echo ensima del susodisho y le metio su miembro beril por el sieso y teniendo lo dentro como si estubiera con una muger cumplio con el y tubo copula carnal por esta parte con el dicho yndio."

13. AHMM, caja 30, exp. 20, fol. 10: "quando acabo de aver tenydo la dicha copula carnal y despranando [desplazando] en el sieso del susodicho."

14. The *Diccionario de autoridades*, vol. 5, defines the word *puto* simply as "el hombre que comete el pecado nefando."

15. Krippner-Martínez, *Rereading the Conquest*, 9–45.

16. See Scholes and Adams, *Proceso contra Tzintzicha Tangaxoan el Caltzontzín*, 14–17: "a que de la prisión donde está, sea sacado, las manos e pies atados, con una soga a la garganta, e con voz de pregonero que manifieste su delito, e sea metido en un zerón, si pudiere ser havido, e atado a la cola de un roçín, e sea tráido en derredor del lugar donde está asentado este real e sea llevado junto al paso de este río e allí sea atado a un madero e quemado en vivas llamas hasta que muera naturalmente e hecho polvos." I thank Karl Appuhn for helping me translate *zerón* from the Italian entry in Martínez Egido, *La obra lexicográfica de Lorenzo Franciosini*.

17. Escobar Olmedo, *Proceso, tormento y muerte del Cazonzi*, 40: "Yten, si saben, vieron, oyeron dezir que Pedro Sánchez Farfán hizo proçeso contra el dicho Cazonzi de sodomía, de lo qual halló bastante informaçión."

18. Arondekar, *For the Record*, 17.

19. Arondekar, *For the Record*, 17.

20. Escobar Olmedo, *Proceso, tormento y muerte del Cazonzi*, 90: "que sabe que tiene indios con quien se echa, que se llama el uno Juanico, que está en Apascuaro que verná agora, y otro que conosció, que es muerto, que se llama Guysacaro. E esto que lo a oido dezir e que es notorio a todos los indios criados del dicho Cazonzi, e que quando está borracho el dicho Cazonzi, le a visto meter la lengua en la boca e besar al dicho Juanillo, e que desde chequito tiene por costumbre el dicho Cazonzi de tener aquellos para aquel efeto, e que así es notorio que los tiene para aquello e por tales son avidos e tenidos entre ellos." Escobar Olmedo reads one largely illegible word in the original document as an abbreviation for *muerto*, "deceased," whereas Scholes and Adams read the largely illegible word in the original document as *mozo*, "young boy." I am uncertain which is correct.

21. Escobar Olmedo, *Proceso, tormento y muerte del Cazonzi*, 36: "han hecho muchas informaçiones e procesos contra él e contra otros muchos prençipales por

los quales han merecido muchas muertes, el dicho Cazonzi, e con sus mañas e con mucha copia de oro e plata se a esemido (exhimido) de las penas que a mereçido."

22. Krippner-Martínez, *Rereading the Conquest*, 30.

23. Lockhart, *Of Things of the Indies*, 99.

24. AHMM, caja 30, exp. 20, fol. 16: "ya que dios [h]a querido declarar y descubrir la verdad."

25. AHMM, caja 30, exp. 20, fol. 16: "el d[ic]ho Joaquin le sirvio de muger ambas a dos beces, y el t[estig]º fue el hombre y ambas a dos le metio su miembro veril por el sieso y desprano y tubo copula carnal con el y q[ue] quando cometio el pecado con el siempre presumio que el d[ic]ho Joaquin hera acostumbrado a cometer este pecado."

26. AHMM, caja 30, exp. 20, fol. 16: "le ha d[ic]ho que heran todos putos y que acostumbravan a cometer el pecado nefando."

27. AHMM, caja 30, exp. 20, fol. 27: "dixo que es cristiano y que puede aver seis años poco mas o menos que siendo este t[estig]º muchacho bibiendo en el barrio de San Fran[cis]ᶜᵒ el d[ic]ho Pedro Quini yndio [h]a cometido a este t[estig]º y persuadio que cometiesse el pecado nefando y este t[estig]º como muchacho no saviendo lo que hazia vino el ello."

28. AHMM, caja 30, exp. 20, fol. 16: "lo convido a dormir con el [Francisco Capiche] y le dixo que se lo hiziese y este t[estig]º [Pedro Quini] se quedo a dormir con el d[ic]ho yndio en la d[ic]ha casa en donde esta un forno y estando alli echados el d[ic]ho Fran[cis]ᶜᵒ Capiche le rrogo que se lo hiziese y siendo como a medianoche y estando juntos, este t[estig]º tubo copula con el y le metio su miembro beril por el sieso y tubo aceso con el d[ic]ho Franᶜᵒ Capiche despranando."

29. AHMM, caja 30, exp. 20, fol. 17: "entraron a dormir en la cosina y estando echados el d[ic]ho Miguel yndio comenzo a insistir a este y atentarle su miembro genital y se convinieron y el d[ic]ho Miguel yndio le sirvio de muger."

30. Davis, *Fiction in the Archives*, 3.

31. Silverman, *Tortured Subjects*, 11.

32. AHMM, caja 30, exp. 20, fol. 17: "es puto y que [h]a cometido el pecado nefando y es antiguo en el ofisio de cometerlo porque se lo [h]a visto cometer puede aver tres años y le vido muchas vezes servir de muger . . . en su casa lo tenia por costumbre q[ue] se lo hizieses . . . y de alli aprendio este t[estig]º a cometer el pecado nefando."

33. AHMM, caja 30, exp. 20, fol. 17: "y un yndio llamado Ticata por sobrenome bibe junto deste d[ic]ho Fran[cis]ᶜᵒ yndio."

34. AHMM, caja 30, exp. 20, fol. 17: "el otro yndio le servía al d[ic]ho Fran[cis]ᶜᵒ Conduyi como si fuese su muger."

35. AHMM, caja 30, exp. 20, fol. 30: "le rrogo que comitiese el pecado nefando y se fueron a un sacatal que esta detras de los corrales de la d[ic]ha carneseria . . . a las nueve antes de mediodia y estando alli este t[estig]º desataco sus calzones y se tendio al suelo . . . y [Quini] despranado como si estuviera con una muger lo qual sintio este t[estig]º."

36. AHMM, caja 30, exp. 20, fol. 2: "tan abominable delito y en tan gran ofensa de dios."

37. Gilberti, *Vocabulario en lengua de Mechuacan*, 136. For more on the problems of translation in relation to sexual sins, see Sigal, "Queer Nahuatl."

38. For scholarship on misinscription of the sodomitical body—though not named as such—see Sigal, *The Flower and the Scorpion*; Sweet, "Mutual Misunderstandings." For colonial cultural, ideological, religious, and linguistic mistranslations, see Burkhart, *The Slippery Earth*; Rafael, *Contracting Colonialism*.

39. Carrasco, *Inquisición y represión sexual en Valencia*.

40. Perry, *Gender and Disorder in Early Modern Seville*, 125.

41. Berco, *Sexual Hierarchies, Public Status*, 35.

42. Penyak, "Criminal Sexuality in Central Mexico," 279.

43. AHMM, caja 30, exp. 20, fol. 23. One marco was equivalent to 136 pesos.

44. AHMM, caja 30, exp. 20, fol. 75: "Que sean sacados de la carcel y prission en que estan en bestias de albarda con sogas a las gargantas atados los pies y manos y voz de pregonero que manifieste su delito y llevados por las calles publicas al lugar donde suelen executarse semejantes justicias. Y alli se les da garrote en la forma acostumbrada hasta que mueran naturalmente y muertos los cuerpos sean quemados en llama de fuego y hechos ceniça y declaro todos sus bienes que de los susodichos se hallaren por perdidos y por la camara de su magestad."

45. Gruzinski based his groundbreaking "Las cenizas del deseo" on incomplete documents found in Seville's Archivo General de Indias—specifically, a few letters from 1658, a list of fourteen men executed for committing sodomy, and a summary of the judicial investigation (the original case is lost)—to partly reconstruct the lives of these men.

46. Martín de Guijo, *Diario de succesos virreinales*, 105.

47. Gruzinski, "The Ashes of Desire," 199.

48. Garza Carvajal, *Butterflies Will Burn*, 9.

49. Gruzinski, "The Ashes of Desire," 199.

50. Monter, "Sodomy: The Fateful Accident," 204–6.

51. Monter, "Sodomy: The Fateful Accident," 212.

52. Perry, "The 'Nefarious Sin' in Early Modern Seville," 67.

53. Monter, "Sodomy: The Fateful Accident," 205.

54. Vainfas, *Trópico dos pecados*; Monter, "Sodomy: The Fateful Accident," 212.

55. Marietta and Rowe, *Troubled Experiment*, 88–89.

56. Ben-Atar and Brown, *Taming Lust*.

57. Bennassar, "El modelo sexual," 297.

58. R. Burns, *Las Siete Partidas*, 1427.

59. López, quoted in Crompton, "The Myth of Lesbian Impunity," 18.

60. See Bennassar, "El modelo sexual," 297; Garza Carvajal, *Butterflies Will Burn*, 40–43.

61. Carrasco, *Inquisición y represión sexual en Valencia*, 41: "establecemos y mandamos, que cualquier persona, de cualquier estado, condición, preeminencia ó dignidad que sea, que cometiere el delito nefando contra *naturam*, seyendo en él convencido por aquella manera de prueba, que segun Derecho es bastante para

probar el delito de herejía ó crimen *laesae Majestatis*, que sea quemado en llamas de fuego en el lugar." The original *Pragmática* is in the Archivo General de Simancas, leg. 1, num. 4.

62. Carrasco, *Inquisición y represión sexual en Valencia*, 41: "y mandamos, que si acaesciere que no se pudiere probar el delito en acto perfecto y acabado, y se probaren y averiguaren actos muy propinquos y cercanos a la conclusion del, en tal manera que no quedase por el tal delinquente de acabar este dañado yerro, sea habido por verdadero hecho del delito, y que sea juzgado y sentenciado, y padezca aquella misma pena."

63. Arondekar, *For the Record*, 14.

64. AGI, Mexico 38, N.57.

65. García Peláez, *Memorias para la historia del antiguo reyno de Guatemala*, 241: "Por acuerdos de 5 y 19 de noviembre de [1]601, en causa de pecado nefando, don Pedro de Carranza y Juan Ucelo, índios de Chiquimula, son condenados á quemar y confiscacion de todos sus bienes para la real cámara, y Andres Perez á tormento de cordeles, agua y toca, reservada la cantidad al señor oidor que asistiese á verle dar."

66. *Boletín del Archivo General del Gobierno*, 33: "Tenemos constancia del incidente en la ciudad de Santiago de Guatemala, el día 10 de diciembre de 1583, fecha en que debió ejecutarse al indio Juan Martín, por medio del fuego, en la Plaza Mayor de dicha ciudad. En esa fecha, tres clérigos y un minorista ayudados de varios particulares, salvaron al sentenciado, Armando gran escándalo en dicha plaza en los precísos momentos en que era conducido el indio Martín al quemadero, por haber cometido 'Pecado nefando.'"

67. Sellers-García, *Distance and Documents at the Spanish Empire's Periphery*, 148.

68. AGN, Jesuítas 1–3, exp. 18, fols. 51–56.

69. BNAH, Archivo Histórico, Gómez Orozco 184, "Annals of Puebla." Townsend, *Here in This Year*, 122–23, 144–45, 148–49, and 150–51.

70. Robles, *Diario de sucesos notables*, 86: "Lunes á las cuatro de la tarde quemaron en el tianguis de San Juan á D. Juan de la Cruz, indio del barrio de la Lagunilla, por el pecado nefando." I thank Sonya Lipsett-Rivera for these references.

71. Robles, *Diario de sucesos notables*, 110: "A 25, jueves quemaron en la albarrada de San Lázaro, dos mulatos y tres negros por sométicos, los cuales trajeron del obraje de Juan de Avila, en el pueblo de Miscoac [Mixcoac]."

72. Robles, *Diario de sucesos notables*, 151: "Siete hombres quemados por sodomitas—Lunes 13, quemaron en la albarrada de San Lázaro siete hombres mulatos, negros y mestizos, por el pecado nefando; estaban en el obraje de Juan de Avila, en el pueblo de Miscuac [*sic*], estramuros de esta ciudad, el cual obraje se fué luego deteriorando hasta que por último se consumió."

73. Robles, *Diario de sucesos notables*, 404: "Lunes 18, entraron en la capilla un mulato y un mestizo para quemarlos, por sométicos. A 19 se publicó la residencia del marques de la Laguna. Quemados. Miércoles 20, quemaron en San Lázaro á los dichos, y sacaron á la vergüenza á un negro por cómplice."

74. AGI, Filipinas 18A, R.6, N.36; AGI, Filipinas 10, R.1, N.7.

75. AGI, Pleitos de la Casa de la Contratación, Escribanía 1075C, fol. 117; AGI, Pleitos Audiencia de Santo Domingo, Escribanía 5B, fol. 95.

76. "Gazeta de México" (1735, no. 87), in León, *Bibliografía mexicana del siglo VXIII*, 518: "El 10. se executó en dos Hombres la sentencia de muerte, y combustion, por el grave delito de Sodomía."

77. "Gazeta de México" (1738, no. 129), in León, *Bibliografía mexicana del siglo VXIII*, 786: "El 27. se executó sentencia de muerte con calidad de fuego, en dos Indios Reos del delito nefando, acompañandolos hasta el Suplicio la Cofradia, y Santo Crucifixo de la Misericordia como (desde los primeros tiempos, antes que año de 1568 se fundasse la Real Sala del Crimen) ha sido costumbre, y consta del Auto de 16. de Febrero de 1565."

78. *Gazeta de México (enero a agosto de 1784)* (30 June 1784), 111: "El 23 se executó la pena de muerte y fuego en un reo nefando de esta Real Carcel de Corte, cuyo cuerpo se reduxo á cenizas en el sitio acostumbrado."

79. Narváez Hernández, *La Idea del Poder Judicial en el proceso constitucional insurgente*, 198. According to Rivera Cambas, *México pintorseco*, 252: "La Acordada era terrible en sus ejecuciones: el 24 de Junio de 1786 aplicó á tres reos la pena de fuego y á otros tres la de horca, penas a que fueron condenados los dos primeros por el crimen de sodomía y bestialidad y los demás por ladrones incendiarios. Las cabezas de estos estuvieron clavadas en varios lugares de la ciudad, en los sitios en que fueron metidos los principales delitos."

80. Farge, *The Allure of the Archives*, 8.

81. Mbembe, "The Power of the Archive and Its Limits," 21.

82. Mbembe, "The Power of the Archive and Its Limits," 19.

83. Eichhorn, *The Archival Turn in Feminism*, 16.

84. AHMM, caja 30, exp. 20, fol. 39: "yndio yncapaz sin entendimiento, sin saber ni entender la grabedad y abominacion."

85. AHMM, caja 30, exp. 20, fol. 38.

86. Mbembe, "The Power of the Archive and Its Limits," 22.

87. Douglas, *Purity and Danger*, 4.

88. Bersani, "Is the Rectum a Grave?"

3. Archiving the Signs of Sodomy

1. AGN, "Unidad de Descripción Documental," accessed October 10, 2017, http://www.agn.gob.mx/guiageneral/contenido.php?CodigoReferencia =MX09017AGNCL01FO005IV.

2. Linda Arnold (personal communication, April 20, 2016) rightly notes that we cannot depend on the national archive's designation of the branch, or even the descriptions, because much of the information was generated largely by a team of recent university graduates, who received social service credit for their work, rather than by trained archivists. The story of how Indiferente Virreinal ended up

as such is complex: It was part of some twenty thousand large moving boxes that in 1977–78 came out of warehouses and into the AGN, and at the time was labeled Indiferente General. As part of the move from Tacuba to Lecumberri, the staff and volunteers (including Linda Arnold and many other scholars) and a group of forty recent graduates began opening boxes and sorting through the papers. Much of the nineteenth- and twentieth-century material was moved into Galleries 2, 3, and 5 and the Cedillo building. With the move to Lecumberri, most of the colonial documents went into Gallery 4, the nineteenth-century material into Gallery 5, and so on. In spite of the official AGN database, there are several boxes, some that contain Nahuatl documents and civil records, that are unaccounted for.

3. AGN, Indiferente Virreinal, caja 5182, exp. 48, fols. 38–68. A reference to this criminal case in another document (AGN, Indiferente Virreinal, caja 1482, exp. 7, fol. 6) gives 1710 as the approximate date.

4. AGN, Indiferente Virreinal, caja 5182, exp. 48, fol. 38: "hizo denuncia Lorenzo Joseph Carrion negro esclabo de Don Gabriel de Macariaga diciendo habia tiempo de nueve meses estaba en el obraje de d[ic]ho Pabia que pasados nueve meses vio en la sala de los solteros que llaman la Clapuchinga se juntaron a cometer el pecado nefando un mulato llamado Juan de Dios libre aprendis de texador soltero un yndio nombrado Joseph de Santiago soltero empeñado en d[ic]ho obraje que el mulato serbia de muger y el yndio de varon y que aunque estaba dormido el declarante, a los mobimientos q[ue] habian hecho habia despertado y vistolos con atencion hasta haber acabado de cometer d[ic]ho pecado."

5. AGN, Indiferente Virreinal, caja 5182, exp. 48, fol. 38: "Y en otra occasion tambien los vido en el lugar de la secreta que llaman la Cuba haviendose lebantado a las 3 de la mañana a una nesesidad natural y en d[ic]ho lugar habia hallado en el mesmo acto el mulato lebantó la cara y vido a d[ic]ho denunciante y el yndio se tapó . . . y este estaba con los calzones puestos y el mulato los tenia quitados hasta los muslos."

6. AGN, Indiferente Virreinal, caja 1482, exp. 7, fol. 6: "les fuesen dado a cada uno docientos azotes; que por todos los dias de su vida estubiesen en carcel perpetua dandoles tan solamente por alimento pan y agua todos los dias por tiempo de siete años ex[ce]pto en las domenicas, y a que en haviendo fallecido se consumiesen sus cuerpos en la parte y lugar donde es acostumbrada." The owner of the mill was also punished—his goods were confiscated—because he did not alert criminal authorities upon hearing the sodomy charges against his employees.

7. K. Burns, *Into the Archive*, 124.

8. Hall, "Encoding, Decoding," 512.

9. Berco, *Sexual Hierarchies, Public Status*, 92.

10. SANM, MF 454, roll 6, frames 830–89 (microfilm accessed at the University of Texas at El Paso Library).

11. SANM, MF 454, roll 6, frame 832: "y reconociendo vien este hecho arrendo el cavallo en que yba hazia donde estaban, y les dio con las riendas unos azotes."

12. SANM, MF 454, roll 6, frame 844: "con el otro yndio estando en el suelo barriga con barriga y que el rreferido yndio preso cojio a este confesante el miembro viril y se lo arrimaba a la parte posterior, y que no se alboroto para meterlo; y que el rreferido yndio se lo estaba manoseando para que se alborotara, y que no pudo alborotarlo; y que por Dios no se le alboroto, y que estando este confessante sobre el otro yndio barriga con barriga, llego el español y que luego se quito."

13. AHET, Judicial Criminal, caja 2, exp. 26, fol. 5: "y sonriendose este declarante se quito los calsones y le palpó todo el cuerpo y las partes con mucha ansia con ambas manos de tal calidad que se deleyto con extremo d[ic]ho mulato de tentarle el miembro a este declarante y le dio muchos besos en el y en los genitales . . . y este declarante le echó semen en las manos a d[ic]ho mulato q[ue] sacó un pañito y estubo limpiando a este declarante disiendole q[ue] como le diese el semen q[uan]do se lo pidiese."

14. AHET, Judicial Criminal, caja 2, exp. 26, fol. 10: "dijo que el haberlo consentido fue por desentreñar su yntencion y darle parte a la justicia para que le castigase como con efecto se la dio a su merced d[ic]ho Señor Governador."

15. Berco, *Sexual Hierarchies, Public Status*, 92.

16. AHMC, caja 6, exp. 39, fol. 6: "como un hombre abrassa a una muger acostados en el suelo."

17. AHMC, caja 6, exp. 39, fol. 3: "bio que las nalgas i trasero del que tenia quitados los calzones lo tenia todo humedecido."

18. AGI, Pleitos de la Casa de la Contratación, Escribanía 1105B, fol. 5: "toda la trasera del muchacho mojada."

19. AGI, Pleitos de la Casa de la Contratación, Escribanía 1105B, fol. 5: "toda untada segun el olor y el tacto del semen."

20. Spurling, "Honor, Sexuality, and the Colonial Church," 47.

21. AHJO, Sección Teposcolula, Serie Penal, leg. 21, exp. 1, fol. 63.

22. White, *Speaking with Vampires*, 58.

23. BPEJ-FE, caja 50, exp. 1, prog. 769, fols. 1–78.

24. SANM, MF 454, roll 6, frames 562–706.

25. BPEJ-FE, caja 81, exp. 10, prog. 1331, fols. 1–146; BPEJ-FE, caja 50, exp. 1, prog. 769, fols. 1–78. For another false accusation, see BPEJ-FE, caja 124, exp. 10, prog. 1856, fols. 1–50.

26. BPEJ-FE, caja 18, exp. 3, prog. 303, fol. 103.

27. AGNP, caja 39A, 1700–1800 Civil, Criminal, Testamentos, unnumbered exp., fols. 1–8: "en donde empezó a meterme la mano en la bragueta haciendo demostraciones y dilixencias para besarle el rostro, y viendome en este peligro me defendi . . . y entonces le di un puñete diciendole no soi dessa calidad no quiero hazer esso y a[h]ora te [h]e de llevar a la cassa de Galves alguacil de bara de la Real Justicia de esta ciudad para que lo castigara."

28. For another example, see AGI, Contratación 72, fols. 1–187.

29. I am grateful to David Lobenstine for this observation.

30. Tortorici, "Sexual Violence, Predatory Masculinity, and Medical Testimony in New Spain."

31. AHET, Judicial Criminal, caja 2, exp. 26, fol. 60.

32. AHET, Judicial Criminal, caja 2, exp. 26, fol. 19: "no [h]ay ningunas de ellas ni señales de q[ue] las pueda haver en el intestino recto de los susod[ic]hos y estar los musculos o muretillos tan sumamente fuertes q[ue] ni aduc. metiendo instrumento hubo orifisio sino solo el natural y q[ue] lo que llevan d[ic]ho es la verdad."

33. AGCA, A2.2, exp. 3471, leg. 175: "quando vivian juntos dormia con él, y por las noches el Viejo le ponia su pajarito arrimando al suio."

34. AGN, Indiferente Virreinal 1182, exp. 31, fol. 9–11: Upon examining the suspect's anus and rectal canal, the surgeon discovered "el ano ilexo pues no tenia señal de equimosis ni plaga." He also asserted, "pues segun Josef Mercado jurisconsulto que la sodomia se prueba cuando los testigos depusieren haver visto las sabanas sangrientas o la camisa teñida de sangre . . . pues estos son indicios mui sospechosos para comprobar . . . en la practica innumerables enfermidades por la corrupcion de los humores."

35. AGNP, caja 39A, 1700–1800 Civil, Criminal, Testamentos, unnumbered exp., fol. 24: "que en quanto no ben los testigos la sangre de tan nefando acto en sabanas [y] camisas, no se puede comprobar semejante delicto."

36. I am grateful to David Lobenstine for making these observations about the arbitrary nature of bodily signs and the undermining of medical expertise through the privileging of non-corporeal signs.

37. AGCA, A2.2, exp. 2888, leg. 152, fol. 2: "no encuentra lesion alguna en el miembro viril y ano del d[ic]ho paciente." Nor were there "manchas de sangre o semen en la ropa."

38. Cutter, *Libro de los principales rudimentos tocante a todos juicios, criminal, civil y executivo*, 38: "reoconoserlo es co vn instrum.to que traheen los ciruxanos, y no habiendolo con vn heubo de Gallina que sea largo el qual se le pone en el ojo de atraz, y se sume, y a este reconosim.to se a de ayar el juez." I thank Chad Thomas Black for this reference.

39. AGI, Pleitos de la Casa de la Contratación, Escribanía 1105B, fol. 103.

40. AGI, Pleitos de la Casa de la Contratación, Escribanía 1105B, fol. 16: "las partes esternas del ano estaban todos ulseradas con unas ulseras sordidas y callosas señales de que havian con el cometido muchas veces el pecado de sodomia."

41. Few, "'That Monster of Nature,'" 161.

42. Martínez, "Archives, Bodies, and Imagination," 165.

43. Martínez, "Archives, Bodies, and Imagination," 160.

44. AGN, Indiferente Virreinal 5216, exp. 12, fol. 7v: "pues no siendo la Juana hombre, ni muger, mal puede Incurrir en un delito que necesariamente exige la existencia de uno de los dos sexos."

45. AGN, Indiferente Virreinal 5216, exp. 12, fol. 2: "se han bautizado por los Anatomicos con el nombre de alas, ó labios: los quales separados se reconoce entre

ellos en su parte superior un pequeño cuerpo algo prominente, muy parecido al miembro viril, llamado *Clytoris*."

46. AGN, Indiferente Virreinal 5216, exp. 12, fol. 6v: "dos cuerpos glandulosos, de figura oval, del tamaño como de un grano de cacao."

47. AGN, Indiferente Virreinal 5216, exp. 12, fol. 1: "contiene en ellos un informe relativo a una d[ic]ha Juana Larga, a q[uie]ⁿ se tenia p[o]ʳ algunos del vulgo p[o]ʳ Hermafrotida . . . p[o]ʳ parecerme obzeno, y provocativo, materia mui agena de andar en Gazeta en manos de todos, y q[u]ᵉ no puede lerse en grave ruina de las almas."

48. For scholarship on Mexican performance artist Jesusa Rodríguez's early performances of Esparragosa, see Martínez, "Archives, Bodies, and Imagination" (and on Rodríguez's infamous orientalist performance of the doctor in 2014, see Siu, "Hemispheric Raciality"). More recently, Juana Aguilar became the satirical target of several problematic cabaret performances at the 2017 Tepoztlán Institute for the Transnational History of the Americas.

49. Monter, "Sodomy: The Fateful Accident," 206.

50. *Diccionario de autoridades*, vol. 3.

51. R. Burns, *Las Siete Partidas*, 1427.

52. AGN, Indiferente de Guerra 45B, fols. 170–214.

53. AGCA, A1.15, exp. 50.049, leg. 5905.

54. AGCA, A1.15, exp. 50.049, leg. 5905: "el d[ic]ho Gaspar difunto que declara que al tiempo que el d[ic]ho su hijo estava cercano a la muerte le dijo que estando jugando con d[ic]ho Alexo junto a la milpa [h]avia raydo . . . y ynpensadamente entrado un troncon o estaca que estava en el suelo por el çiesso."

55. AMMNL, Criminal 26, exp. 465, fols. 1–2: "por ser muchacho le faltaron las fuerzas, y que d[ic]ho Martin lo agarró del pescuezo, y lo medio ahogó y que como ya le havia rebentado la correa de los calzones se le calleron, y quando bolbió en si bolteo la cara atras, y bio que d[ic]ho Martin lo estaba fornicando."

56. AGCA, A2.2, exp. 4500, leg. 216, fols. 4–5: "le puso el pie en el pescueso, en cuyo estado le suplicó el declarante que lo dejase por Dios y por Maria Santissima y Victoriano le dixo *ya no te pego mas como nos forniquemos*, a lo que negaba diciendole que era pecado, por lo que Victoriano le amarró las manos por detras con un orillo que llebaba en la cintura el declarante, y bolteandolo boca abajo (quitado la camisa y los calzones por el mismo que habla antes de que lo amarrasen por mandado del otro) le introdujo el miembro viril por la parte posterior tres ocasiones."

57. AGN, Criminal 98, exp. 2, fols. 25–62.

58. AMMNL, Criminal 52, exp. 848.

59. AGI, Pleitos de la Casa de la Contratación, Escribanía 1075C, fol. 117.

60. AGI, Pleitos de la Casa de la Contratación, Escribanía 1075C, fol. 1: "estavan en el suelo el d[ic]ho Domingo echado de barriga en el suelo quitados los calçones y alzada la camisa trasera y el d[ic]ho Juan Ponze se tapo el rrostro quando llegaron los d[ic]hos Tinoco y Pedro Sanchez."

61. AGI, Pleitos de la Casa de la Contratación, Escribanía 1075C, fol. 14v: López confessed that Ponce grabbed him by the shoulders and "el d[ic]ho Juan Ponze llegó a meterle el miembro por el culo y haciendo fuerza para meterlo y metió la punta del miembro porque lo demas no le cabia por ser gordo y despues de aver acavado de hallo este confesante moxado el culo de la simiente que le avia echado el d[ic]ho Juan Ponze."

62. For other examples of nefarious violence cases, see AGI, Pleitos Audiencia de Santo Domingo, Escribanía 5B, fol. 95 (1648); AHET, Judicial Criminal, caja 7, exp. 18, fol. 11 (1707); AGN, Indiferente de Guerra 45B, fols. 170–214 (18067); AGCA, A1.15, exp. 5373, leg. 247; AGCA, A1.15, exp. 37,051, leg. 4438 (1808); BPEJ-FE 11-7-202 (1813).

63. For several cases of such long-term relationships in colonial Spanish America, see Molina, *Cuando amar era pecado* and "Sodomy, Gender, and Identity in the Viceroyalty of Peru."

64. Rodríguez, *Sexual Futures, Queer Gestures, and Other Latina Longings*, 2.

65. Gruzinski, "Las cenizas del deseo," 278.

66. AGI, Mexico 38, N.57/3/1: "el d[ic]ho mulato se quebrava de cintura y traia atado en la frente de hordinᵒ un pañito que llaman melindre que usan las mugeres."

67. AGI, Mexico 38, N.57/3/2: "que se sentaba en el suelo en un estrado como muger y que hacia tortillas y lababa y guisaba."

68. AGNP, caja 7, 1700–1799 Criminal, unnumbered exp., fol. 51.

69. AGNP, caja 7, 1700–1799 Criminal, unnumbered exp., fol. 13: "aunque es amujerado no por esto enamora a los hombres."

70. AGNP, caja 7, 1700–1799 Criminal, unnumbered exp., fol. 15: "de muchos modos puede incurrir en la nota de afeminada un hombre . . . puede ser afeminado por el nombre, por el aspecto, por la inclinacion, y por el malicioso uso del sexo."

71. AGN, Indiferente Virreinal, caja 1482, exp. 7, fol. 8.

72. AGN, Inquisición 1078, exp. 4, fol. 133: "no era cosa contra la ley de Dios ni de su M[adr]ᵉ SS[antísi]ᵐᵃ ni de los santos, que no era cosa de heregia." See also AGN, Inquisición 1166, exp. 4, fols. 14–142; Penyak, "Temporary Transgressions, Unspeakable Acts," 349–50.

73. AGN, Inquisición 1078, exp. 4, fol. 47.

74. AGCA, A2.2, exp. 2888, leg. 152, fols. 1–17.

75. AGCA, A2.2, exp. 2888, leg. 152, fol. 6: "se le reconvino lo inverosimil que es el que no accediesse a la pretencion de Juan Joseph quando por el contrario es creible que el [Desiderio] fuesse el solicitante atenta la edad tierna del Juan Joseph, y la afeminida condicion y porte que manifiesta el confessante en modo."

76. AGCA, A1.15 (3), exp. 3222, leg. 269.

77. AGN, Inquisición 1349, exp. 28, fol. 18: "Ella es una Muger hombrada, cara fea, triguena, pelo crespo, anulado, cuerpo y andar de hombre . . . es bien conosida por este lado, por Gregoria la Macho, su ocupacion frecuente ha sido jugar a la pelota, al picado y raiuela acompañandose mas bien con Mugeres que con hombres."

78. Quoted in Camba Ludlow, "Gregoria la Macho y su 'inclinación a las mujeres,'" 485.

79. See http://www.agn.gob.mx/guiageneral/contenido.php?CodigoReferencia=MX09017AGNCL01FO006INSE002INUI1349UC0028, accessed October 11, 2017.

80. AGCA, A1.15, exp. 36.600, leg. 4421.

81. Cifor, "Affecting Relations," 10.

82. AGN, Inquisición 212, exp. 1, fols. 1–2: "viniendo de la vela este t[estig]º vido que el d[ic]ho Antonio lipares e cebrian lombardo se besaban con las bocas y que a este t[estig]º le paresio mal y como lo vido."

83. AGI, Mexico 38, N.57/3/2: "le visitavan unos mozuelos a quienes el susodicho llamaba de mi alma, mi vida, mi corazon, y los susodichos se sentavan con él y dormian juntos en un aposento."

84. AGI, Pleitos Audiencia de Panamá, Escribanía 541A, fol. 242.

85. Giraldo Botero, *Deseo y represión*, 33.

86. BPEJ-FE, caja 13, exp. 13, prog. 234, fol. 55.

87. Mott, "My Pretty Boy," 236.

88. Mott, "My Pretty Boy," 132.

89. Earle, "Letters and Love in Colonial Spanish America," 25.

90. BPEJ-FE, caja 11, exp. 6, prog. 64, fol. 2: "en una caxa unas esquelas suscritas por otro hombre que se halla preso en la Real Carcel que segun sus expreciones obscenas y amatorias lo conbensen al sodometico."

91. Lavrin, "Sexuality in Colonial Mexico," 59.

92. BPEJ-FE, caja 11, exp. 6, prog. 64, fol. 3: "Señor Don Nabor de la Encarnación mi muy estimado y querido amigo de mi mayor aprecio y veneración a quien escribo con la mayor subordinación que un cautivo corason le desea con tan soberano dueño mi alma me haras el favor que si se pregunta Don Manuel por la frasada que de quien es, le dices tu que era mia, y la colcha tambien, y tambien te noticio que estoy separado en el quarto oscuro con un par de grillos de lo que me dijiste ante noche lla lo tenia para que fuera a los toros, pero ahora considera como estare sin adbitrio alguno, solo que tu me mandes quatro onsas de hilo y un real de plata para haser un par de medias esto te lo pido enprestado para poder sacar mis trapos para salir al rio, y mandame papel para estarte escriviendo de lo que te encargo no vallas a haser una porquería, la respuesta de esta espero con Polonio, y no mas sino que Dios te guarde muchos años. Tu negro que te estima Apolinario Salmon. [Postscript] No siempre e de estar cautibo. Yo tendre mi libertad, todo el gusto que as tenido gusto pasar se te volvera ay te mando dos dosenas de besos y beinte de abrasos, que tu mano besa. o o o o o o o o o o o o o o o o o o o o o o o o o o x x x x x x x x x x x x x x x x x x x." This letter is also analyzed and transcribed (with some differences) by Miranda Guerrero, "Homosexualidad, derechos, naturales y cultura popular."

93. BPEJ-FE, caja 11, exp. 6, prog. 64, fol. 4: "o o o o = Senor Don Nabor de la Encarnacion mi muy estimado negrito de mi mayor estimacion me alegrare que te halles con la salud cumplida como yo deseo en la compania de las prenas de tu

estimacion mi alma por vida tu lla te encargo que no andes con porquerias porque yo lo [h]éde saber de lo que me dises que lla no ves las horas de que salga, no has de tener mas ganas que yo mi alma no pienses que lo que te mandaba pedir no hera para mi sino para mandarte haser un par de medias por estar osioso ahora, pues aqui tu seda berde la asul y negra con esta no alcansa para aserla, mandamela a la tarde, mandame tambien el hilo que esté retondito, y no mas que Dios guarde tu vida muchos años = Polinario Salmon. o o o o o o o o o o o o x x x x x x, hay te mando esos vesitos y esos abrasos, recibelos con mucho gusto ya me muero de ganas que me des mi lenguita y mis brasitos que estoy con el susidio [*sic*] de no saber que alcahuete estaria mordiendo mi lenguita."

94. BPEJ-FE, caja 11, exp. 6, prog. 64, fol. 5: "las ruedas pintadas en el fin de dichas esquelas significan los vesos, y las exes los abrasos que dirijia a la dicha muger, que con Nabor no ha tenido mas comercio que una amistad lícita que han guardado desde su tierna edad."

95. *Diccionario de autoridades*, vol. 4.

96. BPEJ-FE, caja 11, exp. 6, prog. 64, fol. 6: "la vos publica es de que José Nabor [h]a sido siempre un alcahuete infame inclinado por su viciada propención a afectar modales afeminados tanto como presentarse publicamente vestido con traje de muger."

97. BPEJ-FE, caja 11, exp. 6, prog. 64, fol. 11: "los torpes abusos de un instrumento obseno."

98. BPEJ-FE, caja 11, exp. 6, prog. 64, fol. 13: "el criminal de esta causa Apolinario Salmon resulta convicto y confesó en el abuso del instrumento obceno con que sin nesesidad suplia la aparencia del natural, pero no pidio probarse tan claro como la luz del dia."

99. BPEJ-FE, caja 11, exp. 6, prog. 64, fol. 34: "la correspondencia amoratoria entre los de un sexo no es argumento del connato proximo al crimen de que se trata . . . ygualmente es cierto que el reo por sola su declaracion no puede ser condenado."

4. To Deaden the Memory

1. AGI, Justicia, leg. 248 (microfilm reel no. 191), "Processo contra P[edr]⁰ Na sobre el pecado nefando." I thank John F. Chuchiak, whose "The Sins of the Fathers" brought this case to my attention.

2. AGI, Justicia, leg. 248 (microfilm reel no. 191), fol. 2: "al d[ic]ho Pedro Na yndio que tenya los cazaguelles quitados y sentado en el suelo y entre las piernas una gallina de la tierra y este testigo le hechó la mano e vido como a la d[ic]ha gallina le salia e corria sangre del sieso y del d[ic]ho Pedro Na tenya los caçaguelles desatados e descubierto el myembro engendratibo."

3. AGI, Justicia, leg. 248 (microfilm reel no. 191), fol. 3: "es verdad que ayer tarde en el d[ic]ho camyno topo a estas gallinas [de la tierra] con unos pollos e tomo de ellas la gallina que les mostraba e se entro con ella en el monte e se debaxo los

caçaguelles e con la alteracion carnal que tubo tomo el myembro engendratibo en la mano e se lo metio por el sieso a la d[ic]ha gallina e tubo aceso carnal con ella e della le hizo correr sangre por el sieso a la d[ic]ha gallina e que en esto llegaron un yndio e una yndia."

4. AGI, Justicia, leg. 248 (microfilm reel no. 191), fol. mvcxvi: "condeno que de la carcel e prision en que esta sea sacado en una bestia de albarda atados pies y manos y con boz de pregonero que maniffeste su delito e la justicia que se le manda hazer sea traydo por las calles publicas desta zbdad [ciudad] y sea llebado al suelo que esta en la plaça della y alli sea castrado y le sean cortados los genitales y en destierro perpetuo destas provincias de Yucatan."

5. Fernandez, "The Repression of Sexual Behavior by the Aragonese Inquisition," 472.

6. AGI, Justicia, leg. 248 (microfilm reel no. 191), fol. mvcxix: "la gallina con que delinquyo y cometio el d[ic]ho Pedro Na el d[ic]ho delito esta muerta e se ha tenydo guardada mandaba e mando que para executar la d[ic]ha sentencia se la cuelgen del pescueço al d[ic]ho Pedro Na e sea traydo con ella por las calles acostumbradas desta zbdad e despues de executada la d[ic]ha sentencia el susod[ic]ho mando se quemase la d[ic]ha gallina en llamas bibas e fuese hecha polbos."

7. The second case (AGN, Inquisición 372, exp. 20, fols. 1–24v) is the 1632 Inquisition denunciation of Diego de la Cruz, an Asian slave, who was accused of blasphemy. One of the many charges against Diego de la Cruz was that he had been tempted by the Devil to have sex with a turkey. I am grateful to Tatiana Seijas for this reference.

8. Benson, "Animal Writes," 5.

9. de Hamel, *Scribes and Illuminators*, 17.

10. Benson, "Animal Writes," 12.

11. Benson, "Animal Writes," 6.

12. Whitehead, "Loving, Being, Killing Animals," 330.

13. *Diccionario de autoridades*, vol. 1.

14. For this reference, I am indebted to Vega Umbasia, *Pecado y delito en la colonia*, 33.

15. Martínez de la Parra, *Luz de verdades católicas*, 219: "Pusierale por cabellos enroscadas Vivoras, por frente la de una Cabra, por ojos los de un Escuerzo, por orejas las de un Asno, por narizes las de una Simia, por boca la de un Dragon, por dientes los de un Cocodrillo, por cuello el de un Camello, por pecho el mas apretado de un Galgo, por vientre el de un Cerdon, por manos las de un Oso, por pies los de un Cavallo, por cauda la de una Sierpe, pusierale del Tigre las manchas, del Leon el hediondo aliento. Y toda la figura de un demonio, y de hombre nada: siendolo todo el hombre por la Luxuria."

16. Salisbury, *The Beast Within*, 77.

17. Salisbury, *The Beast Within*, 79.

18. López Austin, *The Human Body and Ideology*, 292.

19. Ruiz de Alarcón, *Treatise on the Heathen Superstitions*, 246.

20. AHET, cédula 197, caja 4, exp. 35, fol. 3v.

21. Sousa, "The Devil and Deviance," 162.

22. AHET, cédula 197, caja 4, exp. 35, fol. 3v.

23. Beirne, *Confronting Animal Abuse*, 113.

24. Trouillot, *Silencing the Past*, 26.

25. See Penyak, "Criminal Sexuality in Central Mexico"; Bazant, "Bestiality."

26. Anderson, *Creatures of Empire*, 96.

27. Fudge, *Perceiving Animals*, 68.

28. Alva, *A Guide to Confession Large and Small*, 107 and 109.

29. BPEJ-FE, caja 62, exp. 12, prog. 1001, fol. 7.

30. BPEJ-FE, caja 104, exp. 2, prog. 1571, fol. 50.

31. Rydström, *Sinners and Citizens*, 18.

32. Bennassar, "El modelo sexual," 304.

33. Monter, "Sodomy and Heresy in Early Modern Switzerland," 47.

34. Penyak, "Criminal Sexuality in Central Mexico," 281.

35. AMHP, Causas Criminales 1718D, "contra Lorenzo Benítez mulato libre por cohabitado con una vaca."

36. AMHP, Causas Criminales 1718D, fol. 5: "preguntadole que le motivó hazer y executar aquel acto tan feo y tan fuera de lo natural; responde que por hazer experiencia y saber si tenia el mismo deleite; teniendolo con la baca; que si lo tuviera con alguna muger."

37. AMHP, Causas Criminales 1718D, fol. 20: "que en todo el tiempo que ha estado en servicio del Capitan Juan Saenz Merino, [h]a sido su travajo tan exsesivo y perpetuo, que no ha tenido dia de fiesta ni de pazeo; por cuia causa nunca tubo ocazion de zaciar el apetito de la naturaleza."

38. BPEJ-FE, caja 145, exp. 6, prog. 2188, fol. 48.

39. AHET, Judicial Criminal, caja 52, exp. 42, fol. 10: "que hubiese sido tan fuerte su tentacion, y que su sensacion hubiese sido incapaz de resistirla, hubiera ido a solicitor a una muger racional, con quien saciarme . . . no dexa por este de conoser la incompatibilidad, y lo chocante que es a la misma naturaleza mesclarse con [h]embra de otra especie."

40. AGN, Inquisición 1042, exp. 34, fols. 238–39.

41. AHCM, Diocesano, Justicia, Procesos Criminales, Bestialidad, caja 832, exp. 1 [exp. 4 in finding aid], fol. 6 (Hacienda del Rincón, 1782): "como hombre fragil, y engañado del demonio no pudo resistir las tentasiones de la carne y se proboco mirando, a la Burra, y consintio miserablemente, en coabitar con ella."

42. BPEJ-FE, caja 62, exp. 12, prog. 1001, fols. 1–28.

43. BPEJ-FE, caja 62, exp. 12, prog. 1001, fol. 22: "se ensendera una hoguera con vaxa por cuias llamas sera pasado violentamente por dos o tres vezes el modo que no llegue a quemarse."

44. AHPJQ, caja 14, exp. 16, fols. 1–12.

45. AGCA, A1.15, exp. 47.595, leg. 5513.

46. AGCA, A1.15, exp. 47.595, leg. 5513: "Suplico a Vuestra Megestad, pregunté al Alcalde Mayor Don Domingo Salgado la cauza porque no castiga mi pecado si lo tengo, y me deja ir a San Martin mi pueblo a vivir con mi mujer porque tanto tiempo estoy padesiendo, siempre estoy preguntando quando viene a la carsel el alcalde mayor y me responde, yo no tengo la culpa su cuenta alcalde mayor de Chimaltenango ya no tengo pasiencia aqui estoy padesiendo ... si tengo mi culpa boy a pagar, y si no boy a bibir con mi mujer."

47. AHMC, caja 9, exp. 42, fol. 4: "tanto que se rebentó por boca, nariz, ojos, y demas partes humedas, y pudendas en su cuerpo: por esa causa queriendo él tener copula con ella, se resistió a hacerlo."

48. Penyak, "Criminal Sexuality in Central Mexico," 281.

49. AGN, Indiferente Virreinal, Acordada 66, exp. 16.

50. Thomas, *Man and the Natural World*, 98.

51. Rydström, *Sinners and Citizens*, 36.

52. AGN, Inquisición 981, exp. 22, fol. 327: "por tiempo de un año frequentemente tuvo accesos torpes con una imagen de N.S. la Virgen Maria es a saber que en estas ocasiones primero tenia estos accesos con bestias, y despues llegaba a la imagen, y tambien procuraba que la mesma bestia tuviese acceso a la imagen."

53. AGN, Inquisición 1042, exp. 20, fol. 168: "que llegó a confessarse conmigo una muger de que avia tenido, por tres veses, tactos torpes con un animal: y que no haviendo, en las dos, sentido delictacion, que procuraba, en la tercera deseó que el Demonio estuviera en el animal."

54. AGN, Inquisición 1042, exp. 20, fol. 168: "por lo tocante a este Santo Officio, no ay embargo, por que pueda absolver a la penitente."

55. AGN, Indiferente Virreinal, Acordada 66, exp. 16: "procesada en aquel Tribunal por sodomia bestial."

56. *Diccionario de autoridades*, vol. 5.

57. AGN, Criminal 62, exp. 20, fol. 469: "lo hayó materialmente introducido en el baso de la dicha burra y luego, que vio al declarante se separó de ella, y esta salio asi al camino derramandose y meando, y el muchacho procuró cubrirse."

58. AGN, Criminal 62, exp. 20, fol. 472: "poseído de los ardores de la concupencia, y no teniendo proporcion de desahogarle, se llegó a una burra parda, de su padre y tubo con ella acto carnal consumado."

59. AGN, Criminal 62, exp. 20, fol. 475: "hechale cargo de la grabedad del delito, odioso a la misma naturaleza ... cohabitar con un desemejante."

60. AGN, Criminal 62, exp. 20, fol. 495: "como criado desde que tuvo uso de razon de pastorcillo entre los animales, e incitado de la brutal concupicensia no supo ni reflexionó seguramente la grabedad del pecado y detestable crimen."

61. AGN, Criminal 89, exp. 6, fol. 155: "vio a el enunciado reo parado en lo mas alto, y el animal en lo mas bajo, este con las nalgas pegadas a los muslos o empeine del reo, y el reo moviendose de manera que no le quedó al que habla la menor duda del acceso bestial que estava consumando."

62. AGN, Criminal 89, exp. 6, fol. 155: "Carajo ¿Que estás haciendo? ¿Que no eres cristiano?"

63. Bazant, "Bestiality," 204–9.

64. BPEJ-FE, caja 104, exp. 2, prog. 1571, fols. 4 and 19: "porque no sabia que era malo" and "que no le pareció pecado."

65. BPEJ-FE, caja 104, exp. 2, prog. 1571, fol. 19: "es verdad que quando se confesaba le daba verguenza decir eso al padre."

66. Bazant, "Bestiality," 205.

67. AGN, Inquisición 1552, fol. 114.

68. W. Taylor, *Drinking, Homicide, and Rebellion*, 65.

69. AGN, Inquisición 787, exp. 26, fols. 133–48.

70. AGN, Clero Regular y Secular 203, exp. 3, fols. 113–47.

71. AGEH, Tula Justicia, caja 51, exp. 22, fol. 21: "se derramó en el suelo, y no dentro de la burra . . . se quedó un rrato mirando su miembro, junto al culo de la burra."

72. AGEH, Tula Justicia, caja 52, exp. 12, fol. 9: "tubo mal pensamento con una burra."

73. AHET, Judicial Criminal, caja 46, exp. 37, fol. 3: "el diablo lo habia engañado."

74. AGEH, Tula Justicia, caja 51, exp. 5, fol. 5: "y solo el Diablo lo pudo mover aquel dia."

75. I thank Martin Nesvig for helping me make sense of these outlying ecclesiastical cases from Michoacán.

76. Penyak, "Criminal Sexuality in Central Mexico," 285; AGN, Criminal 426, exp. 2, fols. 65–170.

77. Penyak, "Criminal Sexuality in Central Mexico," 285.

78. AGN, Criminal 256, exp. 2, fols. 92–158: "delante de el el semen q[ue] aparecia derramando inmediato a la natura de la propria yegua."

79. AGN, Criminal 256, exp. 2, fol. 129: "En ellos no podia variar la configuracion de el fluido seminal, un color, lo glutinoso, y la cantidad de el, removian toda duda."

80. AGCA, A1.15, exp. 28.192, leg. 2972; AGCA, A1.15, exp. 45.808, leg. 5393.

81. AGCA, A1.15, exp. 28.192, leg. 2972, fol. 6: "ovservio tener las partes inflamadas y coloradas y citar que d[ic]ha oveja muy caliente porque alhagaba a quien la tentava."

82. BPEJ-FE, caja 145, exp. 6, prog. 2188, fol. 5: "hasta llegó a desabrocharse un boton de la pretina de los calsones, pero que no pecó pues la mula se resistió que hasta una patada le dio en una espinilla."

83. AMMNL, Criminal 8, exp. 104, fols. 1–7.

84. AGN, Indiferente Virreinal, caja 1482, exp. 7, fol. 2.

85. AHESLP, 1724-2, "Francisco Xavier, indio, preso en la carcel publica de esta ciudad por el pecado nefando": "condeno a que de la prision en que se haya sea sacado en bestia de albarda, y por las calles publicas le sean dados cien azotes hasta llegar a el quemadero en donde sea pasado por las llamas, y la burra se convierta en cenizas, y executado esto se restituya a la prision, y sea vendido su servicio personal

en un obraje por sinco años cuyo producto aplico tercias partes R[ea]l Camara, estrados, y gastos de justicia."

86. AHEZ, Poder Judicial, Serie Criminal, caja 9, exp. 3.

87. AMHP, Causas Criminales 1718D, "contra Lorenzo Benítez mulato libre por cohabitado con una vaca."

88. AHESLP, 1723-1, "Joseph de la Cruz, preso en la carcel pública de esta ciudad por haber cometido el pecado de bestialidad con una yegua."

89. AHESLP, 1723-1: "por mano de Agustín del Castillo, ministro executor de la real justicia, le fue dado garrote de que quedó naturalmente difunto y a la yegua la mató de un palo y fechó sobre el cuerpo del d[ic]ho Joseph. El mismo executor puso una foguera de sobrada leña, y otra retirada de esta sobre la yegua y ambas les dio fuego que asi al referido Joseph como a la yegua convirtió en cenizas."

90. BPEJ-FE, caja 62, exp. 12, prog. 1001, fol. 28.

91. AHPJQ, caja 14, exp. 16, fols. 1–12.

92. The procurador de indios was a legal agent employed by the court who composed petitions on behalf of people with the legal status of "Indian."

93. AHMM, caja 156, exp. 17, fols. 1–5. Leonardo Alberto Vega Umbasia, in *Pecado y delito en la colonia*, discusses a 1615 criminal case in Nueva Granada in which an indio, Hernando from Antioquia, was hanged and subsequently burned for bestiality with a black heifer.

94. AHEZ, Poder Judicial, Serie Criminal, caja 14, exp. 32.

95. I am grateful to David Lobenstine for posing this question.

96. Murrin, "'Things Fearful to Name,'" 142.

97. Beirne, *Confronting Animal Abuse*, 113.

98. SANM, MF 454, roll 10, frames 831–51.

99. AHCM, caja 832, exp. 2, fol. 3: "la baca . . . se degollara y quemara todo lo qual fecho."

100. AMMNL, Criminal 8, exp. 104, fol. 1.

101. AHEA, Judicial Penal 265.2.1.18fs.

102. AGEH, Tula Justicia, caja 20, exp. 21, fols. 1–12.

103. AGEH, Tula Justicia, caja 20, exp. 21, fols. 6 and 11: "membro mojado y lleno de pelos" and "mui mansa mui quieta y sosegada sin alborotarse."

104. AGN, Inquisición 1321, exp. 7, fols. 26–37.

105. Fudge, *Perceiving Animals*, 2.

106. Beirne, *Confronting Animal Abuse*, 201.

107. AGN, Indiferente Virreinal 5980, exp. 21: "haga matar y meter debajo de la tierra la yegua con quien en d[ic]ho Bartolomé Juan cometio el dicho delito para que no quede memoria deste pecado."

108. Penyak, "Criminal Sexuality in Colonial Mexico," 280; AGN, Criminal 62, exp. 20, fol. 500: "mandar que a la burra, se le quite la vida, para que de este modo se amortigüe la rembranza del hecho."

109. R. Burns, *Las Siete Partidas*, 1427, emphasis added.

110. Tomás y Valiente, "El crimen y pecado contra natura," 49.

111. Evans, *The Criminal Prosecution and Capital Punishment of Animals*.

112. Thomas, *Man and the Natural World*, 39.

113. Murrin, "'Things Fearful to Name,'" 117.

114. AHCM, caja 832, exp. 3 [exp. 4 in the finding aid], fol. 15.

115. Douglas, *Purity and Danger*, 6.

116. Liliequist, "Peasants against Nature," 71.

117. AHCM, caja 832, exp. 5, fol. 22: "con una coroza en la caveza, y en ella pintada un hombre y una burra."

118. AHCM, caja 832, exp. 5, fol. 22: "se degollo la burra, y echandose al fuego h[as]ta que se reduxo á zenizas, se dieron al viento."

119. AHCM, caja 832, exp. 5, fol. 22: "mando que . . . ponga en la Puerta principal de esta Yglesia Parrochial, al tiempo de la misa may[o]^r, en Pie con el pelo suelto, la cara descuvierta, soga al cuello, un crusifixo en las manos, Corona de espinas en la Caveza, y solo se hinque al Prefacio h[as]ta las Abbluciones."

120. Fudge, *Brutal Reasoning*, 2.

5. Archives of Negligence

1. AGN, Indiferente Virreinal, caja 5264, exp. 9, fol. 1: "comete el abominable, torpe, y feo pecado de sodomía."

2. AGN, Indiferente Virreinal, caja 5264, exp. 9, fol. 10: "dixo que es verdad y confiesa haver cometido d[ic]ho pecado de sodomía como fragil y miserable, habia como quatro años, poco mas o menos."

3. AGN, Indiferente Virreinal, caja 5264, exp. 9, fol. 7: "y lo echo en la cama forsexeandolo, y le dijo sirviese de muger que no consintio pero como servio forzado, le dixo el testigo serviria de hombre biendo que de un tiron que le dio se corto la sinta de los calzones, y dandole otro tiron le rasgo los calzones por detras a que biendose casi sobre el lo resistio y entonces, le dio d[ic]ho Don Juan dos vezes en cada nalgas, y una mordida con su propria voca, y le dixo el testigo serviria de hombre a que asintio, y acostandose se le subio ensima el testigo y le metio el dedo pulgar, y sintiendo no ocupaba el hueco, le metio dos dedos, juntos, por la parte del intestino o vazo posterior, y sintiendo que estava mas ancho, le metio tres dedos de la mano derecha, y que assi lo reconosio lo havierto, y usado que por dicha parte estava el referido Don Juan."

4. Lea, *History of Sacerdotal Celibacy*, 258.

5. Haliczer, *Sexuality in the Confessional*, 56.

6. AGN, Inquisición 455, exp. 38, fols. 323–30.

7. AGN, Inquisición 455, exp. 38, fol. 323: "le dixo que si queria peccar con él."

8. AGN, Inquisición 455, exp. 38, fol. 324: "y le dijo que si queria yr a su cassa donde le regalaria y dormiria con el."

9. AGN, Inquisición 455, exp. 38, fols. 323–30.

10. Penyak, "Criminal Sexuality in Central Mexico," 262.

11. Petro, "Beyond Accountability," 171.

12. Pérez, *The Spanish Inquisition*, 101.

13. Alva, *A Guide to Confession Large and Small*, 105–9.

14. Lea, *History of Sacerdotal Celibacy*, 251.

15. Foucault, *The History of Sexuality*, 61.

16. Gruzinski, "Individualization and Acculturation," 103.

17. Klor de Alva, "Colonizing Souls," 3; Harrison, "The Theology of Concupiscence," 136.

18. Burkhart, *The Slippery Earth*, 181–82.

19. Alva, *A Guide to Confession Large and Small*, 107.

20. Pardo, *The Origins of Mexican Catholicism*, 111.

21. Pardo, *The Origins of Mexican Catholicism*, 109.

22. Sousa, "Tying the Knot," 38.

23. Sigal, "The *Cuiloni*, the *Patlache*, and the Abominable Sin," 580.

24. Lima, "Aprisionando o desejo," 86.

25. Foucault, *The History of Sexuality*, 44.

26. AGN, Inquisición 445, exp. 3, fol. 420.

27. AGN, Inquisición 464, exp. 7, fols. 149–59.

28. AGN, Inquisición 464, exp. 7, fols. 151–56: "se confesso con el dicho Padre Matheo, y en duda si havia confessado o no quando estaba tan enfermo, le confesso haver cometido el pecado nefando con un yndio panadero de su misma cassa porque tenian panaderia las dichas sus tias, y passo adelante en su confession, y el dicho Padre Matheo empesso a tocarle a este testigo los brazos, los pechos, el rostro, y sus partes vergonsossas, entrandole la mano por debajo de la ropa y no se acuerda este testigo en Dios, y en su conçiençia, si el dicho Padre Matheo se absolvio o no."

29. AGN, Inquisición 1374, exp. 11, fols. 166–254.

30. González Marmolejo, *Sexo y confesión*, 93.

31. Liebman, "The Abecedario," 554. In 1907 Walter Douglas purchased this collection (as a forty-six-volume set of Inquisition documents) for the price of $1,500 from Michael Blake, a dealer of rare books and manuscripts based in Mexico City. Douglas eventually bequeathed all the documents to the Huntington Library, where they remain to this day. Previously, Blake unsuccessfully tried to sell the documents to Henry Charles Lea, a well-known historian whose own massive collection of purchased manuscripts, incunabula, and rare books is now housed at the University of Pennsylvania in Philadelphia.

32. Pardo, *The Origins of Mexican Catholicism*, 110.

33. HUNT, vol. 15, HM 35109.

34. HUNT, vol. 15, HM 35109, fol. 4: "si havia otros pecados con algunas mugeres delante alguna imagen de Nuestra Señora."

35. HUNT, vol. 15, HM 35109, fol. 4: "luego inmediatamente estando todavia de rodillas, le dixo (instando y persuadiendole en la lengua tarasca) que sacasse sus verguenças, y lo rehuso, turbado, temeroso y confuso, respondiendo siempre que no . . . le entro la mano izquierda por la abertura de los calçones por donde se suele

orinar, y le saco el miembro y teniendo con ella, lo tratava y alterava flotandoselo a mano cerrada para hacerle caer en polucion."

36. HUNT, vol. 15, HM 35109, fol. 4: "le queria dezir una oración y tenientole el miembro desnudo asentado, en la palavra dela dicha mano izquierda, tomo con la derecha el cordon de la orden que havia ceñido, y puso el ultimo nudo del atravesado sobre el miembro, de manera que hizo forma de cruz y movio los lábios como que rezaba, intervalo de um Ave Maria rezada, y no le entendio ni percibio palabra."

37. Lea, *History of Sacerdotal Celibacy*, 256.

38. González Marmolejo, *Sexo y confesión*, 61.

39. HUNT, vol. 15, HM 35109, fol. 8: "no bengo padre a que se me altere que no podra de ninguna manera aunque yo quisiera."

40. Jordan, *The Invention of Sodomy*, 59.

41. HUNT, vol. 15, HM 35109, fol. 17: "si [h]abia sido sometico y echó algunos pecados por detras."

42. HUNT, vol. 15, HM 35109, fol. 17: "q[uan]do muchacho jugaba sacando el miembro y los otros muchachos tambien y que q[uan]do se les alteraban los miembros, se topaban con los miembros unos con otros."

43. HUNT, vol. 15, HM 35109, fol. 17: "jugandoselo y tratandoselo con su propria mano el miembro deste denunciante que luego se le altero el miembro, y que no le dexo de la mano el dicho confessor fr. Esteban entregandole el dicho miembro [h]asta que este denunciante vino a tener polucion y deramar la simiente en la mano del dicho fr. Esteban, y que la dicha semilla le cayo al dicho fr. Esteban sobre su proprio habito."

44. HUNT, vol. 15, HM 35109, fol. 22: "Le confesso que [h]avia cometido el peccado de sodomia contra naturaleça con todos generos de animales por aver leido este confessante en la choronita de el glorioso Sant fran[cis]^{co} los muchos milagros que obrava nuestro señor por medio de la cuerda que trajen todos los religiosos le paresio que podria ser de hefecto para apartar al d[ic]ho hombre de tan abominable peccado y diciendosele anssi y viendo que estava muy arepentido le absolvio sacramentalmente y luego inmediatamente le dixo que para aver de tocarle con la cuerda era necesario que sacase su miembro viril como en hefecto le sacó y teniendole con su mano cubierto con la camissa le dio este confessante tres golpes sobre el con la cuerda que traya ceñida diciendo en el interin la oracion de Sant Antonio de Pádua."

45. HUNT, vol. 15, HM 35109, unnumbered fol.: "soy frayle viejo, hijo de buenos padres, y que confeso mis delictos con verdadero arrepentimiento de ellos, y naturalmente puedo vivir pocos años, ya que soy ministro muy necesario para las nuevas conversions por saber quatro lenguas, algunas de las mas dificiles que ay en esta dicha provincial, que son Mexicana, Octomi, Michuacana y Guachichila, en las quales he administrado a tiempo de treynta años."

46. AGN, Inquisición 1128, exp. 14, fols. 427–36.

47. AGN, Inquisición 1128, exp. 14, fol. 427: "si estaba dispuesta a cumplir una penitencia de azotes."

48. AGN, Inquisición 1128, exp. 14, fol. 427: "le mandó bajar los calzones y arrodillandose en cuio acto lo estuvo pelliscando y tocando de lo superior del cuerpo hasta la parte inferior procurando descubrirle sus partes vergonzosas que tenia ocultas con sus manos."

49. AGN, Inquisición 1128, exp. 14, fol. 427: "su confesion era de tiao tiao, esto es de cosa de poco mas o menos."

50. I am extremely grateful to Vicente Rafael for helping me make sense of the historical and linguistic context of this case (and, particularly, of the term *tiao tiao*).

51. AGN, Inquisición 1128, exp. 14, fols. 430–31: "en el idioma de la tierra con la doctrina del catecismo de q[ue] semejante pecado era muy grave a que respondio el padre Maria q aquello era mentira."

52. AGN, Inquisición 1128, exp. 14, fol. 433: "dandoles el confessor su penitentia por su propria mano, como con el dolor de los azotes daban muchas bueltas y descubrian sus carnes, se las tocó deshonestamente a titulo de ponerlos quietos en su lugar y q[ue] no diesen bueltas, en eso estaba su pecado."

53. AGN, Inquisición 1353, exp. 7, fols. 13–14.

54. Terraciano, "The People of Two Hearts," 17.

55. AGN, Inquisición 288, exp. 1, fols. 1–176. I thank Martin Nesvig for alerting me to the existence of this case.

56. AGN, Inquisición 288, exp. 1, fol. 18: "q[ue] era officio de los christianos y obra de los angeles y servicio de Dios y que asi [h]avian de yr al cielo, y ser angeles. Iten declara este declarante q[ue] el d[ic]ho benefficiado le mando q[ue] le metiese su miembro natural en la boca al d[ic]ho benefficiado y que este declarante de miedo lo hizo y q[ue] vino a cumplir aquel acto y derramar su simiente natural en la boca del d[ic]ho beneficiado el t[estig]° se trago, y le dixo a este declarante que ya eran parientes."

57. AGN, Inquisición 288, exp. 1, fol. 18.

58. Chuchiak, "The Sins of the Fathers," 71.

59. AGN, Inquisición 288, exp. 1, fol. 154: "que como miserable ha tenido algunos tocamientos e poluciones con algunas personas hombres en la forma que el capitulo dize."

60. AGN, Inquisición 288, exp. 1, fol. 155: "dixo que en lo que es como miserable haver cometido los peccados de carne que los ha cometido algunas vezes."

61. AGN, Inquisición 288, exp. 1, fol. 174.

62. See AGN, Inquisición 472, exp. 5, fols. 63–891.

63. AGN, Inquisición 388, exp. 22.

64. AGN, Inquisición 388, exp. 22, fol. 340; Gutiérrez, *When Jesus Came, the Corn Mothers Went Away*, 114, 123.

65. Haskett, "'Not a Pastor, but a Wolf,'" 323.

66. Gutiérrez, *When Jesus Came, the Corn Mothers Went Away*, 114.

67. Penyak, "Criminal Sexuality in Central Mexico," 262.

68. AGN, Inquisición 764, exp. 18, fols. 475–93.

69. AGN, Inquisición 1195, exp. 11, fols. 158–72.

70. AGN, Inquisición 368 (vol. 1), exp. 38, fols. 140–42.

71. AGN, Inquisición 291, exp. 4, fol. 5.

72. AGN, Inquisición 353, exp. 2.

73. AGN, Inquisición 529 (vol. 2), exp. 19, fols. 344–46.

74. AGN, Inquisición 552, exp. 13, fols. 67–70: "fr. Joseph encontro al declarante en el patio, y lo subio a su zelda, y alli lo comenzo abrazar y a querer besarle y le quito los calzones, y quito hechar enzima de una caja para tener acto carnal con el, por la parte posterior, y le dezia que aunque era pecado tener aquellas cosas hombre con muger, no lo era tenerlas hombre con hombre."

75. AGN, Inquisición 776, exp. 26, fols. 223–57. See Penyak, "Criminal Sexuality in Central Mexico," 264.

76. AGN, Inquisición 1373, exp. 14, fols. 173–205.

77. AGN, Inquisición 1373, exp. 14, fol. 174: "*no pienses en esso que no es pecado y lo sé porque soy sacerdote.*"

78. AGN, Inquisición 1373, exp. 14, fol. 174.

79. AGN, Inquisición 1042, exp. fol. 97; Gutiérrez, *When Jesus Came, the Corn Mothers Went Away*, 314.

80. AGN, Inquisición 1042, exp. fol. 97: "no toca al S[an]to Officio."

81. AGN, Inquisición 632, exp. 2; AGN, Indiferente Virreinal 6534, exp. 54.

82. AGN, Indiferente Virreinal 6534, exp. 54, fol. 1: "tubo la osadia de decir alli alguna vez que este tribunal habia procedido con injusticia dandole sentencia sin hallar causa, y que le tenia embargados mil y setecientos pesos."

83. AGN, Inquisición 1292, exp. 15, fol. 146: "siempre procuraba que fuera gente rustica y desconocida en quienes huviesse menos peligro de que lo delatassen o infamassen."

84. AGN, Inquisición 781, exp. 13, fols. 155–66.

85. AGN, Inquisición 845, exp. 21, fols. 331–45.

86. AGN, Inquisición 1275, exp. 12, fol. 87.

87. W. Taylor, *Magistrates of the Sacred*, 189.

88. Derrida, *Archive Fever*, 12.

6. Desiring the Divine

1. AGN, Inquisición 680, exp. 2, fol. 19: "olvidado de Dios y creyendo las tentaciones y persuaçiones del Demonio, empesó a delinquir con ocaçion de haver besado repetidas vezes una echura de Santo Christo de bronse que trae al cuello pendiente en una cruz del mesmo metal todas las partes de su cuerpo naturales por delante y por detras pensando que era lícito; y de estas acciones resultó que tambien le besava los pies a la Virgen S[antísi]^ma Nuestra S[eño]^ra devajo de la advocaçion del rosário; y luego passo a las manos, voca, ojos, y las partes naturales estando la Virgen S[antísi]^ma en un lienso pintada y en una medalla que trae al cuello."

2. AGN, Inquisición 680, exp. 2, fol. 19v: "como fragil cayó, trallendo a la imaginacion dos mil desatinos, y que aquellas partes naturales de la Virgen representavan la Santissima Trinidad y las puertas de Esequiel."

3. AGN, Inquisición 680, exp. 2, fol. 19v: "que la Santissima Trinidad lo casava con la Virgen. Y aviendose levantado de la cama creyó que lla estava casado, y llegandose a una cama distinta de aquella en que [h]avia dormido tuvo una polucion creyendo que estava casado con la Virgen."

4. Franciosini, *Vocabolario italiano e spagnolo*, 592: "la corruzione nell'atto venereo"; Sobrino, *Dicionaro nuevo de las lenguas española y francesa*, 291: "pèrdida de la simiente del hombre quando duerme"; *Diccionario de autoridades*, vol. 5: "pecado torpe contra natura."

5. *Diccionario de autoridades*, vol. 5: "mancha corporal que afea."

6. Terreros y Pando, *Diccionario castellano*, 173.

7. HUNT, vol. 15, HM 35109, fol. 34: "cometio gravíssimo peccado mesclando las cosas sagradas y benditas de que ussa n[uest]ra S[an]ta Madre Yglesia como las oraciones de San Antoniode Padua y la cuerda bendita de San Franc[is]o con las torpes y azquerossas de sus sensualidades profanando y violando la pureza del sacramento sancto de la penitencia con sus abominaciones y torpezas."

8. Holler, "'More Sins Than the Queen of England.'"

9. Jaffary, *False Mystics*, 2.

10. Jaffary, "Sacred Defiance and Sexual Desecration," 45.

11. Penyak, "Criminal Sexuality in Central Mexico," 290; AGN, Criminal 385, exp. 15, fol. 296.

12. AGN, Inquisición 680, exp. 2, fols. 17–29: "Angeles. Año de 1690. Denunziazion q[ue] hizo contrassí Ju[an] Esteban Peres, por estar pensando en la Virgen Santísima N[uest]ra S[ant]a, en actos obzenos."

13. Pratt, *Imperial Eyes*, 6–7.

14. AGN, Inquisición 680, exp. 2, fols. 20–21: "sentido descompuesto y el cuerpo miserable" and "este demonio que solicitó estas maldades se fingia que era mi señor."

15. AGN, Inquisición 680, exp. 2, fol. 22: "me hallaba corason enamorado y der[r]am[ad]a la polusion y sudaba."

16. AGN, Inquisición 680, exp. 2, fol. 23: "hizo tanta armonia mirandome con los hojos por donde quiera que yba en la misma casa que me paresio cosa milagrosa y quando me paresia que la estaba fornicando como si fuera mi esposa, me ponia esta ymaxen delante y otros sinco que busco con esse yntento para que fornicara a la que me paresiera y escoxiera."

17. AGN, Inquisición 680, exp. 2, fol. 21: "espera en Dios se a de server perdonarle, y que aunque lo quemen en la Inq[uisici]on esta presto a obedecer."

18. AGN, Inquisición 680, exp. 2, fol. 19: "diga la enfermedad o enfermedades que al presente tiene y [h]a tenido."

19. AGN, Inquisición 680, exp. 2, fol. 19: "y que tambien [h]a [h]echo diligencias por apagar el fuego de la sensualidad con fuego y sevo ardiendo y un tiron y le quemó sus partes naturales de que hoy está lastimado y oferecio hacer demonstracion; y el señor comisario lo impidio."

20. AHPJQ, caja 2, exp. 21.

21. AHPJQ, caja 2, exp. 21: "el proprio con su propria mano fue quien se corto la dicha bolsa de los testiculos con una nabaja que pidio en la misma mañana a Pedro Arevalo que vive en esta propria casa."

22. AHPJQ, caja 2, exp. 21: "que se ba la ocasion de offender a Dios, cuyo hecho lo executo sin decirlo, ni comunicarlo a persona alguna."

23. AGN, Inquisición 680, exp. 2, fol. 19: "creyendo ser lícitas las poluciones que lleva referidas."

24. Weber, *Teresa of Avila and the Rhetoric of Femininity*, 119.

25. AGN, Inquisición 680, exp. 2, fol. 26: "las enfermedades que havia padesido y padesia, parece que el susod[ic]ho está fatuo o por lo menos que tiene lusidos, o padece mucha melancolia."

26. AGN, Inquisición 680, exp. 2, fol. 19: "tiene el juicio alvorotado."

27. AGN, Inquisición 680, exp. 2, fol. 26: "y lo encargué a algun religioso doctor y de su satisffacc[i]ᵒⁿ para que lo confiese y consuele y procure sosegar en los d[ic]hos pensam[iento]ˢ y escrupulosos."

28. AGN, Inquisición 680, exp. 2, fol. 27: "queda desengañado."

29. BANC MSS 96/95, 5:4, fol. 2: "considera que se juntan con ella de diferentes maneras estando ella debaxo dellos y de lado y puesta encima dellos y tambien estando ella boca abaxo y ellos encima teniendo qu[en]ta con ella por ambas partes deshonestas della."

30. BANC MSS 96/95, 5:4, fol. 2: "y q[ue] quando está oyendo missa y vee alçar la hostia se le representa q[ue] vee a Jesu Xpo [Cristo] con su cosa defuera y q[ue] desto tiene ella entonces alteración carnal y peca alli consigo el peccado q[ue] he dicho haciendo q[uen]ᵗᵃ que está en el acto carnal con Jesu Xpo [Cristo]. Y que [h]avia tambien peccado de la mesma manera haziendo q[uen]ᵗᵃ que estava con la Virgen Maria."

31. Lavrin, "Sexuality in Colonial Mexico," 51.

32. Laqueur, *Solitary Sex*, 136.

33. BANC MSS 96/95, 5:4, fol. 32.

34. BANC MSS 96/95, 5:4, fol. 32: "que vino aeste lugar que la enbio aqui un her[ma]ⁿᵒ suio de San Luis llamado Xpobal [Cristóbal] Felipe para que estubiesse en casa del d[ic]ho Alonso de Garibaldi hasta que viniesse por ella."

35. BANC MSS 96/95, 5:4, fol. 4: "malos pensam[ient]os y malas imagenes."

36. BANC MSS 96/95, 5:4, fol. 4: "desde la d[ic]ha edad de onçe años hasta [h]abra los d[ic]hos seis meses ha usado el dicho pecado de cumplir con la mano tocandose en sus partes deshonestas haciendo q[uen]ᵗᵃ que estaba con los d[ic]hos santos Xᵒ [Cristo] y la Virgen y que complia con ellos carnalm[en]ᵗᵉ y ellos con ella y que esto ha sido tres veces poco mas o menos cada dia en todo el dicho tiempo."

37. Bautista, *Confessionario en lengua mexicana y castellana*.

38. BANC MSS 96/95, 5:4, fol. 12: "hazia con ellos quando estava sola y se tocava y cumplia carnalm[en]ᵗᵉ con la memoria dellos, y pa[ra] este effecto dezia las palabras q[ue] le parecian apropiadas significativas deste deseo q[ue] tenia de tenerlos pres[en]ᵗᵉˢ y holgarse con ellos en la forma d[ic]ha."

39. On *mal de corazón* in the early modern period, see Brooks, "The Nail of the Great Beast," 317–21.

40. BANC MSS 96/95, 5:4, fol. 5v.

41. BANC MSS 96/95, 5:4, fol. 12: "venian ellos con sus partes deshonestas alteradas y cada uno la significava q[ue] agora decida de verse amada y deseada della venian desde el cielo a la tierra a cumplirle su deseo pero depues abraçandola y besandola se encendian mas en sus amores y tenian los demas a estas y palabras deshonestas como actualmente los tiene un hombre con una muger teniendo copula carnal con ella, y q[ue] con la virgin [h]avia besarse y abraçarse en la cama y atentarse la una a la otra sus partes deshonestas y q[ue] de los demas Jesu Xpo [Cristo] era el q[ue] mas se señalava en regalarla y regalarse con ella con los d[ic]hos actos y copula deshonestas y obras y palabras deshonestas, y q[ue] le dezia el, que la [h]avia criado tal como era hermosa y graciosa y a su gusto para q[ue] fuese su puta y para gozarla y para gozarse con ella y q[ue] el era su puto y su rufian."

42. BANC MSS 96/95, 5:4, fol. 13: "es verdad catholica q[ue] los santos del cielo y Jesu Xpo [Cristo] y la Virgin Maria no pecan ni pueden peccar ni [h]aver venido del cielo a la tierra hazer y dezir lo q[ue] esta declarante ha confesado q[ue] la han hecho y dicho, y q[ue] [h]avia sido el demonio."

43. BANC MSS 96/95, 5:4, fol. 13: "en su alma de [h]aver estado errada y [h]aver ofendido a dios y a los santos y a la virgen con las torpezas y suziedades y ha d[ic]ho pasar ofensas contra su dios y s[ant]ᵒˢ y le pide perdon."

44. BANC MSS 96/95, 5:4, fol. 3: "se le mostraban agradecidos con palabras que la decian deshonestas y amorosas correspondientes a las que ella decia nombrando ellos las partes deshonestas del hombre y de la muger."

45. BANC MSS 96/95, 5:4, fol. 12: "por q[ue] eres mi alma y mi vida y mi querida mas q[ue] todas las cosas y tienes un coño sabroso y gostoso p[ar]ᵃ mi."

46. BANC MSS 96/95, 5:4, fol. 12: "y antes de tener la copula carnal y teniendola él le dezia y ella respondia, 'mi alma q[ue] te meto' y ella dezia mis ojos el carajo me meto el carajazo, y él dezia por donde? y ella respondia por el coño q[ue] es tuyo, y el dezia y q[ue] te hago? y ella dezia, me hoder, me estas hodiendo."

47. BANC MSS 96/95, 5:4, fol. 12: "y que con la Virgen con los besos y abraços se llamavan de tu y de vos y de mi alma mi vida mis amores y se atentavan las partes deshonestas preguntandose q[ue] te atiento q[ue] me atientas y respondiendose el coño p[ara] q[ue] te refriego y respondiendose la crica y diciendose q[ue] hazian quenta q[ue] la una p[ar]ᵃ la *otra era hombre y el dedo y la mano era carajo y q[ue] se lo metian la una a la otra y q[ue] recibian el gusto q[ue] si hombre las hodiera* y se llamavan de putas meneadoras hodedoras y se dezian lo q[ue] mas el gusto podia pero no se echavan una sobre otra ni juntavan sus partes deshonestas *y q[ue] estos actos con los santos [y] Xpo [Cristo] y la Virgen eran en la cama,* y las palabras sonavan con voz clara como hablando con estos hombres y con muger de manera q[ue] si alguien estuviera presente las oyera y entendiera y q[ue] cada una destas personas con quien esta declarante [Agustina Ruiz] tenia las d[ic]has amistades la hazian en una noche los d[ic]hos actos y tenian la d[ic]ha copula carnal en la forma

referida dos o tres vezes y se yva [iba] y cada una de las d[ic]has personas sanctos [y] Xpo [Cristo] y la Virgen la dezian y darian a entender q[ue] en pago de su amor y amistad se gozarian con ella en esta vida, y despues en el cielo seria esta declarante una gran sancta."

48. Alva, *A Guide to Confession Large and Small in the Mexican Language*, 61: "siendo tan dulce, tan suaue, y sabrosa la ley de Dios."

49. On Saint Rose of Lima, see Graziano, *Wounds of Love*.

50. Avila, *The Life of Saint Teresa of Avila by Herself*, 210.

51. Bataille, *Erotism*, 224.

52. BANC MSS 96/95, 5:4, fol. 33: "con esta imaginacion se fue a su casa y estando acostada en su cama la misma noche y tocandose sus partes vergonçosas para venir en polución se le represento con una imaginacion el d[ic]ho S. Nicolas trayendolo ella a la memória para el d[ic]ho acto y en efecto le tubo consumado como si realmente estubiese pecando con el."

53. BANC MSS 96/95, 5:4, fol. 34.

54. See, respectively, *Diccionario de autoridades*, vol. 4: "complacéncia, deléite o deseo de alguna cosa"; *Diccionario de autoridades*, vol. 3: "Delicia, placer, recreo, gusto especial, contento" and "Se llama el gusto carnal venéreo"; *Diccionario de autoridades*, vol. 4: "tener, posseer, obtener y lograr alguna cosa"; *Diccionario de autoridades*, vol. 4: "celebrar, tener gusto, contento y placer de alguna cosa, alegrarse de ella."

55. BANC MSS 96/95, 5:4, fol. 51.

56. Penyak, "Criminal Sexuality in Central Mexico," 260.

57. AGN, Inquisición 981, exp. 22, fols. 327–46. I am grateful to Jacqueline Holler for bringing this case to my attention.

58. AGN, Inquisición 981, exp. 22, fol. 327: "primeramente hice pacto con el Demonio que se me aparecio en figura visible de hombre obligandome por este pacto á no hacer en adelante exercicio ninguno de virtud, ni traer Rosario al cuello, y confirme este pacto con tres sedulas que el mesmo escibio, y en que á mas de esto se contenia que le entregaba mi alma."

59. AGN, Inquisición 981, exp. 22, fol. 327: "y mantuve torpe amistad con el mesmo por tiempo de dos años, en que siete occasiones poco mas ó menos tuve con el accesos torpes con copula consumada."

60. AGN, Inquisición 981, exp. 22, fol. 327: "Tres veces hablando con el mesmo demonio dixe de corazon, q[u]e yo no creyia en Dios, aunque luego me arrepentia de [h]aver sentido, y proferido esto."

61. AGN, Inquisición 981, exp. 22, fol. 327: "por tiempo de un año frequentemente tuvo accesos torpes con una imagen de N[uestra].S[eñora]. la Virgen Maria es a saber que en estas ocasiones primero tenia estos accesos con bestias, y despues llegaba a la imagen, y tambien procuraba que la mesma bestia tuviese acceso a la imagen."

62. AGN, Inquisición 981, exp. 22, fol. 333: "tres veces tube accesos impuros con la Ymagen de Xpto [Cristo], y muchas veces con la imagen del mesmo señor niño" and "con varias imag[en]es de sanctos tuve accesos torpes."

63. AGN, Inquisición 981, exp. 22, fol. 327v: "esta [López] la despedezó, y las particulas mescló con una yervas [hierbas], y dixo que la virtud que aquel compuesto tenia era provocar á los hombres á cosas obscenas."

64. AGN, Inquisición 981, exp. 22, fol. 327v: "y en otra occasion tuve tocamientos impuros con la mesma forma consagrada."

65. AGN, Inquisición 981, exp. 22, fol. 327: "escupiendo al suelo en presencia de las imagenes en demonstracion de ira, y diciendo a mis solas que los santos no tenian poder para alcansarme de Dios lo que les pedia."

66. Massumi, "The Future Birth of the Affective Fact," 67.

67. Jaffary, "Sacred Defiance and Sexual Desecration," 53.

68. AGN, Inquisición 981, exp. 22, fol. 332: "enfermidades de espiritu y de cuerpo."

69. AGN, Inquisición 981, exp. 22, fol. 332: "una verdadera contricion y serio animo de emmendar su vida."

70. AGN, Inquisición 981, exp. 22, fol. 341: "que esta muger esta poseida del demonio un mes [h]á [h]asta [h]oi dia."

71. AGN, Inquisición 981, exp. 22, fol. 327.

72. Blouin and Rosenberg, *Processing the Past*, 121.

73. AGN, Inquisición 1353, exp. 12, fol. 1: "Denuncia espontanea de Ramon Sanchez de la Baquera por accesos con las sagradas ymagenes, invocaciones del demonio, y supersticiones."

74. http://www.agn.gob.mx/guiageneral/contenido.php?CodigoReferencia=MX 09017AGNCL01FO006INSE002INUI1353UC0012, accessed October 15, 2017: "es un hombre asimplado, insensate, y de aquellos tolerados locos."

75. AGN, Inquisición 1353, exp. 12, fol. 1: "me haver coinsidido por terceira ocasion en el delicto de haver tenido acceso a dos ymagenes de Nuestra Señora la Virgen Maria, que se veneran en la yglecia de religiosos dominicos del convento del dicho pueblo."

76. AGN, Inquisición 1353, exp. 12, fol. 1: "porque no alcansava a reconocer la gravedad a este delicto."

77. AGN, Inquisición 1353, exp. 12, fol. 5: "Ygualmente declara haver ejecutado lo mismo (*cum efusione seminis*) lo que tambien ejecutó en lo yá expresado de las Ymagenes de la Virgen; con San Pedro martir tiempo de un año."

78. AGN, Inquisición 1353, exp. 12, fol. 3: "dijo que es cierto que los acesos que ha tenido con la ymagen de N[uest]ra Señora del Rosario que se venera en la yglesia del conbento de N[uest]ro Padre S[na]to Domingo en cuyo lugar sagrado los ha cometido, ha sido confricando su miembro biril contra el ropaje de la sagrada ymagen, y que en el discurso de ocho años o algo más segun declare despues han sido tantas las ocasiones de su delito que no las puede reducir a numero."

79. AGN, Inquisición 1353, exp. 12, fol. 5: "de quatro a seis ocasiones unas de dia, y otras de noche sin poder aberiguar el dia y ora."

80. AGN, Inquisición 1353, exp. 12, fol. 7: "Dijo estar tan arraigado al pecado de la lascivia, y tan apasionado, a esta calidad de objetos como lo rrefieren los delitos

declarados que no satisf[ec]ho de lo que lleva expresado en los [h]orrorosos ascesos los circunstanciava teniendolos muchas ocasiones en las bocas, y manos de las sagradas ymagenes; y que en los tocamiendos que consigo mismo ha tenido han sido dentro de la misma yglesia figurandose a aquellas ymagenes por objeto de su torpeza, sin poder averiguar el numero de estos pecados y sacrilegios."

81. AGN, Inquisición 1353, exp. 12, fols. 7–8: "nunca ha sentido mal de N[uest]ra Señora la Virgen María y sus santos, y que guiado de su natural simplicidad dirijió mas el culto y veneracion q[ue] tiene a la santisima Virgen."

82. AGN, Inquisición 1353, exp. 12, fol. 8: "rrepetia la imbocacion del demonio principalmente para que le quitara la simplicidad estulticia y locura que tiene, y pecar con las ymagenes y las mugeres del mundo."

83. AGN, Inquisición 1353, exp. 12, fol. 11: "quisiera para satisfacer esta su declaracion ser ahorcado y quemado por dar satisfaction a dios."

84. AGN, Inquisición 1353, exp. 12, fol. 1: "El delincuente es un [h]ombre fatuo al parecer y reputado por demente e inocente en la comun del pueblo."

85. AGN, Inquisición 1189, exp. 16, fol. 117: "y que con este mismo fin quiso quedarse solo en una iglesia e hizo las diligencias posibles para ello, para lograr atuir el sagrario y sacar de el alguna forma para usar de ella con inmundicias y suciedades; y que por el mismo fin de desprecio o incredulidad [h]a querido cometer el mismo pecado de sodomia con las imagenes de Christo."

86. AGN, Inquisición 1189, exp. 16, fol. 121: "que los medicos llaman satyriasis en los hombres, y en las muxeres furor uterino provenido del exesivo calor acrimonia del humor genital y sales de tanta actividad, que redicen al pasiente a tal estremo de impetu libidinoso, que a manera de brutos perden hasta el natural pudor como lo traen los medicos que e leido, y algunos moralistas, y juristas."

Conclusion

1. Arondekar, *For the Record*, 1.

2. "Desplegado sobre la Ley General de Archivos," November 22, 2016, http://www.h-mexico.unam.mx/node/18666. See also the website of the Comité Mexicano de Ciencias Históricas, http://cmch.colmex.mx/.

3. I thank Linda Arnold for providing me with this database in PDF form, "Archivo Histórico del Distrito Federal, Presos en Lecumberri, 1920–1976, alfabético."

4. According to a placard, "Palacio Negro de Lecumberri," in the archive's central foyer.

5. "Ley federal de archivos," January 23, 2012, http://www.diputados.gob.mx/LeyesBiblio/pdf/LFA.pdf.

6. "Desplegado sobre la Ley General de Archivos," November 22, 2016: "la posibilidad de construir una memoria colectiva plural e incluyente."

7. AGN, "Estadísticas sobre el Acervo Documental," accessed October 15, 2017, http://www.agn.gob.mx/guiageneral/estadisticas.html.

8. Mbembe, "The Power of the Archive and Its Limits," 19.

9. Arondekar, *For the Record*, 102.

10. See Arondekar, *For the Record*, 5, 18; Baron, *The Archive Effect*, 7; Dirks, "Annals of the Archive," 60.

11. K. Burns, *Into the Archive*, 124.

12. AGN, Indiferente Virreinal, caja 1482, exp. 7, fol. 9v: "se formó causa de oficio de la jurisdiccion ecl[esiasti]^ca contra J[ose]pha de Garfias por el crimen de sodomia que perpetró con otras mugeres y haviendose rezivido ynformacion sumaria se aprehendió a d[ic]ha reo con auxilio de la R[ea]^l Justicia que impartó el S[eñ]^or Juan Carrillo Moreno alcalde desta R[ea]^l sala del crimen de esta corte y Juez de provincia en ella y sustanciada la causa en forma con aud[iencia]^a del promoter fiscal de este Ar[zobis]pâdo se pronunció sentencia definitiva y por ella condenó el S[eñ]^or Prov[is]^or a d[ic]ha Josepha en que por tiempo de dos años sirviese personalmente a las pobres enfermas del hospital de S^n Ju^o [San Juan] de Dios: le impuso distintas penitencias medicinales y mando entre otras cosas se quemasen siertos instrumentos de que usaba para su torpe delicto: y todo se executó."

13. Vainfas and Tortorici, "Female Homoeroticism"; Black, "Prosecuting Female-Female Sex in Bourbon Quito."

14. Arondekar, *For the Record*, 102.

15. Harris, "The Archival Sliver," 64.

16. VEMC, leg. 57, exp. 30, fol. 87: "[me] metio un poco el miembro . . . pero que fue mui poco."

17. Burton, *Archive Stories*, 8.

18. See Stoler, *Along the Archival Grain*; Dirks, "Annals of the Archive"; Ghosh, "National Narratives and the Politics of Miscegenation"; K. Burns, *Into the Archive*.

19. Stoler, *Along the Archival Grain*, 32.

20. Dinshaw, *Getting Medieval*, 1; Freeman, *Time Binds*, 110.

21. Arondekar, *For the Record*, 1.

BIBLIOGRAPHY

Primary Sources

Alva, Bartolomé de. *A Guide to Confession Large and Small in the Mexican Language, 1634.* Edited by Barry D. Sell and John Frederick Schwaller with Lu Ann Homza. Norman: University of Oklahoma Press, 1999.

Avila, Teresa of. *The Life of Saint Teresa of Avila by Herself.* London: Penguin Classics, 1988.

Bautista, Juan. *Confessionario en lengua mexicana y castellana.* Mexico City: Melchior Ocharte, 1599.

Burns, Robert I., ed. *Las Siete Partidas.* Vol. 5, *Underworlds: The Dead, the Criminal, and the Marginalized.* Philadelphia: University of Pennsylvania Press, 2001.

Covarrubias, Sebastián de. *Tesoro de la lengua castellana o española.* Madrid: San Luis, 1611.

Cutter, Charles R., ed. *Libro de los principales rudimentos tocante a todos juicios, criminal, civil y executivo: Año de 1764.* Mexico City: 1994.

Diccionario de autoridades. Vol. 1. Madrid: Real Academia Española, 1726.

Diccionario de autoridades. Vol. 2. Madrid: Real Academia Española, 1729.

Diccionario de autoridades. Vol. 3. Madrid: Real Academia Española, 1732.

Diccionario de autoridades. Vol. 4. Madrid: Real Academia Española, 1734.

Diccionario de autoridades. Vol. 5. Madrid: Real Academia Española, 1737.

Diccionario de autoridades. Vol. 6. Madrid: Real Academia Española, 1739.

Escobar Olmedo, Armando M., ed. *Proceso, tormento y muerte del Cazonzi, último gran señor de los tarascos por Nuño de Guzmán, 1530.* Morelia: Frente de Afirmación Hispanista, 1997.

Franciosini, Lorenzo. *Vocabolario italiano e spagnolo.* Rome: Paolo Profilio, 1620.

García Peláez, Francisco de Paula, ed. *Memorias para la historia del antiguo reyno de Guatemala.* Vol. 1. Guatemala City: Establecimiento Tipográfico de L. Luna, 1851.

Gazeta de México (enero a agosto de 1784). Mexico City: Rolston-Bain, 1983.

Gilberti, Maturino. *Vocabulario en lengua de Mechuacan.* Mexico City: Juan Pablos, 1559.

Gómez, Antonio. *Compendio de los comentarios extendidos por el maestro Antonio Gómez, a las ochenta y tres leyes de Toro.* Madrid: J. Doblado, 1785.

León, Nicolás, ed. *Bibliografía mexicana del siglo VXIII.* "Gazeta de México." Mexico City: Imprenta Francisco Díaz de León, 1902.

Ligorio, Alphonsi de [Alphonsus Maria de' Liguori]. *Theologia moralis*. Vol. 1. Venice: Bassani, 1785.

Martín de Guijo, Gregorio. *Diarios de sucesos virreinales*. Mexico City: Planeta, 2002.

Martínez de la Parra, Juan. *Luz de verdades católicas y explicación de la doctrina christiana*. Barcelona: Lucas de Bezáres, 1755.

Martínez Egido, José Joaquín. *La obra lexicográfica de Lorenzo Franciosini: Vocabulario italiano-español, español-italiano (1620)*. Alicante: Biblioteca Virtual Miguel de Cervantes, 2002.

Old Testament. New York: Thomas Y. Crowell, 1884.

Robles, Antonio de. *Diario de sucesos notables, escrito por el Licenciado D. Antonio de Robles, y comprende los años de 1665 a 1703*. Vol. 2 of *Documentos para la historia de Méjico*. Mexico City: Imprenta de Juan R. Navarro, 1853.

Ruiz de Alarcón, Hernando. *Treatise on the Heathen Superstitions That Today Live among the Indians Native to This New Spain, 1629*. Edited by Richard Andrews and Ross Hassig. Norman: University of Oklahoma Press, 1984.

Scholes, France V., and Eleanor B. Adams, eds. *Proceso contra Tzintzicha Tangaxoan, el Caltzontzín, formado por Nuño de Guzmán, año 1530*. Mexico City: Porrua y Obregón, 1952.

Sobrino, Francisco. *Diccionario nuevo de las lenguas española y francesa*. Vol. 2. Brussels: Francisco Foppins, 1705.

Terreros y Pando, Esteban de. *Diccionario castellano con las voces de ciencias y artes*. 4 vols. Madrid: Imprenda de la Viuda de Ibarra, 1787.

Secondary Sources

Aggrawal, Anil. *Necrophilia: Forensic and Medico-legal Aspects*. Boca Raton, FL: CRC Press, 2011.

Ahmed, Sara. *The Cultural Politics of Emotion*. New York: Routledge, 2004.

Alberro, Solange. *Inquisición y sociedad en México, 1571–1700*. Mexico City: Fondo de Cultural Económica, 1988.

Anderson, Virginia DeJohn. *Creatures of Empire: How Domestic Animals Transformed Early America*. Oxford: Oxford University Press, 2004.

Arondekar, Anjali. *For the Record: On Sexuality and the Colonial Archive in India*. Durham, NC: Duke University Press, 2009.

Baron, Jamie. *The Archive Effect: Found Footage and the Audiovisual Experience of History*. New York: Routledge, 2014.

Bataille, Georges. *Erotism: Death and Sensuality*. San Francisco: City Lights Books, 1986.

Bazant, Mílada. "Bestiality: The Nefarious Crime in Mexico, 1800–1856." In *Sexuality and the Unnatural in Colonial Latin America*, edited by Zeb Tortorici, 188–212. Oakland: University of California Press, 2016.

Beirne, Piers. *Confronting Animal Abuse: Law, Criminology, and Human-Animal Relationships*. Lanham, MD: Rowman and Littlefield, 2009.

Ben-Atar, Doron S., and Richard D. Brown. *Taming Lust: Crimes against Nature in the Early Republic*. Philadelphia: University of Pennsylvania Press, 2014.

Bennassar, Bartolomé. "El modelo sexual: La Inquisición de Aragón y la represión de los pecados 'abominables.'" In *Inquisición española: Poder político y control social*, edited by Bartolomé Bennasar, 295–320. Barcelona: Editorial Crítica, 1981.

Benson, Etienne. "Animal Writes: Historiography, Disciplinarity, and the Animal Trace." In *Making Animal Meaning*, edited by Linda Kalof and Georgina M. Montgomery, 3–16. East Lansing: Michigan State University Press, 2011.

Berco, Cristian. *Sexual Hierarchies, Public Status: Men, Sodomy, and Society in Spain's Golden Age*. Toronto: University of Toronto Press, 2007.

Bersani, Leo. "Is the Rectum a Grave?" *October* 43 (winter 1987): 197–222.

Black, Chad. "Prosecuting Female-Female Sex in Bourbon Quito." In *Sexuality and the Unnatural in Colonial Latin America*, edited by Zeb Tortorici, 120–40. Oakland: University of California Press, 2016.

Blouin, Francis X., and William G. Rosenberg, eds. *Archives, Documentation, and Institutions of Social Memory: Essays from the Sawyer Seminar*. Ann Arbor: University of Michigan Press, 2007.

———. *Processing the Past: Contesting Authority in History and the Archives*. Oxford: Oxford University Press, 2011.

Boletín del Archivo General del Gobierno. Vol. 3. Guatemala City: Archivo General del Gobierno, 1937.

Boswell, John. *Christianity, Social Tolerance, and Homosexuality: Gay People in Western Europe from the Beginning of the Christian Era to the Fourteenth Century*. Chicago: University of Chicago Press, 1980.

Brooks, John. "The Nail of the Great Beast." *Western Folklore* 18, no. 4 (1959): 317–21.

Brown, Judith C. *Immodest Acts: The Life of a Lesbian Nun in Renaissance Italy*. Oxford: Oxford University Press, 1986.

Burkhart, Louise M. *The Slippery Earth: Nahua Christian Moral Dialogue in Sixteenth-Century Mexico*. Tucson: University of Arizona Press, 1989.

Burns, Kathryn. *Into the Archive: Writing and Power in Colonial Peru*. Durham, NC: Duke University Press, 2010.

Burton, Antoinette, ed. *Archive Stories: Facts, Fictions, and the Writing of History*. Durham, NC: Duke University Press, 2005.

Camba Ludlow, Ursula. "Gregoria la Macho y su 'inclinación a las mujeres': Reflexiones en torno a la sexualidad marginal en Nueva España, 1796–1806." *Colonial Latin American Historical Review* 12, no. 4 (2003): 479–97.

Carrasco, Rafael. *Inquisición y represión sexual en Valencia: Historia de los sodomitas (1565–1785)*. Barcelona: Laertes S. A. de Ediciones, 1985.

Chen, Mel Y. *Animacies: Biopolitics, Racial Mattering, and Queer Affect*. Durham, NC: Duke University Press, 2012.

Chuchiak, John F., IV. "The Sins of the Fathers: Franciscan Friars, Parish Priests, and the Sexual Conquest of the Yucatec Maya, 1545–1808." *Ethnohistory* 54, no. 1 (2007): 69–127.

Cifor, Marika. "Affecting Relations: Introducing Affect Theory to Archival Discourse." *Archival Science* 16, no. 1 (2016): 7–31.

Crompton, Louis. "The Myth of Lesbian Impunity: Capital Laws from 1270 to 1791." In *Historical Perspectives on Homosexuality*, edited by Salvatore J. Licata and Robert P. Peterson, 11–26. New York: Haworth, 1981.

Cutter, Charles R. *The Legal Culture of Northern New Spain, 1700–1810*. Albuquerque: University of New Mexico Press, 2001.

Davis, Natalie Zemon. *Fiction in the Archives: Pardon Tales and Their Tellers in Sixteenth-Century France*. Stanford, CA: Stanford University Press, 1987.

de Hamel, Christopher. *Scribes and Illuminators*. Toronto: University of Toronto Press, 1992.

Derrida, Jacques. *Archive Fever: A Freudian Impression*. Chicago: University of Chicago Press, 1996.

Dinshaw, Carolyn. *Getting Medieval: Sexualities and Communities, Pre- and Postmodern*. Durham, NC: Duke University Press, 1999.

———. *How Soon Is Now? Medieval Texts, Amateur Readers, and the Queerness of Time*. Durham, NC: Duke University Press, 2012.

Dirks, Nicholas B. "Annals of the Archive: Ethnographic Notes on the Sources of History." In *From the Margins: Historical Anthropology and Its Futures*, edited by Brian Keith Axel, 47–65. Durham, NC: Duke University Press, 2002.

Douglas, Mary. *Purity and Danger: An Analysis of the Concepts of Pollution and Taboo*. London: Routledge, 1966.

Dubois, Laurent. "Maroons in the Archives: The Uses of the Past in the French Caribbean." In *Archives, Documentation, and Institutions of Social Memory: Essays from the Sawyer Seminar*, edited by Francis X. Blouin and William G. Rosenberg, 291–300. Ann Arbor: University of Michigan Press, 2007.

Earle, Rebecca. "Letters and Love in Colonial Spanish America." *The Americas* 62, no. 1 (2005): 17–46.

Eichhorn, Kate. *The Archival Turn in Feminism: Outrage in Order*. Philadelphia: Temple University Press, 2014.

Evans, E. P. *The Criminal Prosecution and Capital Punishment of Animals: The Lost History of Europe's Animal Trials*. London: Faber and Faber, 1987.

Farge, Arlette. *The Allure of the Archives*. New Haven, CT: Yale University Press, 2013.

Fernandez, André. "The Repression of Sexual Behavior by the Aragonese Inquisition between 1560 and 1700." *Journal of the History of Sexuality* 7, no. 4 (1997): 469–501.

Few, Martha. "'That Monster of Nature': Gender, Sexuality, and the Medicalization of a Hermaphrodite in Late Colonial Guatemala." *Ethnohistory* 54, no. 1 (2007): 159–76.

Foucault, Michel. *Archaeology of Knowledge*. New York: Harper and Row, 1976.

———. *The History of Sexuality*. Vol. 1: *An Introduction*. New York: Vintage Books, 1978.

Freccero, Carla. "Archives in the Fiction: Marguerite de Navarre's *Heptaméron*." In *Rhetoric and Law in Early Modern Europe*, edited by Victoria Kahn and Lorna Hutson, 73–94. New Haven, CT: Yale University Press, 2001.

———. *Queer/Early/Modern*. Durham, NC: Duke University Press, 2006.

Freeman, Elizabeth. *Time Binds: Queer Temporalities, Queer Histories*. Durham, NC: Duke University Press, 2010.

Fudge, Erica. *Brutal Reasoning: Animals, Rationality, and Humanity in Early Modern England*. Ithaca, NY: Cornell University Press, 2006.

———. *Perceiving Animals: Humans and Beasts in Early Modern English Culture*. Champaign: University of Illinois Press, 2002.

Fuentes, Marisa J. *Dispossessed Lives: Enslaved Women, Violence, and the Archive*. Philadelphia: University of Pennsylvania Press, 2016.

Garza Carvajal, Federico. *Butterflies Will Burn: Prosecuting Sodomites in Early Modern Spain and Mexico*. Austin: University of Texas Press, 2003.

Ghosh, Durba. "National Narratives and the Politics of Miscegenation: Britain and India." In *Archive Stories: Facts, Fictions, and the Writing of History*, edited by Antoinette Burton, 27–44. Durham, NC: Duke University Press, 2005.

Giraldo Botero, Carolina. *Deseo y represión: Homoeroticidad en la Nueva Granada (1559–1822)*. Bogotá: Centro de Estudios Socioculturales e Internacionales, 2002.

González Marmolejo, Jorge René. *Sexo y confesión: La Iglesia y la penitencia en los siglos XVIII y XIX en la Nueva España*. Mexico City: Editores Plaza y Valdés, 2002.

Graziano, Frank. *Wounds of Love: The Mystical Marriage of Saint Rose of Lima*. Oxford: Oxford University Press, 2004.

Gruzinski, Serge. "The Ashes of Desire: Homosexuality in Mid-Seventeenth-Century New Spain." In *Infamous Desire: Male Homosexuality in Colonial Latin America*, edited by Pete Sigal, 197–214. Chicago: University of Chicago Press, 2003.

———. "Individualization and Acculturation: Confession among the Nahuas of Mexico from the Sixteenth to the Eighteenth Century." In *Sexuality and Marriage in Colonial Latin America*, edited by Asunción Lavrin, 96–117. Lincoln: University of Nebraska Press, 1989.

———. "Las cenizas del deseo: Homosexuales novohispanos a mediados del siglo XVII." In *De la santidad a la perversión, o de por qué no se cumplía la ley de Dios en la sociedad novohispana*, edited by Sergio Ortega, 255–81. Mexico City: Editorial Grijalbo, 1986.

Gutiérrez, Ramón A. *When Jesus Came, the Corn Mothers Went Away: Marriage, Sexuality, and Power in New Mexico, 1500–1846*. Stanford, CA: Stanford University Press, 1991.

Haliczer, Stephen. *Sexuality in the Confessional: A Sacrament Profaned*. Oxford: Oxford University Press, 1996.

Hall, Stuart. "Encoding, Decoding." In *The Cultural Studies Reader*, edited by Simon During, 507–17. London: Routledge, 1993.

Harris, Verne. "The Archival Sliver: Power, Memory, and Archives in South Africa." *Archival Science* 2, nos. 1–2 (2002): 63–86.

————. "A Shaft of Darkness: Derrida in the Archive." In *Refiguring the Archive*, edited by Carolyn Hamilton, Verne Harris, Jane Taylor, Michele Pickover, Graeme Reid, and Razia Saleh, 61–81. Cape Town: David Philip, 2002.

Harrison, Regina. "The Theology of Concupiscence: Spanish-Quechua Confessional Manuals in the Andes." In *Coded Encounters: Writing, Gender, and Ethnicity in Colonial Latin America*, edited by Francisco Javier Cevallos-Candau, Jeffery A. Cole, Nina M. Scott, and Nicomedes Suárez-Araúz, 135–53. Amherst: University of Massachusetts Press, 1994.

Haskett, Robert. "'Not a Pastor, but a Wolf': Indigenous-Clergy Relations in Early Cuernavaca and Taxco." *The Americas* 50, no. 3 (1994): 293–336.

Hillman, David. "Visceral Knowledge: Shakespeare, Skepticism, and the Interior of the Early Modern Body." In *The Body in Parts: Fantasies of Corporeality in Early Modern Europe*, edited by David Hillman and Carla Mazzio, 81–106. New York: Routledge, 1997.

Holland, Sharon P., Marcia Ochoa, and Kyla Wazana Tompkins. "On the Visceral." *GLQ: A Journal of Lesbian and Gay Studies* 20, no. 4 (2014): 391–406.

Holler, Jacqueline. "'More Sins Than the Queen of England': Marina de San Miguel before the Mexican Inquisition." In *Women in the Inquisition: Spain and the New World*, edited by Mary E. Giles, 209–28. Baltimore: Johns Hopkins University Press, 1999.

Horswell, Michael. *Decolonizing the Sodomite: Queer Tropes of Sexuality in Colonial Andean Culture*. Austin: University of Texas Press, 2005.

"Inquiring about the Inquisition?" *Bene Legere: Newsletter of the Library Associates* 56 (fall 2000). http://www.lib.berkeley.edu/give/bene-legere/bene56/inquisition.html.

Jaffary, Nora E. *False Mystics: Deviant Orthodoxy in Colonial Mexico*. Lincoln: University of Nebraska Press, 2004.

————. "Sacred Defiance and Sexual Desecration: María Getrudis Arévalo and the Holy Office in Eighteenth-Century Mexico." In *Sexuality and the Unnatural in Colonial Latin America*, edited by Zeb Tortorici, 43–57. Oakland: University of California Press, 2016.

Jeanneret, Michel. *A Feast of Worlds: Banquets and Table Talk in the Renaissance*. Chicago: University of Chicago Press, 1991.

Jordan, Mark D. *The Invention of Sodomy in Christian Theology*. Chicago: University of Chicago Press, 1997.

Klor de Alva, Jorge. "Colonizing Souls: The Failure of the Indian Inquisition and the Rise of Penitential Discipline." In *Cultural Encounters: The Impact of the Inquisition in Spain and the New World*, edited by Mary Elizabeth Perry and Annie J. Cruz, 3–21. Berkeley: University of California Press, 1991.

Krippner-Martínez, James. *Rereading the Conquest: Power, Politics, and the History of Early Colonial Michoacán, Mexico, 1521–1565*. University Park: Pennsylvania State University Press, 2001.

Laqueur, Thomas. *Solitary Sex: A Cultural History of Masturbation*. New York: Zone Books, 2003.

Lavrin, Asunción. "Sexuality in Colonial Mexico." In *Sexuality and Marriage in Colonial Latin America*, edited by Asunción Lavrin, 47–95. Lincoln: University of Nebraska Press, 1989.

Lea, Henry Charles. *History of Sacerdotal Celibacy in the Christian Church*. Vol. 2. London: Williams and Norgate, 1907.

Liebman, Seymour B. "The Abecedario and a Check-List of Mexican Inquisition Documents at the Henry E. Huntington Library." *Hispanic American Historical Review* 44, no. 4 (1964): 554–67.

Liliequist, Jonas. "Peasants against Nature: Crossing the Boundaries between Man and Animal in Seventeenth- and Eighteenth-Century Sweden." In *Forbidden History: The State, Society, and the Regulation of Sexuality in Modern Europe*, edited by John C. Fout, 57–88. Chicago: University of Chicago Press, 1990.

Lima, Lana Lage da Gama. "Aprisionando o desejo: Confissão e sexualidade." In *História e sexualidade no Brasil*, edited by Ronaldo Vainfas, 67–88. Rio de Janeiro: Graal, 1986.

Lockhart, James. *Of Things of the Indies: Essays Old and New in Early Latin American History*. Stanford, CA: Stanford University Press, 1999.

López Austin, Alfredo. *The Human Body and Ideology: Concepts of the Ancient Nahuas*. Vol. 2. Salt Lake City: University of Utah Press, 1988.

Marietta, Jack D., and G. S. Rowe. *Troubled Experiment: Crime and Justice in Pennsylvania, 1682–1800*. Philadelphia: University of Pennsylvania Press, 2006.

Martínez, María Elena. "Archives, Bodies, and Imagination: The Case of Juana Aguilar and Queer Approaches to History, Sexuality, and Politics." *Radical History Review* 120 (fall 2014): 159–82.

Martínez-San Miguel, Yolanda. *From Lack to Excess: "Minor" Readings of Latin American Colonial Discourse*. Lewisburg, PA: Bucknell University Press, 2008.

Massumi, Brian. "The Bleed: Where Body Meets Image." In *Rethinking Borders*, edited by John C. Welchman, 18–40. Minneapolis: University of Minnesota Press, 1996.

———. "The Future Birth of the Affective Fact: The Political Ontology of Threat." In *The Affect Theory Reader*, edited by Melissa Gregg and Gregory J. Seigworth, 52–71. Durham, NC: Duke University Press, 2009.

Mbembe, Achille. "The Power of the Archive and Its Limits." In *Refiguring the Archive*, edited by Carolyn Hamilton, Verne Harris, Jane Taylor, Michele Pickover, Graeme Reid, and Razia Saleh, 19–27. Cape Town: David Philip, 2002.

McLellan, Peter M., and Gordon P. Baker. "Incidence of Allergy in Archival Work." *American Archivist* 28, no. 4 (1965): 581–84.

Miller, William Ian. *The Anatomy of Disgust*. Cambridge, MA: Harvard University Press, 1998.

Miranda Guerrero, Roberto. "Homosexualidad, derechos, naturales y cultura popular: 1790–1820." *La Ventana*, no. 15 (2002): 263–312.

Mirow, M. C. *Latin American Law: A History of Private Law and Institutions in Spanish America*. Austin: University of Texas Press, 2010.

Molina, Fernanda. *Cuando amar era pecado: Sexualidad, poder e identidad entre los sodomitas peruanos (siglos XVI–XVII)*. La Paz: Plural, 2016.

———. "Sodomy, Gender, and Identity in the Viceroyalty of Peru." In *Sexuality and the Unnatural in Colonial Latin America*, edited by Zeb Tortorici, 141–61. Oakland: University of California Press, 2016.

Monter, William E. "Sodomy and Heresy in Early Modern Switzerland." *Journal of Homosexuality* 6, nos. 1–2 (1980–81): 41–55.

———. "Sodomy: The Fateful Accident." In *History of Homosexuality in Europe and America*, edited by Wayne R. Dynes and Stephen Donaldson, 192–215. New York: Routledge, 1992.

Mott, Luiz. "My Pretty Boy: Love Letters from a Sodomite Friar, Lisbon (1690)." In *Pelo Vaso Traseiro: Sodomy and Sodomites in Luso-Brazilian History*, edited by Harold Johnson and Francis A. Dutra, 231–62. Tucson: Fenestra Books, 2007.

Muñoz, José Esteban. *Cruising Utopia: The Then and There of Queer Futurity*. New York: New York University Press, 2009.

Murrin, John M. "'Things Fearful to Name': Bestiality in Early America." In *The Animal/Human Boundary: Historical Perspectives*, edited by Angela Creager and William Chester Jordan, 115–56. Rochester: University of Rochester Press, 2002.

Narváez Hernández, José Ramón. *La Idea del Poder Judicial en el proceso constitucional insurgente*. Mexico City: UNAM, Instituto de Investigaciones Juridícas de la UNAM, 2014.

Pardo, Osvaldo. *The Origins of Mexican Catholicism: Nahua Rituals and Christian Sacraments in Sixteenth-Century Mexico*. Ann Arbor: University of Michigan Press, 2004.

Penyak, Lee. "Criminal Sexuality in Central Mexico, 1750–1850." PhD diss., University of Connecticut, 1993.

———. "Temporary Transgressions, Unspeakable Acts: Male Sodomy in Late-Colonial Mexico, 1744–1843." *Colonial Latin American Historical Review* 17, no. 4 (2008): 329–59.

Pérez, Joseph. *The Spanish Inquisition: A History*. New Haven, CT: Yale University Press, 2006.

Perry, Mary Elizabeth. *Gender and Disorder in Early Modern Seville*. Princeton, NJ: Princeton University Press, 1990.

———. "The 'Nefarious Sin' in Early Modern Seville." In *The Pursuit of Sodomy: Male Homosexuality in Renaissance and Enlightenment Europe*, edited by Kent Gerard and Gert Hekma, 67–89. New York: Harrington Park Press, 1989.

Petro, Anthony M. "Beyond Accountability: The Queer Archive of Catholic Sexual Abuse." *Radical History Review* 122 (spring 2015): 160–76.

Pratt, Mary Louise. *Imperial Eyes: Travel Writing and Transculturation*. New York: Routledge, 1992.

Rafael, Vicente L. *Contracting Colonialism: Translation and Christian Conversion in Tagalog Society under Early Spanish Rule*. Durham, NC: Duke University Press, 1993.

Rivera Cambas, Manuel. *México pintoresco, artístico y monumental: Vistas, descripción, anécdotas y episodios de los lugares más notables de la capital y de los estados, aun de las poblaciones cortas, pero de importancia geográfica ó histórica.* Mexico City: Imprenta de la Reforma, 1880–83.

Rodríguez, Juana María. *Sexual Futures, Queer Gestures, and Other Latina Longings.* New York: New York University Press, 2014.

Rydström, Jens. *Sinners and Citizens: Bestiality and Homosexuality in Sweden, 1880–1950.* Chicago: University of Chicago Press, 2003.

Salisbury, Joyce. *The Beast Within: Animals in the Middle Ages.* New York: Routledge, 1994.

Schwartz, Joan M., and Terry Cook. "Archives, Records, and Power." *Archival Science* 2, nos. 1–2 (2002): 1–19.

Sellers-García, Sylvia. *Distance and Documents at the Spanish Empire's Periphery.* Stanford, CA: Stanford University Press, 2013.

Sigal, Pete. "The *Cuiloni*, the *Patlache*, and the Abominable Sin: Homosexualities in Early Colonial Nahua Society." *Hispanic American Historical Review* 85, no. 4 (2005): 555–94.

——. *The Flower and the Scorpion: Sexuality and Ritual in Early Nahua Culture.* Durham, NC: Duke University Press, 2011.

——. "Queer Nahuatl: Sahagún's Faggots and Sodomites, Lesbians and Hermaphrodites." *Ethnohistory* 54, no. 1 (2007): 9–34.

Silverman, Lisa. *Tortured Subjects: Pain, Truth, and the Body in Early Modern France.* Chicago: University of Chicago Press, 2001.

Siu, Lok C. D. "Hemispheric Raciality: Yellowface and the Challenge of Transnational Critique." *Asian Diasporic Visual Cultures and the Americas* 2, nos. 1–2 (2016): 163–79.

Sousa, Lisa. "The Devil and Deviance in Native Criminal Narratives from Early Mexico." *The Americas* 59, no. 2 (2002): 161–79.

——. "Tying the Knot: Nahua Nuptials in Colonial Central Mexico." In *Religion in New Spain,* edited by Susan Schroeder and Stafford Poole, 33–45. Albuquerque: University of New Mexico Press, 2007.

Spurling, Geoffrey. "Honor, Sexuality, and the Colonial Church: The Sins of Dr. Gonzalez, Cathedral Canon." In *The Faces of Honor: Sex, Shame, and Violence in Colonial Latin America,* edited by Lyman L. Johnson and Sonya Lipsett-Rivera, 45–67. Albuquerque: University of New Mexico Press, 1998.

Steedman, Carolyn. *Dust: The Archive and Cultural History.* New Brunswick, NJ: Rutgers University Press, 2001.

Stoler, Ann Laura. *Along the Archival Grain: Epistemic Anxieties and Colonial Common Sense.* Princeton, NJ: Princeton University Press, 2009.

Sweet, James H. "Mutual Misunderstandings: Gesture, Gender and Healing in the African Portuguese World." *Past and Present* 203, suppl. 4 (2009): 128–43.

Taylor, Diana. *The Archive and the Repertoire: Performing Cultural Memory in the Americas.* Durham, NC: Duke University Press, 2003.

Taylor, William B. *Drinking, Homicide, and Rebellion in Colonial Mexican Villages.* Stanford, CA: Stanford University Press, 1979.

———. *Magistrates of the Sacred: Parish Priests and Indian Parishioners in Eighteenth-Century Mexico.* Stanford, CA: Stanford University Press, 1999.

Terraciano, Kevin. "The People of Two Hearts and the One God from Castile: Ambivalent Responses to Christianity in Early Colonial Oaxaca." In *Religion in New Spain,* edited by Susan Schroeder and Stafford Poole, 16–32. Albuquerque: University of New Mexico Press, 2007.

Tomás y Valiente, Francisco. "El crimen y pecado contra natura." In *Sexo barroco y otras transgresiones premodernas,* edited by F. Tomás y Valiente, B. Clavero, J. L. Bermejo, E. Gacto, A. M. Hespanha, and C. Alvarez Alonso, 33–56. Madrid: Alianza Editorial, 1990.

Tortorici, Zeb. "Against Nature: Sodomy and Homosexuality in Colonial Latin America." *History Compass* 10, no. 2 (2012): 161–78.

———. "Archival Seduction: Indexical Absences and Historiographical Ghosts." *Archive Journal* 5 (fall 2015).

———. "'Heran Todos Putos': Sodomitical Subcultures and Disordered Desire in Early Colonial Mexico." *Ethnohistory* 54, no. 1 (2007): 36–67.

———. "Masturbation, Salvation, and Desire: Connecting Sexuality and Religiosity in Colonial Mexico." *Journal of the History of Sexuality* 16, no. 3 (2007): 355–72.

———. "Reading the (Dead) Body: Histories of Suicide in New Spain." In *Death and Dying in Colonial Spanish America,* edited by Miruna Achim and Martina Will de Chaparro, 53–77. Tucson: University of Arizona Press, 2011.

———, ed. *Sexuality and the Unnatural in Colonial Latin America.* Oakland: University of California Press, 2016.

———. "Sexual Violence, Predatory Masculinity, and Medical Testimony in New Spain." *Osiris* 30, no. 1 (2015): 272–94.

———. "Visceral Archives of the Body: Consuming the Dead, Digesting the Divine." GLQ: *A Journal of Lesbian and Gay Studies* 20, no. 4 (2014): 407–37.

Thomas, Keith. *Man and the Natural World: Changing Attitudes in England, 1500–1800.* New York: Penguin Books, 1991.

Townsend, Camilla. *Here in This Year: Seventeenth-Century Nahuatl Annals of the Tlaxcala-Puebla Valley.* Stanford, CA: Stanford University Press, 2009.

Trouillot, Michel-Rolph. *Silencing the Past: Power and the Production of History.* Boston: Beacon Press, 1995.

Vainfas, Ronaldo. *Trópico dos pecados: Moral, sexualidade e Inquisição no Brasil.* Rio de Janeiro: Editora Nova Fronteira, 1997.

Vainfas, Ronaldo, and Zeb Tortorici. "Female Homoeroticism, Heresy, and the Holy Office in Colonial Brazil." In *Sexuality and the Unnatural in Colonial Latin America,* edited by Zeb Tortorici, 77–94. Oakland: University of California Press, 2016.

Vega Umbasia, Leonardo Alberto. *Pecado y delito en la colonia: La bestialidad como una contravención sexual (1740–1808).* Bogotá: Instituto Colombiano de Cultura Hispánica, 1994.

Weber, Alison. *Teresa of Avila and the Rhetoric of Femininity*. Princeton, NJ: Princeton University Press, 1996.

White, Luise. *Speaking with Vampires: Rumor and History in Colonial Africa*. Berkeley: University of California Press, 2000.

Whitehead, Neil L. "Loving, Being, Killing Animals." In *Centering Animals in Latin American History*, edited by Martha Few and Zeb Tortorici, 329–45. Durham, NC: Duke University Press, 2013.

Wiesner-Hanks, Merry. *Sexuality and Christianity in the Early Modern World: Regulating Desire, Reforming Practice*. New York: Routledge, 2010.

INDEX

Note: Page numbers in *italics* indicate figures and tables.

abjure de levi, for light suspicion of heresy, 167, 183, 188, 193

abjure de vehementi, for serious suspicion of heresy, 113, 188, 193

absent archival referents, 74–76, 248. *See also* archival absences; lost archives

absolution: for bestiality, 143; for eroticized desire for the divine, 218

abuse, sexual, by priests: church inattentiveness to, 164–65; gaps in scholarship on, 23. *See also* solicitation in the confessional

abuse, sexual, in *estupro* and rape, 97, 105

Acamapichi, Cornelio, 145

Acámbaro (Mexico), bestiality in, 156

access. *See* archival access

accusations: exaggerated, in solicitation in the confessional cases, 186–90; false, in sodomy cases, 93–96; false, in solicitation in the confessional cases, 190. *See also* denunciations

Acordada, Tribunal de La, 25, 77

acts, as crimes and sins: vs. beliefs, 39, 201, 210; vs. thoughts, 39, 199. *See also* sexual acts

adolescents, in sodomy cases, 67–68, 92, 105–8

affect: archiving of, 116–23; definition of, 116

affective fornication, sexual acts with dead bodies as, 33

affective signs, as evidence in sodomy cases, 86–88, 100, 116–23

age, of defendants: in bestiality cases, *138*, 138–39; in sodomy cases, 67–68, 92, 105–8

agency: of animals, 130; in sodomy cases, 67–68, 105–10

AGN. *See* Archivo General de la Nación

Aguaya, Pedro de, 58

Agüero, Cándido, 113

Aguilar, Juana, 100–104, 243–44

Aguilar, María Nicolasa, 141

Aguirre, Lorenzo, 108

Ahmed, Sara, 33, 43

Albersuna, Juan José, 141

Albert the Great, 165

alcohol. *See* drunkenness; pulque

Alejo (indigenous defendant), 106

Alfonso X, *Siete Partidas* under, 11, 72, 105, 157

Alonso (indigenous defendant), 146

Alonso, Juan, 181

alumbradismo, 201

Alva, Bartolomé de, *Confessionario mayor*, 136, 172–73, *174*, 215, 249

Álvarez, Máximo, 95

Amador, Tomás, 139, 149

amujerados. See effeminate men

anachronistic language, 246–47

Anderson, Virginia DeJohn, 135

animal(s): agency of, 130; archival, 129–30; bodies of, as evidence in bestiality cases, 125, 126, 128, 147–48; boundaries of category of, 131; centering in history, 130, 156–57; erasure of (*see* animal erasure); European, 133–34, 136; fellatio associated with, 41–42; humans as, 128; indigenous to Mesoamerica, 127, 136; in parchment and vellum, 129–30; in public shaming, 126;

animal(s) (*continued*)

    as raw material of archives, 43, 129–30; subjectivity of, 154; transformation of humans into, 130–34. *See also* bestiality; *and specific animals*

animal erasure, in bestiality cases, 153–60; by burning animal bodies, 126–27; by killing animals, 135, 157–58; types of disappearance in, 130–31

Annals of Puebla, 75

anthropocentrism, 154, 156

Antonio, José, 156

anus: in definition of sodomy, 33; medical examination of, in sodomy cases, 96–100. *See also* sodomy

Apatzi, Antonio Juan, 178–79, 181

Apatzingán (Mexico), bestiality in, 158

appeals: in bestiality cases, 140, 151, 152–53; in Sala del Crimen, 112; in sodomy cases, 70, 73, 118

appetite, in definition of desire, 6

Aquinas, Thomas, Saint: on animals, 132; on bestiality, 128; on sodomy, 41–42, 165; *Summa Theologica*, 5; on unnatural sexual acts, 4–5

Aragonese Inquisition, 67, 71

Arcaya, Patricio de, 191

Archaeology of Knowledge, The (Foucault), 241

archival absences, 233–53; absent archival referents as, 74–76, 248; in el Caltzontzin's sodomy trial, 55–56, 58; created through use of language, 246–48; of female sodomy, 243–45; indexical, 244–45; speculation about, 248. *See also* lost archives

archival access, 233–53; to Archivo General de la Nación, 234–40; classification systems in, 245–48; legal restrictions on, 234, 238–39; protocols for, 238, 251; seduction in, 233, 240–45, 248, 251–53

archival animals, 129–30

Archive Fever (Derrida), 43, 196, 241

archives: classification systems of, 245–48; connections between bodies and, 8–9;

as contact zone for past and present, 7; ethnographic approaches to, 252; gaps in scholarship on, 3, 8; impulses of, 48–49; instability of desire in, 4, 15, 17–19; language of (*see* language of archives); lost (*see* archival absences; lost archives); materials used in production of, 129–30; metaphors of consumption in, 21, 29, 42–45; misinscription in (*see* misinscription); motivations for creating, 3; of negligence, 165; physical aspects of files, 9–10, *10*, 43–44; physical space housing, 239–40; queering of, 15–18; seduction of, 233, 240–45, 248, 251–53; as sepulcher, 77–83; as source vs. subject, 3–4; stages in creation of, 4; subjectivity in creation of, 15; visceral reactions to, 30–33, 44–45

archivists and historians: in archival process, 4; consumption of archives by, 21, 29, 42–45; contact between past and present, 7; desires of, 6; in misinscription, 50, 78–79; seduction of, 233, 240–45, 248, 251–53; visceral reactions of, 30–33, 44–45; voyeurism of, 50

Archivo General de Centro América (Guatemala), 8, 74–75

Archivo General de Indias (Spain), 8, 74, 76, 124

Archivo General de la Nación (AGN, Mexico), 8, 234–40; building housing, 234–39, *235–37*, *240*, 250–51; changes in protocols of, 238; destruction of documents at, 238–39; establishment of, 234, 237–38; *Gazeta de Guatemala* in, 103; Indiferente Virreinal in, 84–85, 161, 271n2; legal restrictions on access to, 234, 238–39; number of volumes in, 168; photographic library of, 236. *See also specific cases*

Archivo General de la Nueva España, 237–38

Archivo General del Gobierno (Guatemala), 74

Archivo Histórico del Distrito Federal, 235

Archivo Histórico Municipal de Morelia, 46–47, *47*

Ardón, Remigia, 115
Arévalo, Francisco de, 181
Arévalo, Pedro, 207
Arnold, Linda, 84, 271n2
Arondekar, Anjali: on archival figuration, 244; on desire for archival access, 251–52; on empty archives, 73, 233; on lost archives, 55; on search for lost sexuality, 19
Arroyo, Manuel, 36–42; confession of, 41; database entry for, 37; denunciations against, 39; descriptions of crime of, 37, 38–39; Lázaro Martínez's case compared to, 28–29, 38–39; location of archives on, 36–38; origins of investigation of, 39–40; sentencing of, 42; trial of, 39, 42; visceral reactions to crime of, 39–42
Asumpción, Beato Juan de la, 246
Atitaliquía (Mexico), bestiality in, 156
attorneys, defense, role of, 14
Audiencia de México. See High Court of Mexico
Augustine, Saint, 4, 132
authoethnographic expressions, 204
autoarchival expressions, 204
Ávalos, Agustín de, 75
Azpilcueta, Martín de, Manual de confesores y penitentes, 175

Bacalar (Mexico), solicitation in the confessional in, 192
Badiola, Josef, 39
Balça, Diego, 181
Bancroft Library: Arroyo case archives at, 36–38; Ruiz case archives at, 37–38, 209
Barres, Bartolomé, 100
Barrosio de Palacios, Cristóbal, 166
Bautista, Juan, Confessionario en lengua mexicana y castellana, 169, 171, 171, 211
Bayarte, Pedro Juan, 92
Bazant, Mílada, 146, 153
Beirne, Piers, 135, 155, 156–57
beliefs vs. acts: as crimes, 39, 210; as sins, 201
Beltrán, José, 148
Benítez, Lorenzo, 139, 151–52
Bennassar, Bartolomé, 138

Benson, Etienne, 128, 130, 155
Bentham, Jeremy, 237
Berco, Cristian, 43, 67, 89
Bersani, Leo, 83
Bertrand, François, 27
bestiality: as heresy, 147; as indigenous crime, Spanish view of, 127, 145–46; as nefarious sin, 1; as sin against nature, 4–5, 128–29; and sodomy, conceptual linking of, 128–29
bestiality cases, 22, 124–60; age of defendants in, 138, 138–39; animals as victims in, 155; chronological breakdown of, 137, 137–38; classification of, 128; common types of animals in, 136; demography of defendants in, 137–44; earliest in New Spain, 124–28; eroticized desire for the divine in, 142–43, 220–21; ethnicity of defendants in, 141, 141–42; explanations and motivations for, 138–40, 144–49; female vs. male animals in, 137; gaps in scholarship on, 19, 135, 143–44; jurisdiction over, 13, 127, 147; killing of animals in, 1, 135, 139, 150, 152, 153, 154–58; legal codes on, 153, 157; in North American colonies, 71, 135, 155; number of, 127, 135, 136–37, 137; official and public reactions to, 1–3; photos of documents of, 129, 159; terminology used in, 128; voyeurism in, 125, 139–40; voyeurism of witnesses in, 125; women as defendants in, 142–43, 220–21
bestiality cases, evidence in: animal behavior as, 156; animal bodies as, 125, 126, 128, 147–48; eyewitnesses as, 148; medical, 144, 147–48; restraint of animals as, 149
bestiality cases, punishments in, 149–53; age of defendants and, 138; castration as, 125–27, 150; death penalty as, 2, 71, 139, 140, 142, 151–53; decline in severity of, 150–51, 153; exile as, 2, 125–26, 150–51; forced labor as, 2, 141, 142, 145, 150–51; imprisonment as, 145; public shaming as, 125–26, 140, 159–60; variation in, 149, 153; whipping as, 141, 149–50

Derrida, Jacques, 17; *Archive Fever*, 43, 196, 241

desecration, in bestiality cases, 143. *See also* divine, eroticized desire for the

deseo, definition and use of term, 5–6. *See also* desire

Desiderio, Cristóbal, 99–100, 113

desire: definition and use of term, 5–6; diverse forms of, 6–7, 53; for the divine (*see* divine); instability of, 4, 15, 17–19; methodology of, 6–7; same-sex (*see* same-sex desire); sexual act vs. procreation as object of, 5; translation of terms for, 52

Deuteronomy, Book of, 158

Devil: animals associated with, 133; in bestiality cases, 143, 147; in eroticized desire for the divine, 197, 213, 219–20, 223, 226

Diario de sucesos notables (Robles), 75–76

Díaz, Domingo, 178

Díaz, Porfirio, 234–35

Diccionario castellano con las voces de ciencias y artes (Terreros y Pando), 198

Diccionario de autoridades, 6, 48, 121, 131, 144, 198, 218

digestion, of archives, 44

dildos, 122, 233, 244

Dinshaw, Carolyn, 16, 252

Dios, Juan de (free mulatto defendant), 85–86

Dios, Juan de (slave defendant), 162

Dirks, Nicholas, 252

Dirty War, 235, 239

divine, eroticized desire for the, 23, 197–32; bestiality in, 142–43, 220–21; challenge of locating cases of, 200–201; church iconography in, 200, 207, 215–16; in claims of sexual intercourse with saints, 208–18; Devil in, 197, 213, 219–20, 223, 226; in female mysticism, 215–17; first-person letter on, 204–6, *205*; interiority in cases of, 229–30; leniency in cases of, 208, 218, 227–28; mental illness in, 197–98, 207–8, 224, 227–28; prevalence of, 200–201; repentance for, 206–8, 218, 222–23, 227, 230; self-denunciations for,

197, 204–6, 225, 228, 230; vague language in archives on, 200; among women, 201–2, 229. *See also* Jesus Christ; Virgin Mary

documentation, of torture, 60

dogs, bestiality with. *See* bestiality

Dolores, Alberto Ramos de los, 112

Domingo, José, 137, 140, 152

Domingo, Juan, 133–34

Domínguez, Juan Francisco, 219–20, 222–23

Donantes, Pedro, 194–95

donkeys: bestiality with (*see* bestiality); in public shaming, 126; ubiquity of, 136

Double Mistaken Identity, 57

doubt, religious, and eroticized desire for the divine, 220, 221–22

Douglas, Mary, 82

Douglas, Walter, 285n31

drunkenness: in bestiality cases, 146–47; in sexual acts with dead bodies, 26; in sodomy cases, 51, 52–54

Dubois, Laurent, 9

dust, of archives, 43–44

ecclesiastical courts, 11–13; bestiality cases in, 147, 159–60; establishment of, 12; jurisdiction of, 11–13, 88, 127; priestly sodomy cases in, 161–64

Edicts of Faith, dissemination of, 12–13

effeminate men, in sodomy cases, 111–14

eggs, in medical examinations in sodomy cases, 100

Eichhorn, Kate, 79

ejaculation: in bestiality cases, 148–49; in definition of perfect sodomy, 70; as pollution, 198

Ek, Clemente, 187

El Salvador, sodomy in, 113

Encarnación, María Paulina de la, 108

epistolary writings. *See* letters

escribano. See notaries and scribes

Esparragosa y Gallardo, Narciso, 101–4

estupro: definition of, 97, 105; medical examinations after, 97; vs. rape, 97, 105

General Indian Court. *See* Juzgado General de Indios

genital mortification, 206–7

gente de razón, 155

gestures: definition of, 110; as evidence in sodomy cases, 86–87, 110–15

Ghosh, Durba, 252

Gilberti, Maturino, *Vocabulario en lengua de Mechuacan*, 64, 65

Giraldo Botero, Carolina, 117–18

Goa: jurisdiction in, 13; sodomy in, 71

goats, bestiality with. *See* bestiality

Gómez, Antonio, 27, 32

Gómez, Ignacia, 25, 34–35, 45

gonorrhea, 41

González, Andrés, 162

Gordillo, Manuel, 113

Granada, Holy Office of, 165

Gregory XV, Pope, *Universi Dominici Gregis*, 166

Gruzinski, Serge, 70, 75, 111, 269n45

Guadalajara (Mexico): sodomy in, 95, 118, 119–22; solicitation in the confessional in, 193

Guanajuanto (Mexico), solicitation in the confessional in, 194

Guatemala: Archivo General de Centro América of, 8, 74–75; Archivo General del Gobierno of, 74; death penalty for sodomy in, 74–75; evidence of sodomy in, 98, 99–100. *See also specific cities*

Guatemala City: cross-dressing in, 115; medical voyeurism in, 100–104; sodomy in, 107–8

Guijo, Gregorio Martín de, 70

guilt: as construct, 230; for eroticized desire for the divine, 222, 224, 230; for masturbation, 249–50. *See also* repentance

Guislain, Joseph, 27

gut reactions. *See* visceral reactions

Guzmán, Nuño de, 55, 57

hacer cuenta, 211

Hacienda del Rincón (Mexico), bestiality in, 140

Hall, Stuart, 87, 111

hanging, of animals, 157

haptic historiography, 44

Harris, Verne, 17, 245

Haskett, Robert, 189

Havana (Cuba), 76, 109, 113, 148

hearsay, in el Caltzontzin's trial, 56

Heredia, Pedro de, 190

heresy: changes in meanings of, 12; combating, as goal of Inquisition, 12–13, 39, 167; vs. crime, 11; in ecclesiastical courts, 11, 13; light suspicion of, 167, 183, 188, 193; serious suspicion of, 113, 188, 193. *See also specific heresies*

hermaphroditism, medical examination for signs of, 100–104

Hernández, Francisco, 117

Hernández, Juan (bestiality defendant), 148–49, 150

Hernández, Juan (sodomy witness), 50

Herrera, Gertrudis, 140

Herrera, Lázaro de, 140, 152

Hidalgo (Mexico), bestiality in, 150

Hidalgo, Miguel, 62, 63, 69

Hidalgo, Nicolás, 189–90

Hidalgo del Parral (Mexico): bestiality in, 139; sodomy in, 94

Hidalgo y Costilla, Miguel, 2

hierarchy, of sins against nature, 128–29, 209

High Court of Mexico, 11

Hiligaynon language, 184

Hillman, David, 44

historians. *See* archivists and historians

historicity, mutilated, 50

historiography: haptic, 44; locating archives in, 9

History of Sacerdotal Celibacy in the Christian Church (Lea), 173

History of Sexuality, The (Foucault), 173

Holland, Sharon P., "On the Visceral," 33–34

Holler, Jacqueline, 201

holy images, pollution of, 197–99. *See also* Jesus Christ; saints, eroticized desire for; Virgin Mary

Holy Office of Granada, 165

Holy Office of the Inquisition. *See* Inquisition

Holy Office of the Mexican Inquisition. *See* Mexican Inquisition

Holy Spirit, illumination by, 201

homosexuality: decriminalization of, 236; historians' focus on, 3; imprisonment for, 236; limitations of classification of, 245; origins and use of term, 246; as term in archives, 29, 246–47, *247. See also* same-sex desire; sodomy

horses, in public shaming, 126

human(s): as animals, 128; boundaries of category of, 131; transformation into animals, 130–34

human bodies. *See* bodies

humanity, of colonized peoples, denial of, 155

Huntington Library, 176, 178, 285n31

iconography, in desire for the divine, 200, 207, 215–16

ignorance, as defense: in bestiality cases, 144–46; in sodomy cases, 81

imagination, in eroticized desire for the divine, 212

immorality: imprisonment for, 236; as term in archives, 203

imperfect sodomy, sexual acts with dead bodies as, 33

imperial power, textual, 3

imprisonment: for bestiality, 145; coercive sodomy during, 108–9; for eroticized desire for the divine, 217; for homosexuality, 236; for immorality, 236; for sodomy, 86

impulses, of archives, 48–49

impurity, pollution as type of, 198

indexical absences, 244–45

Indians. *See* indigenous peoples

Indiferente Virreinal, 84–85, 161, 271n2

indigenous languages: confessional manuals written in, 136, 170–72; priests' proficiency with, 177–78. *See also* Nahuatl language; Purépecha language; translations

indigenous peoples: accusations of solicitation in the confessional by, 186–90; in bestiality cases, *141,* 141–42, 144–47; death penalty for sodomy by, 75–77; jurisdiction over, 12; misinscription in cultural interactions of, 57; misunderstandings of confession among, 174; rusticity associated with, 144–45; Spanish view of bestiality as crime of, 127, 145–46; transformation into animals, 132–34. *See also* Purépecha language; Purépecha men

inhalation, of archives, 43–44

Inquisition: Edicts of Faith in, 12–13; jurisdiction of, 11–13; primary goal of, 12–13; on solicitation in the confessional, 165–66; tribunals of, 12. *See also* Mexican Inquisition

inscription, definition of, 49. *See also* misinscription

interrogations, in criminal investigations, 14

intersex, 97, 103

intimacy, same-sex, signs of, 116–22

Iriarte, Blas de, 94

Isabella of Castile, 72

Ixmiquilpan (Mexico), bestiality in, 147

Jaffary, Nora, 201, 222

jealousy, as evidence in sodomy cases, 118

Jesus Christ, eroticized desire for: bestiality in, 220–21; claims of sexual intercourse in, 208–18; iconography in, 215–16, *216;* inside churches, 225–27; kissing of images in, 198, 204–5; "sordid accesses" in, 220–22

Jiménez, Joseph, 191

Jiménez, Paulo, 98

Joachinque (indigenous defendant), 62

Jordan, Mark, 181

Joseph, Pedro, 152

Juan (Purépecha defendant), 62, 63, 69–70, 81

Juan, Bartolomé, 157

judges, in criminal proceedings, 14

juries, in secular courts, lack of, 11

jurisdiction, 11–13; over bestiality cases, 13, 127, 147; of Mexican Inquisition, 11, 13, 88, 168; over sodomy cases, 13, 88; over solicitation in the confessional, 165
Juzgado General de Indios, 12

labor. *See* forced labor
Laguna, Moreno de, 117–18
language of archives, 21–22; anachronistic/ counterchronistic, 246–47; in bestiality cases, 128; on body positions in sodomy, 63–68; bureaucratic, 63–64; in clas- sification systems, 245–48; first-person voice in, 204–6, 219; naming of acts in, 29, 246–47; in sodomy case against Purépecha men, 48–49, 51, 63–68; third-person voice in, 1, 204; vague, on desire for the divine, 200. *See also* translations
Lares, Nicolás de, 1, 2
Laso, Manuel José, 159
Lateran Council, Fourth (1215), 165
Lavrin, Asunción, 209, 228
lawyers, defense, role of, 14
Lázaro, Juan, 136–37, 140
Lázaro Martínez, José, 25–39; Arroyo's case compared to, 28–29, 38–39; classification of crime of, 27, 30; database entry for, 30, 33; defense used by, 27; interrogation and confession of, 25–26; photo of documents on, *31*; sentencing of, 27–28; trial of, 26, 33; visceral reactions to crime of, 25, 30–36, 45
Lea, Henry Charles, 180, 285n31; *History of Sacerdotal Celibacy in the Christian Church*, 173
leather, 43, 129
Lecumberri Palace, 234–40, *236*, *237*, 251
legal codes: on bestiality, 153, 157; conflicts among, 11–12; sexual acts with dead bodies missing from, 27, 32; on sodomy, 72–73, 88, 105. *See also specific laws*
letters: on eroticized desire for the divine, 204–6, *205*; same-sex intimacy in, 119–23
Leviticus, Book of, 72, 135, 151, 158

Leyba, Ana María de, 219–23; bestiality case against, 142–43, 220–21; encounters with the Devil, 219–20, 223; family of, 220; first-person denunciation of, 219; *mal de corazón* of, 223; photo of documents on, *224*; religious doubts of, 220, 221–22; repentance expressed by, 222–23; title of file on, 223, *224*
Leyes de Toro, 11
Ley General de Archivos, 234, 238–39
Libro de los principales rudimentos tocante a todos juicios, criminal, civil y executivo, 100
Liguori, Alphonsus Maria de', *Theologica moralis*, 33
Liliequist, Jonas, 158
Lipares, Antonio, 117
liquor, camphorated, 41. *See also* drunken- ness; pulque
location: of sodomy, 108–9; of solicitation in the confessional, 179
Lockhart, James, 57
longing. *See* desire
López, Domingo, 76, 109, 110
López, Gregório, 72
López, María Bárbara, 142, 143
López, Teresa, 221
López Austin, Alfredo, 133
Lorenzo, Lucas, 85
lost archives: as absent archival referents, 74–76, 248; on el Caltzontzin's sodomy trial, 55–58; on death penalty for sodomy, 73–77; on female sodomy, 243
love letters, same-sex intimacy in, 119–23
Luebano, Andrés, 95
Luna, Juan José de, 156
lust: as opposite of reason, 132; in trans- formation of humans into animals, 132, 134, 154
Luz de verdades católicas y explicación de la doctrina christiana (Martínez de la Parra), 132, 134, 154

Madrid (Spain), sodomy in, 71
Magdaleno, Diego, 161–62, 164

mal de corazón, 212–13, 223
Maldonado, García, 50
Maldonado, Miguel, 139
manna, 43
Manual de confessores y penitentes (Azpilcueta), 175
Marcos, Mariano, 108
María, Agustín, 184–85
Mariano Suárez, Francisco, 190
married men, bestiality among, 140–41
Martín, Francisco, 133–34
Martín, Juan, 74, 75
Martín, Manuel, 184
Martín, Miguel, 94
Martín, Sebastián, *159*, 159–60
Martínez, María Elena, 7, 101
Martínez de la Parra, Juan, *Luz de verdades católicas y explicación de la doctrina christiana*, 132, 134, 154
Mary. *See* Virgin Mary
Mascorro, Jacinto, 146
masculine (manly) women, 111, 114–15
masculinity: gestures in performances of, 111; in language describing sodomy, 65–68
Massumi, Brian, 31, 34–35, 222
masturbation: act of, vs. sinful beliefs and acts, 201; with Eucharist, 201, 221; female, 201–2, 229; guilt for, 249–50; in hierarchy of sins, 209; mutual, 91, 97, 113; "pollution" as term for, 23, 198, 229; sexual acts with dead bodies as, 33; as sin against nature, 4–5, 128. *See also* divine, eroticized desire for the
Matheo, Father, 175–76
Maturana, Jose María, *129*, 146
Maya, accusations of solicitation in the confessional by, 186–90
Mbembe, Achille, 21, 77, 81, 239–40
medical examinations: in bestiality cases, 144, 147–48; of gender ambiguity, 97, 100–104; in sodomy cases, 96–106, 108
medical voyeurism, 97, 100–104, *102*
Memorias para la historia del antiguo reyno de Guatemala, 74

memory and remembering: archives of sodomy cases as act of, 81; collective, 239; and evidence, in trials, 51; translations of words for, 51. *See also* forgetting
men: effeminate, 111–14; solicitation in the confessional of, 23, 166–67. *See also* sodomy
Mendoza, Leandro Hurtado de, 98–99
Meneque, María, 210, 213
menstrual blood, 201
mental illness, in eroticized desire for the divine, 197–98, 207–8, 224, 227–28
Mérida (Mexico), bestiality in, 124–28
Mesa, Pedro Joseph de, 112
mestizos, death penalty for sodomy by, 76
Metapán (El Salvador), sodomy in, 113
metaphorics, of consumption, 21, 29, 42–45
methodology: of desire, 6–7; of history, problems with, 79–80, 82; queer, 15–17
Mexican Constitution of 1977, 239
Mexican Inquisition: aim of, 11, 39, 167; bestiality cases in, 143, 147; decision making about formal charges by, 168; ecclesiastical courts of, 11, 12; establishment of, 11, 12; jurisdiction of, 11, 13, 88, 168; number of denunciations made to, 168; staffing of, 168. *See also* divine, eroticized desire for the; solicitation in the confessional
Mexican national archive. *See* Archivo General de la Nación
Mexico. *See specific cities*
Mexico City: bestiality in, 143; coercive sodomy in, 105–6; death penalty for sodomy in, 75–76, 117; female sodomy in, 243; priestly sodomy in, 161–64; Real Sala del Crimen of, 243; solicitation in the confessional in, 175, 193; Spanish conquest of, 55
Meza, Gabriel, 118
Michelet, Jules, 43
Michoacán (Mexico): Spanish conquest of, 55; trial and execution of el Caltzontzin in, 54–58
Miller, William Ian, 42
Miranda, Pedro de, 189

misinscription: bureaucratic language in, 63–64; in cultural interactions, 57; gendered language in, 63–68; meaning of, 18, 49–50, 81; in sodomy case against Purépecha men, 49–52, 60–61, 78–79; torture in, 60–61; translations in, 51–52, 61, 63–66

missing archives. *See* lost archives

missionaries, confessional manuals written by, 171–72

Molé, Juan, 92, 100

Mondragón, Carlos Jiménez, 190

Monroy, Felipe de, 191

Monter, William E., 71, 105, 138

Monterrey (Mexico): bestiality in, 1–4, 150; sodomy in, 108

Montesano y Larreaga, Agustín José, 114, 115

Montesinos, Alonso Gómez, 181

Montoro, Andrés de, 213

Montúfar, Nicolás de, 99

Mora, Juan de, 182

Morales, Esteban, 194

Morales, Joaquin, 107–8

Morales, Manuel, 156

Moreira, Pio, 148

Morelia, Archivo Histórico Municipal de, 46–47, 47

Moreno, Juan Carrillo, 243

Morillo, Reducindo, 108

mortification, genital, 206–7

Mott, Luiz, 119

Moya de Contreras, Francisco, 178

mulattos, death penalty for sodomy by, 75–76

mules: bestiality with, 136, 139, 141; in public shaming, 126

Muñoz, Francisco, 59

Muñoz, José Esteban, 17

Murrin, John, 155, 157

Museo Nacional de Antropología e Historia, 75

mutilated historicity, 50

mutual masturbation, 91, 97, 113

mysticism, female, 215–17

Na, Pedro, 124–28, 134–36, 149–50

Nabor de la Encarnación, José, 119–22

nahualli shapeshifting, 133–34

Nahuatl language: confessional manuals in, 136, 171–72; in nahualli shapeshifting case, 133–34; in sodomy cases, 51; translation of term "confession" in, 174; translations of, 51

naming, of corporeal acts, 29, 246–47

Napoli, Ignacio María, 194

Naredo, Antonio, 94–95

Nari, Felipe, 147

natural sexuality, procreation as purpose of, 4–5

nature, sins against. *See* sins against nature

Nava, Fernando de, 188

Navarro, Antonio Joseph, 194

necrophilia, origins of term, 27

nefarious sins and crimes, in language of archives, 64. *See also* bestiality; sodomy

nefarious violence, 105–10

negligence, archives of, 165

negligent favoritism, in solicitation in the confessional, 190–95

Neri, Francisco, 140

New England, sodomy in, 71, 94

New Mexico: bestiality in, 156; sodomy in, 90; solicitation in the confessional in, 186, 189–90

New Spain: as contact zone, 7; end of, 2; establishment of, 2; geographic boundaries of, 2; scarcity of priests in, 174–75

newspapers: on death penalty for sodomy, 76–77; medical voyeurism in, 101–4, 102

Nicholas of Tolentine, Saint, 217, 230–31

nicknames, effeminate, 113

Nicolás (slave defendant), 75

Nicolás, Antonio de, 144

Nicolás, José, 156

North American colonies: bestiality in, 71, 135, 155; sodomy in, 71

notaries and scribes: in archival process, 4; in phases of criminal investigations, 14

Nueva España. *See* New Spain

Nuñez de Villavicencio, Nuño, 143

nuns, pollution by, 201

priests, 22–23; confession to (*see* confession); proficiency with indigenous languages, 177–78, 183–85; scarcity of, in New Spain, 174–75; sexual abuse by (*see* sexual abuse, by priests; solicitation in the confessional); sodomy by, 161–64, *256–60*

prisons: coercive sodomy in, 108–9; Lecumberri, 234–40, *236, 237*, 251. *See also* imprisonment

procreation, as purpose of sexuality, 4–5

procurador de indios, 152, 283n92

profanation: pollution as, 198; sexual acts with dead bodies as, 30, 33, 37

profane and sacred, mixing of, 199, 214–15

Protomedicato, Royal, 96–97

public shaming: animals used in, 126; for bestiality, 125–26, 140, 159–60; for sexual acts with dead bodies, 28, 34; for sodomy, 86, 92, 113, 118; visceral responses to, 34

Puebla (Mexico): desire for the divine in, 197–98; sodomy in, 95–96, 112; solicitation in the confessional in, 194

Puente, Mariano Rafael, 112

Pulido, Francisco, 193

pulque: in bestiality cases, 146–47; definition of, 26; and sexual acts with dead bodies, 26; in sodomy cases, 52–54. *See also* drunkenness

punishments: for bestiality, 2, 3, 125–26; for consumption of semen, 42; for eroticized desire for the divine, 208, 218, 227–28; examples of, 14; for false accusations of sodomy, 94, 95; for female sodomy, 243; for sexual acts with dead bodies, 27–28; for sodomy (*see* sodomy cases, punishments in); for solicitation in the confessional, lack of, 192–93; as stage of criminal proceedings, 14. *See also specific punishments*

Purépecha language: confessional manuals in, 171; term for sodomy in, 64; translations of, 51, 52, 61

Purépecha men, sodomy cases against, 21, 46–83; el Caltzontzin in, 54–58, 74; death penalty in, 48, 54, 55, 69–70, 74, 78–79; drunkenness in, 51, 52–54; as earliest

sodomy trial in New Spain, 62; evidence in, 51, 54; expansion of scope of, 54, 58–63; language used to describe, 48–49, 51, 63–68; misinscription in, 49–52, 60–61, 78–79; origins of, 47–48; photos of documents on, *47, 59*; physical positions of bodies in, 63–68; torture in, 60–61; translations in, 51–52, 61; trial of, 51–54; witnesses in, 48–49, 50–51

putos: definition of, 64; in Purépecha sodomy case, 54, 58–59, 61, 64

queering, of archives, 15–18

queer methodology, 15–17

Querétaro (Mexico): bestiality in, 140, 152; eroticized desire for the divine in, 208–18; genital mortification in, 206–7; solicitation in the confessional in, 181

Quesa, Ángel María, 193–94

Quessar, Juan, 75

Quijada, Diego de, 125–26

Quijano, Julian, 192

Quini, Pedro, 46–83; changes to testimony of, 54; confession of, 54, 58; death penalty for, 69–70; legal argument in defense of, 81; origins of case against, 47–48; other men accused by, 54, 58–63, 64; photos of documents on, *47, 59*; physical position of body of, 66; trial of, 51–54; underwear of, 51, 54, 92; witnesses to crime of, 48–49, 50–51. *See also* Purépecha men

race: of defendants in bestiality cases, *141*, 141–42; as index of animality, 132; rusticity associated with, 144

rape, vs. *estupro*, 97, 105

Real Academia Española, 6

Real Audiencia, appeals of sodomy cases to, 70, 73

reality, vs. fantasy, of eroticized desire for the divine, 211–12

Real Sala del Crimen (Mexico City), 243

reason: in definition of humanity, 131–32; in identity of Spaniards and Creoles, 154–55; lust as opposite of, 132

San Felipe (Mexico), sodomy in, 94

San Francisco, Pedro de, 191

San Joseph, Antonio de, 194

San Luis Potosí (Mexico), bestiality in, 150, 152

San Miguel, Marina de, 201

Santa María de las Parras (Mexico), bestiality in, 140

Santiago, Joseph de, 85–86

Santiago, Pascual de, 94

Santos de Luna, Juan de los, 152–53

Santos Losada, Simón de los, 143

Santo Tomás, Manuel de, 208–9

Sardo, Fernando, 112

Schwartz, Joan M., 19

Scott-Railton, Thomas, 43

scribes. *See* notaries and scribes

Sebastián, Juan, 191

Secretaría de Cámara del Virreinato, 84

secular criminal courts. *See* criminal courts, secular

seduction, archival, 233, 240–45, 248, 251–53

self-castration, 206–7

self-denunciations: in church fight against heresy, 12; for eroticized desire for the divine, 197, 204–6, 225, 228, 230

Selís, Domingo de, 94

Sellers-García, Sylvia, 75, 243–44

semen: as evidence of bestiality, 148; as evidence of sodomy, 92; women's equivalent of, 229. *See also* ejaculation

semen, consumption of, 37–42; act of vs. thoughts/beliefs about, 39; classification of crime of, 38; descriptions of crime of, 37, 38–39; as heresy, 39; punishment for, 42; visceral reactions to, 39–42

sentencing. *See* punishments

sepulcher, archives as, 77–83

Serafin, Father, 195

Servando, Francisco, 246

Seville (Spain): Archivo General de Indias in, 8, 74, 76, 124; sodomy in, 67, 71

sexual abuse, by priests: church inattentiveness to, 164–65; gaps in scholarship on, 23. *See also* solicitation in the confessional

sexual abuse, in *estupro* and rape, 97, 105

sexual acts: naming of, 29, 246–47; vs. procreation, as proper object of desire, 5; vs. thoughts and beliefs, 39, 199; unnatural, church doctrine on, 4–5. *See also specific acts*

sexual coercion. *See* coercion

sexual desecration, 201–2

sexual desire. *See* desire

sexualidad, 5. *See also* sexuality

sexuality: definition and use of term, 5; procreation as purpose of, 4–5

shaming. *See* public shaming

shapeshifting, nahualli, 133–34

sheep, bestiality with, 136–37, 140, 148–49

ships, sodomy aboard, 92, 100, 109, 117

Sicily, sodomy in, 71

Siete Partidas, 11; on bestiality, 157; on sodomy, 72, 105

signs, definition of, 86, 87, 111. *See also* evidence

silencing, of bestiality cases, 135, 143–44

Silencing the Past (Trouillot), 135

Silva, José Guadalupe, 118

Silverman, Lisa, 60

Singuilucan (Mexico): bestiality in, 142–43; eroticized desire for the divine in, 219–23

sins against nature: hierarchy of, 128–29, 209; jurisdiction over, 11–13; origins of church doctrine on, 4–5; preconceived notions of, 20; rarity of prosecution of women for, 209–10; translations of terms for, 64. *See also specific types*

Sixth Commandment, confessional manuals on, *171*, 172–73, 175, 182

social class, in severity of punishment for sodomy, 67, 155

social control, through confession, 173–75

sodomitical subcultures, 70, 80, 83, 111

sodomy: and bestiality, conceptual linking of, 128–29; female, 72, 101–4, 242–45; as heresy, 88; imperfect, 33; as nefarious crime/sin, 46, 72; perfect, 70, 73, 151; as sin against nature, 4–5, 128–29; as unnatural sexual act, 4–5, 42 sodomy cases, 21–22, 46–123; agency in, 67–68, 105–10; coercion through violence in, 105–10; denunciations in, role of, 89; earliest in New Spain, 62; false accusations in, 93–96; gendered language describing position of bodies in, 63–68; jurisdiction over, 13, 88; legal codes on, 72–73, 88, 105; number of, 87; photos of documents of, *47, 59*; priests as defendants in, 161–64, *256–60* (*see also* solicitation in the confessional); procedural norms of investigations in, 14–15; rumors in, 56–57, 94. *See also* Purépecha men, sodomy cases against

sodomy cases, death penalty in, 21, 69–82; as act of forgetting, 21, 81; affective evidence in, 117; age restrictions on, 67–68; vs. bestiality cases, 71, 151; in Guatemala, 74–75; missing archives on, 73–77; newspaper coverage of, 76–77; prevalence of, 70, 74; for priests, 164; in Purépecha case, 48, 54, 55, 69–70, 74, 78–79; in Spain vs. New Spain, 71–73, 76, 109

sodomy cases, evidence in, 85–123; affective signs as, 86–88, 100, 116–23; vs. bestiality cases, 144; of coercion, 105–10; corporeal signs as, 86–88, 92, 96–100; corroboration of, 89, 91–92; criteria for, 87–88; eyewitnesses as, 85, 87, 89–93; false accusations as, 93–96; of female-female sodomy, 101–4; gestural signs as, 86–87, 110–15; love letters as, 119–23; medical, 96–106, 108; physical, lack of, 87; physical, underwear as, 51, 54, 92

sodomy cases, punishments in: in coercive sodomy, 105–10; decline in severity of, 93, 96; forced labor as, 70, 91, 97, 108, 118; imprisonment for life as, 86; position of bodies as factor in, 66–68; public shaming as, 92, 113, 118; social class as factor in, 67, 155; in Spain, 67–68, 71–73; whipping as, 86, 113, 118. *See also* sodomy cases, death penalty in

solicitation in the confessional, 22–23, 161–96; archives of negligence on,

165; church inattentiveness to, 164–65; confessional manuals and, 170–76, 182; consensual, 164–65, 169–70; cover-ups of, 23, 165, 167, 191–92; death penalty for, 165; definitions of, 165–66; exaggerated accusations of, 186–90; favoritism for priests accused of, 190–95; gaps in scholarship on, 23, 168; growth in problem of, 165–66; as heresy, 23, 165, 193; jurisdiction over, 165; location and timing of, 179; men and boys as target of, 23, 166–68; number of cases, 167; in Philippines, 184–85; photo of documents on, *177*; power relations in, 164–65, 167; priests' fluency in indigenous languages and, 177–78, 183–85; prosecution of, lack of, 167, 170, 190–96; summary of cases, *256–60*; time lag between events and reports of, 194–95; women and girls as target of, 23, 166, 167

Sololá (Guatemala), bestiality in, 141

sordid accesses, 219–22

Spain: Archivo General de Indias of, 8, 76; punishments for sodomy in, 67–68, 71–73, 76, 109; solicitation in the confessional in, 194; viceroyalties of, 2. *See also* New Spain; *and specific cities*

Spaniards, reason in identity of, 154–55

Spanish conquest: of Mexico Tenochtitlán, 55; of Michoacán, 55

Spanish language, confessional manuals in, 136, 170–71. *See also* translations

speculation: about archival absences, 248; about visceral responses, 34–36

Spurling, Geoffrey, 93

Steedman, Carolyn: on archival consumption, 43, 44; on discontinuities in archives, 18; on seduction of archives, 233, 238, 241; on voyeurism of archivists, 50

Stoler, Ann, 3, 43, 49, 92, 252

Suárez, Juan Pablo, 112

Suchitlán (Mexico), bestiality in, 146

suicide, alternative terminology for, 29–30

Summa Theologica (Aquinas), 5

superstition, church concern with, 12

syphilis, 41, 141

Tagalog language, 184
Taos (New Mexico), solicitation in the confessional in, 189–90
Taos Indians, 189–90
taxonomies, of the archives, 6, 20–21, 33, 44–45, 49, 82, 101, 243, 248
Taylor, Diana, 24
Taylor, William B., 146, 195
temascal, 47
Tenochtitlán, Spanish conquest of, 55. *See also* Mexico City
Teocaltiche (Mexico), bestiality in, 139
Tepoztlán Institute for Transnational History of the Americas, 19
Terán, Santiago, 148
Teresa of Ávila, Saint, 207, 216, 217
Terraciano, Kevin, 186
Terreros y Pando, Esteban de, *Diccionario castellano con las voces de ciencias y artes*, 198
Tesoro de la lengua castellana o española (Covarrubias), 5–6
Texupa (Mexico), sodomy in, 94
Theologica moralis (Liguori), 33
third-person voice, used in archives, 1, 204
Thomas, Juan, 151–52
Thomas, Keith, 142, 157
thoughts, vs. acts: as crimes, 39; as sins, 199
Tibursio (mulatto defendant), 161–62
Tinoco (witness), 109
Tlatelolco massacre of 1968, 235
Tlaxcala (Mexico): bestiality in, 133; sodomy in, 90–91, 97
Tlaxcalilla (Mexico), solicitation in the confessional in, 178–79, 181
Toer, Pramoedya Ananta, 43
Toledo, Council of (693), 72
Toluca (Mexico), sodomy in, 113
Tompkins, Kyla Wazana, "On the Visceral," 33–34
tongues, 177–78
Torre do Tombo (Lisbon), 73
Torres, Simón de, 156
torture: documentation of, 60; in misinscription, 60–61; secular courts' use of,

11, 14; in sodomy investigations, 60–61; in solicitation in the confessional investigations, 182–83
town criers, after false accusations, 94. *See also* public shaming
Townsend, Camilla, 75
transcriptions: in criminal proceedings, 14; misinscription through, 81–82
translations, 21–22; in bestiality cases, 124, 125; of colloquial testimony into bureaucratic language, 63–64; in confessional manuals, 136, 170–71; in misinscription, 51–52, 61, 63–66; in sodomy cases, 51–52, 61
transvestism, female, 114–15
Treatise on the Heathen Superstitions That Today Live among the Indians Native to This New Spain (Ruiz de Alarcón), 133
Trent, Council of, 170
Tribunal de La Acordada, 25, 77
tribunals, of Inquisition, 12
Trouillot, Michel-Rolph, 143; *Silencing the Past*, 135
Trujillo, Manuel, 90
truth, memory and evidence in, 51
Tulancingo (Mexico), bestiality in, 144–45
Tulane University, Latin American Library at, 246
turkeys: bestiality with, 124–28, 135, 136, 279n7; as indigenous species, 127, 136
Tzintzicha Tangaxoan. *See* Caltzontzin, el

Ucelo, Juan, 74
Ulloa, Vincente, 95
uncleanliness, of bestiality, 157–58
underwear, as evidence in sodomy cases, 51, 54, 92
Universi Dominici Gregis (Gregory XV), 166
unnatural sexual acts, church doctrine on, 4–5. *See also specific acts*

vagina, terms used for, 214
Valencia, Cristóbal de, 186–90
Valladolid (Mexico), bestiality in, 147, 152, 159–60
Vallejo Hermosillo, Juan, 161–64, 193

Vaquera, Ramón Sánchez de la, 224–27
Vásquez, Miguel Antonio, 112
Vega, Francisco Xavier de la, 228
Vega, Juan de la, 111, 117
Velasco y Vargas, Romualdo, 190
Velázquez Rangel, Juan, 47–48, 50, 64
vellum, 43, 129–30, 244
verbal expressions of intimacy, 117
verb tenses, 61, 66
Vicab, Francisco Xavier, 192
Victoriano Ambrosio, José, 107–8
Vidales, Lorenzo, 1–4; killing of animal in case of, 1, 150, 156; origins of case against, 1–2; punishment of, 2, 150; representation of desires of, 18
Villegas, Francisco de, 55, 56
violence, nefarious, 105–10
Virgin Mary, eroticized desire for: bestiality in, 220–21; claims of sexual intercourse in, 208–18; inside churches, 225–27; kissing of images in, 197–99, 204–5; "sordid accesses" in, 220–22
virgins, sexual abuse of (*estupro*), 97, 105
visceral reactions, 20–21, 25–45; in archival studies, 30–33, 44–45; to consumption of semen, 39–42; physical components of, 36; to sexual acts with dead bodies, 25, 30–36, 45
Viveros, Julián, 158
Vivimos, Juan Joseph, 113
Vocabulario en lengua de Mechuacan (Gilberti), 64, 65
voyeurism: of archivists, 50; in bestiality cases, 125, 139–40; encouraged by judicial system, 90; medical, 97, 100–104, *102*; and misinscription, 50; in sodomy cases, 49, 50, 90–91, 161–62

Weber, Alison, 207
whipping: for bestiality, 2, 141, 149–50; for sexual acts with dead bodies, 28, 34; for sodomy, 86, 113, 118; visceral responses to, 34

White, Luise, 94
Whitehead, Neil L., 130
Wiesner-Hanks, Merry, 5
witchcraft: church concern with, 12; and nahualli shapeshifting, 133–34
witnesses: in archival process, 4; in criminal investigations, 14; as evidence in bestiality cases, 148; as evidence in sodomy cases, 85, 87, 89–93; to sexual acts with dead bodies, 25, 34–35. *See also* visceral reactions
witnesses, voyeurism of: in bestiality cases, 125; encouraged by judicial system, 90; in sodomy cases, 49, 50, 161–62
women: bestiality cases against, 142–43, 220–21; eroticized desire for the divine among, 201–2, 229; masculine (manly), 111, 114–15; masturbation by, 201–2, 229; misinscription of bodies of, 50; mysticism of, 215–17; rarity of prosecution of, for sins against nature, 209–10; same-sex desire among, 114, 242–45; sodomy by, 72, 101–4, 242–45; solicitation in the confessional of, 23, 166; transvestism among, 114–15; as victims of *estupro*, 97, 105

Xavier, Francisco, 150

Yturria, Mariano, 39
Yuba, Antonio, 90

Zacatecas (Mexico): bestiality in, 156; solicitation in the confessional in, 181, 194
Zamorano, Cristóbal, 117–18
Zárate, Miguel de, 27–28
Zarzoza, Alberto, 191–92
Zebrian, José Gregorio, 176
Zempoala (Mexico), sodomy in, 108
Zepeda, Miguel Díaz de, 90–91, 97
Zerón, Bernardo, 90–91, 97
Zinzo, Pedro, 62
Ziziqui, Joaquín, 58, 59, 63, 69–70, 81

Printed in the USA
CPSIA information can be obtained
at www.ICGtesting.com
BVHW052002110823
668476BV00005B/17